THE COLOR OF WEALTH

THE COLOR OF WEALTH

The Story Behind the
U.S. Racial Wealth Divide

• • • • • • • • • • •

Meizhu Lui, Bárbara J. Robles,
Betsy Leondar-Wright, Rose M. Brewer,
and Rebecca Adamson

With United for a Fair Economy

THE NEW PRESS

NEW YORK
LONDON

Requests for permission to reproduce selections from this book should be mailed to: Permissions Department, The New Press, 38 Greene Street, New York, NY 10013

Published in the United States by The New Press, New York, 2006
Distributed by W. W. Norton & Company, Inc., New York

LIBRARY OF CONGRESS CATALOGING-IN-PUBLICATION DATA
The color of wealth : the story behind the U.S. racial wealth divide / Meizhu Lui . . . [et al].
p. cm
Includes bibliographical references and index.
Contents: Overview: the roots of the racial wealth divide—Land rich, dirt poor: challenges to asset building in Native America—Forged in blood: Black wealth injustice in the U.S.—Neighbors and fences: Latinos in the U.S.—The perils of being yellow: Asian Americans as perpetual foreigners—Climbing the up escalator: white advantages in wealth accumulation—Rainbow economics: closing the racial wealth divide.
ISBN-13: 978-1-59558-004-7 (pbk.)
ISBN-10:1-59558-004-2 (pbk.)
1. Wealth—United States. 2. Poverty—United States. 3. Income distribution—United States. 4. Equality—United States. 5. United States—Race relations—Economic aspects. 6. Racism—Economic aspects—United States. 7. United States—Social policy. I. Title: Racial wealth divide. II. Lui, Meizhu.

HC110.W4C654 2006
339.2'208900973—dc22
2005057666

The New Press was established in 1990 as a not-for-profit alternative to the large, commercial publishing houses currently dominating the book publishing industry. The New Press operates in the public interest rather than for private gain, and is committed to publishing, in innovative ways, works of educational, cultural, and community value that are often deemed insufficiently profitable.

www.thenewpress.com

Book design and composition by Lovedog Studio
This book was set in Bembo

Printed in Canada

4 6 8 10 9 7 5

CONTENTS

ACKNOWLEDGMENTS

Research and writing by
Sarah Dewees, First Nations Development Institute

Research assistance from
Aaron Bourke, Veronica Burt, Esther Cervantes, Metric Giles, Sam Grant, Megan Headley, Caitlin Howell, Gene Hoover, Stefanie Juell, Cathi Kozen, Joe Linkevic, Nicholas Lydon, David Lysy, Amy Parker, Nieta Pressley, Amelie Racliffe, Kelly Spada, Christina Song, Liz Stanton, Talia Sturgis, Valerie Taing, Chaka Uzondu, Gretchen Weitmarschen, Katherine Winters, Jo-Ellen Yan, Stephanie Yan, Al Wang, Sheronda Watkins

Thanks to
Dr. Roger Betancourt, University of Maryland
Dr. Douglas Dacy, University of Texas–Austin
Dr. Melvin Oliver, University of California–Santa Barbara
Dr. Lodis Rhodes, University of Texas–Austin

And special acknowledgment to
Dr. Rhonda Williams—may her spirit live on.

THE COLOR OF WEALTH

Chapter 1

OVERVIEW:
THE ROOTS OF
THE RACIAL WEALTH
DIVIDE

*"Accumulating wealth—as distinct from making a big income—is key
to your financial independence. It gives you control over assets,
power to shape the corporate and political landscape, and the ability
to ensure a prosperous future for your children and their heirs. . . .
Wealth is used not just to pay the rent or buy groceries, but to create
opportunities, to free you to pursue your dreams."*

—REV. JESSE JACKSON, SR., AND JESSE JACKSON, JR.

For every dollar owned by the average white family in the United States,
the average family of color has less than one dime. Why do people of color
have so little wealth? Because for centuries they were barred by law, by discrimination, and by violence from participating in government wealth-
building programs that benefited white Americans. Understanding the roots
of the racial wealth divide will lead to more understanding of racial
inequities in general and more understanding of how to reach equality.

WHAT IS WEALTH?

In this book, when we use the term "wealth," we mean economic assets. A family's net worth is their assets minus their debts, or what they own minus what they owe. Assets include houses and other real estate, cash, stocks and bonds, pension funds, businesses, and anything else that can be converted to cash, such as cars and works of art.

These are not the only kinds of wealth. Family, social, and community networks, education and skills, public infrastructure and a healthy environment, religion and spirituality: all these not only make us economically more secure, they help us feel well off in ways that money can't buy. But this book focuses on financial wealth, and the story of the government's role in influencing the racial wealth divide.

Our net worth is influenced by the net worth of our parents, grandparents, and earlier generations. Most private wealth in the United States was inherited. And even for people who do not inherit money after their parents' deaths, their family's education and social contacts and financial help from living relatives make a big difference.

The racial wealth gap has continued to grow (see Figure 1-1). From 1995 to 2001, according to the Federal Reserve Bank, the average family of color saw their net worth fall 7 percent, to $17,100 in just six years, while an average white family's net worth grew 37 percent, to $120,900, in the same period.

The gap in financial assets (cash, stocks, and bonds) is even greater, since most people of color's assets are invested in their home (see Figure 1-2).

PERCEPTION AND REALITY OF ECONOMIC INEQUALITY BY RACE

Explicit racial discrimination has been illegal since the Civil Rights laws of the 1960s, so many people now attribute racial differences in financial success entirely to individual behavior. White Americans in particular tend to believe that the playing field is now level. Every year Gallup takes a "minority rights and relations" poll that reveals ethnic differences in perceptions of opportunity. In the 2004 poll, 77 percent of white respondents and 69 percent of Latino respondents said they believe that African Americans have as good a chance as whites do to get any kind of job for which they are qualified. Only 41 percent of blacks felt the same.[1]

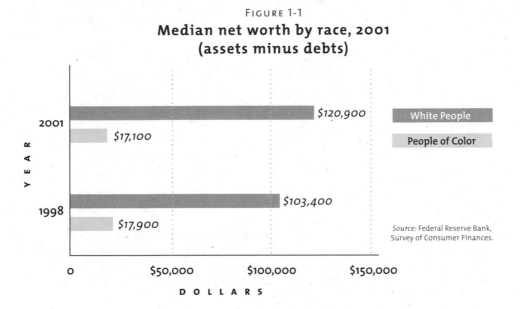

FIGURE 1-1
Median net worth by race, 2001
(assets minus debts)

Source: Federal Reserve Bank, Survey of Consumer Finances.

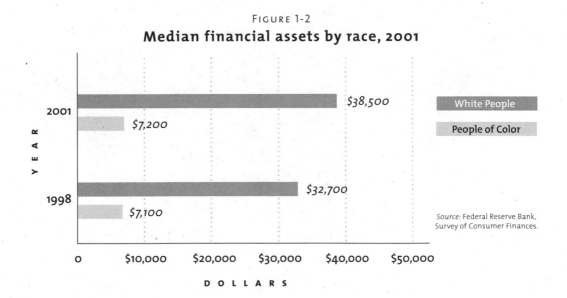

FIGURE 1-2
Median financial assets by race, 2001

Source: Federal Reserve Bank, Survey of Consumer Finances.

A racially mixed group is gathered in a church basement for a workshop on the racial wealth divide. A trainer from United for a Fair Economy has just presented the facts that a typical white family has about $121,000 in assets, compared to the typical family of color, which has about $17,000 in assets.

In response, Ed, a middle-aged white man, raises his hand. "I hear what you are saying—that white people tend to have more money. But I don't like what you are implying—that I should feel guilty about it. I swear, everything I have, I worked hard for."

Ed has a point. He says he studied hard in college, worked hard at every job, and saved steadily until he could buy a home. For the past several years, he and his wife have been contributing to a retirement account.

The trainers ask him who helped him become prosperous, and he says, "No one." When the discussion turns to affirmative action, he says he opposes racial preferences and government handouts.

But then the trainers lead the group in an exercise in which participants put milestones of their family's history on a giant timeline on the wall.

It turns out that Ed's great-great-grandfather got a farm in Nebraska through the Homestead Act—a program only available to whites.

His father, a World War II veteran, got a Veterans Administration mortgage and went to college on the G.I. Bill—programs that black G.I.s couldn't take full advantage of because of housing and education discrimination. Thanks to those boosts to earlier generations, Ed's college tuition as well as the down payment on his home could be paid by his parents.

It may be true that he studied hard, worked hard, saved—and so can claim some credit for his assets. But how much of the credit is his? How much is due to public investments in his family?

A Latina woman, Larisa, asks Ed, "What about me? I studied hard, worked hard, and saved just like you. But I didn't get the same rewards. Doesn't that mean your money comes partly from your race?" Ed admits that it does.

Not surprisingly, there's a similar division on the question of how much the government should try to improve the social and economic status of various groups. Sixty-eight percent of African Americans, 67 percent of Latinos, and only 32 percent of whites said government should play a major role.[2] Our explanation of the racial wealth gap has implications for the solutions we favor: individual failure implies individual responsibility for narrowing the gap, while structural causes require collective efforts for public solutions.

Depending on the particular question asked, between 40 percent and 60 percent of white Americans incorrectly believe that African Americans are doing as well as or better than white Americans in employment, income, education, and health care, according to a 2001 poll by the *Washington Post*, the Kaiser Family Foundation, and Harvard University.[3]

The comments of those polled are revealing. "It's good that the bad days are past and blacks have come up. As a whole, you don't hear about [problems] now as you used to. Now if something occurs, like a black guy being mistreated for a job or something, you hear about it," said Emily Reed of Russell, New York. "I think it's pretty even, but you'd never get blacks to admit it," said retiree Thomas Ripley of Belleville, Illinois. "It keeps the pressure on government for more programs."

Of course, individual effort does make a difference in financial success, compared to how the same individual would have fared without putting forth an effort. But Americans begin the race from different starting lines. Not only do well-off people, primarily whites, have significant head starts, but even many working-class whites have had modest advantages when compared with working-class people of color, most of whom begin far behind whites' starting line.

Income is a short-term measure that shows the effects of education, effort, and talent, as well as the impacts of opportunity and discrimination, on the current generation. But differences in income are dwarfed by differences in wealth, which are far more likely to be affected by the policy environment of previous generations.

Higher incomes have been the primary focus over the past forty years of economic justice activism. One reason is that assets can seem like a secondary concern for people who are incarcerated, homeless, or shut out of decent employment; advocacy has often been concentrated on the causes of people with the greatest need.

Getting into formerly all-white colleges and unions to win access to better paying jobs for people of color, affirmative action, welfare rights, living wage campaigns, and union drives have been worthy goals in the quest to boost the incomes of people of color from their low pre–Civil Rights Era levels. And these efforts have succeeded to some degree. African Americans' median family incomes have risen from $23,514 in 1968 (in 2002 dollars, adjusted for inflation)

As the racial wealth divide workshop progressed, some of the participants seemed uncomfortable with the word "wealth."

One young black man, Max, said, "I think part of what's wrong with this country is that everyone wants to be a millionaire. There's too much greed. What's wrong with just wanting to make a decent living?"

A longtime community organizer, Kate, challenged the workshop's focus on assets, saying, "There's no point in programs for home ownership and savings accounts if people have low incomes and no health coverage."

to $30,134 in 2004, though white incomes have risen even faster.[4] Black per capita income has more than doubled in those same years, as has white income.[5]

But focusing just on income misses much of the problem. People of color are more likely to be tossed on the waves of economic turmoil—and sometimes drowned—because they don't have big enough asset security boats to help them stay afloat. Three-quarters of white people own their homes, while a slight majority of people of color are renters. In times of inflation, housing becomes easier to afford for homeowners with fixed mortgage rates, while renters see their housing costs rise. In times of recession or depression, those with savings accounts can better weather unemployment, while those without savings can be sunk into debt and deprivation. And in times of economic growth, those with assets can invest them or borrow against them to take advantage of business opportunities.

INCOME VERSUS WEALTH

"Income feeds your stomach, but assets change your head. That is, you really do act differently when you have a cushion of assets so that you can strategize around important opportunities in life. When you are living from paycheck to paycheck you just think about how you're making the next day or the next week or the next month happen. But

FIGURE 1-3
1999 per capita income by race

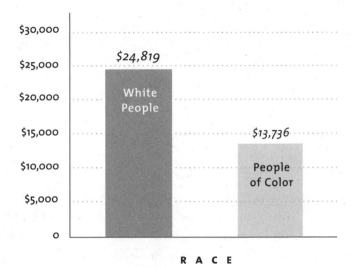

Source: United for a Fair Economy calculations of 2000 Census data.

FIGURE 1-4
Home ownership rates, 2003

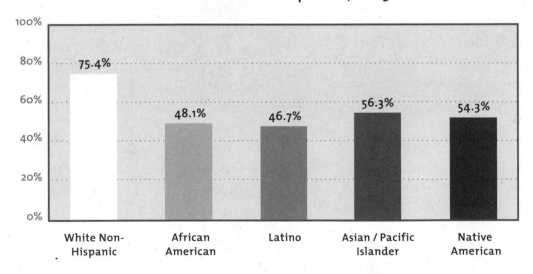

Source: U.S. Census Bureau, *Annual Statistics, 2003, Housing Vacancies and Homeownership,* Table 20.

when you have a set of resources that allow you to think about your future in a positive way, you can strategize about the future, create and take advantage of opportunity. Otherwise you stay in the present."

—MELVIN OLIVER, CO-AUTHOR OF *Black Wealth, White Wealth*[6]

Income can change on a dime, but wealth changes over generations. Our lives are shaped by the wealth—or lack of wealth—of our parents, our grandparents, and our ancestors. As an estimated 80 percent of assets come from transfers from prior generations, the history of the financial situations of prior generations is a primary cause of the racial wealth gap.[7] Until government policy tackles disparities in wealth—not just income—and until it recognizes and compensates for its own responsibility for the racial wealth gap, the United States will never have racial or economic justice.

White people are much more likely to inherit money from deceased relatives than people of color. In *The Hidden Cost of Being African American,* Thomas Shapiro summarizes the research on racial differences in inheritance. One study he cites reports that one in four white families received an inheritance after a parent's death, averaging $144,652, while only one in twenty African American families inherited, with an average inheritance of $41,985. Another study found that as of 1989, one-third of white baby boomers stood to inherit more than $25,000, as opposed to one in twenty black baby boomers.

These numbers show that most white people do not receive any inheritances from deceased relatives' estates. But in interviewing black and white working-class families, Shapiro found that modest amounts of money passed down by living relatives were also far more common in white families than in black families. Whites who get such help often don't think of themselves as inheritors, but consider such transfers to be just a normal part of family life. Contributions to a down payment on a house and college tuition are the most common forms of family financial aid. Shapiro calls these "transformative assets," because they boost lifelong prosperity and security. He estimates a national average of these transfers of $14,000.[8] About half of white families give this kind of head start to young adults, compared with about one in five black families.[9] He found that in white families, money flows from parents to children, while in black families, money flows from adult children to their parents and other relatives.

Shapiro concludes:

The real story of the meaning of race in modern America, however, must include a serious consideration of how one generation passes advantage and disadvantage to the next—how individuals' starting points are determined. While ending the old ways of outright exclusion, subjugation, segregation, custom, discrimination, racist ideology, and violence, our nation continues to reproduce racial inequality, racial hierarchy, and social injustice that is very real and formidable for those who experience it. [10]

SNAPSHOT OF THE 1850s

Think back just a few generations to the 1850s. In that decade, the U.S. government treated people dramatically different based on their race, and the differences present then still affect us today.

For many whites, especially white men, the 1850s were a very exciting time.

➤ Gold had been discovered in California in 1849, and eighty thousand white men had moved there in search of their fortunes, many with government assistance. Only whites were eligible for California land claims, and many who didn't find gold became farmers.

➤ Slave owners were getting rich off of slave labor. The average South Carolina slave owner's income in 1850 was $565, more than ten times the $53 average earnings of all white residents of the state.

➤ White women—for centuries blocked from asset ownership—had recently taken a few small steps toward equal rights. The Women's Rights Convention at Seneca Falls had just happened, in 1848. Married white women had just won the right to own property in New York State. [11]

➤ Anti-immigrant and anti-Catholic groups such as the Know-Nothing Party won elections in the 1850s, but they were never a majority of any legislative body, and thus white immigrant groups, though poor and despised, never lost legal rights.

➤ Congress was discussing plans for distribution of millions of acres of western land to white people through what would become the 1862 Homestead Act.

But if you were a Native American, 1850 was the beginning of one of the most devastating decades in a devastating century.

➤ Throughout the 1850s, the U.S. Army waged battles over land against Indian tribes.

➤ In 1851, the Sioux tribe yielded all of Iowa to the United States.

➤ The state of California appropriated $1 million for bounties for Native American scalps in 1851. In 1853, the California Preemptive Act made all Indian lands available for white homesteaders.

➤ The Native American population of California fell from 310,000 in 1850 to less than 50,000 in 1855, mostly from diseases brought by the "49ers."

If you were African American in 1850, it seemed that slavery would never end.

➤ The Fugitive Slave Law, passed that year, made it a criminal offense to hide or assist runaway slaves. Slave catchers could search for escaped slaves even in free states.

➤ Congress passed the Compromise of 1850, which made the new state of California a free state and ended the slave trade in Washington, D.C., but allowed slavery by popular vote in the other territories that would become Arizona, Utah, Nevada, and New Mexico.

➤ Dred Scott, who had filed suit to win his freedom in 1847, was set free in 1850 by a St. Louis circuit court. But ten years later the Supreme Court overturned that precedent, ruling that African Americans weren't citizens and therefore couldn't file lawsuits.

➤ Free African Americans lost jobs to new immigrants. In 1830 most servants in New York City were black, but by 1850, 80 percent were Irish women.[12]

If your roots were in Latin America, the 1850s were a disastrous decade to live in what's now the United States.

➤ Mexico had lost half of its territory in 1848. In theory the Treaty of Guadalupe-Hidalgo protected Mexican-American landowners. But in fact, one-third of these landowners became landless during the 1850s.

➤ The phrase "manifest destiny," coined a few years before, gained acceptance as a rationale to take much of North America from Mexico.

➤ A "Foreign Miner's Tax" was passed in California in 1850 to stop Mexicans from participating in the Gold Rush.[13] In 1852, it was extended to Chinese workers.

If you were Asian and immigrating to the United States around 1850, you found the country increasingly inhospitable.

➤ As several thousand Chinese men went to California in search of gold, special taxes, fees, and regulations were applied to prevent them from competing with white miners and business owners.

➤ In 1853, a court ruled that Chinese people weren't white, denying them many advantages of citizenship.

SNAPSHOT OF THE 1950s

Now fast-forward a hundred years to the 1950s, within living memory for most Americans or their parents or grandparents. The racial wealth gap widened then, too.

If you were white, the postwar boom meant good jobs and moving to the suburbs.

➤ Thanks to the GI Bill a large number of white male veterans entered college after World War II; many entered professions or got management jobs in the rapidly growing corporate sector.

➤ More than a quarter of all white families shifted from renting to owning their homes in the twenty years after the war.

➤ The new suburbs grew with federal subsidies for roads, infrastructure, and mortgages, and they were almost entirely limited to white home buyers.

➤ The cold war and anticommunism put a chill on the political climate that silenced the voices of many who questioned racism and white advantages.

If you were African American, segregation still ruled.

➤ Hopes raised by the desegregation of the armed forces in 1948 and the integration of professional sports were dashed, as other employers continued to discriminate.

➤ Returning black veterans didn't get the same hero's welcome as white vets. Most black World War II vets found the GI Bill's educational benefits didn't work, except at historically black colleges, which were swamped with far more applicants than they could accommodate. And most colleges were segregated, in practice and in some cases by law.

➤ Rule by terror continued in the South. Fourteen-year-old Emmett Till was murdered in Mississippi in 1955.

➤ Less than 1 percent of all mortgages issued from 1930 to 1960 were issued to African Americans.

➤ In 1948 the Supreme Court banned the restrictive covenants that had limited white home sellers to white buyers. The Federal Housing Administration stopped subsidizing mortgages for homes with restrictive covenants in 1950. But banks, realtors, insurance companies, and white home owners continued to find ways to exclude African Americans from buying homes in white neighborhoods. Too many black families were limited to deteriorating urban ghettos.

If you were Asian American, the U.S. government was still hostile to your presence in the early 1950s.

➤ Asians were still unable to become naturalized citizens in 1950. Not until the McCarren-Walter Act was passed in 1952 were immigrants from Asia able to become citizens.[14]

➤ Japanese-Americans who lost property while in internment camps were awarded some reparations through the 1948 Evacuation Claims Act, but they got only about ten cents for every dollar lost.[15]

If you were Latino and living in the United States or its territories, you were more than likely living in poverty in the 1950s.

➤ Puerto Rico was a territory of the United States, and Puerto Ricans had one of the world's lowest incomes, only 40¢ per day in 1940.[16] Not surprisingly, by 1950 great numbers were moving to the mainland. They came to New York for low-wage factory jobs that disappeared shortly thereafter, leaving them with few opportunities by the end of the 1950s.

➤ Operation Bootstrap enacted in 1947 gave tax incentives for U.S. companies to set up shop on the island, thereby crowding out businesses owned by Puerto Ricans. More than one in eight Puerto Ricans was unemployed.

➤ Most Mexican Americans were landless laborers on land their parents and grandparents had owned.

➤ Mexicans were brought to the United States to fill labor shortages during the war, but in the mid-1950s hundreds of thousands were deported in Operation Wetback.

If you were Native American, you were struggling in 1950 to regain some of what your people had lost.

➤ There had been some progress for Indian tribes in recent decades. The Indian Reorganization Act of 1934 had allowed tribes to regain four million acres by 1950.

➤ But then, in 1953, Congress passed a tribal termination policy that ended federal recognition of and services for over a hundred tribes. The Klamath alone lost over 880,000 acres of timberland. The Menominee tribe went from prosperity to impoverishment after being terminated in 1954.

AND IN 2050?

When 2050 arrives, what will its snapshot look like? Will the rules of the economy still be tilted toward white people's prosperity? Will we maintain an economic order that fosters social divisions?

Or will our country have built a ladder of economic opportunity for Americans of all races to climb? Will we have given those held back for so long a boost to a higher rung? By 2050, a majority of our population will be people of color. Our nation's unity depends on our answers.

WHY NOT JUST FIGHT POVERTY?

Isn't the problem low income and assets, regardless of race? Why not just focus on ending poverty? Why focus specifically on the racial divide?

It's true that the racial wealth divide exists in the context of growing overall economic inequality, now at historic proportions not seen since 1929. And it's true that millions of white people are among those who have fallen backward over the last twenty-five years. More than one in six American children live in poverty, including one in eleven white children.[17] Many progressives of all races advocate organizing against poverty and economic insecurity generally—without highlighting the racial divide—to unite people against the excesses of the superrich.

Recent decades have been a great time for people whose income has come mostly from owning assets, with ten years of explosive growth in stock prices and tax cuts targeted at that group. By 2003, there were 2.27 million millionaires in the United States, up from 1.8 million in 1997.[18] Although major asset owners are disproportionately white, most whites depend on wages for their income. And wage earners did not share in the stock market growth of the 1980s and 1990s.

The wealthiest 1 percent of American families, who own a third of all U.S. wealth, saw their net worth grow by 63 percent, to an average of $12.6 million, from 1983 to 2001, and their financial wealth grow by 109 percent.[19] Meanwhile, the 40 percent with the lowest net worth saw their average wealth fall 44 percent in those same years, to $2,900.[20] Most of this was home equity, and their average financial net worth fell 46 percent to negative $10,000—in other words, more debt than financial assets.[21]

Wealth inequality gaps are much wider in the United States than in other industrialized countries.[22] While the average after tax income of the richest 1 percent tripled from 1979 to 2000, to $863,000, the bottom fifth only rose 9 percent, to $13,700, despite all the economic growth of those decades. The middle fifth gained just 15 percent, to $41,900.[23] The 2.8 million people in the richest 1 percent of American families had more after tax income in 2000 than the 110 million Americans in the lowest income four-tenths of the population.[24] CEO pay grew from 42 times median worker pay in 1980 to 431 times in 2004.[25]

Economic instability has grown among working people of all races. Almost forty-six million Americans lacked health coverage in 2004, and over seven million were counted as unemployed in August 2005.[26, 27] While the uninsured and the unemployed were disproportionately people of color, a majority of them were white. The trade policies, monetary policies, budget decisions, labor rights setbacks, and tax cuts of the last three decades benefited corporations and major asset owners and disadvantaged moderate- and low-income people of all races.

One's impression of the wealth of the average white family depends on which definition of "average" is used. Using the mean, which divides the total wealth owned by the number of white people, distorts the picture by conflating ordinary families with the superrich elite. After all, if you average Bill Gates's assets with a Wal-Mart cashier's, they each have over $20 billion. But using the median—the family in the middle of the line if all white families were lined up in order of net worth (assets minus debts), about $121,000 in 2001—gives a more real-

istic picture of how little benefit white working families get from sharing a race with most of the superrich.

Whites who express resistance to the concept of the racial wealth divide are not necessarily racist but often are working-class people who can't see how government programs have benefited them. The term "white privilege" sometimes falls flat with white people who for reasons of class, gender, disability, or age find themselves living lives that seem far from privileged. One-quarter of white families don't own a home, and more than one in twelve live below the poverty line. Those laid off in the recession of the early 2000s were disproportionately white men in high-tech industries, and they may never recover that lost ground in the new global high-tech economy. The growing economic insecurity faced by more and more white people also cries out for solutions.

The right wing takes advantage of the economic hardships of working and poor white people to recruit supporters for so-called color-blind policies. In 2003, Californians voted on and defeated Proposition 54, a referendum to prohibit public collection of racial information. The Center for Individual Rights has pressed lawsuits against affirmative action in several states. Their suit against the University of Michigan went to the U.S. Supreme Court with mixed results, affirming yet limiting the legality of race-based affirmative action programs.

At the crux of the argument over affirmative action is a historical debate about when discrimination against people of color ended, if ever. "Slavery was a long time ago," goes the argument against reparations for African Americans. And it is true that the best-known transfers of wealth from people of color to white people—taking land from Native Americans and Mexicans, as well as slavery—are no longer in living memory of the people in the United States today. The Civil Rights Movement tackled overt racial discrimination and won broad support for greater equality of opportunity, and the racial income gap and wealth gap shrank in those first postsegregation decades.

So why not disregard race and simply work to eliminate poverty and economic insecurity for everyone?

Because this challenging economy presents more barriers for people of color than for white people. Because past efforts to raise the floor left out most people of color. And therefore the goal of economic security for everyone won't be reached unless we intentionally tackle racism.

In what ways do people of color face more economic barriers than white people? Both outright discrimination and the costs of segregation block the advancement of people of color.

Discrimination

First, despite the denial by conservatives such as Dinesh D'Souza, author of *The End of Racism*, old-fashioned prejudice and dis-

crimination have not gone away. A striking example was portrayed in the episode of ABC's *Primetime Live* in 1991 in which two young men, one black and one white and with similar credentials, moved to a new city.[28] While filmed by a secret camera, they applied for jobs, apartments, and car loans, and met very different receptions. The white young man was offered good deals and rapidly found a position, a home, and a car. The black man was told that apartments had been filled, was rejected for jobs, and was required to pay a higher down payment and interest rate on his car loan. People were rude to his face and security guards followed him around stores.

A 2003 study of job applications showed continuing employer discrimination. Researchers at the University of Chicago and the Massachusetts Institute of Technology sent fictitious responses to help-wanted ads, with either white-sounding names (Emily Walsh, Brendan Baker) or black-sounding names (Lakisha Washington, Jamal Jones). Those with white-sounding names received 50 percent more invitations for an initial interview than applicants with black-sounding names. Black résumés weren't helped much by stronger credentials.[29] Similarly, a sociologist at Northwestern University sent white and black men with and without criminal records to job interviews, and found that white applicants with prison records were more likely to be hired than black applicants without one.[30]

The Costs of Segregation

Even when employers, landlords, and real-tors aren't prejudiced and even when there is no outright discrimination, people of color still tend to be blocked by where they live and who they know from getting as much money as white people. Shapiro's research indicates that homes in neighbor-hoods that are more than 10 percent black have 16 percent less value compared with equivalent homes in overwhelmingly white neighborhoods.[31] Home ownership is worth, on average, $60,000 more to white families than to black families.[32] The asset accumulation method of millions of work-ing-class and middle-class white people—buying a house and letting it appreciate in value until it's sold at retirement—continues to be impossible for most people of color.

Even low-income white people tend to have connections and advantages not avail-able to their counterparts of color. White poor people spend a shorter time in poverty and suffer less extreme deprivation than poor people of color. A good example is a story Dalton Conley tells about growing up as one of the few white families in a poor black neighborhood. When the local school deteriorated, and his parents had no money to move or to send him to a private school, they contacted a friend on the other side of town who let them lie and use his address so Conley could get into a well-funded, high-quality school in that neighborhood.[33] Most

of his black neighbors didn't have that option. He says that he likes to ask white people how they got their jobs. "Mostly people get their jobs through social net-works and connections. Usually it's someone you know—your uncle in the next city or a friend of a friend who knows somebody in your industry. And that is how we get the foot in the door. Unfortunately, because most jobs in businesses are controlled or owned by whites, given the structure of ownership in America, that leads to the per-petuation of racial inequality in the labor market. Whites tend to hire whites because they get them through their personal net-works, which tend to be white."[34]

But wouldn't universal solutions that reach every neighborhood, like single-payer health care, a higher minimum wage, and public investment in affordable housing in fact disproportionately help people of color, while also helping whites in need? These universal solutions are indeed an important part of the answer, as the last chapter will elaborate. But too often universal remedies have been tilted in whites' favor, as with the Social Security Act and other New Deal legislation, which didn't mention race but still managed to give benefits almost entirely to white people in the 1930s and 1940s.

Imagine a first-time home-buyer program that helps two families, one white and one of color, with a lower down payment and a lower interest rate. The white family's "starter home" in a white neighborhood appreciates in value, enabling them to sell it and buy a bigger house in a neighborhood with better schools. Their next house appreciates in value too, and they get a home equity loan against it to send their kids to college. By the time they retire, the mortgage is all paid off. They sell the house, buy a small senior apartment, and invest the difference to give them some income to supplement their social security. Home ownership has given them education and retirement as well as a place to live.

The family of color's house appreciates more slowly or not at all. With lower property values come lower property tax revenues for their city, and so their neighborhood schools are lower in quality. They are more likely to face prolonged unemployment and lose their home to foreclosure. But even if they are able to keep up with the mortgage payments, they can't turn their home into retirement income because there is no cheaper housing to move into. Banks are less likely to give them a home equity loan. Home ownership gave them little more than a place to live.

The first-time home-owner program staff probably thought of the program as color-blind, open to all races. Perhaps they even did extra outreach to make sure they reached people of color. But a program aimed at helping everyone equally ended up helping white people more.

Cultural practices of particular ethnic groups also become barriers with one size fits all white lenders. For example, Vietnamese families who have never incurred debt and pay all bills in cash are sometimes rejected as not credit worthy, and groups of Latino immigrants who pool their resources to start a business are evaluated as individuals instead of as a group.

The 1990s saw a proliferation of local asset-building initiatives, such as pilot Individual Development Account (IDA) programs, innovative approaches to private saving and home ownership, and small businesses that share equity broadly with employees. While these initiatives may help some people of color, without thinking through new initiatives so that they clearly address the racial dimension of wealth disparities, the racial gap may well remain constant.

Melvin Oliver and Thomas Shapiro, in their 1995 book, *Black Wealth/White Wealth*, found that differences in income, occupation, and education only accounted for about 29 percent of the difference between white and black families' assets in 1988; over 70 percent of the difference was related just to race.[35] They called this "the costs of being black," but it could also be called the benefit of being white.

THE UNDERESTIMATED ROLE OF GOVERNMENT IN WEALTH CREATION

"Help from the government" sounds like something poor people and seniors get, not working people or wealthy people. But in fact, all of us depend on public infrastructure such as roads, schools, and laws. And the process of building wealth depends on government programs like social security, Pell grants, subsidized mortgages, and farm loans—and in earlier centuries, land grants.

All these have been more available to white people.

How we try to close the racial wealth gap depends on how we understand where assets come from. If we think well-off white people got their wealth only through individual ability and hard work, then the solution will be to urge low-income people of color to try harder. But if we also see how heavily

At this point in the workshop, it's time to discuss the cause of the racial wealth gap. The trainer asks, "How do people get wealth?" Everyone calls out answers:

"Marrying money!" The group laughs.

"Hard work and saving, that's the only way that works."

"If you're white, maybe. If you're black, forget it—you're not gonna get rich."

"It's all who you know. You gotta have the connections."

"Talent. If you're the best in the world at something."

"Entrepreneurship. Starting a business that takes off."

"Inheriting it. Most rich people got it from Daddy."

The group falls silent, their list complete.

The trainer asks, "What about the government? Is there anything the government does that affects whether people have wealth?"

There's silence in the room.

Finally one young woman, Susan, raises her hand and speaks tentatively. "Do you mean the lottery?"

white people have historically relied on government help to build assets, then we will support expanding assistance to all assetless Americans, and we will work for racial justice for those historically barred from wealth because of their race.

Government racism has not been uniformly applied to all groups of color, but has been manifested through different mechanisms for different ethnic groups over the centuries. Native Americans were displaced from their land by force and then faced constantly changing conceptions of their status dreamed up in Washington, D.C. African Americans were enslaved and then kept at the bottom of the economy by legal segregation and violence. Conquest of Spanish-speaking countries, justified by the Monroe Doctrine, turned Latinos into colonial subjects, both in their formerly independent lands and in the rest of the United States. Asian Americans have been treated as perpetual foreigners no matter how long they've been in the United States. One after the other, these groups were racialized, that is, made into a legal entity subordinate to white people.

Citizenship, as explored by Evelyn Nakano Glenn, is a government-granted status that opens the door to full membership in the society.[36] Citizenship rights ebbed and flowed for each race over the centuries, with all people of color and all women excluded at some times and places. In various ways, lesser political status meant exclusion from better jobs reserved for "free whites": for

example, indentured servitude for Chinese immigrants and Native Americans in California in the 1850s, peonage for Mexican Americans, and of course slavery for African Americans.[37]

This book attempts to tell each of these distinct stories while also pointing out their commonalities in contrast to white Americans' experience. Though many white working-class and poor people, especially immigrants, have struggled with poverty and limited opportunity in the United States, never have they faced these kinds of official obstacles, and frequently the government has given them boosts to prosperity.

In stressing the role of government actions and inactions, we are not claiming that they are the only cause of the racial wealth divide. Ideology, culture, and economic systems are of course woven throughout the history of racial injustice in the United States as well. Government policy does not arise in a vacuum but is formed by voter attitudes and interests and by economic forces, and policy in turn influences beliefs and economic behavior. But as black scholar Adolph Reed Jr. said, "The role of the state is consistently underestimated" in analyzing racism.[38]

The economy is not an invisible hand that operates by its own natural laws. It's a human creation that embodies racial power differences, both caused by and causing discriminatory government policies and individual interactions.

The United States has an economic system based on private ownership and very limited public regulation and public services compared with other industrialized countries. This laissez-faire system did play a role in creating the racial wealth divide. Some scholars emphasize that wealthy white employers and investors always had excessive influence on creating policy in their own interest, despite the officially democratic political system. Manning Marable has said, "The U.S. state apparatus was created to facilitate the expansion and entrenchment of institutional racism in both slave and non-slaveholding states."[39] Theodore Allen documents the role of Virginia planters in steering the colonies and then the new United States away from more direct democracy.[40] William Julius Wilson tells the story of how, when black people were at last allowed to apply for every job, manufacturing jobs disappeared from the northern cities. Just as the ladder of upward mobility was opened to everyone, the ladder broke in half, with new service industries creating millions of nonunion, unstable "McJobs" to be filled by the workers at the bottom of the labor market, who because of historical racism were disproportionately people of color.[41]

In *Faded Dreams: The Politics and Economics of Race in America*, Martin Carnoy says that "every class politics implicitly takes a stand on issues of race," and it's not a coincidence that those disadvantaged by economic policies since the 1980s have been disproportionately people of color. Rather,

antiworking-class policies were sold politically by framing them with racist rhetoric about underclass culture and "welfare queens."[42]

Racial inequality is also perpetuated through what Joe Feagin calls "racial oppression in everyday practice."[43] Cultural, intellectual, religious, and psychological factors help racism permeate through the society.

But the most persistent racist ideologies tend to be those actively promoted by governments. For example, manifest destiny was the rationale for the Anglo conquest of western Native and Mexican lands.

Public policy represents institutionalized attitudes, for better or for worse. Just as segregation laws are institutionalized prejudice, antidiscrimination laws are institutionalized multicultural acceptance. Just as egalitarian whites couldn't legally act on their good attitudes under Jim Crow and antimiscegenation laws, bigoted whites can't legally act on their prejudice under affirmative action laws. The United States needs to institutionalize a multicultural vision of our society in which every group gets the resources and opportunities to thrive.

We see a complex interplay between economics, ideology, and government policies in forming the racial wealth gap. At key moments of U.S. history—after the Civil War, during the Great Depression, and during the turmoil of the 1960s—white Southern landowners and businessmen exerted political pressure to limit or reverse racial progress. Their motivations were pre-

In the next part of the workshop, the trainer asks the group to list ways the government could narrow the racial wealth divide, and is surprised by the resistance she gets.

A longtime black activist calls out, "We've tried that and we've been burned. You can't trust the government to do anything for people of color. We've got to rely on our own community development."

A Native American college student and artist says, "Whatever the government does, there will still be misrepresentations of our people in movies and ads, and white people will still think we're not as good as them. You can't legislate positive images of people of color."

The trainer widens the question to what anyone *could do to narrow the racial wealth divide, and the discussion is off and running.*

sumably a combination of racist prejudice and economic self-interest. Since Southern congressmembers have always had more than their share of leadership roles, the federal government caved in to their pressure and weakened voting rights, the Social Security Act, and Great Society programs. A government not already saturated with institutional racism might have stood up to them.

Similar stories can be found in other parts of the United States, keeping other racial groups at the bottom of the local economy. Southwestern growers in the 1940s successfully lobbied for a guest worker program to bring in short-term contract workers from Mexico, in violation of laws against peonage.[44] In Hawaii, sugar plantation owners influenced policy on who was allowed to

immigrate there, and deliberately stirred up intergroup tensions by putting one Asian group over another as overseers.[45]

There's a circle of causation: economic interests foment prejudice; prejudiced people and self-interested campaign contributors elect racist politicians; racist politicians enact discriminatory policies that further white employers' interests.

However, the government's role is often ignored in popular images of racism. School curricula on the Civil War and for Black History Month often portray the federal government as the savior of black people, intervening on their behalf against slave owners and segregationist mobs. Its capitulations to white Southern racists are overlooked.

Martin Carnoy has seen three different

common explanations for racial inequality, which he calls "individual responsibility," "pervasive racism," and "economic restructuring," and he thinks all three depoliticize racial inequality too much.[46] He thinks politics reinforced the economic and social conditions that impeded black progress.[47]

A political explanation for changes in black progress is not a replacement for all other explanations. Rather, it makes otherwise rigid, depoliticized explanations rooted in racism, changing economic structures, and even individual responsibility more dynamic and coherent. A political explanation also suggests more hope for future improvement. How politics frames racial issues and how government policies treat these issues can be changed and changed more quickly than ingrained individual fears about race or long-established business practices. . . . Politics is shaped by normative rules—how things should be, not how they are. Normative rules can, by their very nature, be shifted, and fairly quickly.[48]

Government Obstacles: Not Only Pre-1964

Legal discrimination was gradually chipped away at from the 1940s to the 1960s, culminating with the Civil Rights Laws. But traces of de jure (in law) discrimination lingered on. For example, the Federal Housing Administration (FHA) continued to exclude most people of color from subsidized mortgage programs, which was legal because the 1964 Civil Rights Act had specifically exempted federal mortgage insurance programs.[49] Enforcement of fair housing laws was so weak as to be almost nonexistent in the 1960s and 1970s.

Disparate treatment by the federal government has also been concealed in seemingly race-neutral policies, as the next five chapters will show. The federal mandate to aid family farms was interpreted by the Department of Agriculture as a mandate to aid *white* farmers. A 1980 class action lawsuit by North Carolina Black Farmers charged that the FHA discriminated in loans to farmers. The Equal Employment Opportunity Commission (EEOC) looked into the charges and found that they were true: white farmers got more help, quicker help, and help on easier terms than black farmers.[50]

President Reagan backed off from even the limited federal commitments to affirmative action and investments in communities of color that were made in the 1970s. Manning Marable describes the racist approach and widespread harm of the Reagan administrations this way:

Reagan's racial agenda was unambiguous to friend and foe alike. He opposed affirmative action, minority economic set-asides, and enforcement of equal employment opportunity regulations. . . . Reagan manipulated crude racist stereotypes in his standard speeches, such as images of "welfare mothers" abusing food stamps and other public assistance programs. Yet despite the deeply racist character of the "Reagan Revolution". . . its essential dynamics were driven by the political economy of capitalism. . . . Reaganism represented a fundamental departure from the liberal welfare state and Keynesian economic policies that had been followed to a great extent by both capitalist political parties. . . . Massive reductions in social programs across the board were mandated . . . 400,000 families were removed from federal and state welfare roles . . . the Department of Agriculture reduced the amount of food served to 26 million children at more than 94,000 schools across the country. Federal housing expenditures and special programs designed for low-income families virtually came to a halt. . . . The number of homeless Americans not surprisingly doubled during Reagan's tenure in office. Most other social programs, such as job training, community development agencies and cooperatives, and public health clinics were either eliminated completely or severely curtailed."[51]

Both the Clinton and Bush administrations have toughened bankruptcy, welfare, and social security rules under the rhetoric of "personal responsibility" and "the free market," but people of color have been disproportionately harmed. For example, the welfare reform law of 1996 was implemented more harshly for recipients of color than white recipients. White people leaving welfare are twice as likely as black and Latina people leaving welfare to receive transitional benefits like child care and transportation assistance.[52] Children of undocumented immigrants, even high school valedictorians whose parents have been paying taxes for decades, are barred from getting in-state tuition rates and public scholarships in many states, excluding some of them from higher education. The gains to people of color from government employment and antidiscrimination policies since the 1960s are counterbalanced by policies that boost white people and hold people of color back.

EVERYONE WOULD BENEFIT FROM CLOSING THE RACIAL WEALTH GAP

In the long run, white people also lose from policies that disadvantage people of color. The lower floor in the United States compared with western Europe, Canada, and other industrialized countries—below poverty minimum wage, weak social bene-fits, lack of guaranteed health care, poor education system—can be attributed to the racial divisions in the United States. The existence of a labor force with substandard wages enforced by racism has enabled employers to pay less to all workers.

Undocumented immigrants are currently the most common group being used this way by unscrupulous employers. Public benefits like welfare and Medicaid are associated with people of color by politicians and media, thus weakening their support among white voters, and then poor whites also suffer when they are cut.

Our vision is not just success for a few, with people of color finally mirroring the class spectrum whites now have. We envision smaller inequality overall, real opportunity for all, and an economy with a higher floor. But within this fairer economy, people of color would be fully enfranchised, with as much economic security as white people. And that will only happen if boosts are given to help the targets of past discrimination accumulate wealth.

There is sometimes queasiness about wealth among progressives who critique the excessive, one-sided rewards to the owners of capital in this economic system. However, we make a distinction between asset ownership made lucrative by exploiting others on the one hand (such as rental housing with excessive rents or inadequate maintenance, or business ownership with low wages and no profit sharing), and basic assets that bring security on the other (such as home ownership and retirement accounts). Of course, there is an enormous gray area, and principled people can disagree about what constitutes exploitation. But it would be hard to argue that owning the home one lives in harms anyone else. It would be hard to argue that having a savings account or retirement account in a credit union or a bank committed to community reinvestment harms anyone else. By making a distinction between modest transformative assets and huge fortunes swollen by exploitation even the firmest critics of capitalism can get behind the goal of asset building for all.

WHY THESE FIVE RACIAL CATEGORIES?

In the next five chapters, we tell the history of government obstacles to asset building for Native American, African American, Latino, and Asian American people, and of government boosts to asset building for white people.

We chose to divide the incredibly diverse population of the United States into these five ethnic groups because they are the largest groups to share a common history of racialization and to face common treatment by the United States government. We tell the histories of groups of color in the order that they began, to show how racism evolved from one group to the next.

Race is, of course, a social construct, not an absolute biological reality. Human beings share 99.9 percent identical DNA. If you look back far enough, all of us have ancestors who traveled the globe and intermingled; and before that we all share an original common ancestor in Africa. The people in the United States could be separated by "race," nationality, and ethnicity into two groups, four groups, eight groups, or a hundred groups, and reasons could be given for each clumping. The categories and words in common use have changed many times over the centuries, and they will change many times in the future.

But if the topic is government actions that affect assets, the five groupings in this book make historical sense. Native Americans of all tribes faced genocide and displacement. Latinos of all nationalities ended up in this country after the United States government invaded, dominated, and/or conquered their lands. Almost all African Americans are the descendants of slaves and of survivors of segregation and mob violence. Asian Americans of all nationalities have been treated as perpetual foreigners. And most European Americans of all ethnic groups have been treated (sometimes reluctantly) as citizens worthy of government assistance. Everyone's story—everyone's reasons for having the amount of assets they own—is different, but most of our ancestral stories fit into one of these five historical streams.

New policies based on race and nationality are still being enacted, such as the post–September 11 detention of over twelve hundred Arab and Muslim men without evidence of wrongdoing, and the registration required for immigrant men from only Muslim countries imposed in 2003. But we have chosen to focus on large groups with centuries-long histories of discrimination in the United States.

And these historical streams have affected each other. As Joe Feagin puts it,

> U.S. society is not a multiplicity of disconnected racisms directed at people of color. Instead, this U.S. society has a central white-supremacist core initially developed in the minds, ideologies, practices, and institutions of those calling themselves "whites" for destroying the indigenous societies and for exploiting African labor. This structure of racialized domination was later extended and adapted by the descendants of the founders for the oppressions of other non-European groups such as Asian and Latino Americans.[53]

Racial inequality used to be regarded as a black/white issue. In 1968, the Kerner Commission, a civil rights advisory board created by President Lyndon Johnson, warned that America was rapidly becoming "two nations," "black vs. white," "separate and unequal." In part, this framing was due to the invisibility of Native Americans, Latinos, and Asian Americans to oblivious white policy makers. But in truth, their numbers were much smaller then. In 1960, whites were 88.6 percent of those responding to the census, blacks, 10.5 percent, Asians, 0.5 percent, and Native Americans, 0.3 percent—almost the identical black and white percentages as in 1910.[54] Questions about Spanish language or Hispanic/Latino origins first appeared in 1970, when they were only about 4.5 percent of the respondents.[55]

Even when Melvin Oliver and Thomas Shapiro wrote their groundbreaking book *Black Wealth/White Wealth* in 1995, the most recent census (widely criticized for under-counting people of color) showed Latino, Asian, and Native American people totaling only 13 percent together, compared with 12 percent black and 75 percent "non-Hispanic white" people.[56] But now it is clear that the United States is a multicultural country, and becoming more so as the global economy displaces more and more people. In 2000, for the first time, the U.S. Census allowed people to identify themselves as more than one race, and 2.4 percent took this multiracial option.[57] The 2000 census also found Latinos more numerous than non-Latino African Americans for the first time, 12.5 percent compared with 12.1 percent. Non-Latino whites had fallen to 69.1 percent, and the other categories had grown, with 0.7 percent American Indian, 3.6 percent Asian, 0.1 percent Native Hawaiian and Pacific Islander, and 5.5 percent "other."[58] In the South, where the historic dynamic has been between black and white, there has been a sudden increase in the population of Latinos. This has brought new attention to the historic racial dynamics among white, Chicano/Mexican American, and Native American people in the Southwest.

As a result of this multicultural trend and growing economic inequality, competition has heated up among communities of color for a slice of the pie. Misunderstandings and mythologies about each race have grown: it is hard to see what they have in common. Their stories are viewed as separate racisms—slavery, Indian genocide, Mexican conquest. In fact, all groups of color have faced the same racism expressed through different mechanisms. Manning Marable describes the issues among groups of color this way:

> With the growth of a more class-conscious black and Latino bourgeoisie, ironically a social product of affirmative action and civil rights gains, tensions between these two large communities of people of color [blacks and Latinos] began to grow. . . . The tragedy underlying this issue is that too little is done either by African American or Latino mainstream leaders who practice racial identity politics, to transcend parochialism and redefine their agendas on common ground. . . . While African Americans, Latinos and Asian Americans scramble over which group should control the mom-and-pop grocery store in their neighborhoods, almost no one questions the racist "redlining" policies of large banks that restrict access to capital to nearly all people of color. Black and Latino working people usually are not told by their race-conscious leaders and middle-class symbolic representatives that institutional racism has also frequently targeted Asian Americans throughout U.S. history. . . . We need to recognize that both perspectives of racial iden-

tity politics, which are frequently juxtaposed as integration/assimilation versus nationalist/separatism, are actually two different sides of the same ideological axis. . . . The ability to create a framework for multicultural democracy intergroup dialogue and interaction within and between the most progressive leaders, grassroots activists, intellectuals, and working people of these communities will determine the future of American society itself.[59]

And after September 11, anti-immigrant sentiment increased among U.S. citizens of all races. Now more than ever racial minorities need to recognize their commonalities in order to implement successful strategies to counter the conservative backlash and to wage the battle for full equality.

In 1903, W.E.B. DuBois named the color line as the key problem of the twentieth century. One century later, we face the same question. How it gets answered will determine our character as a nation. Do we continue to pay lip service to the ideals of our Constitution? Or will we practice what we preach, and truly become a beacon of democracy and equality? First, we must develop a shared understanding of the roots of the divisions, before we can understand how to overcome them. As the saying goes, You can't know where you're going, if you don't know where you've been.

Chapter 2

LAND RICH, DIRT POOR: CHALLENGES TO ASSET BUILDING IN NATIVE AMERICA

*"[Tribes] may . . . be denominated domestic dependent nations . . .
their relation to the United States resembles that of a ward to his
guardian."*

—CHIEF JUSTICE MARSHALL, 1831, *Cherokee Nation v. Georgia*

American Indian tribes are the single largest private landholders in the United States today. But their relationships to this wealth is different than any other group of Americans.

Imagine for a moment that you have inherited a large amount of wealth and property from a rich uncle in Texas. After celebrating your good fortune, you would probably seek to manage and protect this wealth in the best way possible. You may visit with an attorney to set up a trust fund to provide for you and your children. You would receive quarterly statements communicating the particulars of this trust fund—how much wealth it generates in a year, how your money has been invested, how much you are being charged in fees and service costs. More importantly, you would receive regular payments from this trust. If you were dissatisfied with the way your trust fund was being managed, you would have the freedom to hire a new attorney or trust manager, and would seek the most qualified person to manage your valuable assets.

And what about that land in Texas, rich with oil? You would seek to secure the best possible lease for the oil, and would closely monitor the revenues generated from this valuable natural resource. If you felt that you were receiving lower than market rate for your product, you would work to find a new contract that would generate the highest possible return for your goods. If you suspected that your business manager was not finding the best contracts for your oil, you would fire him or her.

These basic principles of asset management are followed by most people who own wealth in America. Yet these basic principles are not available to Native Americans, whose wealth is managed for them by the federal government. The wealth of Native Americans, including the land, natural resources, and income generated from such resources, is "held in trust" for them, meaning that the federal government controls when and how the land is leased, how much money the oil and gas and other resources sell for, and how the money earned is distributed. U.S. courts have ruled that there is

a trustee-beneficiary relationship between tribes and the U.S. government, similar to a guardian and a ward, and from this legal opinion emerged the modern paternalistic relationship toward Indian tribes.

Stemming from the doctrine of trust responsibility, the federal government (through the Bureau of Indian Affairs) controls the management of Indian resources "for their best interest." While in writing it may have appeared that the United States government was interested in "protecting" tribal resources, in reality the federal government has mismanaged them, depriving the tribes of untold amounts of revenue.

The Supreme Court has ruled that the treaties entered into with the federal government create a legal relationship between the Indian tribes and the federal government. The government must respect the sovereignty of the tribes and provide "food, services and clothing to the tribes." In exchange for taking Indian lands and restricting tribes to reservation lands set aside for their use, the federal government would be held under the "moral obligations of the highest responsibility and trust" to the tribes. The *Seminole Nation v. United States* decision in 1942 defined the government duty to keep its promises and act in the best interests of the tribes as "the doctrine of trust responsibility."

While under the doctrine of trust responsibility the U.S. government may claim to manage tribal affairs for the best interests of tribes, this doctrine has in fact been applied in a paternalistic fashion over the past two hundred years. In 1977, the American Indian Policy Review Commission reported to the U.S. Senate that "the Bureau of Indian Affairs . . . has used the trust doctrine as a means to develop a paternalistic control over the day-to-day affairs of Indian tribes and individuals."

This doctrine of trust responsibility has affected American Indian tribes in two important ways: First, the trust responsibility promoted federal control of Indian assets, including land and natural resources, throughout U.S. history. Even in the last twenty years, as Native people have found new ways to create wealth, Congress has legislated new methods of exerting control that undermine Native sovereignty and take money out of the Native wealth pot. Although the original intention of the trust responsibility was to manage tribal resources for the best interests of the tribes, federal appropriation of Native wealth and federal mismanagement has led to lost resources and

stolen funds. These facts are the basis for a $137 billion lawsuit against the U.S. Department of the Interior.

Second, the trust responsibility has led to decades of federal policies intended to help Native Americans assimilate into mainstream white society. These policies included: forcing Indians to sell their tribal land to acquire cash; forcing Indians to adopt Western farming techniques; and removing Indian children from their families to attend schools designed to assimilate them into mainstream society. Such policies have been used for nearly two centuries to coerce Native Americans to accept Western models of property ownership, promoting private property ownership instead of collective tribal property ownership, and have attempted to erode the cultural traditions that formed tribal communities and societies. Beyond the physical genocide practiced in the 1700s and 1800s, these policies result in cultural destruction as well.

TRIBAL LAND, TRIBAL POVERTY

There are over 562 federally recognized tribes in the United States, with reservations that range in size from less than 100 acres to the 17 million-acre Navajo reservation. This includes 333 federally recognized tribes in the lower 48 states, and 229 Alaska Native Villages, now legally recognized as tribes.

In the lower 48 states, reservation lands

account for over 54 million acres, and if the 42 million acres of Alaska Native lands are added, the aggregate amount would qualify as the fourth largest land base by area in the United States, behind Alaska, Texas, and California. Along with the timber, grazing, and croplands, other natural resources include 4 percent of U.S. oil and gas

Largest Tribes and Other Native American Groups

(Population according to the 2000 Census)[1]

Cherokee	281,069
Navajo	269,202
Sioux	108,272
Chippewa	105,907
Alaska Native	95,918
Choctaw	87,349
Pueblo	59,533
Apache	57,060
Lumbee	51,913
Iroquois	45,212
Creek	40,223
Blackfeet	27,109
Chickasaw	20,087
Tohono O'Odham	17,466
Potawatomi	15,817
Yaqui	15,224
Seminole	12,431
Cheyenne	11,191
Puget Sound Salish	11,034
Comanche	10,120

Source: Census 2000

reserves, 30 percent of the low-sulfur coal reserves, and 40 percent of the privately held uranium deposits.

For most people anywhere in today's economy, such property holdings would equal wealth and money. Not so for the American Indian. Defying the economic tenet that property holdings and wealth are two sides of the same economic coin, today's Native Americans have the highest poverty rate in the nation.[2] Native Americans, as a group, have a 25.7 percent poverty rate, and they suffer from disproportionately low education levels[3] and high levels of chronic diseases. Official unemployment on Indian reservations is close to 22 percent annually, with seasonal employment even higher.[4]

Native Americans have the worst housing of any ethnic group. In 2000, 24 percent of households on Indian reservations were overcrowded, almost double the U.S. average.[5] Nearly 24 percent of homes on reservations lacked complete plumbing, substantially higher than the national rate.[6] Among Native American homeowners, the median home value was $81,000 in 1999, or only two-thirds of the white median.[7]

While net worth data are not available for Native Americans, there is evidence that asset ownership is far lower than for white Americans. Only 18 percent of American Indians had any income from interest, dividends, or rents in 1999,[8] compared with 41 percent of whites.[9] There were 197,300 Native American–owned businesses in 1997, but two out of five had revenues of less than

FIGURE 2-1

Median family income, 1999

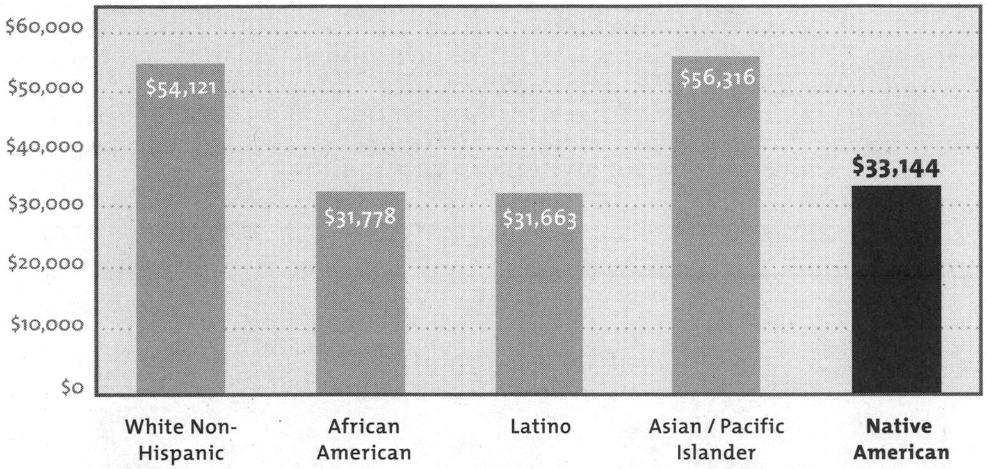

Source: U.S. Census Bureau, *Historical Income Tables*, Table F-5, *Characteristics of American Indians and Alaska Natives by Tribe and Language, Census 2000*, Table 10.

$10,000, three out of five less than $25,000.[10]

How did this group of people that was once so rich come to exhibit such signs of poverty? It is through a long history of federal policy that systematically stripped Native Americans of their assets, including land and natural resources such as gas and oil. Tribes are, in effect, "land rich and dirt poor." This overview of federal policy toward Native Americans shows how it has both systematically removed assets from Native American ownership and also reduced Native control of assets that they rightfully own.

History now widely recognizes that the economic and political structures of colonial rule converted tribal territories into vast wastelands. Yet often unrecognized are the

structural features of colonialism that persist within the legislative, administrative, and judicial processes that continue to govern tribal life. Reservations are viewed as sources of cheap raw materials, food, and labor, and as markets for the surrounding border towns' economies. During the colonial era, up until 1934, and the more recent post–colonial era, up until the present, economic relations and political structures have transformed self-provisioning tribal nations into totally dependent welfare enclaves.

While the cultural, spiritual, and social costs of these government policies were significant and devastating, they are difficult to quantify. However, we can begin to gain an understanding of the economic costs. Westward expansion and land grabs contributed to a loss of over 90 million acres of

Indian territories through land sales, home-steading, and theft. Tribal termination—the U.S. government's decertification of Indian tribes—in the 1950s further removed at least 1.3 million acres from Indian control. The total loss from land grabs and tribal termination, along with the corresponding loss of natural resources from that land,

FIGURE 2-2
Home ownership rates, 2003

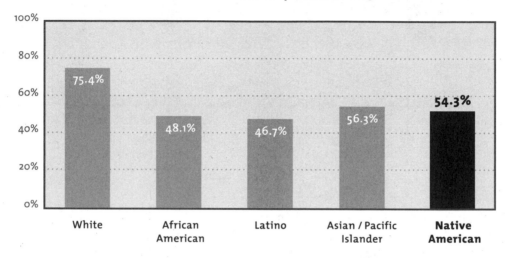

Source: U.S. Census Bureau, *Annual Statistics, 2003, Housing Vacancies and Homeownership,* Table 20

FIGURE 2-3
Home ownership rates, 1994–2003

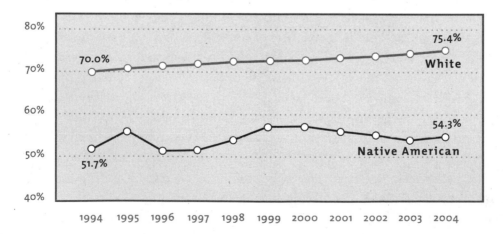

Source: U.S. Census Bureau, http://www.census.gov/hhes/www/housing/hvs/annual03/ann03t20.html.

including timber, energy reserves such as oil, gas, coal, and uranium, and water, is valued at several billion dollars. The trust funds generated by lease of these lands have been severely mismanaged by the federal government, a cost that has been estimated at $137 billion. By the 1960s, competition for and misuse of traditional tribal lands has led to loss of fish stock due to over harvesting, pollution, or damming of rivers. Now, many tribes do not have access to their traditional water rights for agriculture. Environmental degradation has led to decreased land values, all of which have added up to even more billions of dollars of wealth that has been stolen, misappropriated, or mismanaged.

While official and unofficial policies toward Native Americans have historically included murder and forced cultural assimilation, those will not be the focus of this chapter. Instead, this chapter will focus on the ways in which federal policies have systematically removed assets from Native populations. It is only by understanding federal actions that we can begin to understand the conditions that exist in Native America in the current day.

NOT A "MINORITY"

While there is no single definition of "Indian," there are some legal definitions that determine who qualifies for federal and tribal programs aimed at Native Americans. Usually, tribes have criteria based on ancestry for determining who is a tribal member. The federal government also uses certain criteria, often based on ancestry and termed "blood quantum." Most tribes require a one-fourth to one-eighth blood quantum, or that one out of four or one out of eight relatives are tribal members, to be a full-blooded tribal member. Unfortunately, many tribal definitions of tribal members do not match the federal definitions, and this sometimes leads to a confusing situation where an individual may be eligible for a tribal program but not a federal program, or vice versa.[11] The U.S. Census goes with a self-definition approach—anyone who reports that they are Native American on the census is counted as Native American.

It is important to understand that American Indians have a history and a legal status that is different from any other racial group in America. Technically, Indians are not a "minority group," but rather are members of independent, sovereign nations led by sovereign tribal governments. These tribal governments have a unique relationship with the federal government, one that is rooted in American history and federal Indian law. This relationship determines the rights of members of Indian tribes, and determines how the federal government can treat Native Americans given their tribal "citizenship."

As members of a tribe, American Indians are eligible to participate in specific programs sponsored by the U.S. government, including ones designed to take care of the health, educational, and social service needs of tribal members. Individual tribal members may also own land that is held in trust by the federal government. In addition, tribal members can participate in programs related to health, education, and home ownership. These typically are administered by the Bureau of Indian Affairs, which is part of the U.S. Department of the Interior. Historically, the BIA has administered all Indian Health Service programs, all trust funds for tribes, and all land and natural resource leases. More and more tribes are administering programs formerly controlled by the BIA, including health programs, housing programs, and even in a few cases trust funds.

HISTORY OF FEDERAL POLICY TOWARD NATIVE AMERICAN ASSETS

In 1492, the year Columbus accidentally landed in what is now North America, Native populations resided in and controlled the vast land areas of what is now the United States. Different tribes controlled different regions of the continent, and depending on the tribe, were either agrarian populations farming numerous crops, or nomads living off hunting, fishing, and gathering in established territories. The Native population was nearly five million. By 1800, many of these tribes had been forced inland by European settlements, and by 1900 the Native population was less than one million and was residing on less than 4 percent of the original continental United States.[12]

Each tribe in the United States has had a different experience related to treaty making, land theft, and control of tribal resources, but federal policies toward Native Americans on the whole reflect one theme: control of Native assets. Whether it is the relocation of the Cherokee, Chickasaw, and Choctaw tribes in the early 1800s from their rich agricultural land in Georgia and other southern territories, the sale of land on the Osage reservation in Oklahoma to non-Indians to gain access to oil in the early 1900s, or the "termination" of the Klamath tribes in Oregon[13] to sell timber-rich land to a paper company in the 1950s, federal policies toward American Indians have methodically removed wealth from Native populations.

Table 1

History of U.S. Appropriation of Indian Assets

TIMELINE OF INCREASED FEDERAL CONTROL OF INDIAN ASSETS	FEDERAL POLICY/LEGISLATION
Colonization and treaty making (1500–1828)	➤ Numerous treaties
Relocation and reservations (1828–87)	➤ Indian Removal Act of 1830 ➤ California Preemptive Act of 1853 ➤ The Homestead Act of 1862 ➤ The Pacific Railway Act of 1862
Allotment (1887–1934)	➤ General Allotment Act of 1887 (Dawes Act) ➤ The Curtis Act of 1898 (allotment of Oklahoma territories) ➤ Burke Act of 1906
Indian reorganization/Indian New Deal (1934–53)	➤ Indian Reorganization Act of 1934
Termination period (1953–68)	➤ House Concurrent Resolution No. 108 and Public Law 280 (1953)
Modern challenges to tribal wealth (1968–present)	➤ Tribal taxation ➤ *Oliphant v. Ququamish Tribe,* 1977 ➤ *Washington v. Colville,* 1980 ➤ *Rice v. Rehner,* 1983 ➤ *Cotton Petroleum v. New Mexico,* 1989 ➤ *Brendale v. Confederate Takima Tribe,* 1989 ➤ Indian Gaming and Regulatory Act of 1988

COLONIZATION AND TREATY MAKING
(1492–1838)

The first colonists benefited from the knowledge and technology of Native populations in many ways. The pilgrims of Plymouth survived the winter of 1620 with the assistance of the Wampanoag tribe of Massachusetts.[14] Such assistance in the form of food and agricultural help, coupled with a fear of Native populations' often superior military might, contributed to a relationship of respect between the early settlers and Native Americans. As more people from England, France, Spain, and Holland began settling in the eastern colonies, treaties were signed with Indian nations, and for the most part Indian tribes were treated as political equals who were respected for their military strength, advanced agricultural knowledge, and political systems.

As the number of settlers in the "New World" grew, however, conflicts flared between the colonists and the Indian tribes. As the colonists' power increased, they ceased treating Indians as political equals. Conflicts over land led to increased Native resistance, and raids against the European settlements and armed conflicts between settlers and Indians became more frequent.

European colonists in the New World often described the land as barren and empty. This is partly due to their desire to claim ownership of land under the concept of eminent domain, which allowed that if a property was unused it could be claimed by the British Crown.[15] It also stemmed from the settlers' lack of understanding of Native American concepts of property and land use. The Native belief in collective land use, in seasonal agricultural practices in harmony with the environment, and in one's inability to "own" the land often confused the European settlers, who subscribed to individual property rights and strict territorial boundaries. This clash of value systems led to disputes over territorial rights and land use.

In King Philip's War (1675–1676), colonial hunger for land clashed with the Wampanoag chief's growing resentment of the English threat to his sovereignty and power. The Plymouth colony attempted to force the Wampanoags to demonstrate their loyalty to Plymouth by selling their land to the colony.[16] In the resulting war, at least three thousand Wampanoags, Narragansetts, and Nipmucks died, and even more were deported and sold into slavery.[17]

Tensions also ran high in the southern colonies. In the early eighteenth century, European settlers angered the Tuscarora tribe in North Carolina by squatting on their land and kidnapping many Tuscaroras and selling them into slavery. The conflict increased when a band of Swiss colonists established a settlement in a spot already occupied by a Tuscarora village. North

Carolina's surveyor general granted the Swiss permission to drive the Indians off the land without payment. Having been pushed from their lands, the Tuscaroras retaliated by raiding the settlement.[18] War between the Carolinas and the Tuscaroras continued until 1715, when the Tuscaroras were forced to sign a peace treaty and migrate to New York.[19]

Another southern tribe, the Yamassees, also had conflicts with settlers over squatting on tribal lands and enslaving their people. In 1715, only a few months following the end of the Tuscarora War, the Yamassee finally retaliated, attacking several South Carolina settlements.[20] The governor of South Carolina and his militia responded quickly, and drove the Yamassees to near tribal extinction. The land vacated by the Yamassee was then appropriated for the new colony of Georgia.[21] Such constant wars between the colonies and the Indian tribes, conflicts which the outnumbered and outgunned Indians usually lost, resulted in a significant loss of Native land and increasingly weakened Native populations.

Some tribes built strategic alliances with the settlers. As the American colonists began to feud with one another and ultimately with the British Crown, alliances were built with several tribes. The Iroquois Confederacy sided with the British in the French and Indian War, and as a result the English king issued a proclamation to limit colonists taking of Indian land. The colonists largely ignored this proclamation, however,

and when they rebelled against the British Crown in the late 1700s, they preemptively attacked many tribal settlements. Most eastern tribes sided with the British, but the Oneida, Tuscaroras, Mohegans, and Pequots assisted their American neighbors.

After the American Revolutionary War, the tribes that had sided with the British were punished by the new government, while those that had fought on the side of the colonists were rewarded. For example, the Oneida tribe was granted high-quality agricultural land in Wisconsin in exchange for supporting the American colonists. The official position of the new U.S. government after the war was to treat Indian tribes as having status equal to foreign nations, and to respect treaty rights and maintain good relations with them. However, as westward expansion continued, Native Americans increasingly were forced to sign treaties, removed from their land, or relocated to reservations.

Between 1787 and 1871, the United States entered into over four hundred treaties with Indian tribes.[22] These documents represented exchanges or agreements between sovereign powers. During the eighteenth century, most Indian nations were perceived as powerful sovereign governments, and the treaties were perceived as agreements between equals. Before the War of 1812 against England, many treaties were signed voluntarily. After 1812, tribes that had sided with the British Crown were usually forced to sign treaties. For example, the

Creeks, Choctaws, Chickasaws, and Cherokees were forced into a series of treaties between 1816 and 1835 and required to relinquish most of their traditional homelands.

Some tribes have won moderate compensation for these actions and their loss of land. An example is found in the Penobscot and Passamaquoddy tribes of Maine. A 1790 federal law known as the Indian Trade and Intercourse Act prohibited the taking or transfer of any Indian land without the permission of Congress. In several of the eastern states, including Maine and Massachusetts, this law was ignored. In Maine, roughly two-thirds of the state was Indian land improperly transferred (i.e., without congressional approval) to white ownership. The Penobscot and Passamaquoddy tribes filed suit in 1972 for the return of their land. While the tribe had legal right to two-thirds of the state, the target of their suit was really the fourteen largest landowners, all major paper companies. The case was finally settled in Congress and signed into law on October 10, 1980, for a total of three thousand acres. The law authorized the payment of $54.5 million for the land and established a $27 million trust fund for the tribes' economic development.

Another example is found in the Cayuga Indian Nation in New York. In the Cayuga Ferry Treaty in 1795, the Nation ceded most of their sixty-four thousand acres of land to the State of New York. Another three square miles were ceded in an 1807 treaty. Both of these treaties were illegal because they did not have congressional approval. In 1980, the Cayuga Indian Nation, and later the Seneca-Cayuga Tribe of Oklahoma, sued for sixty-four thousand acres of land in the Seneca and Cayuga counties based on the claim that the land had been exchanged illegally. In February 2000, a federal jury awarded the Cayuga $36.9 million, despite the appraised value of $660 million. In October 2001, a judge ordered the state of New York to pay the Cayuga an additional $211 million. An economist at the trial, however, claimed the tribes were entitled to $1.7 billion in interest.[23]

Treaties are the most important legal documents in determining the nature of the federal relationship with American Indian tribes. It is from the texts and proceedings of these treaties that the complex legal and political ideas (subsequently called federal Indian law) have emerged, affecting Indians for over two centuries. The Supreme Court has ruled that the treaties entered into with the federal government create a legal relationship between the Indian tribes and the federal government to respect the sovereignty of the tribes and provide "food, services and clothing to the tribes."[24] This was seen as a fair exchange for taking Indian lands and restricting tribes to reservation lands set aside for their use.

The treaties contributed to a loss of tribal wealth because they forced many tribes to relinquish control of traditional territories, including land and natural resources. They also laid the foundation for the modern-day relationship between tribes and the federal government and for the trust funds that the federal government currently manages for Indian nations. These trust funds were first mentioned in a treaty with the Choctaws in the 1820s, in which they ceded lands west of the Mississippi River, and agreed to have funds set aside to support Choctaw schools. Later treaties would establish trusts to manage tribal wealth, administer leases on tribal natural resources, and manage ownership of land.

The "subject of Indian rights can seem complex and terribly confusing. There are thousands of treaties, statutes, executive orders, court decisions, and agency rulings that play integral roles. Indian law is a subject unto itself, having few parallels."[25] As a subcommittee of the U.S. Senate noted in 1977:

It is almost always a mistake to seek answers to Indian legal issues by making analogies to seemingly similar fields. General notions of civil rights law and public land law, for example, simply fail to resolve many questions relating to American Indian tribes and individuals. This extraordinary body of law and policy holds its own answers, which are often wholly unexpected to those unfamiliar with it.[26]

The U.S. Constitution provides some guidance for the relationship between the federal government and Indian tribes, but unfortunately it does not clearly protect the sovereign rights of tribes. Article I, Section 8, clause 3 (often referred to as the "commerce clause") states that "Congress shall have the power . . . to regulate commerce with foreign Nations, and among the several States, and with the Indian Tribes." This has been interpreted as giving Congress the right to regulate commerce on Indian reservations and commerce between tribes and states. The commerce clause has been interpreted as giving Congress, and the executive branch in the form of the Bureau of Indian Affairs, a great deal of power over Indian tribes and the ability to regulate and control the activities, rights, and obligations of Indians. To this day, the debate continues over the nature of tribal sovereignty, the role of the federal government in regulating Indian affairs, and the rights and responsibilities of tribal members.

RELOCATION AND RESERVATIONS (1828–1887)

When Andrew Jackson was elected president in 1828, federal policy toward American Indians changed dramatically. What had previously been an unofficial pol-icy of increasing control of Indian lands for white settlement became official federal policy. Removal became "the dominant federal Indian policy of the nineteenth century."[27]

GRAND RUSH

FOR THE

INDIAN

TERRITORY !

NOW IS THE CHANCE

TO

PROCURE A HOME

In this Beautiful Country!

Over 15,000,000 Acres of Land

NOW OPEN FOR SETTLEMENT !

Being part of the Land bought by the Government in 1866 from the Indians for the Freedmen.

THE FINEST TIMBER !
THE RICHEST LAND !
THE FINEST WATERED !

WEST OF THE MISSISSIPPI RIVER.

Every person over 21 years of age is entitled to 160 acres, either by pre-emption or homestead, who wishes to settle in the Indian Territory. It is estimated that over Fifty Thousand will move to this Territory in the next ninety days. The Indians are rejoicing to have the whites settle up this country.

The Grand Expedition will Leave Independence May 7, 1879

Independence is situated at the terminus of the Kansas City, Lawrence & Southern Railroad. The citizens of Independence have laid out and made a splendid road to these lands; and they are prepared to furnish emigrants with complete outfits, such as wagons, agricultural implements, dry goods, groceries, lumber and stock. They have also opened an office there for general information to those wishing to go to the Territory. IT COSTS NOTHING TO BECOME A MEMBER OF THIS COLONY.

Persons passing through Kansas City will apply at the office of K. C., L. & S. R. R., opposite Union Depot, for Tickets.

ABOUT THE LANDS.

(small print about the lands)

ADDRESS

WM. C. BRANHAM,

Independence, Kansas.

To parties accompanying my Colony, I would advise them to purchase their Outfit at Independence, Kan., I have examined Stock and Prices of Goods, such as Wagons, Plows, Lumber, Dry Goods, Groceries, and, in fact, everything that is needed by Parties settling upon new Land, and find them as cheap as they can be bought in the East.

RESPECTFULLY YOURS,

Col. C. C. CARPENTER.

P. S.—Parties will have no trouble in getting transportation at Independence for hauling their goods into the Territory.

C. C. C.

Advertisement from the late 1870s. *(Reproduced with permission from Imre Sutteon, et al., editor,* Irredeemable America: The Indians' Estate and Land Claims *(University of New Mexico Press, 1986), p. 2.)*

In the late 1700s and early 1800s, the demand for land had increased even more as new populations arrived and agricultural technology improved. Pressure grew on the federal government to displace many tribes from their rich agricultural land, including the Cherokee, Chickasaw, Choctaw, and Creek. There was also a great deal of interest in newly discovered natural resources in traditional Indian territories. For example, in 1830, the governor of Georgia issued a proclamation that announced that all the lands of the Cherokee, and especially the gold mines, were the property of the state.[28]

The Indian Removal Act of 1830 was drafted to remove eastern tribes to lands west of the Mississippi, thereby opening up former Indian lands in the East for white colonization. Officially, the Native Americans were to be encouraged to move not by force, but by land exchanges. In practice, however, force was often used and the land exchanges were terribly inadequate.

The Cherokee attempted to resist the Indian Removal Act through legal means and brought its case before the United States Supreme Court. In 1832, Chief Justice John Marshall found in favor of the Cherokees in the case of *Worcester v. Georgia*, but President Jackson refused to enforce the court's decision.[29] In the fall and winter of 1838–39, the Cherokee were finally forced westward. Fifteen thousand Cherokee were marched off to "Indian Territory," during what came to be called the Trail of Tears.[30]

During the cold, twelve-hundred-mile march, four thousand Cherokee Indians died.[31] The Chickasaw, Choctaw, and Creek tribes were also relocated from their traditional homelands in the Southeast to the newly created Indian Territory in what is now Oklahoma. Of the twenty thousand tribal Choctaw members forcibly relocated from Mississippi, only seven thousand survived.

When Indians, forced westward by the Indian Removal Act, arrived in the so-called Indian Territory, they often discovered the land areas they were compensated with were even smaller than those in the East. Even this meager land in the newly designated Indian Territory was under contest, however. Before all of the primary removals were completed in the East, the secondary removals had begun in the West, "and the land that was supposed to belong to the Indian in perpetuity was in the white man's market."[32] Again Native American value systems and Western concepts of property rights were in conflict. The land, often considered by Indians to be sacred "mother earth," was increasingly being commodified and sold for profit to benefit white settlers.

Ironically, much of the land to which tribes were relocated was later found to contain great natural resource wealth, as had their traditional territories. When this occurred, the federal government often responded by opening up reservations to white ownership, once again removing Indians to other lands or simply appropriating natural resources.

One example can be found in the Black Hills of South Dakota, formerly on the Lakota Sioux reservation. The Black Hills, located in the traditional territories on the border of what is now Wyoming and South Dakota, was rumored to be full of gold. White trappers and traders appeared in this area in the early 1800s, and by 1819 many Indians had died of measles and smallpox, diseases brought by the white settlers to which Indians had little resistance. White explorers and settlers continued to flock to the Black Hills, eager to find their fortune on Indian land. The Lakota Sioux signed the Treaty of Fort Laramie, which outlined the boundaries of the Great Sioux reservation, against their will in 1868; it included the Black Hills in its border, protected "in perpetuity" for the tribe.

By 1875, a commission had been sent from Washington to "treat with the Sioux Indians for the Relinquishment of the Black Hills."[33] The Sioux were offered $5 million for the Black Hills, but they refused, stating their belief that the Black Hills and Mother Earth should not be bought and sold. In early 1876, in direct opposition to the Treaty of Fort Laramie, troops were sent in to the Great Sioux reservation to find hostiles who were opposed to selling the Black Hills. In late 1876, the Sioux were forced to sign a document that abrogated the Fort Laramie treaty and awarded the Black Hills to white settlers and business interests. This action was codified in the Black Hills Act of February 28, 1877. This act appropriated the Black Hills, together with 22.8 million acres of surrounding territory, for use by the U.S. government. That summer, a gold mine was established in the town of Lead, and ten years later this single enterprise was worth over $6 million.

Other tribes, such as the Choctaw, were pressured to sell their land or provide leases to white business interests when valuable natural resources were found on their reservations. Once the Choctaws arrived in Indian Territory, they discovered that their new reservation consisted of 6.8 million acres, nearly 2 million acres of which were virgin timberland. This continued to attract the interest of white-owned paper companies, and negotiations continued for leases and sales of land. Today the tribe owns only 65,000 acres of their original reservation, and the Weyerhaeuser Paper Company is currently the single largest private landowner in the ten-county region, owning over 1.8 million acres of land that formerly belonged to the Choctaw people. [34]

The Indian Appropriation Act was passed in the mid-1800s and forced more tribes to relocate to reservations. Not only were Indians involuntarily confined to small plots of alien and often inhospitable land, but surveys of traditional Indian territories were notoriously inaccurate. An 1867 presidential executive order established the 1.8 million-acre Fort Hall Indian Reservation in Idaho, to which the Boise Shoshone were relocated from their western territory. The Fort Bridger Treaty of 1868 confirmed the arrangement. However, a survey error reduced the reservation to 1.2 million acres in 1872. [35] The Confederated Tribes of Umatilla Indian Reservation in Oregon had their original, agreed-upon treaty reserve of 512,000 acres reduced to 245,000 acres because of an inaccurate survey.

Throughout the second half of the nineteenth century, colonial settlement continued to push westward. The Homestead Act and the Pacific Railway Act, both passed in 1862, brought floods of settlers to the West. The Homestead Act provided that any white male adult eligible for citizenship could claim 160 acres of government-surveyed western land. [36] The result was that by 1900, homesteaders had filed six hundred thousand claims for eighty million acres of land, mostly in the western Plains states of Kansas, Nebraska, Colorado, and Wyoming, displacing the Sioux, Cheyenne, Ute, Pawnee, and many other tribes. [37]

With the Pacific Railway Act, the government gave huge grants of land to the railroad companies for rights-of-way, and the railroad often cut narrow swathes through the middle of Native American lands. The act itself even encouraged this disruption of Indian land, stating, "The United States shall extinguish as rapidly as may be the Indian titles to all lands falling under the operation of this act and required for the said right of way." [38]

Railroad companies also received many additional square miles of land to gather building materials and establish small settlements to support railroad construction, and the lucrative timber and mineral rights to this land.[39] This permanent grant of land and natural resources benefited many white settlers by providing jobs and transportation corridors, but typically extracted land and other wealth from Indian tribes without compensation.

A compelling example comes from the Zuni tribe in New Mexico. In 1846, the Zuni tribe was one of the wealthiest and most politically secure tribes in the Southwest, and it controlled a 15.2-million-acre aboriginal territory. By 1881, the Zuni had lost over 9 million acres of their territory, and Congress had made a huge land grant to the white-owned railroad companies that were pressing westward. The railroad used their land grant, much of which cut through what had been Zuni traditional territory, not only for railroad construction, but to contract with white-owned lumber companies for tens of millions of board feet of lumber from the newly granted land.[40] Over the next one hundred years, the Zuni continued to lose land to white settlement as the government illegally gave land to traders, missionaries, churches, and government facilities without payment to the tribe. Intensive timber and agricultural operations led to significant land erosion, and attempts to build dams and divert water had a severe negative effect on the entire Zuni watershed. Coal mining was conducted on the Zuni reservation without payment to the tribe, and the improperly managed coal tailings from these mines continue to damage

portions of a local watershed to this day.[41] The Zuni traditional territories had been reduced to less than 3 percent of their original size. By 1995 only 1,370 acres were being cultivated, down from a high of 12,000 acres in the 1850s. The documented costs of government incursions on and mismanagement of Zuni territory include a loss of 11,000 acres of prime irrigable land, millions of board feet of lumber, and tens of thousands of tons of coal, all taken without any compensation to the tribe.[42] In 1990, President George H.W. Bush signed the Zuni Conservation Act into law, compensating the Zuni with $25 million dollars for lost land use and stolen natural resources. The Zuni tribe took $17 million of this, the amount remaining after legal fees and other costs, and established a permanent trust fund for the sustainable development and environmental remediation of the Zuni reservation.

As westward expansion continued, the U.S. Army actively waged battles with tribes to open land for white settlement. In 1845, the U.S. Army clashed with the Sioux in Nebraska, and again in Minnesota in 1862, and also with the Navajo in New Mexico.[43] White settlers often participated in attacks on Native Americans, especially after the U.S. Army went east for the Civil War.[44]

The California Gold Rush, beginning in 1849, was a particularly devastating period in Native American history. Many Indian villages in California were destroyed by order of Congress, and numerous Indians were killed or moved to reservations. In

1853, the California Preemptive Act declared all Indian lands as public domain, open for homesteading.[45] Local tribes were systematically chased off their lands and marched to missions and reservations, and many were enslaved and brutally massacred. In 1851, the California state government provided $1 million for scalping missions. Individuals could get $5 for a severed Indian head in Shasta in 1855, and 25¢ for a scalp in Honey Lake in 1863.[46] All these activities, in addition to the introduction of diseases to the Native populations, reduced the Indian population in California from 310,000 in 1850 to less than 50,000 in 1855.[47] By 1870, there was an estimated population of only 31,000 Californian Indians left. Over 60 percent of the indigenous people died from disease introduced by the hundreds of thousands of so-called 49ers.[48]

ALLOTMENT AND ASSIMILATION (1887–1934)

The loss of Indian land was greatly accelerated in the late 1800s with the passage of the General Allotment Act, also known as the Dawes Act.[49] This piece of legislation, passed by Congress in 1887, was disastrous for tribes and severely reduced their land holdings.

The official purpose of the Dawes Act was to encourage tribal members to adopt a sedentary agricultural lifestyle and to force Indians to assimilate into white society.[50] Other unstated purposes were to break up tribal governments, abolish Indian reservations, promote individual ownership of Indian land instead of traditional collective tribal ownership, and allow white settlers and private business interests increased access to land and other Native natural assets.[51] This was to be accomplished by dividing existing reservations—already diminished by treaties and settlement—into individual Indian allotments of between 80 and 160 acres. Many Indians were given meager farming tools and encouraged to start Western farming practices by Indian Agents dedicated to "civilizing" the Native population. Surplus land not allotted to Indians was typically sold to white farmers and ranchers. This resulted in a massive land transfer from Indians to white settlers over a short period of time. In just one year, 1891, Indian commissioner Thomas Morgan sold off one-seventh of all the Indian lands in the United States to white settlers, over 17.4 million acres.[52]

Native women especially lost property rights under the Dawes Act. The original plan was to distribute land to "heads of families," meaning men, but some tribal leaders objected because women and children had some property rights in their cultures. The plan was changed to a per capita distribu-

Indian
Congress,
1898
(*Library of
Congress*)

tion. However, women and children without men in their families were more often challenged in court by white would-be settlers and usually declared incompetent to own land.[53]

The land allotted to American Indians was inferior in terms of quality and quantity, yet there was no provision in the Dawes Act to compensate for low-quality land. Many individual Indian landholders were not successful at agricultural production, partly because of the low quality of the land, and partly because they were being forced to adopt western agricultural practices. By the turn of the century, whether an individual had received good or poor quality land made little difference, as Indian land increas-ingly fell into the hands of non-Indians through leasing and sales.

Individual Indian allotments were initially to be held in trust for twenty-five years, during which time the state could not tax them nor could they be sold. This was designed to protect individually owned Indian land, as individuals worked to gain economic self-sufficiency through farming. Even this protection, however, was short-lived. The Burke Act, passed in 1890, allowed the Secretary of the Interior to remove allotments from trust before the time set by the Dawes Act to Indian allotees considered competent to manage their own affairs. After allotment lands were taken out of trust, they could be sold and, most importantly, taxed by the state. Many impoverished American Indians sold their allotments or lost them in foreclosures when they were unable to pay the state property taxes. In most instances, this land was quickly sold to local non-Indians, usually for below market value amounts.[54]

Most American Indian farmers received their allotments between 1890 and 1910 when farm prices were growing steadily. This period of prosperity led some Native farmers to make large investments in both land and equipment. After 1920, the prices for agricultural products declined, leaving many Native farmers with unpaid debts. In addition, agricultural production became more intensive with the introduction of irrigated and dry-land farming, which required expensive inputs or large areas of land. By 1930, unable to compete due to lack of available capital and a shortage of loans, many American Indians turned to leasing or land sales. In states such as Kansas, Michigan, Nebraska, Colorado, Oregon, and Minnesota, the number of Indian farms and the total acres dedicated to Indian farms declined dramatically after 1910.[55] Not only had American Indians lost several million acres of land, but also many became unable to use the land that they had.[56]

Allotment occurred most fully in the northern Plains region, where farming and ranching interests were eager to gain access to Indian-controlled land and oil, coal, and other natural resources.[57] One example can be found in the Osage tribe in Oklahoma. The Osage tribe, which had been relocated from their traditional territories in present-day Missouri and Arkansas and forced to relinquish over fifty million acres to the federal government, established a reservation in Oklahoma (then called "Indian Territory") in 1870. Using funds received from the federal government in compensation for lost land, the Osage purchased 1,470,559 acres from the Cherokee tribe to establish their reservation. In 1881, the Osage (through the federal government) signed their first oil and gas lease, allowing for oil and mineral exploration on the reservation. An oil boom started in 1895 when more and more white business interest applied for leases on the reservation and were successful in drilling for oil. By 1906, there were 783 wells on the reservation, 544 producing oil, 41 producing gas, and 198 dry wells. In 1906 alone, over 5 million barrels of oil and a blanket lease for oil exploration on the Osage reservation had yielded $2,686,627.[58] Interest in gaining access to Indian oil led to increased intermarriage between Osage and whites. The Osage had been excluded from the Dawes Act, but by 1892, many mixed-blood tribal members began pressuring the federal government to support private land ownership. After a long period of negotiation, Congress approved the Osage Allotment Act of 1906, and by the early 1900s the land was allotted and individuals began to collect significant revenues from oil wells. By 1908, a total of 1,465,380 acres of the reservation had been converted to individual ownership, and in most cases sold to non-Indians.

During the early 1900s, more and more new natural resources were being discovered on Indian land. The land containing the natural resources was often sold off, or the natural resources were extracted, with permission from the commissioner of Indian Affairs but without tribal consent. In many cases, the resources were extracted with little consideration for the environmental impact. An example can be found in Oklahoma, where once the Quapaw tribal lands in Oklahoma consisted of rolling prairie dotted with trees. The prairie sod produced excellent hay, and led to the area being referred to as the "hay capital of the world." Mining within the boundaries of the Quapaw tribal lands converted this landscape into a low-vegetation terrain consisting of abandoned mines and mountainous piles of mine tailings. Lead and zinc ores were discovered in Ottawa County in 1904, and in almost every year from 1918 until 1945, Oklahoma led the world in zinc production. Production highs for both lead and zinc mining were recorded in 1925.[59] Few Indians benefited from the revenues generated from these mining operations. However, the pollution from this mining continues to this day.

A few tribes were unaffected by the General Allotment Act because their lands were not perceived as valuable for settlement or business interests or their land was not held in trust by the federal government. None of the nineteen Pueblo Indian tribes in New Mexico were subject to the General Allotment Act, partly because they owned their land and had never signed a treaty with the federal government, and partly because the desert location of the tribes' land was considered inhospitable for agricultural interests.[60] Other southwestern Indians also avoided allotment for the most part, as their land was considered too arid for productive agriculture and too remote for productive settlement. Allotment did occur in the region of Phoenix because of the perceived value of the Salt River Valley, but most other Southwest tribes were able to keep their reservations intact.

Through the Dawes Act, the Confederated Tribes of Umatilla Indian Reservation in Oregon was reduced from 245,000 acres to 148,000 acres because of allotment. In 1897 and 1904, the United States Indian Bureau allotted the Uintah and Ouray reservation, and reservation and tribal land holdings fell from nearly 4 million acres to 360,000 acres.[61] Total tribal ownership of land fell from 138 million acres in 1887 to 48 million acres by 1934. Allotment and the subsequent loss of land to non-Indians meant that tribes lost 80 percent of their land wealth, including the value of the associated resources, by the early twentieth century.[62] By 1989, more than 50 percent of all former reservation land in the United States was owned by non-Indians.[63]

Instead of the culturally appropriate, tribally owned collective land, the Dawes Act forced private property ownership upon tribal members. The push to individual allotments also resulted in a checkerboard

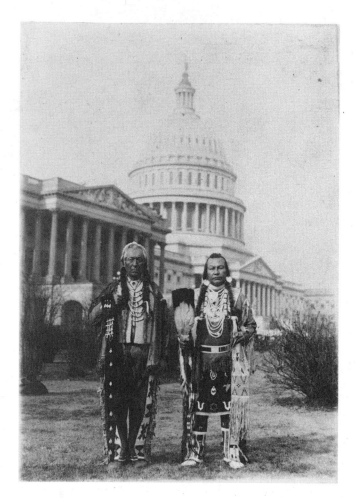

Yakima chiefs Frank Seelatse and Jimmy Noah Saluskin at U.S. Capitol, 1927 *(Library of Congress)*

implementing effective economic development strategies.

For the allotments that were not sold or encumbered, the land was partitioned among the heirs upon the original allottee's death, or sold and the money divided. This aspect of the allotment policy, in particular, has been extremely disruptive to Native land ownership patterns. It has resulted in highly fractionated heirships, where dozens or even hundreds of heirs to the original allottee own partial interests in a single 160-acre allotment. Years of government mismanagement of these land trust accounts has led to great confusion over who owns what parcels of land. The parcels of land were supposed to be managed for individuals and their heirs, but these parcels of land have become highly fractionated with each generation. Some original allotments are now owned by over three hundred people, rendering the land useless for homesteading or development. In addition, mismanagement by the federal government has resulted in lost records pertaining to land ownership, so many tribal members have no record of the land they rightfully own.

Today, there are over eleven million acres of land held in trust for over 387,000 beneficiaries in the Individual Indian Monies

pattern of ownership within the boundaries of many reservations, where Indian allotments were interspersed with non-Indian land plots. This checkerboard pattern of ownership has lead to serious problems on many reservations to this day related to jurisdiction and tribal control of land. Without a unified land base, tribes have had difficulty creating economies of scale or

(IIM) system. More than $300 million are earned annually from agricultural and oil leases, mining and water rights, rights-of-way and timber sales that are collected by the Interior Department's Bureau of Indian Affairs for distribution to Native owners. In addition to Individual Indian Monies, there are some two thousand Tribal Trust Accounts, which include per capita annual payments and compensation for rights-of-way and court settlements, which total $2.3 billion. All trusts managed by the Department of the Interior include about $3 billion in Individual Indian Monies trust funds, about fifty-four million acres of land, and numerous oil, gas, coal, timber, and other natural resource leases.[64]

Unfortunately, these trusts have been severely mismanaged by the federal government. In 2003, the General Accounting Office stated:

> Management of Indian trust funds and assets has long been plagued by inadequate financial management, such as poor accounting and information systems; untrained and inexperienced staff; backlogs in appraisals, determinations of ownership, and record-keeping; the lack of a master lease file or accounts receivable system; inadequate written policies and procedures; and poor internal controls. As a result, account holders have no assurance that their account balances are accurate or that the trust assets are managed properly.[65]

In 1996, the Native American Rights Fund and Eloise Cobell, a treasurer for the Blackfeet tribe, sued the federal government for mismanagement of the trust funds. Ms. Cobell's goals were twofold: to force the government to account for the money it owed her for her individual allotment, and to bring reform to the federal government's management of the trust funds.[66] In 1999, Judge Royce C. Lamberth ruled that the government was in breach of its fiduciary role as a trustee for the Indian accounts. He ordered the program, including twelve thousand backlogged probate cases, to be placed under his jurisdiction for five years so that he could ensure that the Department of Interior complied with his orders. In the spring of 2001, the Department of the Interior set up a division called the Office of Historical Trust Accounting. This office issued a report in July 2002 that stated it would cost $2.4 billion to do an effective audit on the trust funds, and even this may not produce a usable result.[67] In January 2003, the lawyers representing Eloise Cobell submitted a historical analysis of the trust fund that revealed that nearly $137.2 billion might have been stolen, lost, or misallocated since the passage of the General Allotment Act.[68] Litigation in this case is ongoing.

There are numerous other examples of mismanagement of tribal leases. The Quinault reservation, established in 1873, consists of many acres of high-quality forestland in western Washington. Forest resources on the tribal lands have been managed by the Department of the Interior since the late 1800s, which has sold timber leases and administered the revenues from the sales. In 1971, the Quinault tribe alleged that the Secretary of the Interior had mismanaged the timberlands and owed the tribe funds for sale of timber to commercial interests. In *United States v. Mitchell* and *United States v. Mitchell II*, tribal members contended that they are entitled to recover money damages for the United States, as trustee under various statutes, had breached its fiduciary duty. The litigation, which began in 1971, was finally settled in 1989 for $26 million.[69]

Another example can be found in a recent Supreme Court case addressing a coal lease negotiated for the Navajo Nation by the Department of the Interior. In 1964 the federal government assisted them in arranging and approving a lease with the Peabody Coal Company to mine coal on Navajo land in return for a royalty of 37.5¢ a ton. The Navajo now claim that the federal government acted through a pliant tribal council in order to reach this agreement, and point to a 1978 study by the Interior Department, that shows that the Navajo had received only $2.7 million for coal that Peabody resold for $141 million.[70]

After the 1964 lease lapsed, Navajo leaders began pushing to renegotiate. A Bureau of Indian Affairs official suggested raising the royalty to 20 percent of revenue, but while Peabody was notified of this proposal, the Navajo were not. The Navajo claim that as a result, Peabody hired a friend of Donald Hodel, who was then the secretary of the interior, to lobby Hodel for a chance to negotiate a lower royalty. No one informed the Navajo of the meeting between the lobbyist and Hodel. When negotiations ended in 1987, the Navajo, under severe economic pressure, settled for a 12.5 percent royalty.

In 1993, the Navajo sued the federal government for $600 million for breach of trust, claiming that Donald Hodel, as secretary of the interior during the Reagan Administration, colluded with Peabody Coal Company to cheat the tribe out of millions of dollars in royalties. The Navajo tribes lost the case in 2003, when the Supreme Court ruled in favor of the federal government.[71]

Many similar cases are being litigated in federal court today.

INDIAN REORGANIZATION: THE INDIAN NEW DEAL (1934–1953)

John Collier, appointed commissioner of Indian Affairs in 1933, held views contrary to most other Indian advocates of the time

and believed that all efforts to acculturate and assimilate Indians into white society had failed, and had only served to destroy the

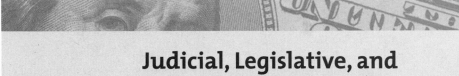

Judicial, Legislative, and Administrative Actions

"From birth to death his land, his reservation, his schools, his jobs, the stores where he shops, the tribal council that governs him, the opportunities available to him, the way in which he spends his money, disposes of his property, and even the way in which he provides for his heirs after death—are all determined by the Bureau of Indian Affairs acting as the agent of the United States government."

— *Cahn and Hearne,* Our Brother's Keeper: The Indian in White America[72]

The body of law that defines Native Americans' relationship to the federal government consists of judicial, legislative, and administrative actions. The United States court system continually interprets and reinterprets the original tribal treaties and the trust responsibility, and these decisions by the Supreme Court and lower courts define such important issues as the boundaries of traditional hunting and fishing grounds, access and ownership to traditional water rights, and liability for the management of funds and resources held in trust for Native people. This body of court cases makes up the judicial law that has affected Indian tribes and their control over assets such as land, natural resources, and hunting and fishing rights. Court cases regarding the trust responsibility, the sovereign powers of tribal governments, and tribal government control of land and other natural resources continue to this day.

Similarly, legislation passed by Congress is constantly redefining the rights, responsibilities, and powers of tribal governments in the United States. These different policies make up the legislative actions that have affected tribes and their control over assets. Congress has plenary power, or full and complete power, over all Indian tribes, their assets, and their governments. Although Congress is not legally required to follow the doctrine of the trust responsibility, this doctrine has guided policy over the past two centuries. The last two centuries of legislation have moved from an era of federal government control of Indian land and assets, to tribal termination, and more recently to attempts to

(continued)

provide Native Americans with more control of their land and other assets. Much of the current legislation is addressing the issues of tribal-state jurisdiction.

Because of the unique relationship between tribes and the federal government, the Bureau of Indian Affairs (BIA) in the Department of the Interior controls many of the actions of tribal governments. Through a series of administrative actions, including mismanagement of leases, trust funds, and other programs, the federal government has contributed to the extraction of assets and wealth from tribal control.

inherent strengths of Indian tribal life.[73] Upon assumption of office, Collier acted quickly to try to reform federal Indian policy and guarantee a land base for future generations. As the allotment policy had turned Indians into paupers instead of making them responsible, self-sufficient farmers, and due to strong support for those previous policies, Collier presumed that legislation would be necessary to guarantee the land protections he sought. His extensive plan, known as the Wheeler-Howard Act, was introduced in Congress in 1934, and an amended version was passed in June of that year. This legislation, also known as the Indian Reorganization Act, became the heart of the Indian New Deal.[74] The Indian Reorganization Act prohibited further allotment of reservation land and extended the trust periods for allotments remaining in trust. Remaining "surplus" land was returned to tribal ownership and held in trust. This policy had a positive impact on many tribes. By 1950, tribes had reacquired four million acres of previously alienated lands.[75]

In its conception, the Indian Reorganization Act, or IRA, was intended to benefit tribes by revitalizing tribal governments, bringing an end to allotment while helping to create new reservation lands, and strengthening relationships between tribal and federal governments. Under the act, tribes would be able to draw up charters for the creation of business corporations, giving tribes a chance for economic expansion and control over corporation affairs independent of the BIA. A revolving credit fund would be established to further aid in economic development while financial aid would assist in providing for college education and technical training. Preference would at last be given to Native Americans for employment in the BIA, allowing tribes greater control over their own affairs. Tribes would be granted the ability to hire attorneys in order to defend their own interests. Moreover, since few tribes were experienced in dealing with modern government affairs, the act provided a model constitution as a guide in restructuring tribal governments. Each tribe had the option of voting on acceptance of a constitution and on the Indian Reorganization Act as a whole.

In practice, however, the IRA quickly made evident a new way of imposing a non-Native system upon tribes. Though the IRA was used to produce much good through the protection of Native lands, its approach also played a part in destroying traditional ways of life and governance, by imposing such foreign concepts as a majority rule government, an adversarial system of justice, a one-person-one-vote concept, and the separation of church and state.[76] Many tribes found themselves willing to reject the promise of federal loans after adoption of the IRA upon learning of a stipulation that they felt continued the influence of the BIA in tribal affairs: for a constitution to be adopted, the Act stated, the document must contain a provision wherein the Secretary of the Interior must give approval over the final constitution and any amendments. The Secretary was further able to veto new laws, overrule certain council actions, call elections and settle election disputes, oversee economic affairs for the tribe, and approve their choices of legal counsel. The tribes recognized that the Secretary essentially maintained a say over any legislation that might significantly affect the tribe.[77] With these powers, tribes felt that the secretary would

maintain considerable control over tribal affairs. For instance, should a tribe wish to hire an attorney who would help it contest any aspect of the Secretary of Interior's control, the attorney simply would not be approved.

In the end, 181 tribes voted to accept the IRA, while 77 opposed it.[78] Records reveal, however, that votes were frequently mismanaged. The votes of any eligible tribal members who abstained were counted as affirmative ones. This deliberately unorthodox practice took advantage of the traditional right of signifying no by actively boycotting the vote. On the Santa Ysebel Reservation in California for example, forty-three tribal members voted against the IRA, while nine voted in favor. However, sixty-two eligible voters chose to boycott the proceedings; their absences, counted as favorable votes, meant the act was considered passed on the reservation.[79] In other cases, Native voters were ill informed or even subjected to electoral fraud in order to obtain a positive outcome. For instance, the Hopi people were told that the vote was for retention of their land not for reorganization. In addition, many Hopi votes and registration papers were falsified.[80] More controversial still was the Lakota vote, swayed to the affirmative when enough dead persons were registered as having voted changing the outcome of the IRA.[81]

One school of thought suggests that the Founding Fathers of the United States discovered in Native systems such as the

League of the Iroquois a model for the United States Constitution.[82] Even if true, by 1934 vast differences existed between traditional models of tribal government and the governmental model imposed upon the tribes. Being unfamiliar with a European/U.S. form of government, tribes generally accepted model constitutions that could not allow for the differences in governance systems among tribes that were sometimes merged together under one constitution.

While large variations exist between modern tribal governments, general similarities can be found across tribes under IRA constitutions. For instance, legislative power is typically established within a tribal council, an often small governing body that can exercise great power. Council members are elected by the people, nominated with few guiding qualifications other than a minimum age, and the requirement to serve out a set term in office. Duties of the legislative body, however, vary widely, as either specifically stated or implied by each tribal constitution. Such duties frequently include the establishment of a judicial system, delegation of powers to committees, management of business enterprises, enacting ordinances and resolutions, and in all cases providing for the tribe's welfare.[83]

A typical example of a tribal council can be found in the Pueblo of Santa Clara in New Mexico. Eight elected representatives, a governor, lieutenant governor, secretary, treasurer, interpreter, and sheriff make up the Pueblo council and as a whole wield legislative power. Such powers include the rights to employ chosen legal counsel, to prevent loss of land through sale or lease, and to pass ordinances within the Pueblo, although only after such laws have been approved by the Secretary of the Interior. Within the Pueblo, the tribal council also fulfills a judicial role, a common occurrence in other tribal governments.[84] While tribes usually have both a legislative and executive branch, not all tribal governments have a separate judicial branch.

The Pueblo of Santa Clara is also typical in placing at the head of its executive branch an elected governor. The governor, in other tribes referred to as either president or chairperson, is charged with enforcing all laws passed by the council as well as leading organized council meetings. Moreover, the Pueblo governor, as is typical, acts as both leader and spokesperson for the tribe.[85]

Although the IRA was intended to provide tribes with the power to govern themselves and protect their own interests, the new systems of government were largely criticized. At the core of the act remained the issue that foreign concepts of government were replacing tribal traditions. How could an imposed government appropriately represent its tribal constituents? The very manner in which power rested in the hands of a few was inherently foreign to tribes accustomed to communal-based forms of Native government. In instances where the tribal council found itself concerned with all aspects of governance, the placement of power in the hands of a few individuals could lead to mismanagement of the tribe's interests by their own tribal members.

Some tribes were able to protest this new structure by pursuing traditional ways of governing. The Crow Tribe of Montana, for instance, created a general council consisting of all female tribal members over eighteen and male tribal members over twenty-one.[86] Decision making in that case remained in the hands of the people. Certain members of the Hopi communities, although organized under an IRA constitution, simply refused to acknowledge the imposed government form.

The very act of enforcing a unified tribal government on a reservation held its own difficulties. In the creation of reservations, earlier government policies had ignored differences among tribes and frequently situated several ethnic groups together on a single land base. Factionalism over differing interests consequently emerged when the IRA was used to attempt to establish a formal government over such reservations. Moreover, management problems remained a constant issue, ranging from merely inefficient to criminal administration.[87] In some instances, attorneys appointed by the tribal council members or chairperson allowed for the possibility of acting against the interests of the tribe in order to benefit individual leaders.[88]

An example of the devastating consequences of imposed governments can be found in the Hopi tribe. In 1934, the twelve Hopi villages situated on Black Mesa in Arizona, under great pressure, organized under an IRA constitution. Before then, no central government had existed for the Hopi. The villages had made decisions separately under the leadership of separate Kikmongwi and advisers. The Kikmongwi, an authority figure and a life-appointed "village chief," held responsibility for making decisions on traditional religion and to preserve the welfare of the villagers, his children. This religious authority did not transfer to secular matters, and the Kikmongwi was strongly prohibited from dealing with worldly disputes; such disputes were delegated to the levels of advisers.

The new IRA constitution unified the twelve villages under a single tribal council, giving the Hopi people a strong voice that would make it possible for them to deal with modern development. Indeed, development came to the very doorstep of the tribe; even as the votes were being counted, coal companies were seeking to negotiate with the Hopi people for a land lease, in hopes of mining the fuel-rich and traditionally sacred Black Mesa.[89]

As a nod toward tradition, a provision in the tribal constitution maintained the authority of the Kikmongwi, giving the village leaders power to certify the appointment of members to the tribal council. The result proved disastrous. Drawing the religious figure into a secular role compromised the Kikmongwi position. For years the

Kikmongwi refused to certify tribal members, leading to the disbandment of the tribal council in 1943. Factionalism between traditionalist and modernist interests emerged among the distinct voices of the villages that had been unified under one government. In 1955, the Secretary of Interior gave approval to the formation of a new Hopi Council. Only nine of the seventeen positions were filled, and entirely by modernists supporting United States–style development. Many of the Kikmongwi refused to certify council members.[90]

The constitution, by placing authority in one council, made it possible for coal companies to obtain one signature and, through that, permission to open mines on the reservation. Not only did the mines lead to the destruction of sacred sites and damage supplies of groundwater, but the Hopi were cheated out of millions in revenue through mismanagement of their affairs.[91]

THE TERMINATION PERIOD (1953–1960)

Beginning in the 1940s, war-related industrialization and attempts to terminate the legal recognition of some tribes meant that many Native Americans lost control of more land and natural resources. In 1949, the Hoover Commission issued a report that called for the "complete integration" of Native Americans into mainstream society.[92] In 1953, with direct support from President Dwight D. Eisenhower, Congress passed House Concurrent Resolution No. 108. This resolution, often called "the termination resolution," sought to remove governmental power from tribal governments, discontinue the relationship between the federal government and tribal nations, and discontinue federal benefits and support services that accompanied the trust responsibility. Many of the supporters of the new policy argued that it represented "emancipation" because it would "free" Indians from the oppressive, day-to-day control of the Bureau of Indian Affairs.[93] The resolution stated that

all of the Indian tribes and the individual members thereof located within the States of California, Florida, New York and Texas, and all of the following named Indian tribes and individual members thereof, should be freed from Federal supervision and control and from all disabilities and limitations specially applicable to Indians.

The policy was implemented by individual congressional acts for each tribe that was slated for termination and was accompanied by a termination plan that transferred tribal land into private ownership and discontinued tribal government powers.

Termination had a devastating affect on tribes. When the federal government terminated a tribe, it once again forced individual

Unfair Compensation: The Indian Claims Commission (1946–1978)

In 1946, Congress passed the Indian Claims Commission Act, allowing tribes to sue the federal government for compensation of Native lands unfairly purchased or taken, through treaties or force, by the United States government. The commission was established in order to clear the backlog in the Court of Claims as well as to once and for all end the question of land claims, thereby moving along the process of "tribal termination and Indian assimilation."[94] From the beginning the commission acknowledged that only monetary compensation would be offered to tribes. By accepting payment, the tribe would agree to give up all claims of land or money lost.[95] Through the duration of the commission, over $800 million was awarded to nearly three hundred claimants—in reality, a fraction of what was owed. A stipulation of the act forbade the payment of interest, so the compensation received by tribes was at the nineteenth century value of the land, far less than its worth at the time of the settlement. Moreover, the full amount of the allotted money did not always reach tribes.

In 1951 the Western Bands of Shoshone Nation, represented by the Te-Moak Bands, filed suit with the Indian Claims Commission addressing the taking of their lands and the mishandling of money in trust. After the disbandment of the commission in 1978, these claims were passed to the U.S. Court of Claims, which settled the land claim in 1979 for $26.1 million. In 1991 the court awarded a second claim to settle the mishandling of the Western Shoshone people's trust funds by the U.S. government.

The awards have yet to be paid to the Western Shoshone people. On February 25, 2003, Representative Jim Gibbons (R-Nev.) introduced a bill in the House "to provide for the use and distribution of the funds awarded to the Western Shoshone . . . under Indian Claims Commission."[96] However, the Shoshone people are themselves split over whether they want to press for the return of the appropriated money. Accepting the payment means receiving $142,472,000 (the original awards plus interest) from the land claim for distribution to sixty-five hundred

(continued)

eligible individuals within the Western Shoshone community, and the establishment of an education trust fund with the funds from the accounting claim.[97] If the payment is accepted, however, the Shoshone acknowledge an end to any legal claim to land set aside by the purported 1863 Treaty of Ruby Valley. Many members of the Western Shoshone tribe have refused to accept the payment because they believe that they have aboriginal title to the land and have never signed a treaty or agreement for any of the land in question. Therefore, the claim is ongoing until questions of sovereignty and self-determination are resolved.

private property ownership upon tribal members, often against their will or interest. Individual tribal members, once they became private property owners, were forced to pay taxes to the state. Many Indians either sold their land to whites or were swindled out of it, and many individual Indians lost land that they were not able to pay taxes on. This further contributed to the erosion of the Native land base.[98] By selling Indian land, Congress destroyed the economies of many tribes, reducing them to poverty and dependence on public assistance. In total, approximately 109 tribes and bands were terminated under the policy, and a minimum of 1,362,155 acres and 11,466 individuals were affected. While some of these tribes have since been reinstated, most tribes are still struggling to this day to recover from such a devastating economic blow.

The shameful nature of this period in U.S. history is further reflected in the fact that once again the motivation for tribal termination appeared to be wholly economic, rather than simply misguided social policy. Tribal termination across the nation resulted in the surrender of over twenty million acres of prime timber and farmlands to the United States government. In addition, terminated tribes were cut off from valuable federal services that accompanied the trust responsibility, including health, education, and housing. These terminated tribes have never been compensated for the loss of these services, valued at about $148 million. [99] Because tribal sovereignty is a federal guarantee that insulates tribes from taxation and other economic burdens imposed by the state and local non-Indian governments, the loss of this protection also had high costs. The Native American Rights Fund estimates that these costs may be over $100 million over the period from 1961 to 1986. [100]

One case dating from this time can be found in the Menominee tribe in Wisconsin, although their history of exploitation begins earlier. The Menominee land base was drastically reduced in 1831, when they were forced to sell three million acres, territory that would become some of the state's most valuable agricultural and industrial land. The Menominee tribe was then relocated to their current reservation elsewhere in Wisconsin in the mid 1800s, with the boundary of their reservation defined by an 1854 treaty. The land they were relocated to was described as "wilderness where no white man would live." [101] Most of the land was wooded, and much of the soil was of poor quality for agriculture. The Menominee were given 13.5¢ an acre for the rich agricultural land they relinquished to white farmers and settlers, and the landholdings of the tribe were reduced from 9.97 million acres to 233,092 acres. [102] Although beset by disease spread by newly arriving settlers in the 1860s, and by encroachments on their traditional territories, by the late 1800s the tribe was finally able to develop a vibrant economy mostly due to their harvesting and the sale of tribal timber resources. For the most part, the Indian Bureau at the Department of the Interior managed the harvesting and the sale of the timber, because the Menominee were still considered wards of the state, like all other Indian tribes. Many of these timber projects managed by the Indian Bureau were characterized by waste, corruption, inefficiency, and violations of statutory and contractual requirements. [103] Despite these and other setbacks, the Menominee were able to generate a fair revenue from their timber harvest. By 1951, the Menominee had grown relatively prosperous compared to other tribes, and had moderate economic development on their reservation. However, private, white-owned timber companies became increasingly interested in the timber resources on Menominee lands. In 1954, the Menominee tribe was one of the first tribes to be slated for termination by the federal government. Although tribal forest resources were mostly protected by the formation of a tribal corporation, termination led to a drastic decline in tribal employment, increased poverty, and devastating reductions in basic services and health care. The Menominee economy was devastated, and deaths from diseases skyrocketed. Many Menominee left the reservation in search of work. Criticism of the termination program and recognition of its devastating impact led to the reinstatement of the Menominee tribe in December 1973. The lands of Menominee County reverted back to reservation status in 1976. The tribe has since sued the federal government for the costs associated with termination, as well as for mismanagement of tribal timber resources, but has not been successful in its lawsuits.

There are many other examples of tribes that were never compensated for the high costs of termination and the wealth that such termination generated for other private interests.

CHALLENGES TO HUNTING AND FISHING RIGHTS (1960–1980)

Historically, tribes controlled vast land areas where they actively hunted and fished for food. As tribes increasingly were forced to cede land and accept relocation to reservations, access to these traditional resources became more limited. Competition from corporate interests led to challenges to traditional harvest rights. In addition, the construction of dams, environmental pollution, and other factors seriously diminished the amount available to the tribes. However, since many tribes continued to rely on these natural resources as an important food supply, they have had to work to defend their rights.

In the 1960s, competition from commercial fishing interests and sport hunters and fishermen began to grow. The salmon runs and other fish stock in the Pacific Northwest of the United States were increasingly attractive to corporate interests. In the 1980s, a legal battle erupted over traditional fishing rights in Wisconsin. A series of court cases was heard by the state and federal courts that ultimately upheld access rights of tribes to their traditional fish harvest. The backlash from corporate interests and sport hunters and fisherman was significant, however, and protest continues to this day.

Indian hunting and fishing rights were the focus of some of the fiercest anti-Indian agitation by sportsmen, who were vocal, active, and even violent in their opposition. Yet the greatest injury from legally allocating a percentage of the catch to Indians was not to sport fishermen, but to the commercial fishing industry. So while the campaign against Indian fishing rights was expressed entirely in terms of sportsmen's interests and environmental protection, the campaign organizers were in fact mostly commercial fisheries. They blamed Indians for smaller fish runs, that were actually caused by normal cyclical patterns and stream pollution from corporations. The response to court protection of tribal fishing rights included fishermen in their boats with guns and the refusal by the state of Washington to enforce the court decision.

Case study:
The Klamath Tribe[104]

No tribe in America has been more victimized by the vagaries of federal Indian policies than the Klamaths of Oregon. These resourceful and productive people have been
twice decimated by federal policies designed to deliberately destroy their economy and
undermine their culture.

The prosperous and powerful Klamath, Modoc, and Yahooskin Band of Snake
Paiute people (known as the Klamaths) once controlled twenty-two million acres of
territory in south central Oregon and northern California. Their lifestyles and
economies provided abundantly for their needs and their cultural ways for over fourteen thousand years. Contact with invading Europeans, however, quickly decimated
their numbers through disease and war and resulted in a treaty reserving to the tribes
a diminished land base of 2.2 million acres. Once traditional rivals, the three tribes
were forced to live in close proximity to one another on these drastically reduced
reserved lands.

The tribes' economy and trade were wiped out and the people were forced to survive on a subsistence basis, dependent almost entirely on the fish, wildlife, and gathering provisions of the reservation and the meager services of the federal
government—a subsistence that was further diminished by the destruction of the
abundant salmon runs by the construction of hydroelectric dams in the early 1900s.
They were forced to engage in a continuous struggle with the United States over its
relentless efforts to diminish and ultimately wipe out the Klamath homeland—a
struggle further exacerbated by federal encouragement of strife among the tribes.

In spite of these obstacles the Klamaths thrived on the remaining fish and wildlife
resources, and revived their vigorous economy with timber resources and imported
livestock. They soon became one of the nation's wealthiest and strongest tribes. In
1953 the Klamath people were nearly at economic parity with mainstream society.
Tribal individual income was approximately 93 percent of the average national
income. Moreover, the tribe was no burden on taxpayers. The Klamath tribes were the
only ones in the country paying their BIA administrative costs. In 1957 there were

(continued)

only four Indians on welfare in the Klamath basin—three on old-age benefits and one on disability. The Klamath tribes were by every measure not only not a burden, but were a significant contributor to the local economy.

The Klamath tribes were terminated against their will in 1953. Termination led to a loss of over 880,000 acres of ponderosa pine, 90,000 acres of which was immediately sold to timber company Crown Zellerbach. The remaining land was taken through condemnation by the United States to contribute to Winema National Forest and part of Fremont National Forest. Both national forests have been opened for logging by national timber companies. In the forty years following termination, this timber resource produced over $450 million in revenues for the United States.

The effect on the tribe was devastating. The economy of the Klamaths was destroyed. They lost their land to the federal government for a fraction of what would prove to be its real value. The culture and social fabric of the people was seriously disrupted. Their government was critically undermined and all but dysfunctional. Their consistent requests for assistance in preserving a small portion of their heritage went largely unheeded. They were dispossessed from the very land-based enterprises at which they had been so successful. They were sent to participate in a society for which they had few of the skills or inclinations necessary to succeed, a society ill-prepared and largely unwilling to accommodate them.

Faced with growing demoralization, the social profile of the Klamath people reflected increasing evidence of all of the indices that have come to characterize one face of Indian America—poverty, alcoholism, high suicide rates, low educational achievement, disintegration of the family, poor housing, high dropout rates from school, disproportionate numbers in penal institutions, increased infant mortality, decreased life expectancy, and more. Data compiled for the years from 1966 through 1980 showed that 28 percent died by age twenty-five, 52 percent by age forty. Forty percent of all deaths were alcohol related. Infant mortality was two and one-half times the statewide average. Seventy percent of the adults did not have a high school education, and poverty levels were three times that of non-Indians in Klamath County, the poorest county in Oregon. Over half of those and 30 percent of those over sixty-five had no health insurance.

The once self-sufficient Klamath people had not realized the dream of assimilation that the federal officials and bureaucrats had crafted and forced upon them. They had, instead, had their land and resources stripped from them.

WHO BENEFITS FROM TRIBAL NATURAL RESOURCES?

In the lower forty-eight states, tribes hold about 30 percent of the nation's coal resources, 10 percent of the natural gas resources, and 5 percent of the oil resources. According to some estimates, 10 percent of the nation's energy resources lie within the tribal land base.

The electric power industry is a $280 billion per year business in the United States. Coal, natural gas, and some oil are used as the fuels for this industry. If you take the 10 percent of energy resource holdings owned by Indian tribes, then one could assume that the total amount of revenue generated from the tribal energy resources should be around $28 billion per year. Yet in 1999, the annual income to the tribes was less than $1 billion ($900 million).

Until 1962, the Department of the Interior held that it was not legal for Indians to develop their own mineral properties. In practice, Indian mineral owners were simply leaseholders with little say over such matters as air and water pollution and preservation of sacred sites. As the Council of Energy Resource Tribes states:

It was no longer necessary to move Indians off their land or necessary to send in troops to protect trespass mining; all that was necessary was to induce the Indian landowner to sign a minerals lease, or the government to sign it on behalf of the owner. The location of roads, storage facilities, the use of timber, water, gravel, and the minerals themselves in support of the mining operations become solely the province of the lessee. Until the early 1970s, the only legal role for the Indian mineral owner was that of a passive royalty owner. Under such a scheme, tribes had no opportunity to develop their managerial, technical, or business skills but remained, under the law, wholly dependent upon the integrity of federal institutions for the protection of their interests.

More recently, some tribes have taken a more active role in managing the leases for their natural resources. Only one tribe, the Southern Ute (located in Colorado, New Mexico, and Utah) has complete control of their energy resources. Most tribes have had their energy resources leased to outside corporations, mostly owned by non-Indians. The Bureau of Indian Affairs usually negotiates the leases, often without tribal input, and the corporations pay a percentage in royalties to the tribes. These royalties range from 12 percent to 25 percent of total revenues earned from the resource. While this is changing, the majority of leases for tribally

The issue is control

by Rebecca Adamson

My grandmother was not allowed to speak her Cherokee language in school, and so my mother never learned it. I was brought up with the message, "Be less Indian."

My father moved us to Ohio, where I went to good public schools. That community invested in me. Every summer I stayed in North Carolina with my grandmother, and she regretted not being able to teach me her Indian language. My cousins knew the best fishing holes, but they didn't know fractions or how to read a ruler. So that's how I came to work on education, because it just wasn't right. Why weren't the schools investing in my cousins like they invested in me? Indian schools at that time were run by missionaries, by the Bureau of Indian Affairs, or by all-white school boards.

The first five Indian-controlled schools ever were funded by President Kennedy under the Indian Education Act. But President Nixon impounded the money, and the five schools sued, won, and founded the Coalition of Indian Controlled Schools. They used some of the money to hire me to promote Indian-controlled schools.

I was in and out of jail in many podunk racist towns. In Hoopa, California, and Duckwater, Nevada, I was charged with disturbing the peace. In Hammon, Oklahoma, a school district with 85 percent Indian kids, they said proudly that they had never had an Indian student graduate since the 1940s. There was an eighth grade teacher who taped all the Indian students' mouths shut during her classes. We took every kid out of that school and enrolled them in our school, and the old school folded. We founded thirty-two new Indian-controlled schools.

In the 1970s, with the American Indian Movement on the scene, we were not exactly welcomed. Once I noticed a ceiling tile that was ajar, and I stood on my desk and found twenty-three microphones up there.

Finally, in 1975, the Indian Education Self-Determination Act was passed, giving a legal basis for Indian control. Under the Bureau of Indian Affairs, bad

(continued)

> *decisions were always getting made and imposed on schools—for example, that computers were just a fad so they wouldn't fund them.*
>
> *So I realized that self-determination means not negotiating a better contract with the BIA but walking to the table with our own money. That's why I founded First Nations Development Institute in 1980. Our number-one priority has to be control of our own assets.*

owned natural resources are granted to non-Indian companies. Recently, many lawsuits have emerged that claim the federal government has historically mismanaged these natural resource leases. Litigation in many of these lawsuits is ongoing.

CHALLENGES TO NATIVE WEALTH TODAY

In the 1980s, in an effort to promote economic development on Indian reservations, the Reagan administration encouraged tribes to pursue revenue-generating activities that took advantage of their tribal sovereign jurisdiction. Such activities as cigarette sales and gaming that took advantage of the tribes' unique tax and legal status were promoted. As tribes began to use their governmental status as a vehicle for income-generating activities, however, courts were increasingly called upon to clarify the scope of tribal regulatory and jurisdictional authority. Eyeing profits being generated on Indian reservations, states were eager to impose taxes on tribes.

Taxation

Indians are subject to federal taxation on income, whether it is earned on or off a reservation or tribal lands. However, tribes can operate tribally owned companies that are exempt from federal taxes, even if the company conducts business off the reservation. In addition, most tribes are not subject to state taxation, and therefore tribal businesses can benefit from a significant tax savings. The origin of this legal right is the 1832 opinion by Chief Justice Marshall in *Worcester v. Georgia*, which declares that state laws "can have no force" on an Indian reservation without the consent of Congress. [105] Marshall referred to tribes as "domestic dependent nations" and stated:

Indian nations had always been considered as distinct, independent political communities, retaining their original natural rights, as the undisputed possessors of the soil.

The U.S. Constitution mentions Indians as distinct and separate identifiable groups twice: once, in the provision for representation in Congress, and the second time in the Fourteenth Amendment, when Indians are exempted from some federal taxation. For the most part, the rights of Indians who live and work on Indian land to avoid state taxation have been upheld including in a 1973 decision. [106] In addition, Indians who buy goods on their reservations, regardless of whether they buy it from an Indian or a non-Indian, do not have to pay state sales tax. This is not true for non-Indians purchasing goods on the reservation. In 1980, the Supreme Court ruled in *Washington v. Colville* to allow states the authority to tax cigarette sales to non-Indians, effectively stripping tribes of a profit margin for taxing such sales. In *Rice v. Rehner*, in 1983, the Supreme Court ruled that states can regulate the sale of alcohol by requiring tribes to purchase state permits to sell packaged liquors on the reservation.

The special tax status of tribes continues to be eroded. Ironically, just as tribes are finding ways to develop business enterprises to aid in economic development on their reservations, the states and the federal government are promoting policies to require tribes to share their resources. Most court cases have required tribes to enter into compacts, or legal agreements, with states to negotiate payment to states as a result of tribes' commercial activities.

The state of Oklahoma provides a case study. Increasing pressure from the state government caused many tribes to enter into compacts to levy taxes on cigarette sales on reservations. [107] Today, tribes with tobacco compacts pay the state $0.0575 per pack, or a little less than 25 percent of the state excise tax at the wholesale level. The state requires $0.1725 per pack from tribes without tobacco compacts, but does not collect this amount. In 2000, tribes paid over $8 million to the state in taxes on cigarette sales, accounting for 15 percent of the total $55 million grossed by the state that year. (Native Americans account for 12 percent of the population in Oklahoma.) [108]

Another example comes from the state of Idaho. In February 2003, the state legislature of Idaho announced their intention to impose taxation on tribal enterprises and collect cigarette taxes on the four reservations in the state. The governor, battling a budget shortfall, predicted that sales taxes by tribes on all reservations could add about $3 million to the state's revenue. [109]

Gaming

As gaming has become increasingly profitable, states have become more aggressive in their attempts to regulate or tax gaming profits. It all started in 1979, when the Seminole tribe of Florida became the first Indian tribe to operate a high-stakes bingo game.[110] With the advent of more profitable gaming in the early 1980s by the Cazabon Band of Mission Indians and the Morongo Band of Mission Indians, which opened high-stakes poker parlors, tribes began to recognize the income-generating power of gaming operations. More and more tribes began to open casinos or other gaming operations.

Federal Indian law means that Indian reservations are generally exempt from regulation by the states and this, in turn, puts the federal government into a dilemma over the issue of gaming. The issue came to a head in 1987 with *California v. Cazabon Band of Mission Indians.* The Supreme Court found that by allowing any gambling within the bounds of the state, the state could not prohibit gaming on the reservation. In other words, the state could not prohibit gaming on a reservation while it endorsed or participated in similar gaming off the reservation.

As a result of the decision in *Cazabon,* in 1988 Congress enacted the Indian Gaming Regulations Act (IGRA) to provide a statutory basis for the operation of gaming by Indian tribes as a means of promoting tribal economic development, self-sufficiency, and strong tribal governments. IGRA provided a shield from organized crime and other corrupting influences, and it established federal regulatory standards.[111] The Indian Gaming Regulatory Act specified that funds from gaming can only be used for:

- funding tribal government operations or programs;

- providing for the general welfare of the tribe and its members;

- promoting economic development for the tribe;

- donating to charitable organizations;

- helping fund operations of local government agencies.[112]

Many tribes believe that that IGRA infringed upon tribal sovereignty because it required tribes to enter into compacts with states before it could offer certain types of gaming, and it restricted the use of gaming funds. While the legislation clearly indicates that states do not have the right to collect taxes on Indian reservations, the state compacts that tribes must participate in often require that the tribes pay the state a large portion of their revenues. Rarely does Congress place such restrictions on state or local governments, and privately owned casinos have no such obligations.

As a result of state compacts, state governments around the nation are benefiting from revenues earned by gaming enterprises on Indian reservations. In Connecticut two gaming tribes give 25 percent of their slot machine revenue to the state, which amounts to no less than $160 million per year.

In Wisconsin, tribal gaming creates just over $68 million in payroll, and almost half of the 4,500 tribal casino employees are non-Indian. Casino employees paid more than $380,000 in state income tax and $2.1 million in federal income tax in 1992. A state compact required the Forest Country Potawatomi to create a foundation, and the Forest County Potawatomi Community Foundation donated a total of $3.6 million to Milwaukee organizations in 2001, and more than $44.6 million has been paid in federal, state, and local taxes. [113] In 1998, the state of Wisconsin collected $83 million in tax and compact payment revenues, with total gains of about 24,400 jobs and approximately $170 million spent by gaming enterprises on goods and services from Wisconsin vendors. [114]

In Minnesota, approximately $62 million in taxes and payments have been made to the state, federal, and local governments. [115] Nationally, the total estimated impact of Indian gaming in terms of output of final goods and services was approximately $4.4 billion in 1997. [116]

The efforts to force tribes to share gaming revenues increased as many states experienced severe budget crises in the early 2000s. In January 2003, the California state government announced that it expected gaming tribes to contribute an annual amount of $1.5 billion from their gaming revenues. As of 1998, the Indian gaming opportunities in California had already contributed approximately $120 million in state and local taxes, and employed approximately 14,571 California residents, approximately 90 percent of them non-Indian. Given the state budget crisis at the time, the state appeared to be using the upcoming state compact renegotiation to extract significant funds from gaming tribes to help pay down the state's approximate $35 billion budget deficit. This action was especially upsetting given the state's historical lack of support for some of the poorest tribes in the nation.

LOOKING FORWARD

Native Americans have a history that is different from every other racial group in the United States. While many of the policies that forced tribes to relocate from traditional lands and sell their land and natural resources to whites and non-Natives occurred many years ago, a new set of policies have emerged in the last twenty years that continue to extract newly acquired resources from Indian people.

It is only by understanding the federal policies and actions that led to wealth transfer from Native Americans to white Americans that we can understand why

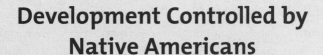

Development Controlled by Native Americans

First Nations Development Institute (FNDI) has provided funding and technical assistance to Indian efforts to reclaim control of their assets. The Eagle Staff Fund of FNDI awarded five $20,000 grants to Indian land allottee associations—in Oklahoma; Quinault, Washington; Fort Hall, Idaho; the Navajo reservation in Arizona; and the Pine Ridge reservation in South Dakota—to build their land management capacity and increase control over their assets, and another grant to a technical assistance group. The goals were to verify and update ownership records and to secure fair market value for their assets including oil royalties in two cases, timber sales in one case, and land leases in two others.

This project bore remarkable results. In Fort Hall, Idaho, the Bureau of Indian Affairs had been leasing some of the tribe's land for $50 an acre, when the next cheapest lease was $200 an acre. The lease was increased from less than $1 million to $3.9 million, and the tribe was awarded an additional $2.5 million in agricultural subsidies.

Navajo oil had been priced at $3 a barrel when the market price was $5.75. Pine Ridge land was leased for half the local going rate. In both cases the tribes won an increase to market value.

Before this project, the five grantees had $1.4 million in annual revenue from their assets, and afterward, it rose to $34.6 million. Quite a return on a $120,000 investment! This success shows how important control of assets is to prosperity.

American Indians are "land rich and dirt poor" today. Federal actions, including legislative, judicial, and administrative policies that extracted or mismanaged tribal wealth, have contributed to the current condition of poverty and underdevelopment that many tribes find themselves in today.

Native Americans would be well off if they had gotten the fruits of their assets. It would be simple to make this happen; by extending the protections enjoyed by other asset owners to Indians as well.

The United States has a body of law regulating trustees' responsibilities to beneficiaries. The Securities and Exchange Commission (SEC) protects shareholders from conflicts of interest and requires trustees to maximize the benefit to the beneficiary. The Department of the Interior should be held to these same standards, instead of being allowed to cut sweetheart deals with Peabody Coal and other corporations at tribes' expense.

To enact these reforms, Native Americans should become legal beneficiaries of their own assets, instead of wards of the government. Indeed, why are Native Americans defined as wards, given that wards are usually children or mentally incompetent adults?

Today tribes have started to build and consolidate their land holdings.

In earlier centuries Native Americans were assumed by white policy makers to be incompetent savages, but now the debate about Native competence should be over. The SEC or another neutral, third-party ombudsman should have the power to audit the Department of the Interior and other trustees managing tribes' assets.

Being land rich should not mean being dirt poor.

Chapter 3

FORGED IN BLOOD: BLACK WEALTH INJUSTICE IN THE UNITED STATES

"You can give a man some food and he'll eat it. Then he'll only get hungry again. But give a man some ground of his own and a hoe, and he'll never go hungry again."

— FANNIE LOU HAMER, 1960's CIVIL RIGHTS ACTIVIST
AND BLACK FREEDOM FIGHTER.

The story of black wealth inequality begins with the trauma of violence: the violence of enslavement, underpaid labor, land theft, and discrimination. Governmental policies have systematically created a deep and abiding black/white wealth split over a long historical time. The government has always played a central role in creating this divide. African Americans have always resisted.

African Americans were encoded as property, first in colonial legislation and later in state and national laws. The three-fifths compromise, defining an African American man as three-fifths of one whole male, institutionalized Africans as part human, part property in the United States Constitution. Considered assets or property and as producers of wealth for others, African Americans were bought and sold to enrich northern and southern elites.[1] African slavery produced the initial start-up capital for what ultimately would become the basis for capitalism in the United States. Over time, government policies ensured national stability by lifting whites' status and providing them protection, while excluding African Americans.[2]

FIGURE 3-1

Median net worth, 2001 (in 2001 dollars)

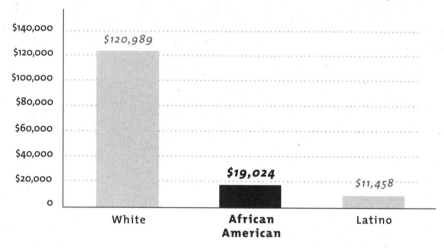

Source: Bárbara J. Robles's analysis of Federal Reserve Bank Survey of Consumer Finances data.

FIGURE 3-2

Median net worth, 1992–2001
(in 2001 dollars)

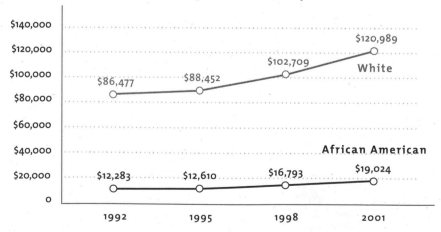

Source: Arthur B. Kennickell, *A Rolling Tide: Changes in the Distribution of Wealth in the U.S., 1989-2001,* Levy Economics Institute of Bard College, November 2003, Table 23.

Even now, a large number of African Americans continue to be marginalized from the economy and denied access to wealth-producing assets. In New York City, for example, only 52 percent of working-age black men were employed in 2003, the lowest percent since the Bureau of Labor Statistics began recording employment-to-population ratios in 1979.[3]

The racial wealth gap has widened, according to the Federal Reserve Bank's most recent Survey of Consumer Finances, which found that African Americans were 13 percent of the U.S. population in 2001, but owned only 3 percent of the country's assets.

Data examined to determine median net worth—that number at which half the population is above and half below—show that in 1989 whites had a median net worth of $97,800, and blacks, $5,300. A little over a decade later in 2001, whites had a median net worth over $120,000, while that of blacks was under $20,000. While both levels had increased, given the sorrowfully low overall level for African Americans, too little had changed.

Mean net worth—the average calculated by adding everyone's wealth together and dividing by the number of households—is even more unequal. African Americans' average of $75,748 in 2001 is only one-sixth of whites' average of $482,534. For every dollar the average white family has, in other words, the average black family has less than 17¢.

In every measure of assets and wealth, African Americans own far less than whites.

FIGURE 3-3

2001 mean net worth,
(assets minus liabilities in 2001 dollars)

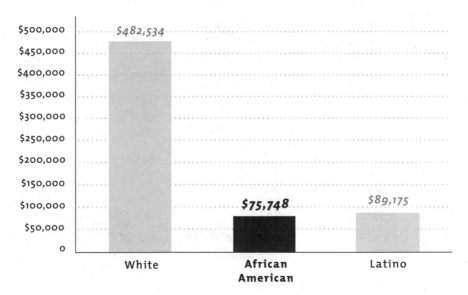

Source: Bárbara J. Robles's analysis of Federal Reserve Bank Survey of Consumer Finances data.

FIGURE 3-4

Percent owning each type of asset, 1989 and 2001

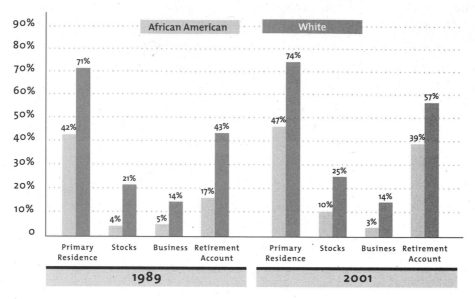

Source: Arthur B. Kennickell, *A Rolling Tide: Changes in the Distribution of Wealth in the U.S., 1989-2001*, Levy Economics Institute of Bard College, November 2003, Table 23.

FIGURE 3-5

Mean asset ownership, 2001 (in 2001 dollars)

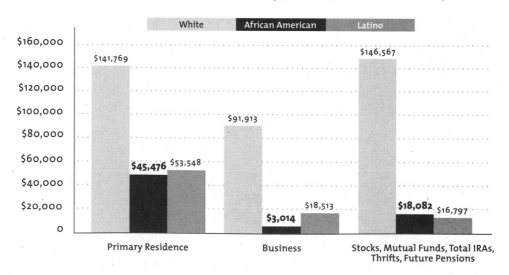

Source: Bárbara J. Robles's analysis of Federal Reserve Bank Survey of Consumer Finances data.

FIGURE 3-6

Median family income, 1999

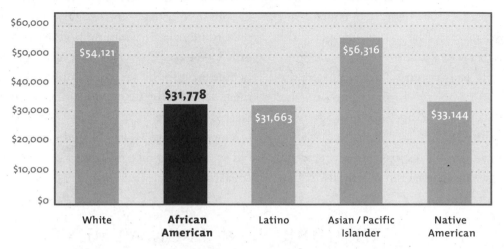

Source: U.S. Census Bureau, *Historical Income Tables*, Table F-5, *Characteristics of American Indians and Alaska Natives by Tribe and Language, Census 2000*, Table 10.

In 2001, only 10 percent of African Americans owned shares of stock.[4] For many who did, those shares of stock were worth very little.[5] What's more, stock ownership for upper income whites remained steady at 80 percent of families from 1997 to 2004, while the share of upper income African Americans with stock fell from 75 to 60 percent in 2004 alone.[6] Only 39 percent of blacks had private retirement accounts in 2001. And the mean value of those retirement accounts for a black family was $12,247, compared to $65,411 for a white family.

Half of all white families, but only one-fifth of black families, have parents who can help them buy a home. According to the Federal Reserve Bank, the average inheritance plus financial gifts given to a white family in 2001 was $20,685, which is enough for a down payment. That's ten times more than the average African American legacy, which was around $2,000.

Why have these wealth and income gaps persisted for so many centuries? There are many reasons, but government actions and inactions have been central in creating and maintaining black wealth inequality in the United States. They have been intertwined with persistent and virulent racism, based on the idea that African Americans were an inferior race, even subhuman, and that that justified the economic exploitation that has occurred during slavery, after emancipation, under the racial apartheid of the twentieth century, and into the twenty-first century. Clearly the plantation owners and factory owners who profited from free or cheap black labor had a deep interest in maintaining such a racist ideology, and too often they convinced working-class whites to identify with them by race, instead of identifying with black workers by class.

The earliest state actions, of course, were the laws making Africans into property. But long after slavery, and even after segregation laws were for the most part eliminated, discriminatory policies involving housing and land, farm aid, hiring, and public benefits have continued.

African Americans have not accepted this private and public racism quietly. Part of the story of black people is of resistance to wealth inequality. Over and over again, black people have spoken up for their fair share, only to be met by white mob violence and official silence. Over and over again, black people have built up assets, only to have them destroyed by white violence or by laws created by white men. Over and over again, black people have moved to find better jobs, only to find job discrimination or jobs disappearing south.

MAAFA: THE HORROR OF ENSLAVEMENT AND THE THEFT OF AFRICAN LABOR

From the fifteenth century to the nineteenth century, the expropriation of African labor was the great engine of Europe's wealth. *Maafa*, the Kiswahili word for disaster, describes this African holocaust of enslavement that ironically grew from the desire for sugar. The New World in the Caribbean and Brazil were the sites of this ultimately wretched, labor-intensive crop; they became the places for the cultivation of this sweetest of products and this bitterest of *maafas*. Tremendous profits flowed from Africans cultivating sugar.[7] Europe also colonized North America, and the colonies ultimately became the site of a burgeoning slave trade. The wealth of the new nation of the United States was built on this labor and its production of tobacco, rice, indigo, and, of course, cotton. Africans were bought and delivered to South America, the Caribbean,

and the United States in exchange for sugar, tobacco, rice, and other goods. These goods were then shipped to Europe for sale. Some of the proceeds from European goods went to Africa and were exchanged for more slaves.[8]

Over time, Africans' status in the English colonies of North America shifted from being nearly free of slavery, to a highly stigmatized permanent servitude, to full-scale lifelong enslavement.

Black enslavement flies in the face of the purported values of the founding of the United States. Political theorist Charles Mills rightly points out in *The Racial Contract*[9] that political doctrines framing this nation were actually a particular kind of contract, with liberty and justice and freedom just for some, not for all. He calls this the racial contract that underpins U.S. society. All white men would eventually have guarantees of citizenship—life, liberty, and the pursuit of happiness—which were not meant for the enslaved, nor for Native Americans, nor for the Japanese, Chinese, and Mexicans, nor for all women.[10]

Slavery: State Policies and Early Racial Thinking

Racial thinking was constructed over time rather than immediately appearing in the colonies.[11] But by time of the establishment of the new nation in the eighteenth century, it was clear that blackness was heavily stigmatized.

The earliest white settlers of the eastern colonies were stratified by religion (Christian versus heathen) and social position (master versus dependents of various kinds—women, children, servants—who were required to obey their master). Nonetheless, a narrative of black inferiority emerged, heavily rooted in the idea that physical difference, especially skin color, marked Africans as inferior and as slaves. Blackness became synonymous with slavery which solidified the idea of black inferiority.

In the colonies, the institution of slavery began in Virginia, the first colony to inscribe an inferior status for blacks into law. Servants who ran away had their terms of indenture extended, white servants for a few years and black servants for decades or for life. In the 1640s, colonial courts in Virginia made rulings that began to refer to black men and women and their children as property. The first recorded sales of human beings in North America took place in that decade.[12]

The Slave Codes, laws passed in Virginia between 1680 and 1705 that specifically singled out Africans, defined the children of slaves as slaves, and limited the political rights of free black people as well.[13] These codes emerged as a specific response to revolts by black and white servants, in particular Bacon's Rebellion, in which Jamestown was burned down during an insurrection in 1676.[14] This began a pattern that became consistent over the life of the nation: to divide black and white workers from one another. Race was used to modulate class tensions among whites, and this pattern has continued up until the present time.[15]

In 1670, South Carolina was founded as the first colony with institutionalized slavery established in its charter.[16] The Royal African Trading Company of England, with a history of trafficking slaves in the New World, went into business in North America, and the numbers of Africans enslaved and transported across the Atlantic increased dramatically. The proportion of slaves in the Virginia population, for example, grew from one-twelfth in 1700 to one half in 1763.

Governmental decisions both created and responded to racial divisions. The creation of unjust laws was central to building the racial state and the U.S. social order. White elites generated privileges such as differential citizenship rights for white males. Racism deflected attention away from class and gender inequalities. This is the racial contract that excluded African Americans from citizenship rights, land, and wage labor. It was also the catalyst for black resistance to these injustices over the past four centuries.

Building a Nation Based on Slavery

At the constitutional convention of 1787, the debate centered on whether there would be slavery in the emerging nation. The founding fathers were a mix of slave owners and slavery opponents. Some of them spoke against slavery but owned slaves themselves. Indeed, the signers of the Declaration of Independence and the writers of the Constitution were mostly wealthy landowners, and much of their wealth came from the labor of slaves. Thomas Jefferson was a slaveholder and articulated various public stances toward blacks that justified slavery by asserting the superiority of whites and the inferiority of Africans. If George Washington's wealth were adjusted for inflation, today he would be the fifty-ninth richest American of all time, according to a 1996 survey that put Bill Gates thirty-first. George Washington's house, Mount Vernon, had five plantations totaling eight thousand acres. He ran a huge fishery with slaves catching the fish, and a distillery run with slave labor. At his death

he owned 123 slaves, rented 40 from a neighbor, and his wife's estate had 153.[17]

As the white male elites negotiated the Constitution in 1787, the representatives of the southern slave states made concessions to northern merchants in exchange for not making slavery unconstitutional. The Constitution recognized slavery in three ways. First, the infamous three-fifths compromise, which established blacks as part human and part property, was a compromise between southern slaveholders who wanted more representatives in Congress because of their large nonvoting slave population, and northern states who wanted only voters (white men with property) to count. The compromise counted slaves as three-fifths of a person in determining the number of state congressional representatives. Second, the Constitution said that Congress would prohibit the slave trade in 1808 and not before, and third, it said that a slave held under the laws of one state could not be discharged from slavery after escaping into a nonslave state.[18] This last provision was strengthened in 1793 by the Fugitive Slave Law, which gave slave owners more rights to capture runaway slaves in northern "free" states.[19] This deal sealed the fate of Africans for the century.

A ban on importing slaves into the United States passed in 1808, the deadline set in the Constitution, and the transatlantic traffic slowed to a trickle, though slaves were still imported illegally.[20] Demand for cotton was great, and the potential for profit was great, so the trade continued. The cotton gin

Engraving of slave auction in Harper's Weekly, 1861 (*Library of Congress*)

and British textile manufacturing created an insatiable demand for cotton, and the interplay between governmental practice, economic exploitation, and racist justifications assured that some form of the trade would continue, even if illegal under the law.[21]

Whether to allow slavery in new states was a heated public policy debate in the hundred years before the Civil War. In 1787, the Northwest Ordinance banned slavery in the Northwest Territories.[22] The 1820 Missouri Compromise let Missouri be a slave state, but permanently outlawed slavery north of 36° 30' latitude. In the Compromise of 1850, California became a free state but Utah and New Mexico were allowed to write their constitutions as either slave or free states. Similarly, in 1854, the Kansas–Nebraska Act let Kansas and Nebraska decide whether to be slave or free states.[23]

Southern members of Congress represented slave owners' interests at the federal level. They won some concessions before the Civil War that worsened slaves' conditions, such as a new and stronger Fugitive Slave Act that passed in 1850, which compelled northerners to return runaway slaves to southern states.[24]

The Supreme Court's decision in *Dred Scott v. Sanford* in 1857 made runaway slaves' predicament even worse. Dred Scott was a slave in Missouri whose owner took him to live in Illinois, a free state. He sued for his freedom, but the Supreme Court decided he had no right to file a suit because he was property, not a citizen. This ruling allowed slave owners for the first time to take slaves to free states without losing ownership of them.[25] It was then interpreted as giving the Court's stamp of approval on "black laws" in the North and Midwest that kept free black taxpayers from voting, receiving relief payments, making contracts with white people, attending public schools, and other citizenship rights.[26]

Free Blacks Lose Ground

The free black population carried the stigma of the enslaved. It was difficult for them to obtain property, education, or jobs. Gradually, from 1660 to 1776, free black men lost the right to vote, the right to join local militias, the right to hire white servants, and the right to testify in court cases at different places in various southern colonies. But these rights had always been very precarious.

Nonetheless, between Caribbean immigration, population growth, and freed slaves, the numbers of free black people grew from 319,000 in 1830 to 488,000 in 1860, divided fairly evenly between southern and northern states.[27]

A tiny number of free blacks prospered, including landowners and skilled tradesmen. As Manning Marable describes,

The origins of Black Capitalism are found in the development of a small but affluent propertied Black elite which emerged before the Civil War. In Northern cities, some Blacks owned surprisingly large amounts of real estate. Properties owned by Blacks in Philadelphia were valued at $400,000 in 1847 and $800,000 in 1856. In 1840, Blacks in Cincinnati had accumulated real property, excluding church and personal property, valued at $209,000. Real estate owned by Blacks in New York City and Brooklyn in 1853 was valued at $755,000 and $79,200 respectively.[28]

Land ownership was the basis of almost all wealth in the nineteenth century, and free African Americans faced formidable obstacles in their attempts to get land. In Georgia, free black men were prohibited from owning land until 1818. Homesteading legislation in the 1850s usually excluded African Americans.

Thus, so-called free states did not give full freedom to African peoples, but found many ways to discriminate against them. Although a handful became prosperous and owned property, the majority did not. By 1804, all northern states had passed gradual emancipation laws, but the laws defined the children of slaves as slaves until they reached adulthood.[29] Black laws limited the citizenship rights of free African Americans, and local and state governments frequently refused to hire black applicants for jobs or give licenses to black tradesmen.[30] Incarceration and arrest were common practices.

Resistance, however, was alive and well among free blacks. They fought valiantly to end slavery. They built institutions in the wake of intense racial exclusion. The work of Richard Allen and the founding of the African Methodist Episcopal Church is a case in point. In 1787, when black

Philadelphia worshippers in the white Methodist church suffered the indignity and humiliation of having to sit in the back, they refused to do so one Sunday morning: they founded their own church, the African Methodist Episcopal (AME). In addition, there were numerous appeals by the free black population to exclude slavery from the new nation. The most notable of the appeals was that of David Walker. His *Appeal . . . to the Coloured Citizens of World* was published in 1829.

Black Women's Reproductive Labor

Enslavement is typically treated as a system of labor theft that contributed directly to white wealth. But what is less often featured is the reproductive role black women played in building white wealth. The seamiest side of the institution involved the forced reproduction of slave labor.

The expectation in 1787 of a ban on the importation of African slaves in 1808 had a side effect that worsened conditions for black women: they were increasingly regarded as breeders of more slaves to supply the market after the slave ships stopped coming. As the importation of Africans subsided, slaveholders understood that increasing black labor from within was central to the prosperity of the institution. African American women were often raped by their slave owners or forced into cohabitation

with male slaves to produce more slaves for the owner.[31]

As W.E.B. DuBois sorrowfully noted in 1903 in his *Souls of Black Folk,* he could forgive the South much, but not the horror of the system they inflicted on African women. Angela Davis, in her article "Black Women in the Community of Slaves," powerfully argues that rape and assault on enslaved women was calculated to instill fear into the entire slave community. Nonetheless, African enslaved women resisted in many ways.[32]

Reconstruction, the Beginnings of Jim Crow, and the Long Struggle for Human Rights

In the wake of the Civil War, the first federal efforts to give basic rights to African Americans were the Thirteenth and Fourteenth Amendments to the Constitution and the Civil Rights Acts of 1866, 1870, and 1875. In 1865, the Thirteenth Amendment outlawed slavery throughout the United States The Civil Rights Act of 1866 gave black men, including former slaves, legal rights to enforce contracts, own property, sue in court, and have legal protection for themselves and their property. The Fourteenth Amendment, ratified in 1868, made everyone born or naturalized in the United States a citizen, and forbade states from depriving any person of life, liberty, or property.

In 1870, the Fifteenth Amendment gave all male citizens the right to vote, and the Civil Rights Act of 1870 added enforcement provisions to the 1866 law.[33] Voting and other citizenship rights were not extended to black women. Another Civil Rights Act passed in 1875. These acts were enforced by federal troops that remained stationed in the South after the Civil War.

The new rights were promptly subverted by southern states, but they would be used as weapons of resistance, as African Americans fought for freedom over the years. Black candidates were elected to southern state legislatures and to Congress. They supported the expansion of free public education for both black and white children.[34]

But in 1877, a deal was struck in which Republicans got the presidency in exchange for concessions to southern politicians. As part of this deal, Union troops were removed from the South, and white supremacists regained control of the region.[35]

In 1883, the Supreme Court overturned the Civil Rights Act of 1875, saying that the Fourteenth Amendment covered only state action and did not prohibit individual discrimination.[36] Then, in 1896, in a case about segregated railroad cars in Louisiana, *Plessey v. Ferguson*, the Supreme Court ruled again that "separate but equal" was legal.[37] By 1900, all southern states had segregated schools and laws separating blacks from whites. They also passed laws preventing black citizens from voting—including new poll taxes, literacy requirements, and property qualifications that disenfranchised many poor southern whites as well.[38]

Other so-called black codes mandated that African Americans who quit their jobs or were absent from work could be arrested and imprisoned for breach of contract. Blacks couldn't testify in court except in cases where all parties were black.[39]

Clearly the goal was to prevent black prosperity. As early as 1865, the South Carolina legislature made any "person of color" who was an artisan, mechanic, or shopkeeper, or who was engaged in any other trade or business "on his own account and for his own benefit," obtain annual licenses for $100, while whites paid nothing.[40]

Most of these Jim Crow laws stayed in effect for at least two generations, until the Civil Rights Act of 1964 outlawed them.

During Reconstruction, blacks had begun to get jobs in local government—the same road to advancement that white immigrants would use a few decades later—but the white reaction in the 1870s put an end to public employment for blacks.[41]

FORTY ACRES AND A MULE

Perhaps more than anything else, African Americans wanted land in the post–Civil War period. This would be a difficult and, in most cases, futile effort as it became clear that government policy would be used to forge white political unity—the North with the South—rather than protect the right of freed people. As law professor Robert Westley wrote in his 1998 article on the case for reparations for African Americans:

> If the land distribution had not been undermined by President Johnson, if Congress' enactments on behalf of political and social equality for blacks had not been undermined by the courts, if the Republicans had not sacrificed the goal of social justice on the altar of political compromise, and Southern whites had not drowned black hope in a sea of desire for racial superiority, then talk of reparations—or genocide—at this point in history might be obtuse, if not perverse. As things stand, however, the south pursued a policy of racial separation with the sanction of the Supreme Court and the silent consent of Congress for a century after the official abolition of slavery.[42]

In 1865, during the Civil War, General Sherman issued Special Field Orders No. 15, promising forty acres and a mule to slaves who fought for the Union Army, and saying that part of South Carolina and the Sea Islands in Georgia were "reserved and set apart for the settlement of the negroes [sic] now made free by the acts of war and the proclamation of the President of the United States."[43] Unfortunately, the order was rescinded. And sorrowfully, the hopes of millions of newly freed Africans for land and self-determination were dashed. The order is excerpted below:

Special Field Orders No.15

IN THE FIELD,
SAVANNAH, GEORGIA,
SPECIAL FIELD ORDERS,
No. 15, January 16, 1865—
sections one and two

- The islands from Charleston, south, the abandoned rice fields along the rivers for thirty miles back from the sea, and the country bordering the St. Johns River, Florida, are reserved and set apart for the settlement of the negroes now made free by the acts of war and the proclamation for the President of the United States.
- II. At Beaufort, Hilton Head, Savannah, Fernandina, St. Augustine and Jacksonville, the blacks may remain in their chosen or accustomed vocations—but on the islands,

and in the settlements hereafter to be established, no white person whatever, unless military officers and soldiers detailed for duty, will be permitted to reside, and the sole and exclusive management of affairs will be left to the freed people themselves, subject on to the United States military authority and the acts of Congress. By the laws of war, and orders of the President of the United States, the negro is free and must be dealt with as such. He cannot be subjected to conscription or forced military service, save by the written orders of the highest military authority of the Department, under such regulations as the President or Congress may prescribe. Domestic servants, blacksmiths, carpenters and other mechanics, will be free to select their own work and residence, but the young and able-bodied negroes [sic] must be encouraged to enlist as soldiers in the service of the United States, to contribute their share towards maintaining their won freedom, and securing their rights as citizens of the United States.[44]

Congress created the Freedmen's Bureau in 1865 to distribute abandoned Confederate lands to freed slaves. There was no budget appropriation for the Bureau; its revenue came from renting abandoned land to freedmen and refugees.[45] While over forty thousand black families moved onto this land immediately, after Lincoln's assassination, President Andrew Johnson helped white plantation owners get back the land distributed by the Freedmen's Bureau.[46] This even involved evicting some black farmers at bayonet point,[47] although sparing some farmers with titles given by General Sherman.[48] Congress abolished the bureau in 1872, and the weak land distribution efforts were ended.

The other federal effort to provide ex-slaves with land was also ineffective. In the summer of 1866, the Southern Homestead Act of 1866 opened eighty-acre plots in Alabama, Arkansas, Florida, Louisiana, and Mississippi for settlement, and said former Confederates could not apply for homesteads before January 1, 1867. This gave freed slaves six months to buy the land at low prices without competition from white Southerners or Northern speculators. But most freemen didn't have enough money to buy the land. Three thousand African Americans did start homesteads in Florida. Sadly, most of the land was of poor quality, far from transportation lines, and far from towns where freed people could have jobs until farming began to turn a profit. With no money to tide them over until crops came in, or even to buy tools, most of the homesteaders abandoned their land.[49]

Sharecropping, Tenant Farming, and Debt

Southern plantation owners still found ways to get free labor after emancipation. Unemployed black men would be arrested for "vagrancy," ordered to pay an impossible fine, and jailed. Black people had to carry proof of employment at all times and could be prosecuted for vagrancy if caught without it.[50] Plantation owners would pay their fines and hire them as peons, working to pay off the fine. Bloodhounds chased peons if they ran away; the only significant way the workers differed from slaves was that their employers lost no capital investment if a peon was killed.[51]

Nonetheless, in the 1860s and 1870s, African Americans took advantage of the few opportunities that emancipation and Reconstruction provided to buy land, get local government jobs, and build black institutions. New laws gave them the rights to vote and run for office,[52] and black candidates were elected to state legislatures and Congress.[53]

Sojourner Truth worked for the Freedmen's Bureau, which helped former slaves find jobs and land. It paid for the construction of black schools, mostly on land bought by freed slaves themselves. Despite long hours working for white landowners, former slaves gave their time to building churches, schools, benevolent societies, and political groups.[54] By 1869 they had built 650 schoolhouses.[55]

By the mid-1870s, four percent of the freed families in the South owned their own farms, and this number continued to grow until 1910, when 14 percent of farm owners were African American and owned fifteen million acres.[56]

As the Ku Klux Klan and other terror groups acted to ensure black submission, violence against African Americans actually became worse in some areas than under slavery.[57] There were 4,742 documented lynchings between 1890 and 1960;[58] most people murdered by mobs were black men in the South. The courts remained biased toward protecting white people and property and away from stopping the lynching or exploitation of African Americans. Lynching and other violence terrorized black people who objected to being restricted to the very bottom of the Southern economy,[59] and the police and courts sided with the lynch mobs.[60] The height of lynching was 1892, with 154 lynchings.[61] Lynchings were usually unpunished,[62] and in 1934 an antilynching bill died in Congress.[63]

In 2005, Congress finally approved an apology for lynching. Ninety of one hundred senators signed on as sponsors, but not the two senators from Mississippi, the state with the most lynchings.[64]

By 1890, sharecropping was used by roughly 90 percent of all black tenant farmers.[65] The Freedmen's Bureau had advocated

Lightnin Washington and other black prisoners, Texas, 1934 *(Library of Congress)*

sharecroppers by charging them for tools and other necessities, pushing them off the land right before the harvest, and breaking contracts.[68] Sharecroppers who left were often captured, punished, and threatened with death. Some were jailed and then rented out to white landowners in the penitentiary chain-gang system.[69]

Black and white small farm owners became tenant farmers after merchants took their land to repay debts accrued under the crop lien system, which charged interest as high as 25 percent on store purchases.[70]

So many left to go north that there was a labor shortage, which caused a depression in Southern agriculture that lasted until World War I.[71]

Before the Great Depression, 90 percent of African Americans lived in the South, and only 10 percent of them owned land, while half were sharecroppers and a fourth were farm workers.[72] During the Great Depression sharecropping enjoyed a resurgence: when tenant farmers couldn't pay their rent, farm owners lost their farms, and some former farm owners and some tenant farmers became sharecroppers again.[73]

that sharecroppers receive a minimum of one-quarter of the harvest and later increased the recommendation to one-half.[66] Some landowners violently resisted these criteria, while others had fair contracts with sharecroppers.[67] Unscrupulous planters cheated

THE GREAT MIGRATION AND THE GOLDEN AGE OF BLACK CAPITALISM

Historians call the phenomenon of African Americans moving away from the South between the two world wars the "Great Migration."[74] The oppressive sharecropping system, violence, disenfranchisement, increasing mechanization, and less need for black farm labor pushed African Americans out of the South. At the same time, the prospects of greater freedom, more money, and a chance for their families pulled them north, where they gained a slender foothold in the industrial working-class economy.

Between 1900 and 1930, over a million and a half black people left the South.[75] In the 1920s alone, 872,000 migrated to the North and West.[76] With this migration, African Americans became a predominantly urban people, whether located in the North or the South. Three cities alone—New York, Chicago, and Philadelphia—held a quarter of the black people in the North in 1920.[77] African Americans from the rural South often moved to southern cities first, before heading north.

In Detroit, Chicago, and other northern industrial towns, many blacks, especially men, got decent-paying jobs in auto plants, steel mills, and other manufacturing industries. Thanks to union contracts, some of these jobs came with the health benefits, retirement plans, and job security that had been very rare for Southern jobs held by blacks. Some African Americans reached middle-class standards of living thanks to these jobs.

In these new northern communities, self-reliance among blacks became not just a virtue, but also a necessity. Due to residential segregation, the black middle and working classes lived in the same communities as poor African Americans. Separation from whites and the need for self-reliance led to what is sometimes called the "Golden Years of Black Capitalism," between 1919 and 1929.

There were over seventy thousand black-owned firms during this period. They were largely service businesses: barbers and beauty parlors, laundries, restaurants, grocery stores, newspapers, automotive shops, funeral parlors, insurance companies, and banks.[78] Between 1900 and 1914, the number of black-owned banks grew from four to fifty-one, and black retail merchants went from ten thousand to twenty-five thousand. Between 1919 and 1929, more than seven hundred thousand black firms provided for black consumers. The black middle-class, which included doctors, lawyers, and teachers, grew. Well-off African Americans vacationed at black resorts on Martha's Vineyard and Sag Harbor, among other places. Other black institutions besides for-profit businesses, such as colleges, churches, hospitals, and social clubs, were built or grew during these years.

The period's seventy thousand black-owned firms were vulnerable to economic and social upheaval. Both black businesses and black consumers were largely (and legally) frozen out of the white market. Together with the relatively small numbers of blacks in the North and the difficulty of getting financing (unless it was from a black-owned bank), economic segregation helped keep black firms small. A 1928 National Business League survey of 1,534 black businesses found that nearly half recorded an annual gross of less than $5,000. Only 9 percent grossed more than $25,000 per year. And black prosperity, no matter how small or separate, still sometimes attracted the violence of white envy and competition.[79]

Racism and the competition of white businesses defined the social structure in which black entrepreneurs had to function. That social structure limited the amount of wealth they could accumulate. The black businesses of the period strengthened black communities, but they did not uplift most African Americans.

World War I opened up a bit of economic space for black male workers, but as white workers returned to reclaim those jobs, racial tensions increased. The growing black populations in cities like Detroit, St. Louis, and Chicago flamed the racial hatred of whites in these cities.

The summer of 1919 was called "the Bloody Summer" because of the many violent assaults by white mobs on black communities, which continued through 1925, hitting Chicago, Detroit, Pittsburgh, Tulsa, and St. Louis, among others.

In 1923, white vigilantes lynched more than twenty black residents of Rosewood, Florida, and mobs burned down the entire black neighborhood, including homes, businesses, churches, meeting halls, and schools. These brutal actions removed billions of dollars in today's currency from these communities. The governor's office, the courts and legislatures, the county and local sheriffs, white newspapers and middle-class professionals often looked the other way.

Some employers invited black workers to come north as a way to break unions.[80] Walter White, writing about the notorious Tulsa riot just after it occurred, said:

What are the causes of the race riot that occurred in such a place? First, the Negro in Oklahoma has shared in the sudden prosperity that has come to many of his white brothers, and there are some colored men there who are wealthy. This fact has caused a bitter resentment on the part of the lower order of whites, who feel that these colored men, members of an "inferior race," are exceedingly presumptuous in achieving greater economic prosperity than they who are members of a divinely ordered superior race.[81]

The Great Depression hit black businesses especially hard. Many of the small businesses of the golden years failed, and only twelve black-owned banks remained by 1934. This, plus discrimination at white-owned banks, contributed to the undercapitalization of many more black-owned businesses.

Tulsa: Racial Terrorism in the City of My Birth

by Rose M. Brewer

I grew up in Tulsa, Oklahoma, but the elders rarely spoke of that time when homes went up in flames. Deep racial inequality continued in the aftermath of the racial terrorism of 1921.

There was a large Klan membership in post–World War I Tulsa, and the state of Oklahoma overall incorporated the racial practices of the Jim Crow South: segregated schools, housing, and public accommodations. A prosperous entrepreneurial sector called Greenwood emerged in North Tulsa. However, the majority of black Tulsans were locked in the racially stigmatized work of domestics, and dirty, poor-paying manual labor. But the symbols of black prosperity did not sit well with white supremacist thinking. So the Greenwood neighborhood was destroyed.

As with many such stories of blacks and white violence, it began with the supposed attack of a white woman by a black man, Dick Rowland, a shoe-shine "boy," as the term was then. White vigilantes attacked Greenwood on May 31 and June 1, 1921. One survivor of the riot said, "All the black community was burned to the ground, and three hundred people died." The wealth that belonged to the black community literally went up in flames—property, homes, and memories. In so many ways it represents so clearly black racial injustice in the United States.

The truth was finally exposed on this horrific event through a special commission. But the city remained segregated, and the underdevelopment of the black community was intentional.

My family understood the dangers as well as the possibilities of "being somebody." But that was always encouraged. Thus, I grew up in the cauldron of racism, but also in the midst of a community that expected much from her children, believed in us, and expected us to fly.

BAD DEAL FROM THE NEW DEAL

Because of the pressure of the Great Depression of the 1930s, the federal government created a general welfare state. Some government support was extended to African Americans, but unfortunately, racism marked the New Deal programs. Many African Americans were not served by the programs and received highly unequal treatment. Indeed, social welfare in the United States has always been splintered along racial, class, and gender lines.[82]

Southern committee members in Congress blocked efforts that would have included rural Southern workers in the social security legislation that was the centerpiece of the New Deal. Domestic work, in which black women were heavily concentrated, was excluded, as were agricultural jobs that many black men occupied. Nationally, 60 percent of African American workers did domestic or agricultural jobs in the 1930s, but in the South those occupations employed almost three-quarters of black workers,[83] and 85 percent of black women.[84] Deep into the twentieth century, domestic work was known as black women's work. Especially notable was the way that African American women were not deemed reputable enough to qualify for "mother's pensions."

Even among black workers in covered occupations, 42 percent did not earn enough to qualify for benefits, compared with 22 percent of white workers.[85] Southern maids earned less than $5 a week for seventy hours of work.[86]

Southern congressmen, committed to preserving the prevailing social order, wanted to keep their maids, sharecroppers, and field hands desperate, without any other options. Fifteen dollars a month in Social Security old-age benefits would have been well above a sharecropper's income of $38 to $87 per person per *year*.[87]

For those who qualified, social security made a huge difference in black well-being. In 1940, 2.3 million African Americans were eligible for old-age insurance, the greatest number of blacks ever to get any kind of government assistance.[88] In some Northern states, benefits were actually slightly more for black retirees than white; in the South the reverse was true, with ten states paying black retirees less than $10 a month.[89]

Other programs favored whites as well. Unemployment insurance and the minimum wage also didn't apply to domestic workers or farm workers. Unemployment benefits were limited to those who had had steady employment before being laid off, a restriction that continues to this day.

New Deal relief programs, though they were 70 percent federally funded under the Federal Emergency Relief Administration, were administrated by local authorities who could set their own benefit levels and eligibility rules. Southern congressmen prevented two rules from being passed, one requiring states to set relief levels at "a reasonable subsistence compatible with decency and health," and the other centralizing relief in one state agency.[90] While in Northern cities relief payments went disproportionately to blacks,[91] based on their greater need, in the South a smaller percentage of blacks than whites got federal relief payments, even though average black income was less than half of the average white income.[92] African Americans got no relief at all in some counties in Georgia.[93] Grant amounts also varied widely: while they averaged almost $30 a month in 1935, many Southern states paid $15 or less, and in some areas the Works Progress Administration found that black families got $2 to $6 less than white families.[94]

In 1936, the Aid to Dependent Children (ADC) program was similarly amended to exclude children in poor two-parent families for fear that able-bodied black workers, who on average earned far less than white workers, would stop working. Only children with dead, absent, and incapacitated breadwinners were eligible. States set their own benefit levels, and in Southern states they were very low. Some states, such as Texas, Kentucky, and Mississippi, declined to set up an ADC program.[95] In Georgia, one study found that 14 percent of eligible white families and 1.5 percent of eligible black families got benefits in 1935.[96] In 1940,

two-thirds of eligible children were not getting ADC benefits.[97] Outside the South, however, significant numbers of black families did get help from ADC.[98] Nationally, the program and its successors (AFDC and TANF) have always been used disproportionately by African Americans, though a majority of welfare recipients have been white.[99]

Survivor benefits were added to the social security program in 1939, so widows of employed men (mostly white) were transferred away from ADC to social security, which paid twice as much in benefits. ADC became stigmatized as a program mostly for black women and unmarried single mothers when white widows began collecting social security benefits.[100] ADC was the only public program with a "morals tests" for recipients: having men living in the household and unmarried births were grounds for termination from the program.

Farm aid from the Agricultural Adjustment Administration went mostly to white farmers.[101] The number of black-owned farms fell dramatically, from about 900,000 in 1930 to 682,000 in 1939.[102] Sharecroppers and tenant farmers were displaced as well. When white farmers got cash to make up for the drop in cotton and other prices, many used the money to purchase tractors and evict sharecroppers.[103] The federal government responded by amending the law to say that half the money should go to tenants, but planters often stole the checks outright.

Some poor black people got their own farms through federal programs, but these programs were small compared to the disruptive forces of the Depression, technology, and intimidation by whites. Briefly, in the mid-1930s, the Farm Security Administration had a tenant purchase program that allowed some tenant farmers to buy farms they had worked as sharecroppers.[104] The Resettlement Administration (RA) gave farms to former sharecroppers and unemployed urban former farmers. In Macon County, Georgia, a black town grew up and flourished, with cooperative marketing, a school, and a health clinic, after 106 families were given eleven thousand acres by the RA in 1935.[105]

Attempts to raise wages generally backfired against black workers in ways similar to the attempted agricultural assistance. The National Recovery Administration (NRA) set wages of $12 a week for the cotton industry, but many black workers had jobs not covered by the law, so employers reduced black wages to save the money needed to pay white workers more. In other industries, such as coal mining and tobacco stemming, minimum wages led to mechanization,[106] and displaced black workers were less likely than whites to find other work. Black workers covered by higher wage laws were often fired, and white workers hired instead.[107] Some African Americans called the National Recovery Act "the Negro Removal Act" and blamed minimum wages for increasing black unemployment.[108]

Labor unions won legitimacy in the National Labor Relations Act (also called the Wagner Act) and other New Deal legislation at a time when most unions not only were white-only, but also, in some cases, actively campaigned to keep black workers out of their trades.[109] Again, agricultural and domestic workers were excluded from the many newly granted labor rights.[110] By banning "open shops" with a mix of union and nonunion employees, the black workers were effectively kept out of workplaces with white-only unions.[111] The NAACP advocated a clause barring racial discrimination by unions, but the American Federation of Labor said it wouldn't support the bill if that part weren't removed.[112] Since black workers were often used as strikebreakers, a clause that kept strikebreakers out of unions allowed some unions to organize only white workers with the National Labor Relations Board's blessing.[113]

The public works programs of the New Deal did give some opportunities and some antidiscrimination protection to black workers. In the Public Works Administration, the federal government specified the minimum number of black craft workers on public construction projects.[114] The Civilian Conservation Corps had segregated labor camps in the South, but some black workers did learn skilled trades by participating in them.[115] Federal jobs slowly opened up to black workers, including twelve subcabinet positions in the Roosevelt administration during the 1930s.[116]

The Home Owners' Loan Corporation was created in 1933 to help home owners avoid foreclosure, but not a single loan of approximately one million, went to a black person, and a greater proportion of black people lost their homes during the Depression.[117] Home ownership actually became more difficult for African Americans to achieve because of New Deal housing programs. Since their goal was to reassure banks that they would be protected from the waves of defaults that happened when the Depression hit, the Federal Housing Administration (FHA) insured only economically sound loans, which in practice meant redlining low-income neighborhoods, including most neighborhoods of color and mixed-race areas. Soon banks would only lend with FHA insurance. Realtors, restrictive covenants and neighbors kept black families out of white areas.

The New Deal housing programs essentially backed white home ownership and black tenancy. HOLC is has been cited as originating the practice of "redlining." HOLC used an appraisal and rating system that outlined neighborhoods on a color-coded, alphabetically rated map. Blue, or "A," neighborhoods were most desirable, yellow "B" neighborhoods were not as affluent, green "C" neighborhoods bordered black neighborhoods, and red "D" neighborhoods were black areas.[118]

Thus, FHA redlining meant that many black families couldn't even buy a home unless they were prosperous enough not to need a mortgage at all.[119] Public housing was built in segregated neighborhoods, and public housing authorities selected tenants by race.[120] In many towns, including Northern suburbs, municipal ordinances prohibited black people from living within city limits, or even from staying in town after sundown.[121]

On the eve of World War II, the black unemployment rate was twice as high as the white rate, compared with half again as high in 1930.[122] Racial inequality had grown during the Depression.

A 1943 study found that average black annual family income in the rural South was $565, a third of what poor whites earned. In urban areas of the South, black income averaged $635 a year, white income, $2,019.[123] The basic cost of subsistence at the time was about $1,200 a year.[124]

In this context, the war looked like an opportunity for black advancement. The Selective Service Act of 1940 banned racial discrimination in the Armed Services, and in 1943 wage differentials by race were eliminated.[125] After A. Philip Randolph of the Brotherhood of Sleeping Car Porters proposed a march on Washington for defense jobs, President Roosevelt banned discrimination in defense industries and government jobs.[126] Many employers refused to comply, but for those who did get them, defense jobs were a big step up. The hypocrisy of the United States in fighting racist fascists in Europe played a role in these reforms: the National War Labor Board accompanied the equal wages with a statement saying that the treatment of black soldiers "is a test of our sincerity in the cause for which we are fighting."[127] About a million black people served in the war, half of them in combat.[128]

However, when they returned from the war, they didn't get the hero's welcome that white GIs got. Only in 1948 did President Truman issue an executive order mandating equal treatment in the armed services.[129]

UNEQUAL TREATMENT FOR BLACK GIs

The Servicemen's Readjustment Act of 1944—nicknamed the GI Bill—made education and home ownership affordable to veterans. It was a huge program, costing 15 percent of the federal budget in 1948, and involving 80 percent of all American men born in the 1920s.[130] Over $95 billion was spent by the federal government from 1944 to 1971 on the largest public benefits program in history.[131]

In theory, veterans of all races were eligible, but in practice mostly white veterans enjoyed its full benefits. A higher proportion of white men than black men had served in World War II, as early in the war Southern states rejected most black volunteers, and even when a shortage of troops led to inducting black soldiers starting in 1943, black rejection rates were always higher, largely based on illiteracy.[132] Half of age-eligible African Americans served in World War II, compared with three-quarters of whites.[133] But even among veterans, blacks had lower rates of participation in GI Bill programs. Dishonorable discharges excluded a veteran from benefits, and one ploy was to exclude black vets with a general

discharge on the grounds that it wasn't an honorable discharge. Black vets who protested military discrimination and mistreatment had their discharges downgraded, so they were more likely than white vets to not have honorable discharges.[134]

More than two million of sixteen million veterans had attended college under the GI Bill by 1955.[135] How did black veterans lose out on these education benefits?

First, most white colleges didn't accept black students. Historically black colleges, most of which were small and under-equipped, were swamped with far more applications than they could handle. By 1947, black colleges had between fifteen thousand and twenty thousand more black veterans applying than they could admit,[136] despite expanding their enrollment from twenty-nine thousand in 1940 to seventy-three thousand in 1947, with federal assistance.[137] Fifty-five percent of applicants to black colleges were turned away for lack of space.[138]

Eager black veterans also applied to white schools, and while some Northern colleges accepted them, in most cases they were rebuffed. All Northern and Western colleges combined never had more than five thousand black students in any year of the late 1940s.[139] The GI Bill is often credited with creating a new black middle-class of college-educated home owners, but its size was tiny compared with what it could have been.

Second, the average black veteran had a fifth-grade education. World War II soldiers overall had an unusually high education level, with 40 percent, mostly white, having completed some college.[140] This left many white veterans better able to take advantage of the college benefits.

Vocational education and job placement was covered, but was locally administered by United States Employment Services centers, which in the South especially, only wanted African Americans to get menial jobs.

White counselors at Southern USES centers gave black vets job referrals mostly for unskilled jobs. One study, done in October 1946, shows that 86 percent of white vets were referred to professional jobs, while 92 percent of black vets were referred to unskilled and service jobs, even if they had more advanced skills.[141] Refusing a job beneath their skill level, such as a janitorial job offered to a carpenter or a porter's job to a radio repair expert, was grounds for denial of unemployment insurance.[142]

To get vocational training, black vets often had to find an employer willing to train them, and then get this employer approved by the state coordinator of educa-

tion. According to the Southern Research Council, in 1946, blacks represented about one-third of the South's World War II veteran population. However, they could only enter one out of every twelve on-the-job training programs.[143]

Southern blacks who did get into training programs often faced trainers who took advantage of them; many found their experience useless. If they complained about the conditions, they would often be thrown off the job, and denied other GI benefits, such as unemployment checks. Some black vocational schools were poor quality outfits thrown together to take advantage of federal funding, with little actual job training.[144]

The home ownership benefits of the GI Bill were even harder for black veterans to take advantage of. In theory, veterans who were first-time home buyers of all races were able to get low-interest mortgages guaranteed by the Veterans Administration or the Federal Housing Authority. With these loan subsidies, home ownership often became more affordable than renting. But to get such a loan, a veteran needed a willing lender and a willing seller—both difficult to find, especially in the South. Loans were limited to single-family homes, not urban apartments or town houses. Sometimes collateral was required, which few African Americans had.

In the summer of 1947, *Ebony* magazine did a survey in thirteen Mississippi cities and found that of 3,229 VA loans, only two went to African Americans.[145]

One effect of federal home-ownership assistance was to create the suburbs and to increase residential segregation.[146] Because FHA and VA guarantees made mortgages safer for lenders, most banks stopped lending to anyone without them. Over $120 billion in home loans were financed by the VA and the FHA by 1962; less than 2 percent went to buyers of color, and only in segregated neighborhoods.[147]

Overall, less than 1 percent of all mortgages went to African Americans between 1930 and 1960.[148] Bankers received the FHA *Underwriting Manual* which included a ban on lending in integrated neighborhoods. The millions of African Americans who moved north after the war encountered opposition from white developers, lenders, realtors, local officials, and white mobs determined to keep them out of white areas. Restrictive covenants were attached to deeds to require white owners to sell only to white buyers. In the 1940s, a publication of the National Association of Real Estate Boards advised realtors to be on guard against "a colored man of means" who thought that his children "were entitled to live among whites," comparing such a man to a gangster who wanted to hide his activities by living in a better neighborhood.[149]

Black net worth was driven down by segregation. Black home owners didn't have as many buyers for their properties, and their properties didn't appreciate in value the way white-owned properties did, costing them billions in assets.[150] African Americans paid more for poorer quality housing. A severe housing shortage in black neighborhoods forced many black families into overcrowded conditions.[151] A study in the late 1960s by the Commission on Urban Problems and the President's Committee on Urban Housing found a shortage of twenty-six million units.[152]

The Housing Act of 1954 funded "urban renewal," called "Negro removal" by its critics because it destroyed mostly black rental housing without replacing much of it. Of the 400,000 homes razed by 1960, only 10,760 low-rent replacement units were built.[153]

In theory, discrimination in real estate was illegal. In 1940, the U.S. Supreme Court outlawed banning black people from buying in white areas.[154] And in 1948, it ruled that restrictive covenants were illegal. Additionally, the FHA stopped subsidizing mortgages for homes with such race restrictions in 1950.[155] In 1962, President Kennedy banned racial discrimination in federally owned or funded housing, but less than 1 percent of all housing in the U.S. was covered.[156]

THE STRUGGLE FOR EQUALITY

After World War II, African Americans began a determined effort to overturn segregation and poverty that transformed the nation. The first sit-ins by the Congress On Racial Equality (CORE) were in the late 1940s. By 1954 a million southern blacks had registered to vote, often risking their lives to register.[157] In 1955 the Montgomery bus boycott brought the Civil Rights Movement to national prominence.

As the NAACP filed lawsuit after lawsuit, the courts aided African American struggles. In 1949 and the early 1950s, the state universities of Kentucky, Texas, Virginia, and Louisiana were forced by court decisions to let in black students.[158]

But there were limits to what courts could do without cooperation from other government bodies. In 1954 the Supreme Court struck down "separate but equal" schools in the *Brown v. Topeka* decision, but local school authorities were allowed to determine the pace of integration.[159] The phrase "at all deliberate speed" included in the decision was interpreted to mean "slowly" in many areas. School desegregation progressed so slowly in the deep South that some dual school systems—one black, one white—persisted into the mid-1970s. More common was de facto segregation due to white flight into private schools and suburban school districts.

In Prince Edward County, Virginia, in 1959, rather than integrate the public schools, officials chose to close them for four years, providing vouchers for whites to attend public schools in other counties while denying blacks an education. In 2005, reparations in the form of college scholarships were given to blacks excluded from Virginia schools.[160]

The federal government is given a hero's role in many portrayals of this era, but, in fact, federal protection of Civil Rights activists was slow in coming. Promotion of equal rights by the federal government came only after massive organized pressure.

In 1960, the Democratic Party platform included strong language supporting civil rights. But what President Kennedy actually did was far less. In 1961 he issued an executive order outlawing racial discrimination in government employment and public contracts, and accelerated Justice Department enforcement of discrimination lawsuits. He delayed honoring his campaign promise to end discrimination in federally funded housing until 1962, and he didn't press Congress on civil rights legislation.

When the governor of Mississippi led a mob trying to prevent James Meredith, a black student, from registering at the University of Mississippi in 1960, Kennedy sent in too few federal marshals to control the rioters. Only after two people were killed and thirty-five marshals injured were federal troops sent in. A year later, federal marshals were sent to protect the first Freedom Riders only after they had been beaten by mobs in both New Orleans and Montgomery.[161]

In 1962, President Kennedy avoided dealing with Civil Rights legislation by supporting a less controversial option, an amendment to the Constitution outlawing poll taxes, which was passed after his assassination, and became the Twenty-fourth Amendment. In 1963, the pressure grew even more, with demonstrations in eight hundred municipalities and the March on Washington, which drew a quarter of a million protesters.[162] Despite filibusters by southern senators, the Civil Rights Act passed in 1964. The act provided for equal access to public accommodations. It gave the federal government the ability to sue school districts and public facilities to force them to desegregate; employers and unions were required to provide equal opportunity; and it allowed the federal government to cut off funds from agencies if they discriminated. It created the Equal Employment Opportunity Commission and strengthened the Civil Rights Commission.[163]

Almost immediately hundreds of complaints were filed with the Justice Department over segregated public accommodations. Although segregation wasn't eliminated, there was a visible change the first year, when black people in the South finally were able to freely patronize restaurants, department stores, bus and train stations, hotels, and even water fountains and public restrooms.[164]

In 1965 President Johnson publicly supported the Voting Rights Act, which finally passed after Alabama state troopers attacked peaceful marchers, shooting a black protester and beating another to death.[165] There was an immediate rise in black registration and voting. Ten years later, almost a thousand African Americans had been elected to public office in the six states with the worst histories of excluding black voters.[166] By 1977 there were over two thousand.[167] But that represented only 3 percent of elected officials, and African Americans were twenty percent of the population.[168] In 2001, there were over nine thousand African Americans holding office nationwide.[169]

Federal agencies also made covert efforts to weaken and destroy the Civil Rights and black power movements. Through the counterintelligence program, (COINTELPRO) the FBI took 295 actions against black groups from 1956 to 1971, including agent provocateurs, wiretaps, planting false rumors and information, and murders.[170] The victories of these movements were won despite federal interference, as much as with federal help.

One of the accomplishments of the Civil Rights Movement was that the federal government has not instituted policies with the explicit intent of disadvantaging African Americans since. The official policy

The Freedom Farm Co-op

Fannie Lou Hamer is best known as a civil rights pioneer. She was a field organizer for the Student Nonviolent Coordinating Committee, where she registered black people to vote in her native Sunflower County. She led the delegation of the Mississippi Freedom Democratic Party, which challenged the all-white state delegation to the 1964 Democratic Convention.

Less known is her economic development work, of which the highlight was the Freedom Farm. Her own life experience led her to prioritize ending poverty and developing assets in the black community in her Mississippi county.

Hamer was the youngest of twenty children of sharecropper parents on a cotton plantation. She picked cotton starting at age six, when the plantation owner offered her goods from his store to lure her into debt, which she never got free of. She left school after the sixth grade. Her parents saved enough money to rent land and buy animals and equipment to farm independently, but someone poisoned their animals and they were forced to return to the plantation.

Very few African Americans owned land in Sunflower County, Mississippi: only seventy-one of thirty-one thousand families in 1967. The median black income in the Mississippi Delta was $456 a year. Malnutrition and even starvation were common. By the end of the sixties, 32 percent of blacks were on public assistance; 12.6 percent were unemployed; families averaged 5.69 members; residents received on average only a sixth-grade education; 70 percent of homes were dilapidated, and 60 percent lacked plumbing.[171]

Hamer had the idea for the farm in 1969, after hearing of the death of her neighbor's eighteen-year-old son, who was so malnourished that he was never able to walk.[172] Through fundraising and generous contributions, Hamer purchased forty acres of land with an $8,000 down payment.[173] She then set up a "pig bank" with the help of the National Council of Negro Women, which donated fifty pigs. The bank loaned pregnant pigs to poor families, who could keep the "dividends," in the form of piglets, and return the original pig to the

(continued)

bank. When the first pigs from the litter became pregnant, the family would donate them to another family.[174] By 1973, three hundred families had almost three thousand new pigs.[175]

Everywhere Hamer went, she would ask for donations for the Freedom Farm. In Chicago, 176,000 white high school students "March[ed] Against Hunger" to raise money for the farm. Eventually five thousand people participated in growing their own food through the co-op. The Freedom Farm also helped thirty-five local families, living in shacks, with down payments on FHA-financed home purchases. They helped people fill out the FHA applications for a total of $800,000 in loans.[176] In 1971, there were thirty-three plots of land totaling 1,940 acres owned by blacks in the county, with the Freedom Farm comprising 33 percent of the land owned by blacks in the area, and by 1972 they had built seventy affordable homes. They built streets and laid down water and sewer pipes and electrical and gas lines.[177] Hamer and her family were one of the families who got a home through the housing co-op. Hamer would frequently overhear her neighbors speak about the benefits of their new houses: "You'll see two men walking out their front doors. One will kind of stop, look around, and say, 'Phew! I didn't realize how cold it was outside!' Every place they ever lived in before, it was always just as cold inside as it was outside."[178]

Sadly, the Freedom Farm was sold in 1974 to its creditors. Fannie Lou Hamer strived hard to bring economic well-being to many living in the Mississippi Delta. L.C. Dorsey, who ran the North Bolivar County Farm Cooperative, remembered Hamer's compassionate nature and said that "when she'd wake up in the morning, there'd be people with problems and in the evening when she'd come home, they'd be there with their problems. She just tried to address those problems."[179] When Hamer died of cancer in 1977, she was buried at the site of the Freedom Farm.

of the legislative and executive branches, as well as of many state and local governments, became nondiscrimination, with some degree of uplift offered to Americans of color. That does not mean, however, that no policies with negative impacts on African Americans were enacted. Sometimes harmful policies have started as attempts to help black communities or families. Discrimination shifted away from de jure to de facto, from intentional laws to just common practice.

Fair housing was a major demand of the Civil Rights Movement, and it had won antidiscrimination laws covering private housing in twenty states by 1966.[180] Federally, Title VI of the 1964 Civil Rights Act banned discrimination in housing financed with federal subsidies, but by that time there were fewer VA or FHA mortgages; only 20 percent of new housing in 1963 had such federal assistance.[181] Less than 4 percent of housing was covered by federal bans on discrimination.[182]

The Fair Housing Act of 1968—which was passed less than a week after Dr. Martin Luther King, Jr., was assassinated—was more comprehensive, banning discrimination in home sales and rentals, covering over 80 percent of all U.S. housing.[183] But in fact redlining continued, and there was virtually no enforcement of laws against discrimination by realtors, banks, and zoning boards.[184]

A U.S. Commission on Civil Rights investigation revealed the FHA's collaboration with blockbusters and unscrupulous speculators who sold substandard housing to people of color and then profited from the foreclosures when the properties deteriorated.[185]

The new Department of Housing and Urban Development (HUD) set criteria for loan risk that basically redlined urban neighborhoods, once again making them ineligible for federally assisted loans and driving down their property values.[186] The 1964 Civil Rights Act had specifically exempted federal mortgage insurance programs from antidiscrimination laws.[187]

In 1970, the Uniform Relocation Assistance and Real Property Acquisition Act said that local housing authorities had to replace any low-income units they destroyed in the course of urban renewal. Congress responded by eliminating the urban renewal program altogether and replacing it with more flexible community development block grants.[188] Even after urban renewal was over, African American urban neighborhoods continued to lose 80 percent as many housing units as during the devastation of the 1960s, while white neighborhoods lost housing units at the slower rate of the 1950s.[189]

After revolts in some cities in the late 1960s, some experienced builders and lenders pulled out of inner-city development, and the FHA turned to inexperienced and, in some cases, dishonest developers who created substandard housing units. Poor people who bought them and couldn't afford to repair them defaulted in large numbers, and the federal government ended up owning thousands of defective apartments.[190] After a 1971 report on this scandal, the program was shut down. To slow the avalanche of foreclosures, the HUD redlined inner cities, making it difficult for homeowners there to sell, as buyers couldn't get loans.[191]

White property owners mounted a backlash against integration. In response, President Nixon declared that he would not force local governments to accept construction of federally subsidized housing against their will.[192] Violent mobs burned crosses, a Ku Klux Klan tactic, on the front lawns of black families who moved into white neighborhoods in major northern cities. "Property owners' rights" laws passed in thirteen states, superceding fair housing laws.[193] Ronald Reagan became governor of California after campaigning against the state fair housing law.[194]

Ten years after the Fair Housing Act was passed, the National Committee Against Discrimination sent black and white testers to try to buy or rent homes, and found discrimination against black buyers 48 percent of the time, and even more against black renters.[195]

Federal housing policy continued along two tracks, with generous subsidies for the development of white suburbs but only limited, underfunded, and segregated urban public housing, some for white and some for black renters.[196]

As a result, by 1984, only 40 percent of African Americans were homeowners, compared with 70 percent of whites, and their homes were worth less than $30,000 on average, compared with $52,000 for white-owned homes.[197]

How much wealth was lost to African Americans due to these decades of housing discrimination? One estimate is that the current generation of African Americans will lose about $82 billion in home equity due to discrimination, and the next generation will lose $93 billion.[198]

While home ownership obviously has a direct positive impact on net worth, an affordable rental apartment can facilitate asset development as well. The guarantee that comes with public or government-subsidized housing that rent will not rise above 25 percent or 30 percent of household income is an important buffer against rising rents in private housing.

Affordable housing was supposed to be a centerpiece of the "War on Poverty," but the results fell far short. President Johnson proposed a major program of rent subsidies that would have allowed poor people to live in nonpoor neighborhoods, and would have helped working poor people, not just the extremely poor then eligible for public housing. But southern members of Congress opposed this proposal because it would have led to racial integration, and because of its cost.

The final bill, the Housing Act of 1965, included rent supplements only for very poor people, controlled by local housing authorities able to keep housing segregated.[199] Subsidies for low-income renters tripled in the 1970s, reaching 2.2 million families, but they still reached only 10 percent of all renters and only 22 percent of poor people.[200]

President Nixon put a moratorium on all subsidized housing programs in 1973 and then shifted federal spending from home ownership to rental subsidies.[201] Some towns disbanded their public housing authorities altogether rather than integrate. By the mid-1970s, most new subsidized housing was built for white and elderly people.[202]

BLACK FARM BLUES

Starting in the 1960s, black farmers began losing their land at a dramatic rate. In 1969, African Americans owned only 5.5 million acres of farmland, less than half of what they had owned 20 years earlier.[203] By 1990, only 1.5 percent of all farmers were black, compared with 11 percent in 1960, about the same percentage as African Americans in the U.S. population.[204] By 1999, black farmers owned less than one million acres.[205] White farmers were losing their farms during these decades as well, but the rate of loss of black farmers has been estimated at two and a half to five times the rate of white-owned farm loss.[206]

The loss of black-owned farms had started slowly a generation or two earlier. In 1920, a million black farmers owned fifteen million acres.[207] With 14 percent of all farms, black people were more likely to own farms than white people,[208] although in size they were smaller than white-owned farms, at an average of 63 acres, compared with 145 acres for whites in 1935.[209] For a few decades African Americans slowly and steadily left and lost farms, so that twelve million acres were black-owned in 1950.[210] This rate of loss sped up after 1960.

What did state policy and inaction have to do with black farmers losing their farms? Black-owned farms were smaller and poorer than white-owned farms and so

more vulnerable to weather and technological and economic change.[211] These factors were connected to institutionalized inequality, which generated an unequal playing field for black farmers. For example, in the 1930s, the Farmers Home Administration (FH) authorized local white farmers to decide who got loans.[212] FH boards increased their rejection rates for loans to black farmers after the 1954 *Brown v. Board* of Education Supreme Court decision to desegregate public schools, especially to those who joined the NAACP or tried to register to vote.[213] A 1964 study by the Johnson administration found racial discrimination in every program of the U.S. Department of Agriculture (USDA).[214]

The federal government has been propping up struggling farmers with subsidies since the 1800s, and the aid has been directed to white farmers. The Department of Agriculture was established during Reconstruction, and when Southern members of Congress asked for provisions that would steer agricultural assistance away from black farmers; the USDA complied.[215]

In 1980, the North Carolina Black Farmers organization filed a lawsuit against the FH, charging racial discrimination in farm aid.[216] The Equal Employment Opportunity Commission investigated the complaint and found differences in aid to black and white farmers. Black farmers got fewer loans for smaller amounts. They were less likely to get deferred loan payment schedules, and more likely to have to agree to liquidation of their property if they defaulted.[217] A USDA investigation found that white farmers typically waited 88 days for loan decisions and black farmers waited 222 days.[218] Of white applicants for loans, 84 percent were approved; of black applicants, 56 percent were approved.[219]

In 1983 President Reagan eliminated the division of the USDA that handled civil rights complaints. Local USDA officials continued to tell farmers whose loans were denied to send their complaints to Washington, where they piled up in a room in the USDA building.[220]

A second class-action lawsuit in 1997, *Pigford v. Glickman*, was successful in winning a settlement: a $375 million restitution program for black farmers denied loans from 1981 to 1996, but the payouts have been small and limited.[221] If black farmers could prove past discrimination to the USDA's satisfaction, their government debts were forgiven and they got a one-time tax-free $50,000 settlement. Since their average debt was over $75,000, and many had already lost their land, this settlement didn't solve problems exacerbated by discrimination. Farmers also have an option of going to an arbitrator for more compensation, $100,000 to $800,000.[222] Of eighteen thousand farmers who had filed claims by the year 2000, 40

percent were rejected,[223] sometimes for minor errors like misspellings.[224]

To win a claim under the settlement, farmers have to find a similar white farmer who was approved for a loan when they were denied. Many claims of discrimination that occurred before 1989 have been denied because the USDA says it can't find the records of the white farmer's loan. The reason is that pre-1989 records are on microfiche, and so the USDA needs the borrowers' Social Security numbers to find the loans, which the black farmers have no way of knowing.

Many black farmers felt betrayed by the settlement. The president of the Black Farmers and Agriculturalists Association said in 2001, "*Pigford v. Glickman* should be thrown out, as it has done nothing more than continued to ruin the lives of black farmers across the country. . . . We have already unsuccessfully attempted through the courts to have this case amended and reexamined to make it more plaintiff-friendly. . . . Of the few farmers who receive the $50,000, most still have substantial debt to the USDA and therefore will have to give up any money they receive; their state taxes will increase and put them in a bind; they have someone else who has a judgment against them, and they won't be able to get the money; or they are in bankruptcy and the money goes to the court to pay old debts, ... so the $50,000 is virtually of no help to the farmer. . . . Even Tim Pigford stated as recently as June 24, 2001, in a North Carolina newspaper, 'I'm ashamed my name is on this case. . . . It has probably hurt more black farmers than it has helped." [225]

The U.S. Commission on Civil Rights concluded after a 1982 study that the USDA was the main reason black farmers had lost their land. [226] In 1990, $10 million a year was authorized by Congress under the Minority Farmers Rights Act, but not once has the full amount been appropriated or spent. [227] In 1997, 91 percent of farm loans went to white farmers and only 2 percent to black farmers.

As rural black farmers struggled for freedom and justice, the transformation of urban black America was proceeding apace. As workers, they always had to struggle against racially biased wages. Black labor has always been paid less than what white labor made. This racial wage differential, or the split of the labor market along racial lines, has been a key piece of white labor's racial wage. [228] This structural division has continued to the present; the economic position of black labor has seen some gains and frequent reversals over the decades.

BLACK JOB GAINS AND LOSSES

The 1960s and 1970s are widely remembered as the decades in which people of color made great strides forward in employment. That's largely an accurate perception, although there was never the creation of a "level playing field" that many whites assume was the result. The Civil Rights and black power movements did result in federal policies that allowed people of color to break into more and better paying jobs, but not without considerable struggle and frequent reversals.

The 1964 Civil Rights Act was supposedly given teeth by the formation that same year of the Equal Employment Opportunity Commission, created to eliminate discrimination in the workplace, promote equal employment programs, and oversee compliance with the federal law.

The federal government attempted to lead by example with 1965's Executive Order 11246, requiring all employers with federal contracts of more than $50,000 to file with the government written plans for eliminating discriminatory staffing practices. The plans were required to include minority and female hiring goals and timetables, and committed contractors to making "good faith" efforts. The 1972 Equal Employment Opportunity Act Amendment targeted the federal government directly, mandating affirmative action hiring and employment policies by all federal executive departments and agencies.

As a result of the flurry of legislation, federal, state, and local government agencies hired more African Americans, and paid them more than private employers did.[229] In 1970, the majority of black college graduates were government employees, and 18 percent of the overall labor force worked in the public sector, compared with 26 percent of African Americans. The percentage of blacks among all workers employed in government rose from 13 percent to 21 percent between 1960 and 1970 due to strong affirmative action recruitment efforts.[230] This surge in black government employment helped expand public sector unions, which in turn expanded the share of union members in the black population.

Jobs in the new suburban areas were usually inaccessible for African Americans and other people of color, because of housing costs, job and housing discrimination, lack of public transportation, and lack of informal social networks with suburban employers.[231] At firms that moved to the suburbs from the central cities, black employment fell 24 percent, while white employment fell less than 10 percent.[232] Some employers were looking for a labor force not used to unions and not trained in assembly-line production, and that meant leaving the mostly black cities and moving to mostly white or Latino areas like the Boston suburbs, Albuquerque, Austin, and Boulder.[233] Some employers admitted that avoiding black workers was a factor in their location decisions.[234] A study of the causes of black unemployment in forty-five urban areas found that 25 percent to 50 percent resulted from jobs shifting to the suburbs.[235] Even the

federal government shifted jobs to the suburbs: while the number of federal civilian jobs grew by 26,558 from 1966 to 1973, federal jobs in central cities fell by 41,419.[236]

President Johnson launched the War on Poverty with the Economic Opportunity Act of 1964, which created the Office of Economic Opportunity (OEO) to coordinate federal antipoverty programs. Its funding wasn't much, but it did have a new and radical feature: it bypassed the New Deal welfare system that underserved African Americans, and instead attempted to go directly to poor communities.

Unlike the New Deal and post–World War II programs, the federal government kept direct control of these new OEO antipoverty programs and didn't delegate them to local governments. Community Action Agencies (CAA) were required to have the maximum feasible participation from poor people themselves. Across the country, especially in the South, and most especially in Mississippi, white politicians and welfare agencies tried to control where this new federal money went, and OEO resisted mightily, withholding funds from organizations that weren't community based enough. CAAs bypassed local patronage systems by hiring African Americans, many of them Civil Rights activists.[237]

After the Watts riots in 1965, the OEO began to focus on adult education and job training programs aimed to increase the skills of African Americans with little formal education and few chances for better jobs.

According to Jill Quadagno in *The Color of Welfare: How Racism Undermined the War on Poverty*, "In deciding to change the characteristics of the individual rather than the structure of the economy, federal officials initially ignored barriers impeding the right to work, emphasizing instead barriers impeding the ability to work. Between 1964 and 1970 federal expenditures on job training increased from $200 million to $1.4 billion."[238]

CAAs did succeed in delivering some services to African Americans in southern states, despite resistance from southern white officials.[239] Black community activists gained experience at CAAs and went on to be elected political officials.

Integrating blacks into the federal government proved to be a cakewalk compared to integrating them into construction trade unions. Title VII of the Civil Rights Act of 1964 contained a clause specifically targeting union discrimination in admission of members, apprenticeship programs, and job referrals, and the Bureau of Apprenticeship and Training within the Department of Labor was charged with enforcing this clause. Former trade unionists staffed the bureau, however, and managed to delay any enforcement for several years. Finally, in 1967 an Ohio court ruled that the Labor Department had to withdraw federal contracts from projects where African Americans were denied equal opportunity for apprenticeships.[240]

The AFL-CIO and the Labor Department collaborated in 1967 on a program called "Outreach" to draw people of color into union apprenticeships. Still, by the end of 1969, there were only 5,304 minority apprentices in the program.

In 1969, the Nixon administration put training and apprenticeship programs under federal control, effectively forcing construction unions to accept black workers. President Nixon's Philadelphia Plan required each trade to have a certain percent of minorities on each job by a certain timetable. The plan worked. Minorities accounted for less than 6 percent of all trade union apprentices in 1967, 14 percent by 1973, and 17 percent by 1979.

Nixon's motives were far from pure: he was looking to reduce inflation by increasing the supply of construction workers and so lowering their wages, just as the federal government was constructing more housing.

The term "affirmative action" entered the American lexicon in 1968 when the Labor Department coined the phrase to describe what unions had to do to get people of color proportionately represented or else lose federal contracts. The 1972 Equal Opportunity Act Amendment followed closely on the heels of a 1971 Supreme Court ruling that said, "Employers had the responsibility to justify policies that resulted in a statistical imbalance of minorities or women among their employees."[241] The EEO Amendment applied only to the federal government, but it opened the door to a number of subsequent Supreme Court rulings that established affirmative action as a powerful legal concept that propelled people of color into unions, technical jobs, and management positions that had never before been available to them.

Affirmative action was never a magic bullet, and was sometimes successfully rebuffed. From 1974 to 1989, the Supreme Court ruled on eleven major affirmative action decisions; in four it found that "counting-by-race remedies" were not allowable because they caused harm to the white males involved, while in seven cases race-conscious remedies were deemed valid as ways to overcome past discrimination.[242] In practice, affirmative action was only approved as a remedy for past discrimination by a specific employer or school.

In 1979, for example, the Supreme Court upheld a plan under which Kaiser Aluminum and Chemical Corporation reserved half of its positions in a skills-training program for minorities. At the time, only 1.8 percent of Kaiser's aluminum craft workers were African-American. Brian Weber, a white employee, had sued after being passed over for promotion. In 1980, the Supreme Court upheld a federal program requiring 10 percent of public works contracts to be awarded to minority-controlled enterprises.

While the goal of equal opportunity became an article of faith for a majority of Americans after the Civil Rights Movement, quotas and numerical goals have never been fully embraced, and their effectiveness has always been debated, even among people of color. Nonetheless, numerical goals clearly boosted black employment in the trade unions, and have helped increase black employment in white-collar jobs. Employers with federal contracts, and therefore under Office of Federal Contract Compliance affirmative action rules, had a greater increase in black male employment from 1974 to 1980 than did those employers not under federal contracts, and the difference was even greater for more skilled jobs. Number goals also played a role in doubling the percentage of black officers in the U.S. military from 2 percent in 1971 to 5 percent in 1981.[243]

Affirmative action had impressive results in higher education in particular. In 1964, fewer than one in twenty students enrolling in college were African American; in 1990, the number was one in eight, the same as the black proportion of the whole population. From 1970 to 2000, the number of black doctors doubled, and the number of black engineers and lawyers tripled.[244]

Enforcement of Civil Rights laws was erratic from the start and had weakened nearly to the point of uselessness by the 1990s, but there is no doubt that they were responsible for substantial economic gains by blacks. It must be remembered that these gains were only substantial relative to the deep economic hole blacks had started from. Large gains do not, by any means, suggest that blacks have caught up with white people economically, much less that blacks had an advantage.

PRESIDENT REAGAN TURNS BACK THE TIDE

Affirmative action began to lose steam under the Reagan administration, and was essentially a thing of the past by the late 1980s, by which time Reagan appointees had tipped the Supreme Court in a decidedly conservative direction. In 1984 the Court ruled in a case in Memphis, Tennessee, that firefighters with more seniority could not be laid off to keep African American firefighters with less experience who had been hired to satisfy a racial discrimination charge against the fire department. Justices said the African American firefighters were not victims of illegal discrimination by the department.

Affirmative action essentially ended its usefulness as an employment tool in 1989, when the Supreme Court reversed its stand by ruling that when the plaintiff was "a category of workers [blacks, Latinos, etc.], the burden of proof is on the plaintiff to prove that the employer actually practiced discrimination and not a policy that could be justified as necessary to the employer's business."[245]

Antipoverty programs begun as part of the Johnson's War on Poverty disintegrated under Reagan. Of the ten federal programs most severely cut in 1985, six had more than 45 percent beneficiaries of color.[246] For example, the Comprehensive Education and Training Act (CETA), which provided on-the-job training, with 45 percent of the ben-

eficiaries being people of color, was completely eliminated. The Urban Development Action Grant program fell from $675 million in 1981 to $216 million in 1988, and then was eliminated all together.[247]

Public sector employment grew more slowly under President Reagan, and that slowdown reduced job opportunities for people of color who were shut out of private-sector employment by employer discrimination. A quarter of a million more black men and half a million more black women would have had jobs in 1984 if government employment had continued to grow at its 1962 to 1976 rate through the early 1980s. In addition, one-half of the gap between black and white unemployment for men and the whole gap for women would have been eliminated by continued public sector growth.[248]

President Reagan began cutting domestic spending immediately after taking office. Affordable housing—more urgently needed by more people of color than white people[249]—was the first and most severely cut area, falling by 77 percent and accounting for more than one-third of all cuts. Spending on housing subsidies fell from $26 billion to $2 billion after 1981.[250] Federally financed production of subsidized housing fell by over 82 percent, to only fifty thousand units a year in the late 1980s. Rents in public and subsidized housing were raised from 25 percent of income to 30 percent, taking income directly out of the pockets of the lowest income tenants.[251] The political clout to stop these cuts was difficult to muster because subsidized housing was perceived as serving only poor black people. In 1979 38.5 percent of tenants in subsidized housing were African American, triple their share of the overall U.S. population.[252] Throughout the 1980s, waiting lists for public housing often had twice as many names as the total number of units.[253]

Reagan declared his intention to "get the government out of the housing business," but he didn't touch the most expensive federal housing subsidy, the mortgage interest deduction, which disproportionately benefited white people. In 1983, 68 percent of white people owned their homes, compared with 44 percent of African Americans and 33 percent of Latinos.[254] Home ownership was a great investment in the 1980s, as home values were rising. The median price of a home grew 230 percent from 1970 to 1985, compared with overall inflation of 117 percent.[255] Most of this increased net worth went to white people.

Michael Stone, in *Shelter Poverty: New Ideas on Housing Affordability,* originates the term "shelter poverty," meaning insufficient income to cover other needs after paying for housing. High housing costs, after all, are not a problem if incomes are high enough to afford them comfortably, and low incomes can be survivable if housing costs are low enough. He argues that shelter poverty is

more common among African Americans than white Americans, and that shelter poverty rose to a peak rate of 60 percent of African Americans in 1983, up from 55 percent in the 1970s.[256]

One attempt by the federal government to encourage asset creation within economically distressed African American communities has been empowerment zones, an idea first introduced by Jack Kemp, a former U.S. congressman and the secretary of Housing and Urban Development under Reagan. Thirteen years later, in 1993, Congress finally established Empowerment Zones and Enterprise Communities (EZ/EC) as part of the Omnibus Budget Reconciliation Act. It was argued that EZ/ECs could be effective ways of revitalizing economically depressed communities.[257] Basically, businesses were encouraged to locate and operate in targeted communities through a system of incentives that reduced labor costs, taxes, and regulatory burdens. In return, businesses were supposed to provide employment opportunities and increase economic prospects.

The EZ/ECs have not been a particularly successful tool for building assets in African American communities for a number of reasons. First, EZ/ECs tend to attract what are called traditional line black businesses, such as barbershops and beauty parlors, rather than construction, wholesaling, and manufacturing businesses. Unfortunately, traditional line black businesses tend to have a small number of employees, and the employment opportunities they create fail to significantly reduce unemployment in their communities.[258] EZ/ECs also tend to promote jobs that offer low wages, rely on minimal technology, and are generally nonunionized.[259]

Further, EZ/ECs do not address discriminatory financing practices. Generally, banks are more likely to finance businesses in the suburbs rather than in the inner city. When they do provide loans it tends to be at discriminatory rate. These are major issues since a serious obstacle to the development of African American businesses is access to capital.[260] Therefore, even if EZ/ECs can provide limited opportunities for income generation, they have not been very successful in creating opportunities for asset building among African Americans.

Similarly, efforts to turn ownership of public and subsidized housing over to residents, such as some of the Homeownership Opportunities for People Everywhere (HOPE) programs at the U.S. Department of Housing and Urban Development, have been mired in delays, budget cutbacks, and profiteering by developers.

LIVING OUTSIDE THE LABOR MARKET

African Americans have always had high poverty rates, in part because of low wages, but also because of high unemployment. At all points in U.S. history, millions of black adults have lived outside the labor force, outside the mainstream economy. In times of recession or government cutbacks, their ranks swell. Policies that might seem to have nothing to do with building wealth, such as welfare, bankruptcy, and criminal justice, in fact have everything to do with whether or not a family survives a period of unemployment and rises to work and save again.

Since the 1980s, the policy context for poor unemployed people has become steadily harsher. While middle-class African Americans got ahead during the economic growth of the 1990s, poor black people at times became more numerous, and at times even poorer, with an ever-shrinking safety net to catch them.

Welfare Reform

The 1996 welfare reform law eliminated the entitlement to cash income for the poorest single parents and children, a disproportionate percentage of whom are black women. The new program, called Transitional Assistance for Needy Families (TANF), also put new obstacles in the path of unemployed single parents seeking help: time limits, work requirements, vaccination requirements, and many others, varying by state. The number of families on welfare plummeted in response. Only about half left to take paying jobs. Where all the others turned for subsistence isn't well documented, but in the first eight years of the new welfare rules, the number of women in prison and the number of children in foster care both rose rapidly.[261] The transitions to employment were not all happy endings either. Hundreds of thousands of children lost their eligibility for health insurance under Medicaid with nothing to replace it when their parents took jobs with no benefits.

Women of color face an even harsher job market than most white women after leaving welfare. Employers are more likely to hire a white welfare-leaver.[262] The median wage for white welfare-leavers from 1997 to 1999 was $7.31 an hour, compared with $6.88 for African Americans and $6.71 for Latinas.[263] One study found that black TANF job applicants are more likely than whites to be asked to work nights or weekends, and are more likely to be required to take pre-employment and drug tests.[264] And white welfare-leavers are twice as likely as black and Latina welfare-leavers to receive transitional benefits such as child care and transportation assistance.[265]

Implementation of welfare rules has always been more arbitrary and stricter for women of color, but it appears that this has become even truer under the new law. White women have an easier time getting cash benefits and transitional benefits such as child care, and are more often "tracked" into education programs leading to decent-paying jobs. Women of color are more often illegally prevented from getting benefits or education, sanctioned for minor infractions, and tracked into dead-end situations. Researchers at the University of Illinois at Chicago and the Illinois Department of Human Services found that almost half of all white recipients in that state were referred to education programs, compared with only 18 percent of African American recipients.[266] The Urban Justice Center studied illegal practices by staff at welfare offices, such as telling applicants that benefits did not exist, and found them practiced less often on white applicants.[267]

In Virginia, a 1998 study found that child care and transportation assistance have been offered more consistently to white welfare recipients.[268] Two adjacent counties in Georgia offer a telling contrast: in Forsyth County, 98 percent of TANF recipients are white, and 95 percent of them get child care support; in Fulton County, 96 percent of TANF recipients are black, and only 25 percent get child care support.[269]

The Economics of Criminal Justice

Incarceration is an obstacle to family asset accumulation because it takes away years of earnings, and because a criminal record makes it harder to get any work, especially higher paying work.

The War on Drugs started in the 1980s.

Ostensibly this was not a race-based crack-down, and it shouldn't have been, as illegal drug use has not been more commonly found among any racial group. A 1990 study by the National Institute on Drug Abuse found that 15 percent of habitual drug users were black and 77 percent were white, approximately their proportions in the total population, with a bit heavier drug use among whites.[270] Similarly, a 1998 federal household survey found that 72 percent of all illicit drug users were white, 15 percent were black, and 10 percent were Latino, very close to their proportion of the general population.[271]

However, most drug arrests have been of people of color, and the number of prisoners of color jailed for drug offenses has soared since the early 1980s. The number of people in prison almost tripled from 1985 to 1997. Seventy percent of the new inmates have been African American, Latino, or other people of color.[272]

White people are treated more leniently by the courts. In the federal prison system, sentences are 20 percent longer for African Americans than for whites for the same crime.[273] In ten states and the District of Columbia, black men are ten times as likely to be imprisoned as white men convicted of the same offense.[274] Black men are one-third of those arrested for drug use but 57 percent of those convicted.[275] Of those convicted of felonies, 32 percent of white defendants were sentenced to prison, compared to 46 percent of African American defendants.[276]

A crack cocaine epidemic devastated urban areas in the late 1980s, and in 1986, mandatory minimum sentences were imposed for offenses involving crack, most committed by people of color. No such mandatory minimum was imposed on the version of the same drug used by most white drug abusers, powdered cocaine. The results of this disparity were devastating. In 1986, the average federal sentence for drug offenses was 11 percent higher for black than for white offenders, but in 1990, the average sentence was 49 percent higher for black drug offenders.[277] Millions of black and Latino men have languished in jail, while their white equivalents, guilty of the same crimes, were free and in the labor market.

Black men and women are used as exceedingly low paid labor in the context of incarceration and the growth of the prison industrial complex.

At the end of 2003, of the 1.4 million people in prison with a sentence of more than a year, about 44 percent were African American and 35 percent were white.[278] The Justice Department estimates that if current trends continue, almost a third of black men, over a sixth of Latino men, and one in twenty white men will enter state or federal prison in their lifetimes.[279]

RECESSIONS AND OUTSOURCING

During each economic recession over the last twenty years, job loss has hit black workers harder than white workers. Black unemployment rose twice as fast as that of whites during the recession of the early 2000s.[280] By 2004, one in nine African Americans was unemployed.[281] This rise in unemployment came on the heels of the tight labor market of the late 1990s, which was very beneficial for African Americans. Their unemployment rate fell from 18 percent in the 1981–82 recession to nearly 13 percent in the early 1990s, down to below 7 percent in 1999 and 2000, the lowest black unemployment rate on record.[282] After the 2001 recession, black unemployment did not fall below 10 percent for over three years.

Of the more than two million jobs lost from 2000 to 2003, nearly 90 percent were manufacturing jobs. In 2000, there were two million African Americans working in factory jobs, representing 10.1 percent of all manufacturing workers, about the same as the black share of the total workforce. By 2003, two million manufacturing jobs had been lost in the United States. White workers lost 1.7 million factory jobs, about 10 percent of the number they held before the recession.[283] Blacks, on the other hand, lost about 15 percent of their manufacturing jobs. By the end of 2003, the share of all fac-

tory jobs held by African Americans had fallen to 9.6 percent.[284]

The National Urban League (NUL) issued a report on black unemployment in 2004. Summarizing its findings, NUL President and CEO Marc H. Morial said, "The last recession has had a severe and disproportionate impact on African Americans and minority communities, and the creation of jobs must be the first and foremost agenda of the nation's business, labor, and political leaders." The Urban League found that the double-digit unemployment rates for fourteen months from late 2002 through 2003 were the result of the worst labor market for African Americans in twenty-five years. The median income of black families fell 3 percent from 2001 to 2003, while white families lost just 1.7 percent.[285]

In 2003, when Autoliv closed its seat-belt plant in Indianapolis, more than 75 percent of the laid-off workers were African Americans. Many of them were young adults hired in the late 1990's labor shortage despite lacking a high school diploma, and who had few options after losing their jobs. "They were taken from the street into decent-paying jobs. They were making twelve to thirteen dollars an hour. These young men started families, dug in, took apartments, purchased vehicles. It was an up-from-the-street experience for them, and now they are being returned to their old environment," said Michael Barnes, director of an Indiana AFL-CIO training program for laid-off workers.[286]

Official unemployment figures, of course, greatly understate the actual number of adults without jobs. The definition doesn't include discouraged people who have stopped looking for work, underemployed part-timers, students, or imprisoned and other institutionalized people. A recent study of men in New York City, done by the nonprofit Community Service Society, found that a little less than half of all African American men between sixteen and sixty-five had no jobs in 2003. The 2003 employment-population ratio reported by the Bureau of Labor Statistics was 51.8 percent for black men, 57.1 percent for black women, 75.7 percent for white men, and 65.7 percent for Latino men in New York City. The black male number was the lowest on record for the years since 1979.[287] In February 2002, the *New York Times* reported that African Americans make up only 27 percent of those collecting unemployment benefits in New York City, even though they make up 37 percent of the officially unemployed.[288]

Jobs moving overseas account for a sizable share of the job loss. In the never-ending quest for cheaper labor and the easy flow of capital and goods, multinational corporations have outsourced skilled and unskilled labor to new shores, exploiting the economic labor markets of Asia, Africa, the Caribbean, and Central and South America. With jobs transplanted, American workers, and especially African American laborers, too often have been reduced to unemployment or jobs with barely sustainable wages. A study by the Bureau of Labor Statistics found that almost one-third of people laid off when their jobs moved abroad still were not fully re-employed even years later. Of those who did get new jobs, more than half were earning 85 percent or less of their previous wages.[289]

Job growth has been concentrated in the low-wage service sector, which pays less than the shrinking manufacturing sector. In Michigan, for example, growing industries like health care pay 26 percent less than those like the auto industry that are losing jobs.[290] African Americans represent a disproportionate share of this eliminated or displaced labor.

BLACK CLASS COMPLICATION

In 2005, the heads of Merrill Lynch, American Express, and Time Warner were black men —Stan O'Neal, Ken Chenault, and Richard Parsons. Oprah Winfrey had a net worth of $940 million in 2002,[291] and the second-highest income in the country in 2004, according to Forbes.com. Though the Census Bureau's 2005 report on income gives no good news for African Americans—median income didn't rise at all from 2003 to 2004[292]—a few blacks are obviously prospering.

As within other races, power and class divisions among African Americans mean that an elite profits while many people are marginalized. In fact, according to the Survey of Income and Program Participation, the disparities between the wealthiest blacks and the poorest are greater than the disparities within any other race. In 2000, the typical black household in the highest income quintile had a net worth 8.7 times that of the median black household. Whites with the highest incomes held only 2.6 times their race's median net worth.

In his 1978 book, *The Declining Significance of Race,* sociologist William Julius Wilson argued that, once official segregation ended and overt racism declined, a person's economic opportunities depended more on their class than on their race.[293] Wealth accumulation by some African Americans while others are excluded is one of the peculiar legacies of the Civil Rights Movement. Polices such as affirmative action have helped enlarge the black middle class. At the same time, middle-class status and upward mobility have often meant moving to the suburbs, draining businesses, jobs, and tax revenues from the cities where poor blacks are still concentrated.

In 2001 Robert Johnson, the founder of Black Entertainment Television and worth $1.45 billion in 2002,[294] took out a full-page *New York Times* ad advocating repeal of the estate tax, calling it a "double tax" on the wealth of those blacks who have amassed plenty. (Supposedly the first taxation comes when the money is earned, the second when the earner dies, though in fact the bulk of most large estates is untaxed capital gains, the appreciated value of unsold assets such as stocks and real estate.) In Johnson's case, this is a patently false claim. When Viacom bought BET in 2000, the SEC classified the transfer as a "tax-free transaction."[295] None of Johnson's earnings on the sale became tax revenue that could provide public services or otherwise help the less wealthy. African Americans who have not amassed wealth like Johnson may wonder where their taxable estates are supposed to come from in the first place when those who have climbed the ladder pull it up behind them.

Although it is crosscut by issues of class, race still matters. Robert Johnson may be worth $1.45 billion and Oprah Winfrey worth $940 million, making them the two wealthiest African Americans, but when whites are added to the list, neither makes the top ten. For that, they would have to have at least $13.8 billion.[296] And though the highest-earning African Americans may hold 8.7 times more wealth than those who earn the median income for their race, their net worth is only one-third that of the highest earning whites. The lowest-income quintile among blacks had a median net worth of only $57 in 2000,[297] while the lowest-earning whites had a median net worth of $24,000 that year.[298]

And while income affects wealth, race affects income. With every level of educational achievement, whites earn more than blacks.[299] Both race and class inequality mean that the central problems of the great majority of African Americans are problems of bread and butter: too few jobs, low wages and wage discrimination, too much poverty, too few assets, and too little access to quality education. The devastation caused by Hurricane Katrina in Louisiana and Mississippi revealed to a shocked nation not only how many people were too poor to escape, but especially how many were African American.

The social effects of class division—such as living in separate urban and suburban neighborhoods, unlike the old days of segregation, mean that inequality both within and between races will not end unless the government enacts and acts on policies to end it.

NEW CENTURY, STILL A RAW DEAL

The 2001 recession was followed by the first jobless recovery since the Great Depression. After the recession of the early 1990s, during the George H. W. Bush administration, black unemployment rates fell below their prerecession levels within two years, and continued to drop during the economic boom of the Clinton years. But there was no similar decrease in unemployment for blacks in the three years after 2001.

One reason was the federal government's reluctance to help states with their fiscal crises. In an ironic coincidence, during the economic downturn of 2001, state spending fell from 5 percent of the Gross Domestic Product to 4.6 percent.[300]

While the recession and state tax cuts are certainly the immediate causes of the drop in state spending, the federal government's reluctance to help states with their fiscal crises also played a role. In an ironic coincidence, the George W. Bush administration's 2002–2004 tax cuts gave the wealthiest 1 percent (overwhelmingly white) almost exactly the same amount of money as the deficits of all fifty states in the same three years—197.3 billion compared with $200 billion.[301]

This political choice had racial implications. Public services are disproportionately used by people of color. When Georgia cuts pregnant women and infants off Medicaid, when Florida and Massachusetts reduce child care subsidies, when California, Maryland, and Texas spend less on public higher education,[302] low- and moderate-income African Americans are overrepresented among the people harmed.

Median income fell for all racial groups from 2000 to 2003, but it fell faster for people of color than for white people, widening the racial income gap. After slowly increasing from 56 percent of white income in 1988 to 65 percent in 2000, black median income fell again to 62 percent in 2003, according to the Census Bureau. About half of the progress in median income from 1996 to 2000 was wiped out in the following four years. African Americans finally broke the $30,000 barrier in 1999, with the typical household getting $31,636, but then lost more than $2,400 between 2000 and 2004. The typical white household lost over $1,000 in income from 1999 to 2003.[303]

Black workers are more likely to be in jobs with pay too low to lift a family of four above the poverty line. African Americans make up one-ninth of the workforce but hold one-seventh of these low-wage jobs. White Americans, by contrast, make up almost seven-tenths of the workforce, but hold fewer than six-tenths of the low-wage jobs.

Real estate prices have risen steadily since the 1990s, not falling even during the 2001 recession. This so-called housing bubble highlights the irony that asset growth for some can mean more economic insecurity for others. Many black urban neighborhoods, undervalued because of decades of disinvestments, face gentrification as well-off home seekers, developers, and speculators buy up properties and convert them from low-rent apartments to condos or luxury rentals.

The tastes of many middle-class professionals of all races have changed from preferences for suburbia to the city. The targeted areas are often highly prized because they are well located, frequently connected to both the major business and cultural areas by public transportation. Accompanying these changes are a rise in property values, an increase in rents, and the displacement of families and individuals with limited assets. Typically, home owners benefit and renters suffer, although low-income homeowners can face hardship from rising property taxes. While the home owners are disproportionately white and the renters disproportionately black, the assets of some African American families have grown because of gentrification as well.

Take the example of Harlem. Many still think of Harlem as a major center of African American intellectual production and artistic genius, site of the Harlem Renaissance of the 1920s and 1930s. Unfortunately, Harlem has more recently been associated with poverty, drugs, unemployment, and general despair. This is now changing, because Harlem is experiencing intense gentrification. In 2002, for example, at a ribbon-cutting ceremony, town houses selling for $300,000 to $600,000 were described as "affordable housing."[304] Affordable for whom? The median income in Central Harlem in 2002 was $26,000 per year.[305] No wonder Nellie Bailey, a Harlem tenants' rights activist, asked, "Exactly who is the Empowerment Zone empowering?"[306] It was obvious that the Upper Manhattan Empowerment Zone (UMEZ) was not revitalizing Harlem for its residents. How else can one understand the development of luxury apartments, the real estate boom, and huge rent hikes?

If your rent increases from $500 to $1,200 what can you do? For the majority of renters their only option is to relocate—to search for scarce affordable housing—or to become homeless. Typically, those without assets are displaced. The economic hardships faced by many African Americans living in inner cities limit their ability to benefit from the development of their communities. Gentrification may benefit real estate developers, banks, and the new landlords, but for the asset-poor, it creates unwanted burdens.[307] In fact, the asset-poor find themselves in a catch-22. On the one hand, dilapidated neighborhoods remain in that state if they are not rehabilitated. On the other hand, rehabilitation brings displacement and denies inner-city residents the benefits of better housing and social services.

Gentrification brought Lenox Lounge, that new jazz Mecca, and the Studio Museum, wonderful additions to Harlem. The recent investments in Harlem have created some employment opportunities and have positively transformed the urban landscape. However, this has come at a cost, and the cost has been borne mainly by the asset poor.[308]

Recent studies by the U.S. Small Business Association (SBA) showed that businesses owned by people of color made great gains in the 1990s, growing at four times the rate of white-owned firms.[309] But when broken out by race, the data present a less optimistic picture for black-owned businesses. For instance, in a 1999 study, the SBA reported that "black-owned businesses represented a little over one-quarter of the [minority-owned] businesses (27 percent) but less than one-eighth of the revenue ($59 billion or 12 percent)."[310] Nearly 90 percent of black-owned businesses had no employees other than the owner, who, on average, earned only $16,000 in annual revenues.[311] Black-owned businesses with employees had the lowest survival rates of all businesses, 61 percent, compared with 72.6 percent for nonminority-owned businesses.[312]

Historically, businesses owned by people of color have received a markedly lower share of government and private financing. In 2000, a mere 4 percent of loans from the Small Business Investment Company (SBIC) and 4 percent of venture capital funds found their way to people of color, in spite of the proven success and rapid growth of many minority-owned firms.[313]

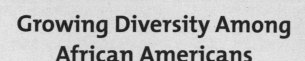

Growing Diversity Among African Americans

Perhaps more than any other group, African Americans are a people united by a history in the United States. Of the thirty-six million black people in the 2000 Census, the vast majority are descendants of slaves.

However, growing numbers of African and Caribbean immigrants have made the black population increasingly diverse. In 2002, the United States received 94,240 legal immigrants from the Caribbean and 56,135 Africans.[314]

Afro-Caribbean Immigrants

Voluntary black immigration from the Caribbean to the United States existed before the Civil War, but it greatly expanded afterward. Afro-Caribbean immigrants were generally well educated and highly skilled. In the United States, they were businessmen, craftsmen, and activists; in fact, the racism they encountered here often radicalized their politics, and many whites regarded them as a race of troublemakers. A separate stream of working-class Afro-Caribbean immigrants moved to Central America to work on projects like the Panama Canal, United Fruit banana plantations, and railroads before coming to the United States.

Notable Afro-Caribbean immigrants of the nineteenth century include Prince Hall, believed to be from Barbados, who founded black freemasonry in the United States, John Russwurm of Jamaica, who with African American Sam Cornish cofounded the country's first black newspaper, and Edward Blyman, a black nationalist activist who was born in the U.S. Virgin Islands. W.E.B. DuBois and poet and activist James Weldon Johnson also had Caribbean ancestry.[315]

By the 1920s, congressmen such as Ellison DuRant Smith of South Carolina were debating whether the United States "had sufficient population . . . to shut the door [to] the denizens of Africa [in order] to breed up a pure, unadulterated American citizenship."[316] The Quota Act of 1921 limited the number of immigrants who could come to the United States in a given year to 3 percent of their population here as counted by the 1910 Census. The Immigration Act of 1924 lowered the quotas to 2

(continued)

percent of the foreign-born of a given nationality counted in the 1890 census. Both acts favored immigrants from northwestern Europe and greatly reduced the numbers arriving from all other parts of the world, including the Caribbean and Africa. In fact, Senator James Reed of Missouri won Senate approval of an amendment to the 1924 act that would have banned black immigration outright. Booker T. Washington led the campaign that defeated the amendment in Congress.[317] One of Washington's tactics was to remind Americans of the indispensable role of Afro-Caribbean immigrants in building the Panama Canal.[318]

Immigration restrictions relaxed during World War II. As the United States experienced a shortage of workers, Caribbean, as well as Latin American, immigrants arrived to fill the gap. By the end of the war, the United States was hosting more than forty thousand workers from the Bahamas, Jamaica, Barbados, Saint Vincent, Saint Lucia, and Dominica. Many were able to change their status from contract worker to legal immigrant.[319]

The 1952 Immigration and Nationality Act limited new Caribbean immigration to a small number of farmworkers each year and virtually stopped other black immigration. Many who might have immigrated to the United States made their way to Great Britain instead. The Hart-Celler Act of 1965 lifted the ban three years after Great Britain closed its doors, and Afro-Caribbean immigration to the United States has been steady since.[320] In 2004, the Census Bureau's American Communities Survey counted 1.5 million foreign-born immigrants from the non-Hispanic Caribbean living in the United States. The largest groups were from Jamaica (582,500), Haiti (443,700), Trinidad and Tobago (220,100), and Barbados (54,100).[321] In 2004, 2,164,000 people living in the United States claimed non-Hispanic Caribbean ancestry.[322]

Among Afro-Caribbean immigrants to the United States, Haitians have faced particular difficulties. Since the 1960s, successive U.S. administrations have claimed that poor economic conditions in Haiti and easy access to asylum from its highly unstable and often abusive political leadership would lead to a mass migration that would be a threat to public order and national security.[323]

The United States's treatment of Haitian refugees contrasts with its welcoming treatment of Cuban refugees. The U.S. Coast Guard has attempted to intercept boatloads of Haitian immigrants before they leave Haitian waters, and a disproportionate number of undocumented Haitians who do make it to the United

(continued)

States are jailed. Haiti is economically the least developed country in the Western hemisphere, and the U.S. immigration agency tends to consider economic conditions more important than political repression in Haitian migration. And since economic hardship is not an accepted basis for asylum, it rejects their applications for asylum at a higher rate than any other national group.[324]

African Immigrants

In 2004, the American Community Survey estimated that just over 824,000 foreign-born sub-Saharan Africans lived in the United States.[325] Most have immigrated here since the 1980s, when the Reagan administration offered asylum to Ethiopians and Eritreans fleeing Ethiopia's repressive regime. In 2001, most African refugees in the United States came from Sudan and Somalia.

United States immigration policy has contributed to the growth of the African immigrant population in ways beyond admitting refugees from countries in unrest. The Immigration Act of 1990 started an immigration lottery that favored immigrants from underrepresented countries—including all of sub-Saharan Africa. Since 1995, the United States has accepted an average of forty thousand legal immigrants from Africa each year. Though Africans represented only 3 percent of the foreign-born population of the United States in 2002, they were 6 percent of the immigrants who obtained legal permanent residency that year.

African immigrants to the United States tend to be well educated and belong to the middle class in their countries. Almost half have at least a bachelor's degree, compared to 23 percent of the U.S. population as a whole. Almost all are high school graduates. This high rate of education among African immigrants and the related ability to obtain professional employment in the United States means that they tend to live apart from Caribbean immigrants and African Americans.

Nevertheless, African immigrants contend with the racism against black people that African Americans face. For many, racism against blacks causes shock and indignation. Blackness is not part of their identity. In dealing with this new, imposed identity, African immigrants also work to maintain their own identity as Africans and members of their own nationalities.[326] [327]

The median income of African immigrants in the United States in 1999, $31,300, was very similar to other African Americans, $31,778, and slightly higher than the

(continued)

$30,000 for all foreign-born people. But it is lower than the $36,100 median for native-born Americans, and $54,121 for all white Americans.[328]

There has been debate about how African and black Caribbean immigrants have fared in the U.S. economy. Thomas Sowell, a noted black conservative who believes cultural differences explain income differences between groups, argued that black immigrants achieved more and did better than native-born blacks.[329] Others say that while some West Indians and Africans have succeeded in some occupations where U.S.-born African Americans have not, there are other areas where native-born blacks are ahead.

While clearly black immigrants face racism and discrimination, questions have also been raised about whether they are treated as badly as U.S.-born African Americans or whether the cultural differences lead to different and less virulent stereotypes.

It remains to be seen whether over the long haul these new immigrant groups will acquire significant wealth. But it is clear that for descendants of African slaves, the road to wealth has been rocky.

WHAT CAN BE DONE?

African Americans have proposed many varied strategies to reach prosperity. The impulse to build from within, to focus on community economic development funded by black dollars, is an appealing one for people bitter at being betrayed by governments again and again. But approaches that focus on purely entrepreneurial, single proprietor strategies have not worked.

Instead, the goal must be to build the collective wealth of the community. W.E.B. DuBois pioneered the idea of cooperative economics early in the twentieth century and there have been many such attempts in African American communities. Revolving loan funds, modeled on those created by Asian immigrants to start new firms, have begun in several large cities. One successful new business gives the seed capital for another one to start, so that profits lift up the community as a whole.[330]

Not all are convinced that cooperative strategies alone, without some deeper transformations in the economic order, are enough. For example, longtime organizer Sam Grant contends that the fundamental source of black wealth inequality for African Americans is the search for profit in a system of private ownership of wealth. He asserts:

If you look at the history of capitalism and look at the history of white supremacy . . . you see violence, fundamental violence, violence to human beings, violence to the community, violence to the family. These are all necessary aspects to the dynamic called capitalism, imperialism, racism, sexism—necessary.

Manning Marable too contends that the twin systems of racism and capitalism are the sources of black wealth inequality.[331] As do other leftist thinkers (W.E.B. DuBois, Angela Davis, and Cornel West, to name a few), he believes that some form of socialism is in order.

Other activists and scholars have pressed for a reckoning within the current economic arrangement. What should we call this process? Some say it is about reparations, that is, about repairing the damage done to African Americans over several hundred years of slavery and racist oppression. Others use the word "restitution," a legal concept that requires the thief to pay back what he has stolen. Bill Fletcher, director of TransAfrica, calls for "reconstruction assistance," emphasizing the failure to make good on promises to blacks in the post–Civil War period. A Native American concept of justice that has been winning support is the idea of "restorative justice," in which perpetrators of crimes are seen to damage not the individuals, but their whole community. Their connection to the community must be restored through a process involving their victims and other community representatives.

Congressman John Conyers, Jr. (D-Mich.), has introduced H.R. 40, the Reparations Study Bill, each year since 1989; the bill would require a study on the impact of slavery in the United States.[332]

In March 2002, a group of lawyers led by attorney Deadria Farmer-Paellman filed a federal class-action lawsuit in New York against FleetBoston (now owned by Bank of America), Aetna, CSX, and sixteen other companies to force them to compensate African Americans for wealth created using slave labor. The lawsuit was filed on behalf of all African American descendants of slaves. This strategy is part of a broader movement for reparations that seeks to make public the historical role that governments and corporations have played during slavery and the era of legal discrimination that followed it.

In response to the lawsuits, the Los Angeles and Chicago city councils have approved ordinances that require any company that wants to do business with the two cities to investigate and disclose any profits from the American slave trade. A similar measure is being considered in New York City and Detroit.

The Reparations Coordinating Committee, a group that is co-chaired by

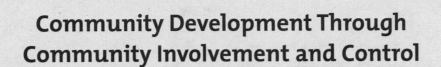

Community Development Through Community Involvement and Control

Not too long ago, the Dudley neighborhood in Boston's Roxbury area was considerably dilapidated and depressed. Deserted buildings filled the landscape.[333] It had even become a dumping ground. A stranger could easily be excused if they believed that some hurricane had struck this part of Boston, but Dudley's state of destruction was not the result of a natural disaster. Instead, the devastation of a community was the result of deliberate human decisions. The disinvestment and abandonment of the Dudley neighborhood was the result of white flight, bank redlining, and government neglect.

The people living in this neighborhood faced daunting challenges. They lived in one of the most economically impoverished areas of Boston.[334] Many of the people were unemployed and/or underemployed. Approximately one out of two children lived below the official poverty line. Further, the Dudley neighborhood was overwhelmingly people of color—mostly African-Americans, but also Cape Verdean immigrants and Latinos. The community was a powerful reminder of the depth of racial wealth inequality. In fact, the magnitude of wealth inequality in the Dudley neighborhood could easily break spirits, stifle imaginations, and kill dreams.

But in the Dudley street neighborhood, spirits refused to be broken, imaginations would not be stifled, and people continued to dream. The Dudley Street Neighborhood Initiative (DSNI) emerged to realize shared hopes. The diverse leadership of this multiracial and intergenerational organization mobilized residents to initiate a "Don't Dump on Us" campaign.[335] This campaign ended illegal dumping and cleaned up vacant lots. But it did something more important: It helped the formation of a shared identity and feeling of community power. Determined to control their destiny, the DSNI became one of the first community groups to get eminent domain authority; they now had the power to control the land in their neighborhood. This new form of power was then used to transform burned-out lots in the Dudley neighborhood into community-controlled wealth[336].

(continued)

The DSNI quest for community power continued on. They developed community gardens, parks and playgrounds, a town common, and housing. In fact, they were the first inner-city neighborhood to win a state grant to create a town common.[337] The DSNI also engaged in tenant organizing and health, safety, and environmental campaigns. In the 1990s, they developed, among other things, a college mentoring project, the Magnolia Housing Cooperative, and the Orchard Commons housing.[338] They have completed the deleading of existing homes and yards and continue to develop new businesses. Further, their vibrant alternative model for development has been studied and copied by community groups all over the United States.

These words from the preamble to DSNI's Declaration of Community Rights are a powerful reminder of the ability of people to envision a new world and work toward its creation.

> *We—the youth, adults, seniors of African, Latin American, Caribbean, Native American, Asian and European ancestry—are the Dudley community.... Today, we are on the rise! We are reclaiming our dignity, rebuilding housing and re-knitting the fabric of our communities. Tomorrow, we realize our vision of a vibrant, culturally diverse neighborhood, where everyone is valued for their talents and contributions to the larger community.*[339]

Harvard law professor Charles J. Ogletree, has a strategy that targets corporations as well as private institutions that have been clearly linked to the slave trade, such as Brown University, Yale University, and Harvard Law School. Ogletree does not advocate for payments to individuals; instead, he believes that the damage has been done to a group—African American slaves and their descendants. The legacy of slavery and racial discrimination in America is seen in well-documented racial disparities in access to education, health care, housing, insurance, employment and other social goods. The reparations movement, he says, must therefore focus on the poorest of the poor. It must finance social recovery for those stuck at the bottom, providing an opportunity to address comprehensively the problems of those who have not benefited substantially from affirmative action.[340]

Similarly, Randall Robinson, author of *The Debt*, a book about reparations, calls for the development of a generational trust rather than checks to individuals. This trust could provide resources over time for education, housing, and other acquisitions of assets that will benefit African Americans over generations.

Taxing Wealth to Broaden Wealth

Taxing very wealthy people and large, profitable corporations would be necessary to pay reparations without cutting back on other federal spending. Instead, tax policy is moving the other way. The four tax cuts enacted from 2001 to 2004 favored the wealthiest 1 percent, who are overwhelmingly white. Repeal of the federal estate tax alone would cost the federal treasury almost a trillion dollars over the next twenty years, and as of 2001,[341] less than one-third of 1 percent of the multimillion-dollar estates that pay the tax were left by deceased black people.[342] Imagine if those trillion dollars were instead invested in the black community as reparations for slavery.

Just as African Americans and other people of color started to have access to public programs, a conservative backlash began against progressive taxation and against social policies that would provide opportunities to people of color. This conservative movement has been far too successful in preserving the racial wealth divide in this country. Is it a coincidence that the very same programs that helped expand the

white middle class suddenly began to be called wasteful and nonessential when people of color began to benefit?

Recently the tax burden has been shifted to moderately paid individual workers, disproportionately black, while tax cuts have been given to the wealthy, corporations, and investors. Progressive taxes, such as the estate tax, the Earned Income Tax Credit, and the federal income tax, are constantly under attack.

Since 1962 the total money collected in payroll taxes (FICA) has proportionately come more from low-income than high-income workers, because the payroll tax is capped (in 2005 earnings over $90,000 were untapped). It doesn't apply to investment income at all.[343]

If the current tax cut trend continues, it will dismantle the progressive tax system needed to help raise poor and low-income blacks into the middle class. Only a progressive tax system can provide the revenue to fund the many programs and services needed to build a real ownership society. The same revenues now used for loopholes and subsidies for corporations and wealthy investors could be used to enable African Americans and all low-income Americans to develop wealth. As Dr. Martin Luther King, Jr., said, "The poor can stop being poor if the rich are willing to become even richer at a slower rate."

The GI Bill after World War II created the vast white middle class. Its programs were supported through a progressive taxation system—the federal progressive income tax, corporate taxes, and the estate tax—based on the principle that people who earn more pay more in taxes. This system has allowed many of those who were in the bottom of the society an economic ladder of opportunity. The same kind of policies that expanded the white middle-class—affordable college, affordable mortgages, and unionized and public jobs—can lift black families into greater economic security.

Chapter 4

NEIGHBORS AND FENCES: LATINOS IN THE UNITED STATES

"La mentira esta, mientras la verdad llega."
"Lies are told until the truth arrives."
—*dicho (saying) attributed to Don Patricio Sanchez*

"La riqueza no es dinero, sino amigos."
"Wealth isn't money, but rather friends."
—*folk dicho (saying)*

Latinos in the United States tend to be described as one large, predominantly immigrant community that displays lagging socioeconomic status compared to the white population. This media-driven perception of the Hispanic population in the United States is misleading. Latinos are diverse in a variety of ways: country of origin; generational status (many were here prior to the establishment of the first thirteen colonies); and class mobility.

Most Americans don't realize that a Latino has played the role of the U.S. president in the popular television series *The West Wing* (Martin Sheen). Most consumers don't realize that salsa is more popular than ketchup. Instead, Americans are more knowledgeable about the nanny problem—using undocumented workers for child care—than about the tremendous diversity within the Latino community in the United States.

Taken as a whole, without regard for length of time in the United States (first generation versus fifth generation), 57.35 percent of all Latino families fall into the zero to $40,000 income bracket.[1] Approximately 40 percent of the Latino population in the United States is foreign born. And contrary to popular belief and the recent book *Who Are We? The Challenges to America's Identity,*[2] native-born Latinos have a 73.5 percent high school completion rate.

In 2004, Latino consumers' purchasing power soared to $686 billion, according to the Selig Center at the University of Georgia. The majority of Latinos in the United States are bilingual and bicultural, with strong patriotic and family-oriented values combined with a deep desire to see their children succeed in the United States.

Wealth building behaviors among Latinos in the United States rest squarely on a strong work ethic, on collective family and extended kin efforts, and a strong entrepreneurial spirit. These are exactly the behaviors demanded in an ownership society. Yet, the gap between Latino families (13.6 percent) and white families (34 percent) earning $80,000 or more is substantial, as is the home ownership rate, which for whites is 74 percent and for Latinos is only 44 percent. This chapter explores Latino wealth and traces the government policies and actions that contribute to the persistent wealth divide affecting Latinos in the United States.

LATINO WEALTH INDICATORS

Indicators of asset ownership—such as the percentage of people who own stocks, bonds, and real estate, and the average value of those assets—tell us much about the Latino community's share in the much publicized ownership society of the United States. We see a sizable gap between the values of Latino and non-Latino homes, stocks, businesses, retirement portfolio accounts, and mutual fund investments. These mean asset indicators provide us with a snapshot of the collective well-being and the standard of living of the Latino population in the United States today.

The ownership of assets of the growing Latino community clearly lags behind the non-Latino white population. The implications for such continuing wealth inequality has ominous overtones for retiring baby boomers, the capacity for the country to pay

FIGURE 4-1
Mean asset ownership, 2001

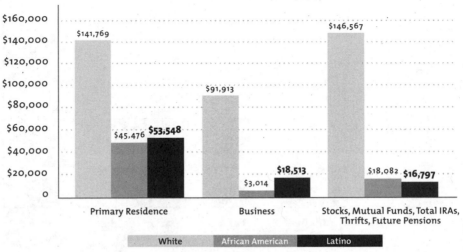

Source: Bárbara J. Robles's analysis of Federal Reserve Bank Survey of Consumer Finances data.

FIGURE 4-2
Median net worth, 2001 (in 2001 dollars)

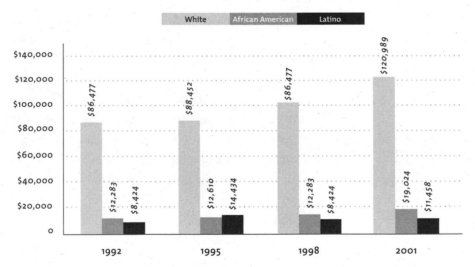

Source: Bárbara J. Robles's analysis of Survey of Consumer Finances, Board of Governors, Federal Reserve System.

down the growing deficit, as well as the current and future growth and health of the economy. When we speak of "wealth" we generally refer to asset ownership most often symbolized by the enduring belief in the American Dream: a home, a retirement portfolio, an investment or savings account, business investments, and ultimately, passing

FIGURE 4-3
Home ownership rates, 2003

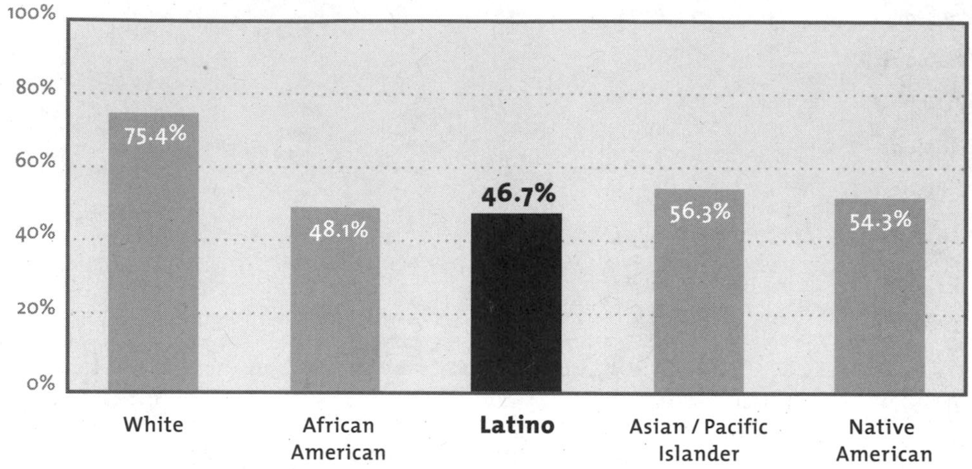

Source: U.S. Census Bureau, http://www.census.gov/hhes/www/housing/hvs/annual03/ann03t20.html

on these financial advantages to offspring—an inheritance. In this notion of wealth, we factor in relatively low total debt if any to derive net worth.

In 2001, median net worth for Latinos (in 2001 constant dollars) was $11,458 compared to $120,989 for whites and $19,024 for blacks. The percentage of net worth attributable to home ownership is significant for white Americans. Much of the lagging net worth indicators for the Latino and black communities rests squarely on the absence of home ownership and, consequently, home equity.

As a country, we have pursued a policy of home ownership that has left behind the working poor and low-income communities. In so doing, we have tacitly agreed that home ownership can only be attained provided you demonstrate a stable and signifi-

cant level of income. These prequalifying and qualifying criteria for entry into the ownership society have not been questioned or considered unjust. Indeed, as a nation, we have indicated that a family must first demonstrate worthiness through stable employment. However, if U.S. workers are facing employment at minimum wage and without long-term security, they do not meet standard home ownership criteria. In essence, our home ownership policy has excluded hard working minimum wage earners (now labeled the working poor) and low-income families from securing the most essential element of the American Dream: a home of their own.

Latinos in the United States seek economic security and mobility similar to all other communities. However, because of historical and recent immigrant experiences,

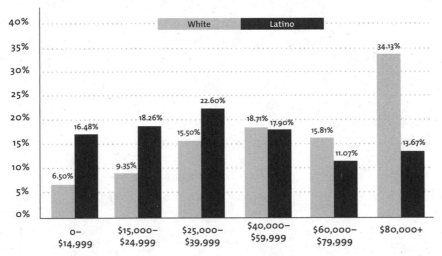

FIGURE 4-4
White and Latino
family income distribution, 2003

Source: U. S. Census Bureau, Curent Populition Survey, 2004 Table FINC-03.

Latinos have stronger intergenerational memories of building wealth through tangible acquisitions, not financial assets such as stocks and bonds. This type of immigrant memory of economic mobility was common for many waves of immigrants. Families wanted "real value" for their hard-won efforts and physical assets such as land, rental property, and business interests are forms of savings and investments that can be a visual bricks-and-mortar confirmation of economic security and mobility. These types of assets continue to be viewed by a majority of the Latino community as safe assets.

Many Latino families and communities continue to pass on their intergenerational memories to their children with traumatic family stories about experiences with financial services and institutions in their country

of origin; developing countries often suffer from exchange rate fluctuations, and volatility that can devastate the value of the country's currency, leaving many upwardly mobile and middle-class families facing severe financial losses. These memories tend to be long-lived. For Latino families living in the United States, a degree of suspicion and distrust stems from the lack of contact with mainstream U.S. financial institutions. Moreover, the desire not to hold debt or be indebted to institutions that may suffer losses leads many Latino families to a very conservative position with respect to a variety of debt instruments: credit cards, installment loans, and other forms of borrowing. Still, the most significant reason for the lack of wealth mobility among Latinos has its roots in government policies toward immigration based on the political philosophies of manifest destiny and the Monroe Doctrine. These two perspectives have had reverberating effects on other government institutions and policies. For example, the lack of retirement security for Latinos can be traced both to the exemption of domestic and farm labor occupations from the passage of the 1933 Social Security Act, and to numerous temporary worker policies like the Bracero Program that allowed Latino workers, mostly Mexicans, to enter the country during U.S. labor shortages, notably during wartimes. Additionally, the ability of families of color to access the government's housing programs was severely limited by realtors and other housing agents, who were disinclined to encourage integration in affordable neighborhoods. Such government policies continue to have an impact on the wealth status of Latinos.

THE IMAGE OF LATINOS

Simplistic images of Latinos in the United States as one large immigrant or recently arrived community persist in the media. The reality is quite different. Generations of Latinos point to a history that spans the exploration and settlement of the southern United States before the arrival of the *Mayflower*.[3] Latinos as both U.S. citizens and noncitizens have served in military campaigns, from the Revolutionary War to the current war in Iraq. During the Vietnam War, Latinos represented 10 percent of the U.S. population but accounted for approximately 20 percent of the war's casualties.[4] Rarely do we see images of Latinos at every juncture of history, but indeed Latinos were present then as they are today.

Who Are Latinos?

Of the more than forty million Latinos living in the United States, approximately 67 percent are of Mexican origin (Mexican Americans/Chicanos), 4 percent are Cuban, 9 percent are Puerto Rican, 14 percent are from Central and South America, with Central Americans more numerous than South Americans, and 6 percent are classified as "Hispanic or Latino other."[5]

The "Hispanic or Latino other" category is a unique U.S. Census category that includes many Spanish-speaking peoples who do not self-identify with those general terms but instead call themselves by their nationality. It is in many ways a catchall category. While including Dominican Americans, who have many socioeconomic indicators in common with Puerto Ricans and other low-income groups, the "other" category is nevertheless numerically dominated by the many Spanish-speaking origin Americans whose socioeconomic profile is closer to non-Hispanic whites.

There has been confusion and controversy over the terms used for people with Latin American roots. The Census Bureau has recently released official documents using the term "Hispanic/Latino," indicating that they are aware of the growing use of the term "Latino" to self-describe the Spanish-speaking population.

"Hispanic" is a term of ethnic origin used to describe Spanish-speaking populations. Hispanics can be of any race: white, black, Asian, American Indian, or other. The Census Bureau introduced this term in the 1980 Census, and it has become the generic category for all Spanish-speaking peoples. The term "Latino," is used interchangeably with the term "Hispanic" in this chapter.

Many non-Latinos are also confused by the use of the term "Chicano," which arose in the late 1960s and early 1970s, and was used by U.S.-born Mexican Americans and foreign-born Mexican nationals residing in the United States. Cesar Chavez's United Farm Workers movement and activist student organizations used the term to bring attention to the plight of Latino farmworkers laboring under feudal conditions in the produce industry; they also publicized the lack of educational access and inadequate public school resources for Mexican American children in the Southwest. The use of the term "Chicano" indicates a self-ascribed political awareness, continued commitment to social and economic justice through political and community activism, and recognition of the importance of indigenous roots.

Because Spanish colonialism in Latin America included waves of immigrants from Europe, who brought with them slaves from Africa, black Spanish Moors, and people from Asia, Latin America today is predominantly *mestizo* (mixed ancestry). The Spanish colonization of Latin America differed from the British, Dutch, German, and French colonization of the U.S. in an important way: the early Spaniards did not bring their families with them. This produced a policy that did not include antimiscegenation laws for indigenous peoples nor an aversion to intermarriage with the conquered natives. This does not imply that the color spectrum in formerly Spanish-colonized countries does not follow class stratification, but rather that there is a significant *mestizo* and mulatto (Euro-African) population among Latino communities. This creates significant diversity of ethnic/racial characteristics within the U.S. Latino community, which in turn has an impact on economic mobility today.

One reading of the 2000 Census data indicates that past history and legacies of immigration to the United States are still with us, in the form of ethnic-racial diversity and continued country-of-origin solidarity. For example, in the 2000 Census almost forty-three million residents declared German as their ethnic origin or ancestry and a mere twenty million self-identified with the American category.[6] In fact, over 80 percent of Census 2000 respondents specified their ancestry, indicating that ethnic/racial roots and cultural identity con-

Family Legacies

by Bárbara J. Robles

My great-aunt, Lucresia [left], and my grandmother, Barbarita Grande [right], were women raised at the turn of the century with Victorian values and yet with a strong will to better their lives and those of their extended family. Both were born in Zapata, Texas, and had seven brothers and sisters. All settled in Texas and northern Mexico, mostly to raise children.

What is interesting about my childhood caretakers is that each chose a different life: my grandmother, marriage and a family, my great-aunt, a working life as a maid to wealthy families in Laredo, Texas and then as my caregiver. Neither spoke English. My grandmother could read and write in Spanish; my great-aunt was illiterate. As a child, I accompanied her to Laredo and Pharr, Texas, and negotiated trips by bus to the local grocery and dry goods stores, changing money for her and acting as her personal interpreter.

My mother often lent me to other family members in need of an interpreter to travel with them to conduct their business or shopping. I would miss school to accompany my grandfather's sister to negotiate bus travel and interpret for her with her suppliers in San Antonio, Texas. This particular great-aunt ran the only Spanish-language movie theater, located in a bodega [warehouse], Teatro Haydee, in our small south Texas town, until 1970. As an adolescent, I ran the popcorn machine, soda pop stand, and cash register.

Grandmother and great-aunt of Bárbara Robles

(continued)

Growing up in south Texas, it never occurred to me to see my great-aunt Lucresia as "limited" by her illiteracy. She was wise and knowledgeable about human nature and people. As a maid, she had acquired a deep understanding of wealth differences among people and could spot arrogance and "airs" a mile away. She was able to read people and situations well and admonished me to avoid situations where being treated "like a Mexican" might occur.

My great-aunt and grandmother witnessed many changes and technological advances. The single most important advice I received from them was: get educated. Often, it was a daily directive. With it, came the advice: "You cannot get ahead today [in this fast-paced time and place] without it." For them, opportunities to get ahead without an education were now scarce; with an education, anything was possible.

My grandmother, like my great-aunt, was frugal, and knew how to manage and run a household on a shoestring. Growing up, I watched these women barter, give gifts, and exchange, all the while engaging in what is called "social capital" in ways that increased the well-being of all in our extended family. Their skills included saving, budgeting, sewing, upholstering, doll making, canning, and gardening: life skills and common-sense financial management practiced at the home level.

tinue to be an important aspect of how Americans identify themselves. In 2000, the Census Bureau began counting the number of individuals who self-identify as multiracial. There are over twenty-two million self-identified racial "Others," comprising almost 8 percent of the total population. The fastest-growing racial category between 1990 and 2000 was "Other." The percent change over the ten-year interim was 58 percent. The growth in the multiracial category clearly chronicles an increasing diversity and inclusiveness, giving rise to a hope of combating the continuing segregation and isolation of communities of color in the United States.

Latinos and U.S. Policies in Historical Context

The link between past and present U.S. government policies toward Spanish-speaking peoples is directly related to the low median wealth in Latino communities today. In order to fully understand the impact of policies affecting the current state of Latino human, social, financial, and cultural capital, we must go back in time. Tracing the series of events that occurred in the social, political, and economic construction of the United States helps us frame the remedies still needed to proactively craft present and future policies that result in sustainable economic equality and social justice. The Latino community in the United States has a rich and complex history in the New World: today, almost one-third are foreign-born; roughly one-third are second generation; with the remaining third having roots that go back several generations. From this last group, many can trace their ancestors to the discovery of the "Americas" and the exploration and settlement of the southern United States prior to the arrival of the English, Dutch, French, and German Pilgrims at Plymouth Rock. Despite the history of Spanish settlements in the New World prior to the arrival of the Pilgrims in New England, Spanish colonists merely pre-empt northern European settlers, illegitimately claiming land appropriated from indigenous people (American Indians).

Spanish Explorers and the Settling of the New World

After discovering the New World in 1492, Spanish explorers arrived to establish outposts, settlements, and missions in the southern U.S. before the *Mayflower* or the founding of Jamestown, Virginia. The oldest Spanish settlements were established in San Miguel de Guadalupe, Georgia (1521); Santa Fe, New Mexico (1555); Tucson, Arizona (1560); and St. Augustine, Florida (1565). Mexico, at the time a part of New Spain,

became a colony of Spain after Cortes conquered the Aztecs in 1521. By the end of the 1500s, Spanish colonies extended into an area that is now the southeastern and southwestern United States, as well as into a number of Caribbean islands.[7] During the 1600s and early 1700s, Spain continued to settle Mexico and points south, as well as northern territories that included parts of present-day Texas, New Mexico, Arizona, California, Nevada, Utah, Oklahoma, Kansas, Wyoming, and Colorado. The *hacendados* (sheep and cattle estate owners) were the largest landowners in the Southwest for centuries, with most Indians forced into peonage on haciendas.[8] During the mid-1700s and early 1800s, the French and Spanish fought over the Louisiana Territory (Spain ruled it from 1762 to 1801). The Louisiana Territory included land in present day Louisiana, Arkansas, Oklahoma, Missouri, Kansas, Iowa, Nebraska, Minnesota, North Dakota, South Dakota, Wyoming, Montana, Colorado, Idaho and the Canadian provinces of Alberta and Saskatchewan. Spanish governor Berndardo Gálvez, who was in charge of the Louisiana Territory, sent money, supplies and materials to George Washington in support of the Americans during the Revolutionary War. Ultimately, France maintained a larger presence in the interior of the territory, but sold its claim in 1803 to the United States in the Louisiana Purchase.

By 1776, Spain was the largest landowner in North America. Unlike the English, the Spanish settlers intermingled with the native population, so that by the 1800s the majority of the population was *mestizo/a* (mixed race), with only a minority *criollo/a* (claiming only Spanish ancestry). The border between Spanish and English colonies became a socially constructed divide predicated on ethnic/racial differences. As the newly formed U.S government solidified its eastern seaboard presence, land purchases such as Florida from Spain under the Adams-Otis Treaty of 1819 began to gain favor among the executive and legislative members of the U.S. government. The widespread justification for land acquisition and expansionism was not philosophically, politically, and militarily adopted until the passage of the Monroe Doctrine (1824) and the emerging support of a policy of manifest destiny.

Mexican-Americans/ Chicanos: Marrying the Monroe Doctrine to Manifest Destiny

By the end of the 1700s, French and British trappers and traders began to appear in the Southwest. As early as 1785, traders operating in Texas expressed a desire to settle there. Initially, the Spanish government viewed new non-French settlers favorably. This was the first time that Latinos of any race and whites encountered each other in the United States in "settlements" and "as neigh-

bors," and initially relations were amicable. However, Mexico was struggling for its own independence from Spain, and the arrival of Anglo-American settlers in large numbers in Spanish colonized territories caused additional political unrest and turmoil.

In 1821, Mexico won its independence from Spain, and in 1829, abolished slavery. The Monroe Doctrine (1824) pledged U.S. "protection" toward the newly emerging independent republics of Mexico and Central and South America. This political doctrine was intended to ward off European interests, and to indicate to Europe that attempts at further colonization of the New World territories was at an end. Interestingly, as part of the Monroe Doctrine, the United States reserved for itself the right to intervene in the southern part of the Western Hemisphere. In 1830, Mexico banned further Anglo-American immigration to Texas and the importation of slaves. However, by this time Anglo settlers in Texas outnumbered the Mexican. Anglo-Americans wanted self-determination and were joined by a number of Mexican landowners who were disaffected by the ruling party in Mexico City. Both groups were frustrated with the lack of effective Mexican frontier authority, and were outraged over the executive order from Mexico City, effectively combining the province of Texas with Coahuila (a bordering northern Mexico state). In 1837, the Texas settlers defeated the Mexican Army, and set up the Lone Star Republic of Texas. Citizenship was granted to all men living in Texas on the day of independence, "Africans, the descendants of Africans, and Indians excepted." The Republic gave public lands to landless white Texans. Most land grants of black Texans were nullified, except for a few rewarded for military service and a few huge landowners.[9] Seventy-seven percent of Mexicans who weren't black or Indian were able to keep their land under the Republic, compared with 86 percent of Anglos.[10]

The term "manifest destiny" is first used during the 1845 congressional debate over the statehood annexation of Texas into the United States, in journalistic reports conveying the American position toward expansionism: "it was our *manifest destiny* to overspread the continent allotted by Providence for the free development of our yearly multiplying millions."[11] This expansionist sentiment had a profound effect on relations between Latinos in the United States and the newly emerging independent Latin American countries. The marriage of the Monroe Doctrine to manifest destiny in the nineteenth century provided the "Providential" rationale for the United States to maintain a policy of economic and political dominance in the Western Hemisphere. This dominance was to delay economic development and impede natural resource sovereignty in Mexico and Central and South America, creating conditions for a continuing flow northward of Latino immigrants in search of economic opportunity.

After a short period of independence, the Lone Star Republic was annexed as the state of Texas by the United States in 1845. President James Polk initiated the U.S.-Mexico War (1845–48) over a disputed border issue in 1945, "one of the most unjust ever waged by a stronger against a weaker nation," according to General Grant.[12] The War ended with Mexico ceding half of its landmass to the United States in exchange for $15 million.[13] The new U.S. territory—including California, northern Arizona, New Mexico, Nevada, Utah, parts of Colorado, and small sections of what are now Oklahoma, Kansas, and Wyoming[14]—was home to a quarter million Native Americans and eighty thousand Spanish-speaking *mestizos* and *criollos*.[15] Southern Arizona would be acquired later in the Gadsden Purchase in 1854. Adding Texas to the Union gave the slave states a two-vote margin that made it easier to get proslavery laws passed in Congress.[16] Put another way, the United States gained a third of its current landmass as a result of the U.S.-Mexican War and the Gadsden Purchase (also known as the Gadsden Treaty). The United States established control over former Mexican settlers on these lands with the ratification of the Treaty of Guadalupe Hidalgo (1848–1850). The treaty ultimately resulted in a massive transfer of land from Mexican Americans to Anglo Americans.

Transfer of land to the United States in the 1800s

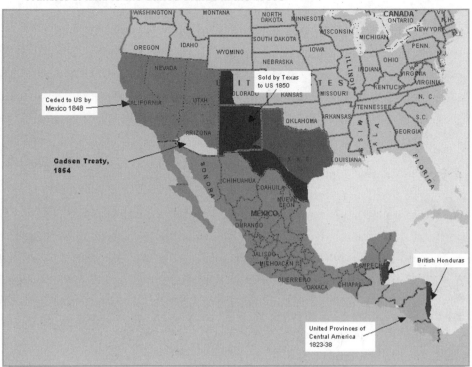

Mexican Land Loss, Lassen County *(Council of Indian Nations)*

The loss of land owned by Mexican Americans after the war can be characterized as one of the most significant barriers to current Mexican American wealth creation. The Treaty of Guadalupe Hidalgo obliged Mexico to cede upper California, Texas, and New Mexico, including what is now Arizona; it also contained a provision (Article X) that guaranteed "protection of all prior and pending titles to properties of every description." Article X maintained that land belonging to Mexican Americans was protected under law, and Mexican land grants would be recognized by American courts. However, when U.S. Congress later ratified the treaty, Article X was omitted. Congress assured Mexicans that "the American government by suppressing the 10th article . . . did not in any way intend to annul the grants of lands made by Mexico in the ceded territories," but the omission of Article X in the ratification of the Guadalupe Hidalgo Treaty presented Mexican-Americans with an economic disaster. Land loss then forced Mexican Americans into American courts with Anglo judges and officials. Many Mexican Americans could not speak English and were unfamiliar with American laws, and therefore, they were unable to legitimate their land titles. In addition, Mexican Americans needed attorneys to defend their land in court; oftentimes, even those who were fortunate enough to keep their land lost money because of excessive attorney fees. Historians have estimated that 80 percent of Mexican land grants went to Anglo-Americans.[17] Under the Mexican government, Mexicans residing in Texas, Arizona, California, and New Mexico had paid taxes on total yield from the land. Thus, in times of distress, Mexicans would pay less in taxes than in times of prosperity. When Mexican farmers fell under American jurisdiction, however, they had to pay a tax based solely on the lands value, and not on the value of the land's yield. Thus, when crops failed, so did Mexican farmers.

Under Anglo legal jurisdiction, racial categories were used to determine who got to keep their land: political rights and land rights were given only to those categorized as white. *Mestizos*, Indians, and African Mexicans had fewer or no rights, depending on the state.[18] A year after the Treaty of Guadalupe Hidalgo was signed, Congress reversed its guarantees of rights to all Mexicans and gave state and territory governments the right to determine the citizen status of Mexicans in each area.[19] Although Article VIII of the treaty stipulated that conquered Mexicans and their heirs could keep their property, the U.S. Congress decided that that provision was invalid for Native

Americans under the Northwest Ordinance of 1787, which took all property rights from Indians.[20] Mexican landowners lost their land rapidly after this reversal. In 1850, over 60 percent of Mexican households in the new states and territories owned land worth more than $100. By 1860, only 29 percent owned land.[21] Between 1848 and the turn of the century, Mexican communities were dispossessed. Legal trickery was backed up by courts, threats of lynching, and the Texas Rangers.[22] By 1851, 13 Anglos had bought 1.3 million acres from 358 Mexicans in sales of dubious legality.[23] Other Anglo men married wealthy Mexican women, which gave them ownership of their land. In the 1850 Census, Texans of Mexican ancestry were a third of the workforce and owned a third of the land, but just twenty years later they were 48 percent of the workforce and owned 11 percent of the land.[24] In 1835 in Nueces County, 100 percent of the land was owned by Mexicans, and in 1883, 100 percent of the land was owned by Anglos.[25]

In New Mexico, some major *criollo* (white Spanish) ranchers kept their land and stayed in political power by allying themselves with Anglo leaders.[26] But for people of color in New Mexico, the story was different. Black people were prohibited from living in the new state at all.[27] Pueblo Indians were allowed to stay, but Apaches were chased out or killed.[28] Anglo real estate investors came to New Mexico and bought up land at low prices from people who didn't have the right documents to prove their title. The New Mexico Surveyor General for the most part approved only the claims of Anglo investors.[29] The claims depended on documents from the Mexican and Spanish governments that claimants weren't allowed to see.[30] Even most of those who had their title confirmed lost their land by the turn of the century due to unpaid back property taxes, assessed retroactively for the time that the title was in dispute.[31] Most Mexicans in New Mexico went from being small farmers to landless wage workers, often on Anglo-owned farms.[32]

The Gadsden Treaty, which turned Arizona over to the United States in 1854, affirmed only the property rights of Mexican landowners whose deeds were registered with the Mexican government, which excluded most landowners. As elsewhere, Anglos poured into the new state and settled on Mexican land. Claims approved by an official surveyor then faced years of delay for confirmation by Congress, and most Mexican families sold their titles to Anglo investors during the wait.[33] Copper and other mines employed landless *mestizos* from the territory and migrant Mexican workers, and they brought large profits to their Anglo bosses. Between 1838 and 1940, over $3 billion in metal was extracted from Arizona mines.[34]

California allowed black and *mestizo* Mexican landowners to file petitions to keep their land, thanks to an antislavery state government. But landless people of color couldn't file new land claims, as federal law limited homesteading to citizens, and under California law only white people could be citizens.[35] White settlers got encouragement and assistance to move to California in the 1840s. By 1900, the boundaries of the continental United States were finalized, with the United States acquiring land that included access to both the Atlantic and Pacific coasts.

During the Mexican Revolution (1910–1920), many Mexican nationals fled the civil war in Mexico and settled in the United States. In 1915, with the Mexican Revolution spilling over the border into the United States and land acquisition by white settlers in south and central Texas at a pitch, many Mexican families sold land titles at gunpoint. An exodus of Mexican families from Texas occurred at the same time immigration north from Mexico was taking place.

Prior to World War I, all U.S. communities were allowed to choose the language of instruction for schooling. In 1900, over 4 percent of the elementary age children were instructed in German. Upon entering World War I, a fierce backlash against "foreign" language instruction in public schools occurred, and by 1919, fifteen states had legislated English-only school instruction in order to root out aliens and contain the "radical labor movement."[36] Nonwhite immigrant students with little or no English-language proficiency were tracked or tested "mentally deficient." In Texas, between 1890 and 1930, the curriculum focusing on the three Rs (reading, 'riting, and 'rithmetic) was replaced with the three Cs (common cultural norms, civics instruction, and command of English) specifically for Mexican-American children. Article IX of the Treaty of Guadalupe Hidalgo had also provided that former Mexican citizens now living in conquered territories had the right to educational instruction in their native language. This article was never enforced.

In 1924, the U.S. Border Patrol was created. Between 1929 and 1935, massive deportations of Mexicans, and exportations of Mexican Americans, who were legal U.S. citizens, and their families occurred as a result of the economic pressure of the Great Depression.

The U.S. Census Bureau identified Mexicans as colored in the 1930 Census.[37] As the U.S. Congress debated and then passed the Social Security Act of 1933, millions of workers were required to fill out applications where the choices were limited to white, Negro, and other: Indian, Mexican and Asian. The Social Security Act disallowed coverage for farmworkers, laborers, housemaids, and others in the service sectors. Since there was a large number of Latino workers in these occupations, a majority of Latino workers were not covered by the Social Security Act. The legacy of this egregious policy, which punishes domestic and field workers, remains with us today; countless of families with live-in maids and nannies do not pay social security taxes for their help. The political vetting

process that includes financial disclosures such as employers' payment (or lack of payment) of social security taxes for maids, nannies, and groundskeepers has ruined political aspirations. Yet media coverage of these politically titillating events does not focus on the distressing lack of retirement funds for these Latino and other racial/ethnic domestic and field workers.

During the Depression years and leading up to World War II and after, segregation of Latino students in public schools was widespread in the southwestern United States. By the 1940s, Texas had 122 segregated public schools for Mexican Americans in fifty-nine counties.[38] During World War II, a labor shortage in the United States encouraged agribusiness owners to lobby for the *bracero*[39] program through an agreement between Mexico and the United States. The program created "temporary" farmworkers who came to the United States to harvest crops and presumably returned to their country of origin when agribusiness no longer needed them.

In 1954, Operation Wetback[40] was launched by the U.S. Immigration and Naturalization Service (INS). INS officials and local officers stopped Mexican-looking individuals and asked for identification papers. This occurred throughout the Southeast and Southwest United States. Many families with native-born children were deported.

The Civil Rights Movement of the 1950s and 1960s and President Johnson's Great

Society legislation spurred a growing political movement for social and economic justice among Latino student and community-based organizations nationwide. During the late 1960s, striking farmworkers organized by Cesar Chavez and Dolores Huerta in California and later throughout the Southwest brought national attention to the working conditions of Latino migrant farmworkers—U.S. and foreign born. The use of DDT, toxic pesticides, the lack of sanitary portable outhouses, and most important, and perhaps most significantly for economic well-being, the lack of minimum wage coverage, and health and retirement benefits for agricultural and migrant farmworkers were exposed.

Currently, Mexican Americans are the largest Latino community in United States, with 25.1 million individuals reported in March 2002.[41] Mexican Americans taken as a whole—meaning the data does not correct for native born and foreign born—have some of the lowest educational attainment rates of any group. However, if we account for generational status, which

also reveals integration and acculturation into mainstream society, we find that underneath the aggregate statistics a different story emerges, with a clear pattern of valuing educational attainment. For example, the percentage of the Mexican American population with at least a high school diploma is 52.9 percent for all Mexican Americans in 1999. However, parsing the Mexican American population by generation, these educational attainment rates change substantially: foreign born, first generation, 36.6 percent; native born, second generation, 68.7 percent; and native born, third generation or more, 74.1 percent have a high school diploma.[42] These data indicate that educational opportunities for Mexican Americans continue to be the path toward more financial stability and a dynamic generational movement into the middle class. The key to fully capturing the dynamism in each Latino community with an immigration experience is to assess the empirical data not in the aggregate, but by generation: foreign born, native born, and third generation plus.

THE CARIBBEAN

Puerto Ricans: A Colonial Past, A Colonial Present

Spain conquered the island of Borinquen in 1510, enslaving much of the native Taino

population to begin cultivating the land for their interests. African slaves were also imported to set up crops. As Puerto Rican land became more important in the sugar and coffee trade, Spain helped support large landowners by backing laws, such as one in

1838, which grafted the name *jornaleros* onto all persons without enough land for subsistence and forced them "to be engaged at the services of someone that can take care of their needs."[44]

In 1898, at the climax of the Spanish-American War, Spain withdrew from Puerto Rico, ceding it to the United States as finalized in the Treaty of Paris. In his famous first speech addressing the Puerto Rican people, General Miles expressed, "We came here not to make war upon the people of a country that for centuries has been oppressed but, on the contrary, to bring you protection, not only to yourselves, but to your property, to promote your prosperity."[44] However, unlike under Spanish rule, there would be very little American settlement of Puerto Rico, and the general treatment seemed to be one of absentee rule, absentee ownership, and caprice. The Spanish-American War of 1898 allowed the United States to annex Puerto Rico, Guam, the Philippines, and Hawaii, leaving Cuba an independent country.

Two years later, all Puerto Ricans, white, *mestizo,* and black saw their oppression reshaped by the Foraker Act of 1900. The outline for the new colonial government included: a governor for the island and a ten-member upper legislative chamber, all appointed by the U.S. president, and a lower chamber elected by Puerto Ricans. Although laws had to be approved by both chambers, the governor had veto power, and if that were not enough to protect U.S. interests, the president had final veto

power.[45] The Foraker Act reinforced the protection of American interests and not surprisingly contradicted the claims set out by General Miles. The island was officially opened to U.S. economic domination.

Puerto Ricans were not afforded U.S. citizenship status until the Jones Act of 1917. Puerto Ricans residing in Puerto Rico are not allowed to participate in U.S. presidential elections, despite Puerto Rico's Commonwealth status. Puerto Rican representation in the U.S. Congress is provided by a commissioner, who advises on Puerto Rican affairs but is not allowed congressional voting rights. Puerto Rican men became eligible for U.S. military service and the draft during World War I.

From the Foraker Act until 1930, United States absentee investment reached $120 million,[46] equivalent to the estimated profits that the U.S. was expecting to extract from the island. This period allowed for the massive switch of assets out of Puerto Rican hands and into American industrial and financial capitalist's control, which by 1930 monopolized at least 60 percent of sugar production, 80 percent of the tobacco industry, 60 percent of all public services and banks, and 100 percent of the maritime lines.[47] The five hundred small and medium-sized farms that existed in 1910 had consolidated into forty-six large corporations by 1930. The unskilled workers in sugar plantations turned to wage labor, but those wages afforded very little purchasing power. For example, at the end of the 1920s, Puerto Rican sugar workers were spending 94 percent of their wages on food.[48] Moreover, women, who were concentrated in the garment industry, were making between one-third and one-quarter of the average male wage.[49]

As the U.S. shaped Puerto Rico into a one-crop and export-producing economy, owners profited nicely, while pushing Puerto Ricans further away from enjoying the benefits.[50] The added effect of this design was that Puerto Rico's land was committed only to export crops that could not be farmed for the people themselves, resulting in the island's increased dependency on U.S. imports.[51] The "*independistas*" of Puerto Rico have pointed out that this method of foreign investment has ultimately meant the impossibility of a "national industrial bourgeoisie," and has only taken profits away from the island, which in turn has created greater dependence.[52] By 1941, Puerto Rico had one of the world's lowest average incomes—a whopping 40¢ per day.[53]

Immigration from Puerto Rico to the mainland increased between the world wars, and continued in a cyclical fashion, peaking during the 1950s. After commonwealth status was confirmed in 1952, a comprehensive economic development plan called Operation Bootstrap was initiated, creating an influx of rural agricultural workers into cities. The restructuring of the Puerto Rican economy by mainland social engineers from agriculture to manufacturing created double-digit unemployment—37 percent—leading to an exodus of displaced workers to

U.S. cities, specifically New York and Chicago.

Operation Bootstrap was designed to increase foreign investment in Puerto Rico by allowing income in Puerto Rico to be exempt from federal income taxes. This program was meant to create jobs and stimulate the Puerto Rican economy, but instead it made Puerto Rico even more dependent on the United States. In addition, Operation Bootstrap diverted attention away from the agricultural sector. The new jobs in industry could not keep up with those lost in agriculture. Another consequence of Operation Bootstrap was to create unfair competition between American tax-exempt firms and those native businesses that were not tax exempt. Operation Bootstrap in Puerto Rico foreshadowed what was to happen in several former colonies and developing countries, namely the development of offshore operations by foreign capital or multinational corporations, which siphon off profits so that there is little to no economic benefit to the island.[54] The government offered ten to twenty-five years of tax exemption, and a population with wages only a quarter of U.S. wages, and other subsidies for infrastructure costs.[55] This was designed to boost profitability and therefore incentives for businesses, but also to alleviate some of the unemployment problems created in the past by uprooting Puerto Rican peasants. However, the result of industrializing the island only created work for approximately 11 percent of its population, and official unemployment reached into the high teens for both men and women in the 1950s.[56]

Operation Bootstrap had the adverse effect of reinforcing Puerto Rico's dependence on the United States.[57] Of all the firms created in Puerto Rico, 78 percent were owned by foreign shareholders.[58] The program may have worked for Puerto Ricans if they had had the ability to own more of the means of production and access to more of the profits. Because of the relationship between Puerto Rico and the United States, however, capital was allowed to flow back to the mainland and to out-compete Puerto Rican capital without controls.[59]

Some of the old white elites left over from the Spanish rule managed to retain some economic power by working for the new "colonial" authority more directly.[60] Whites therefore held some of the only possibilities to retain and gain wealth in the face of American big business. Economic development had been denied Puerto Ricans, and profits had been allocated mainly to white capitalist owners in the United States, although a small, white Puerto Rican elite has retained some influence.

At the same time, Puerto Ricans were being recruited to work in United States industry elsewhere. The combination of Puerto Rican unemployment and displaced agricultural workers who were being encouraged to fill low-skill, low-paying industrial jobs on the East Coast led to a mass migration, predominantly to the New York City area. Some said that emigration was encouraged to defuse social unrest among the island's many unemployed people.[61] It has also been suggested that the headway made on the island during Operation Bootstrap can be attributed to the mass emigration rather than industrial development. Roughly 25 percent of the population left between the 1950s and the 1970s.[62]

The poverty of Puerto Rico laid the foundation for difficulty on the mainland.[63] With unemployment surrounding them on the island, Puerto Ricans were recruited for jobs to help prop up the New York industrial economy,[64] because their low wages helped to leave "substantial profits" to industry owners, and they were also deemed "excellent workers."[65] Puerto Ricans were specifically targeted to fill these jobs because they were U.S. citizens, and because they would take lower paying jobs than mainland Americans.[66] However, as in most cases, Puerto Ricans were again left powerless and unemployed, as most of these industrial jobs left the city, and the profits they helped to build moved elsewhere. New York City lost 40 percent of its manufacturing jobs during the fifties and sixties, within years of and even overlapping with the arrival of so many recruited Puerto Ricans.

In 1956, U.S. pharmaceutical companies ran clinical trials of a high-dosage progesterone/estrogen oral contraceptive, "the pill," at thirty times its current potency on women in Puerto Rico, Haiti, and Mexico. These clinical trials were so "successful" in

Puerto Rico that by 1971 one-third of Puerto Rican women in their childbearing years were "voluntarily sterilized."[67]

Faced with economic dominance, Puerto Ricans have struggled with extreme poverty both stateside and on the island. Wealth, especially in their own island, has been allocated to U.S. companies and investors, the majority of whom are white Anglos, thereby forcing Puerto Ricans to work to generate profits that are not reinvested in their economy and do not help them build assets. Stateside, Puerto Ricans find themselves faced with discrimination beyond these economic barriers. In 1994, Puerto Ricans overall had a 24 percent home ownership rate, by far the lowest of all Latinos and shockingly low when compared to the 70 percent rate of non-Latino whites, according to the U.S. Census *Current Population Survey*.[68] But this figure is exacerbated when examined by race. In one finding: "Of those [Puerto Ricans] who marked themselves as white or European, 35 percent own a home or are making payments on a home. This is distinctly different from those who marked themselves off as 'other race' or 'black' who have a 24 percent and 19 percent home ownership rate, respectively."[69] Furthermore, "Those who marked 'other race' or 'black' are ten percent more likely to live in poverty than those who marked 'white.'"[70]

Taken as a whole, Puerto Ricans have not faired well on the mainland, leading some social researchers to call them "uniquely disadvantaged."[71] Puerto Ricans have seen their position worsen since the 1960s. They are the only Latino group who have not shown any gains during this period. In 1995, the number of Puerto Ricans living in poverty was nine percentage points higher than Mexican Americans, and six percentage points higher than all first-generation Latino immigrants.[72] This has translated into a dismal economic position, indicating their low net worth and home ownership rates. Additionally, more Puerto Rican men in their twenties were incarcerated than enrolled in colleges in 1990 in New York State.[73] Of all the Latino groups in the United States, Puerto Ricans report the highest poverty rates (36 percent), the highest unemployment (37 percent), one of the lowest homeownership rates (35.1 percent), and the lowest annual income, at $29,984.[74] The number of total Puerto Ricans on the mainland reached 3.22 million in March 2002.[75]

Cuban Americans: Independence, U.S. Interests, and the Politics of Embargoes

Following the Spanish-American War, the Platt Amendment in 1901 allowed the United States the unilateral right to intervene in Cuban affairs. The Roosevelt Corollary (1905) provided the United States with the role of policing the Caribbean.

Between 1958 and 1973, there was an exodus of many Cubans after Fulgencio

Batista's fall from power and Fidel Castro's rise to power. The Russian-Cuban alliance so close to U.S. borders during the cold war provoked a challenge to the Monroe Doctrine and a hard-line response by the Kennedy administration toward Cuba, escalating tensions between the United States and the Soviet Union. The ensuing Bay of Pigs fiasco led to increased disaffection by Cuban immigrants in the United States, and a sentiment of betrayal among the Cuban exile community toward the Kennedy administration and the Democratic Party in the United States. The failure to support the Cuban participants in the Bay of Pigs operation by the CIA and United States military produced an unprecedented U.S. immigration policy toward Cuban immigrants in the United States.

In response to the Bay of Pigs, the U.S. government initiated the first "immigrant-friendly" policies for transitioning and aiding Cuban refugees as they relocated in the United States: the Cuban Refugee Assistance Program, the Migration and Refugee Assistance Act of 1962, and the Cuban Adjustment Act of 1966 all contributed to a supportive government initiative toward Cuban immigrants. The single most important factor that uniquely defined the Cuban immigrant experience in the United States was their flight from a "communist-declared" regime in the Western Hemisphere. This prompted a unique immigrant policy response by the federal government in the form of low-interest business loans, low-interest housing loans, special social services, cash, and medical assistance to Cuban refugees. Additional federal aid for public education to state and local governments was also provided, along with the first bilingual education programs before the passage of the 1968 Education Reform legislation. This response by the U.S. government toward Latino refugees fleeing from a "dictatorial" regime established an unprecedented example of "effective and efficient" immigrant-friendly policies that transitioned displaced persons in a relatively short period of time. It further signified that government programs *can* be employed to effectively mitigate economic losses by immigrants. This was the most successful immigration policy in America's history and present-day Cuban American economic indicators attest to the success of such an effective government policy response.[76] For example, in 2001, Cuban Americans had the second highest high school and college completion rates of all Latino population groups—70.8 percent and 18.6 percent, respectively—while also having the highest advanced-degree completion rates, 6.2 percent.[77] In 2001, Cuban Americans had higher home ownership rates (58.8 percent), a higher percentage of families earning $75,000 and over (20.9 percent), and lower unemployment rates (6.1 percent) than Mexican Americans, Puerto Ricans, and Central and South Americans.[78] In March 2002, Cuban Americans totaled 1.38 million people.[79]

Dominican Americans: Old Transnationalism, New Transnationalism

Between 1905 and 1910, the Dominican Republic was placed under customs receivership in the Roosevelt Corollary, which is similar to reserving the right to intervene or invade if events require such action. In 1965, the Dominican Republic saw the automatic implementation of the Monroe Doctrine when President Lyndon Johnson sent in over twenty thousand U.S. troops to quell political unrest. U.S. intervention came after the long reign of Dominican dictator Rafael Trujillo (1930–1961) had ended with his assassination. After thirty years of dictatorship, the country was attempting to implement democratic rule. In 1962, Juan Bosch and the Dominican Revolutionary Party, a broad coalition of parties, were democratically elected with 64 percent of the popular vote. In 1963, a constitution was drafted, allowing for separation of church and state, guaranteed civil and individual rights, and endorsed civilian control of the military. Conservatives and the church viewed these reforms as radical. A military coup occurred in September 1963 and a civilian junta was installed, sending Bosch into exile. A triumvirate was installed, but never gained popular support. The Constitutionalists, a group of young military officers supporting Bosch's reforms and the 1963 constitution, clashed with the Loyalists, conservative senior military officers. A new provisional president was installed, Rafael Molina, but he had no popular support. The Johnson administration, believing the Constitutionalists had the support of communist elements, sent in U.S. troops to maintain order. Between 1961 and 1986, an estimated four hundred thousand Dominicans migrated to the United States.

The Dominican American community is concentrated on the northeastern seaboard but a diaspora is occurring southward. In 2000, the Dominican American community comprised 2.2 percent (approximately 750,000) of the total Latino population in the United States.[80] The Dominican American community reports a substantial 12.4 percent of Latinos in the Northeast, but only eight percent of Latinos in the South (with Florida reporting a 2.6 percent Dominican American population), 3 percent of all Latinos in the Midwest, and only 0.2 percent of all Latinos residing in the West. Research on Latino wage rates and occupational status indicates that for many Dominican Americans, the color line becomes an important factor in repressed wages and job discrimination.

Immigration Policies and the Fear of Being Overrun by Foreigners

➤ The Naturalization Act of 1906 required knowledge of basic English for citizenship. In 1907, legislation was passed that increased the head tax on immigrants and excluded immigrants with physical or mental defects, tuberculosis, and children unaccompanied by parents. The Immigration Act of 1917 excluded illiterates, persons of psychopathic inferiority, and immoral persons.

➤ The 1965 Immigration and Naturalization Act set yearly limits on immigration to the United States by people from other Western Hemisphere countries. In 1976, the Act was amended to set limits country by country.[81]

➤ In 1986, the Immigration Reform and Control Act, also known as the Simpson-Mazzoli bill, was passed. One year later, in 1987, the amnesty portion of IRCA was initiated. The Supreme Court ruled that alien refugees showing well-founded fears of persecution in their country of origin could be eligible for U.S. asylum in *INS v. Cardoza-Fonseca*.[82]

➤ Proposition 187, a California anti-immigration referendum measure, passed in 1994. Its provisions required California law enforcement, social services, health care, and public personnel to: verify the immigrant status of persons with whom they come in contact; notify certain defined persons of their immigration status; report these persons to state and federal officials; and deny these persons social services, health care and education.

➤ Despite the economic boom years of the 1990s, an anti-immigrant backlash occurred amid growing economic prosperity. The passage of the 1996 Personal Responsibility and Work Opportunity Act (PRWOA, also known as the Welfare Reform Act of 1996) denied immigrants access to a variety of public assistance programs. Legal immigrants for the first five years of residency in the United States were also denied public social and health care services. Anti-immigrant attitudes during the last decade of the twentieth century appeared to be directly related to growing demographic shifts and concern over the "browning of America." *(continued)*

> At the end of the twentieth century, several U.S.-Mexico border initiatives were launched: Operation Hold the Line (El Paso), Operation Rio Grande (South Texas), Operation Gatekeeper (California), Operation Safeguard (Arizona). These initiatives were strengthened by increased allocation of federal budget resources to the Immigration and Naturalization Service, renamed in the early twenty-first century the U.S. Bureau of Citizenship and Immigration Services (BCIS), after the attacks on the World Trade Center and the rise of citizen vigilante groups along the southern U.S. border.

Central and South Americans: Seeking Political Asylum

From 1912 to 1933, the United States invaded and intermittently occupied Nicaragua. The democratically elected government of Guatemala was destabilized with CIA covert aid and with the support of the United Fruit Company. Guatemalan President Jacobo Arbenz, elected in 1951 to replace the corrupt government of General Jorge Ubico, presided over a coalition government. Land reform was initiated in 1952 with compensation to United Fruit for public lands it had acquired as a gift during Ubico's reign. Although the plan for land reform was moderate and the lands in question were originally public lands, the prevailing anticommunist sentiment during the McCarthy years in Washington viewed the reform as a precursor to more "socialist" government programs. Arbenz's democrati-

cally elected government was overthrown in 1954. Immigration to the United States began subsequently, and the 1980 census indicated that 71,000 Guatemalans were living in the United States.

The 1980s and 1990s civil wars in Guatemala (conservative political regimes against the non-assimilated indigenous peoples) and in El Salvador (land-poor workers and farmers against the landed aristocracy) created economic and political instability in the region. The number of Guatemalan refugees to the United States was reported at 230,000 in the 1990 census, and over 370,000 in the 2000 census. Many Guatemalans' first language is Maya, with Spanish as a second language. For El Salvadorans, the 1980–1992 civil war created an exodus of 215,000 legal immigrants during the 1980s, raising the overall Salvadoran population in the United States to 565,000. In 1985, Salvadoran refugees in the United States filed a class-action suit against the INS for its massive dismissal of political refugee status applications. In settling the case, the INS revamped its political refugee status procedure and application process. Currently, the 2000 Census reports more than 650,000 Salvadorans in the United States, even after many returned to El Salvador at the end of the civil war.

The 1979 civil war in Nicaragua reached a turning point with the fall of President Anastasio Somoza. Once the Sandinista Party democratically took power in Nicaragua, many of the countries' wealthy landowners left for Europe and the United States. Because the Sandinistas had close ties to Cuba and the Soviet Union, and because they appropriated Somoza's land holdings under government jurisdiction, and initiated land reforms, the United States government began funding what it called *contra* "freedom fighters" based in Honduras and Costa Rica. This also created more pressure for Nicaraguans to emigrate. One tenth of Nicaraguans left during the 1980s. Many arrived in the United States fleeing a "communist" regime, which allowed for quick INS processing for

United States resident status. The precedent set by the Cuban refugees during the 1960s was instrumental in processing many Nicaraguans quickly under political refugee status.

Congress passed the Refugee Act in 1980 and the Supreme Court ruled in 1984 that nondocumented refugees/immigrants must show clear probability of facing torture, death, or persecution upon deportation. In 1980, the Census reported twenty-five thousand Nicaraguans in the United States. By 2000, the number had increased to 175,000.

The continuous immigration since the 1900s from Central and South America has increased the diversity of the Latino population in the United States. Current data indicates that 31.5 percent of all Central and South Americans reside in the Northeast, 34 percent reside in the South, 29.9 percent reside in the West, and 4.6 percent reside in the Midwest. The total population numbers for Central and South Americans reached 5.35 million in March 2002.[83]

POLICIES AFFECTING ALL LATINOS

The advent of affirmative action policies in the late 1960s and 1970s increased the number of Latino students in universities and colleges. The presence of a diverse student population reflecting the population of the United States brought different perspectives and voices to higher education. However, the

legacy of inaccessibility of higher education for Latinos is reflected in the current disparity between the non-Hispanic white rate of college graduates (29.4 percent) and Latino graduates (11 percent).[84] During the Reagan years, poverty rates for the Latino population spiked. The two recessions, 1980 (six months) and 1981–1982 (sixteen months), led to poverty rates for Latino families with children under eighteen years of age of 27.2 percent in 1980, 28.5 percent in 1981, and 32.6 percent in 1982. Many social service budgets were slashed and programs started during the 1960s War on Poverty were discontinued. The impact of the Reagan administration initiatives continued to show up in the poverty statistics of the first Bush administration. The recession in 1990–1991 (eight months) again hurt Latino families with children: poverty rates for Latino families soared and remained high at 31 percent in 1990, 33.7 percent in 1991, 32.9 percent in 1993, 34.3 percent in 1994, and 34.2 percent in 1995. The safety nets were long gone before the 1996 Welfare Reform Act. Proposition 209, a California referendum that repealed affirmative action for underrepresented groups in government institutions, most notably in contract bidding and higher education admissions processes, was passed in 1996. The same year, the Fifth Circuit Court ruled in favor of the plaintiffs in *Hopwood v. University of Texas School of Law*. These measures originally held to be constitutional have now been superseded by the Supreme Court decision in June 2003 concerning the University of Michigan's affirmative action admissions program.

Initial legislative responses to the dismantling of affirmative action programs in public universities resulted in programs being replaced with percentage plans. In California, the legislature passed a 4 percent plan and later a 12.5 percent plan, and in Texas, a 10 percent plan. These percentage plans allowed graduating seniors from state high schools admission to public universities of their choice. In the case of California, additional criteria were imposed, and when instituting the 12.5 percent plan, graduating high school seniors had to complete their freshman and sophomore classes at a community college and then were allowed to proceed to the University of California campuses to complete their degrees. In Texas, the top 10 percent of graduating seniors from state high schools were automatically accepted into the public university of their choice. Neither the program in Texas nor the California program reflected the diversity of student populations in relative proportion to the diversity within each state's population.

WHAT CAN WE LEARN FROM THE PAST?

The legacy of racial/ethnic hostilities of the Anglo and Spanish colonizers in the New World, and in North America in particular, is reflected in the present-day ambivalence in white-Latino relations. The subsequent western expansion relegated the racially mixed Latino communities in the United States to an ethnic category. The dilemma of how to describe an ethnic people with a similar colonizing history has not been thoroughly explored by ethnohistorians. What we do know is that the stories of Latinos and Latino immigration to the United States brought with them their own mixed colonial pasts from Mexico, the Caribbean, Central America, and South America. The color line among Latinos is as complex and varied as the history of Latinos in the United States. The Latino community mirrors the diversity of racial characteristics and suffers the consequences that the color spectrum has on economic mobility.[85] Studies indicate that black and indigenous-looking Latinos fare far worse in the labor market than do more European-looking Latinos, when controlling for English language ability.[86]

Policies that attempt to remedy past discrimination such as affirmative action have become controversial and, for many, divisive. The lack of media coverage of the continuing inequality experienced by communities of color is telling. As a country, we don't want to be reminded of an unequal or unfair past, much less present-day economic and wealth inequities. Yet it is exactly our past that continues to affect the current economic well-being of struggling communities of color today. The growing wealth divide in the United States is a direct consequence of past policies toward people based solely on observable differences.

Compelling social movements, such as the Civil Rights Movement and La Causa (the Chicano movement) from the 1950s, 1960s, and 1970s led to the creation of governmental policies aimed directly at changing an unacceptable wealth divide. These past national priorities can frame a new affirmation of a common goal of access to opportunity and a decent standard of living. The alternative to closing the wealth gap will lead to increasing erosion of democratic institutions and civic participation, a reversal of middle-class gains and a loss of economic prosperity for the nation. Recall, communities of color totaled 32 percent of the U.S. population in 2002.[87] Add to this the two communities with high rates of growth, the Asian and Latino populations, and by 2010, people of color may well top 38 percent of the total US population.

For Latinos with generational roots in the Southwest, there are numerous instances of accommodating white expansion and colluding with Anglo land grabbers to hold onto family "land" and wealth from the Spanish colonial past. Possession of wealth, specifically documented landed wealth, tended to confer "white" attributes. Anglo settlers distinguished between the "noble olive complexion" of the "Spaniard" from the "*mestizo*" traits of the Spanish-Amerindian (*mestizo*) landless worker. What is only now being brought to light by historians of color is the history of Anglo-European settlers refusing to acknowledge working Latinos in the Southwest as citizens with full voting, landowning, and civic participation rights. This history of passive and active discrimination toward laboring *mestizo* populations has contributed to the perception of nondeserving Latino populations in the United States.

Our public school systems have also institutionalized an attitude of low expectations toward communities of color, leading directly to a public education system that socially and economically sorts future leaders and workers, thus perpetuating who will have access to wealth-building opportunities and who will not.

CURRENT POLICIES AFFECTING THE ECONOMIC MOBILITY OF LATINOS

Recent policies affecting Latino economic well-being arise in a variety of wealth-creating areas: immigration, education, labor, community development (housing and business formation), health services, and civic participation. Each of these areas is crucial to the economic mobility of the Latino community, since they are interrelated. For example, one cannot create secure wealth without lawful status. Consequently, immigrant status is part of one's ability to create and own wealth without the fear of deportation and having assets frozen or confiscated. Without educational or human capital in the form of a high school, GED, or vocational diploma, one cannot access higher education nor can one obtain a living wage job with health benefits. Without an education and a living wage job, owning a home or business becomes remote. Without legal status or a living wage job, one cannot access health care services.[88]

Finally, there is a direct relationship between education, income, and voter participation. Being poor and semi-educated increases the rate of political disenfranchisement and, too often, results in low voter registration and turnout. We have seen the consequences of past government policies contributing to the ongoing economic distress in Latino communities. Currently, the progressive policies enacted in the 1960s and 1970s to remedy barriers facing racial and ethnic communities are being overturned. These policies were meant to create economic and social justice for the disenfranchised. At issue now are policies that deny Latinos access to education, housing, and full participation in all aspects of economic life. What contributes to this troubling wave of antifamily, antiworker legislation is the focus on the color line and the legitimacy of current immigrant populations. We have seen the rise of racial and ethnic profiling after September 11, and a growing acceptance of passive public institutions in the face of legislative and judicial rulings intent on dismantling hard-won gains in civil and labor rights. Assessing current economic and wealth indicators along with policies that have affected these indicators may provide clues to closing the growing wealth gap in the United States.

Income and Latino Families

Between 2000 and 2003, Latino median household income declined 4.8 percent, from $36,032 to $34,272.[89] Of the 11.8 million Latino households in 2003, 9.4 million are families, and the income distribution for families indicates that 57 percent of these families annually earn $40,000 or less. Thirty percent of Latino families have five or more members. Moreover, 35 percent of the Latino population is eighteen years of age or younger—fourteen million. Of the

almost forty million Latinos, over half—21.5 million—reside in states along the U.S.-Mexico border in Texas, New Mexico, Arizona, and California.

Family formation among Latinos continues to display non-nuclear and extended-kin or pseudo-kin arrangements. Family formation among Latinos has implications for income parity, budgeting for necessary family expenditures, and wealth-building opportunities. In 2003, Latino families without children had an average of three people in the household; for those with children, the average number of people in the family unit totaled five compared to non-Hispanic white families, which had an average of three people in families with children. Family status plays a significant role in normalizing immigration status, in sponsoring

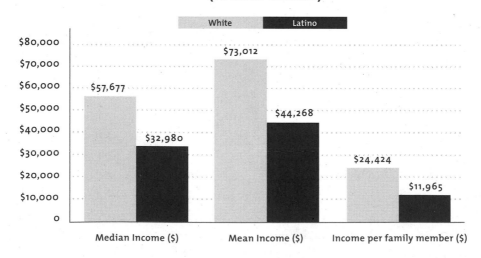

FIGURE 4-5

Family median, mean, and per capita income (in 2001 dollars)

Source: U.S. Census Bureau, *Current Population Survey, 2004*, Table FINC-03

family members, and in reunifying families. Moreover, living arrangements in large families contribute to economies of scale, lower-ing the costs of housing and transportation. Larger families generally have more earners in the household, which contributes to

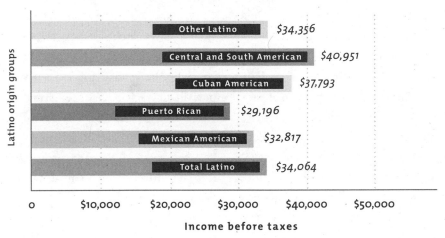

FIGURE 4-6

**Latino groups annual income, 2000–2001
(consumer expenditure survey in 2001 dollars)**

Source: Paulin, G., *Monthly Labor Review*, August 2003.

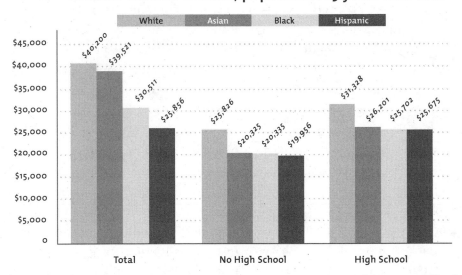

FIGURE 4-7

Median income in 2002, population 25 years and over

Source: U. S. Census Bureau, Curent Poplultion Survey, 2003, Table 10-8.

THE COLOR OF WEALTH

income flow and wealth accumulation. The downside of extended and pseudo-kin family arrangements is the communal nature of pooling resources to acquire assets. In the United States, most laws, financial products and services, housing and housing services, insurance and binding contracts are between individuals. The emphasis on individual property rights, and correspondingly individual liability, devalues communal property and communal asset-building activities. The communal pooling of resources is not recognized by financial data collection agencies and government social services. The collective manner in which family economic survival strategies have evolved in the working-poor Latino community are not within the scope of what the U.S. government defines as a nuclear family, which poses a significant problem for Latinos transitioning from poverty status into financially stable circumstances.

Latino income stability, as for other communities, continues to depend heavily upon access to educational opportunities. The income earned based on educational attainment—the financial return on education—still reflects a disparity across different racial and ethnic groups. These lingering inequalities remind us that education is one route out of poverty, while not a guarantee of equal pay.

Legislation, policies, and judicial rulings at the federal, state, and local levels have adversely affected the income and eco-

nomic stability of Latino families. These include rules barring Latino workers from speaking Spanish on the job; laws preventing undocumented immigrant Latino workers from being treated as native-born workers (in the U.S. Supreme Court decision of March 2002, *Hoffman Plastic Compounds, Inc. v. National Labor Relations Board*); laws setting state minimum wage laws at the federal minimum wage level or below; policies creating regressive sales and payroll taxes for those earning minimum wage and setting asset eligibility requirements for the Earned Income Tax Credit and other social service programs that do not take into account Latino families' communal asset building.

Migrant workers, day laborers, seasonal workers, and recently arrived Latino immigrant families pool their resources in order to purchase assets as a group, while listing the asset under an individual name to meet financial requirements such as getting auto loans. For example, three brothers pool their funds together for the purchase of a van that can transport their families to their place of employment during the harvest cycle. The oldest brother purchases the vehicle, which can cost from $28,000 to $32,000. This asset makes the oldest brother ineligible for subsidized low-income housing and possibly for the Earned Income Tax Credit. Federal and state asset eligibility rules do not take into account the communal pooling of resources that occur among many Latino working families and extended kin.

FIGURE 4-8
Latin home ownership rates, 2000–2001

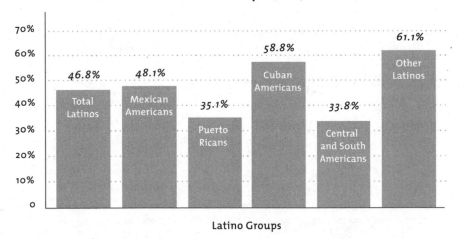

Latino Groups

Source: Paulin, G., *Monthly Labor Review*, August 2003.

Home and Business Ownership

A home is the most important asset a family owns in their lifetime, and becomes an important source of wealth, especially in leveraging educational and business opportunities. Moreover, family home ownership is an important indicator of educational attainment for children of home owners, regardless of neighborhood characteristics.[90] It is also an important predictor of civic participation[91] as well as an indicator of financial stability.[92] Nationally, Latinos lag behind other groups in their rates of home ownership. For Latinos nationally the rate of home ownership is 47 percent. For the various ethnic groups, the rate of home ownership varies with rates of educational attainment, self-employment and median age.

Puerto Ricans have lower home ownership rates for reasons that are similar for Central and South Americans. Puerto Ricans reside predominantly in New York City and Chicago—urban areas—where affordable housing is severely limited. Central Americans (1.8 million), who outnumber South Americans (1.5 million), have lower educational attainment levels and are more recent arrivals than the South Americans. Additionally, six hundred thousand Central Americans live in Los Angeles where the housing market is exorbitantly expensive and six hundred thousand South Americans reside in New York City, which has similarly high housing costs. These factors contribute to the lower home ownership rates of these two groups. Other Latinos and Cubans have economic profiles that closely parallel those of non-Hispanic whites, so it's no surprise that they have the highest home ownership rates.

FIGURE 4-9
Mean housing debt (in 2001 dollars)

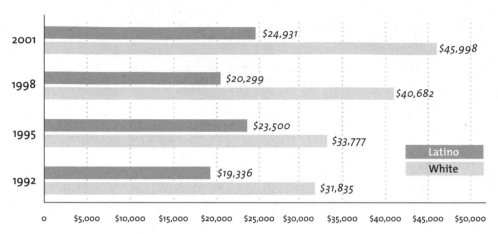

Source: Calculations, Survey of Consumer Finances, Federal Reserve Bank, Board of Governors, 1992, 1995, 1998, and 2001.

Federal housing policies and agencies promoting home ownership have not supported two important legislative reforms necessary for Latino families seeking to become home owners: creating mortgage products that allow extended family workers' income to be included in an evaluation of family income; and instituting wider criteria in the underwriting assessment of credit scoring. If these two legislative and lending industry reforms were spearheaded by government agencies such as the Department of Housing and Urban Development, Fannie Mae, and Freddie Mac, we would see an increase in Latino home ownership rates without a corresponding increase in subprime mortgages. Moreover, evidence continues to confirm the presence of redlining in Latino communities[93] by banks and other financial institutions.

U.S. Latinos have an affinity for entrepreneurship, and when owning businesses and microbusinesses, family involvement in running and expanding the enterprise is well documented.[94] Latino business owners and entrepreneurs are subject to the same market forces that other business owners face. However, because their share in businesses tends to be at the micro and small firm level, the adverse impact on a family's well-being becomes amplified. Government policies have not kept pace with the micro-enterprise phenomenon that exists in many communities of color.

The Small Business Administration recently suffered debilitating budget cuts and simply cannot meet the needs of many microbusiness entrepreneurs. Not-for-profit microfinance lending organizations—community development financial institutions (CDFI)—have become crucial lending entities in communities of color with growing microbusiness owner activity.

Self-employment rates among the various groups indicate that push factors—the inability to find work—and pull factors—high rates of self-employment in one's native country—are present. Latinos overall have a 3.6 percent self-employment rate, whereas the "Other Latino" communities together have a 6.3 percent self-employment rate. Puerto Ricans (1.9 percent) and Cubans (2.1 percent) have lower self-employment rates than do Mexican (2.9 percent) and Central and South Americans (5.9 percent). However, information on many self-employment economic activities such as baby-sitting, lawn care, day labor, and maid services is unavailable. This may mean there is a higher self-employment rate among

Latinos than official data suggests. Recent research indicates that self-employed Latinos have a higher probability of home ownership than Latino wage earners.[95]

During the 1990s, an explosion in Latina self-employment rates occurred. The reasons behind this are cultural, yet driven by economics. Latina entrepreneurship overwhelming involves family members.[96] This alleviates many child care problems associated with full-time wage-earning employment. Micro-enterprises proliferate along the U.S.-Mexico border and in Latino ethnic enclaves in urban areas. Many Latinas find that barriers to entry in the general labor markets force them to turn to entrepreneurial activities to supplement or patch their family income.[97] Between 1990 and 2000, self-employment among Latino women doubled. Small business formation

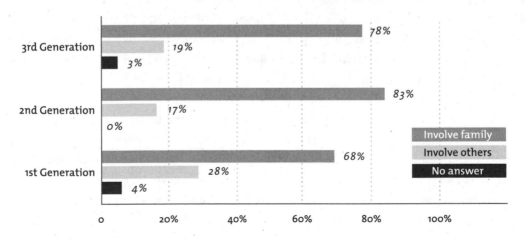

FIGURE 4-10
Latina-owned businesses involve family, regardless of generation, 2000

Source: Center for Women's Business Research, *The Spirit of Enterprise: Latina Entrepreneurs in the U.S.*, September 2000

grew 232 percent between 1988 and 1997.[98] Emerging microbusinesses are another phenomena that policy analysts view as a form of supplementing wage income and minimizing poverty. These micro-entrepreneurs are supported by CDFI that in many ways have replaced banks and credit unions as sources of capital for micro- and small businesses in the Latino community.

Policies promoting and supporting microenterprise owners are desperately needed. Currently, the funding for pre-existing programs sponsored and monitored by the Small Business Administration to encourage and support small business owners have been slashed. No new funding has been allocated to the Treasury Department's CDFI division, which funds microfinance lenders and nonprofit micro-enterprise programs.

Additionally, budgetary assistance for the Internal Revenue Service's Low-Income Tax Payer Assistance Program is not a priority. Simply because working-poor, self-employed, or low-income migrant workers generate small amounts of income does not mean they file 1040EZ forms. Volunteer Individual Taxpayer Assistance (VITA) programs generally do not train volunteers for the more complicated tax preparation of self-employment forms (Schedules SE, C and F). This has the unintended but tragic result of sending many low-income and working-poor taxpayers to commercial tax preparation sites that pressure taxpayers to take rapid anticipation tax loans at high fees. Community-based organizations that offer tax preparation service at nominal fees or for no fee need IRS support. Policies that encourage the SBA, the Treasury Department's CDFI division, and the IRS to partner with community-based organizations would result in wealth retention in communities of color.

Educational Attainment

Two communities stand out among all other Latino communities in approaching non-Hispanic white educational attainment rates: "other Latinos" and Cuban Americans. The *Current Population Survey* done by the Census Bureau in March 2002 indicates that 19.7 percent of "other Latinos" hold a bachelor's degree or higher, while 18.6 percent of Cuban Americans hold postsecondary education degrees. Bachelor's degrees among Mexican Americans are lower, at 7.6 percent, Central and South Americans, at 17.3 percent. Forty-nine percent of foreign-born South Americans have a high school degree or higher and 24 percent of foreign-born Central Americans having more than a high school degree, and for Puerto Ricans, 14 percent.

Among Americans, Asians and Pacific Islanders had the highest proportion of college graduates (47 percent), followed by whites (29 percent), and African-Americans (17 percent), with Hispanics (11 percent) trailing behind. The proportion of Hispanics born in the United States who had a bachelor's degree or more (13.5 percent) was

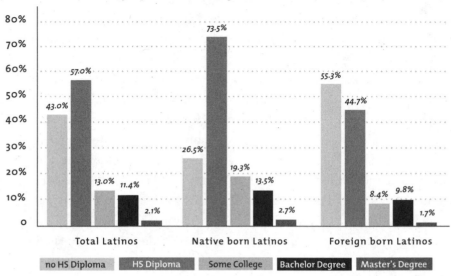

FIGURE 4-11

Latino educational attainment, 2003
(population 25 years old and over)

Source: U. S. Census Bureau, Current Population Survey, 2003, Table 10-06.

higher than that of foreign-born Latinos (9.8 percent).[99]

Several state legislatures have enacted percentage plans in response to federal court–mandated repeals of affirmative action programs in higher education (*Hopwood*, Fifth Circuit Court, 1996, Texas, and Proposition 209, 1996, California). These percentage plans have worked in large part because high schools with high Latino enrollment are *de facto* segregated. Moreover, no corresponding legislative response has occurred to remedy the demise of affirmative action admissions in graduate and professional programs in affected public universities. This has resulted in a loss of Latino,

African American, and American Indian leaders in business, law, policy, medicine, and other graduate fields. Current admissions policies after the June 2003 Supreme Court ruling in the University of Michigan cases indicate a trend towards a "wholistic" evaluation of applications. Each application is reviewed as part of the whole student profile, as opposed to receiving points for particular attributes, such as race or ethnicity. No similar lawsuits have been brought against legacy admits or veterans admits—students admitted on the basis of their parents' alumni status or military service. What this implies is a fundamental social acceptance that children of former alums or those who serve in the military are deemed to be outside the normal competitive process.

Policies that promote a pipeline approach to educational opportunities are needed in public education. This implies rethinking K–12 programs to incorporate pre-K-to-16 options. In a rapidly changing economic environment driven by technological advances and global market connections, the nation requires more innovation and imagination in crafting educational policies that recognize and cultivate all our young. The changing demographic shifts in the population of school-age children have already occurred. Our policies toward public schooling cannot afford to lag behind this reality. In order to prepare the young for a rapidly changing work and career environment, policies must be flexible enough to accommodate societal needs. Policies that create educational programs that increase apprenticeships in the arts, engineering, computer technology, crafts, health, business, and communications could be the high school curricula needed to integrate our youth into a learning process that provides equal opportunity to all communities. Such an overhaul does not track our students into single-skilled employment or educational opportunities but rather prepares them for the reality of our current career and work environment that requires multiskilled individuals. Moreover, communities of color bring a high degree of natural assets to the educational environment.[100] If instead of deficit thinking policies, we approach multilingual and culturally diverse children as assets to and in the educational process, we can then build educational spaces and places that reflect our communities, that make use of the communities' real resources, and that recognizes the global nature of what communities contribute.

NET WORTH, RETIREMENT, AND INHERITANCE INDICATORS

Wealth inequality is not as simple a task to uncover as income inequality. Our national data collection efforts focus on the earnings capacity of different communities and indicate that only income and earnings matter. But this tends to focus our attention toward labor and job discrimination and away from barriers in the housing and real estate markets, financial services access, such as credit opportunities and small business loan availability. But perhaps most disturbing is the lack of information on the retirement income of the elderly in communities of color. Federal Reserve data indicate that the net worth of communities of color is intimately tied to educational attainment, occupational status, financial market sophistication and participation, home ownership, and pension participation.

Latino communities display the same immigrant and recent immigrant memories as many other ethnic communities, resulting

FIGURE 4-12

Mean retirement pensions—IRAs, thrifts, future pensions (in 2001 dollars)

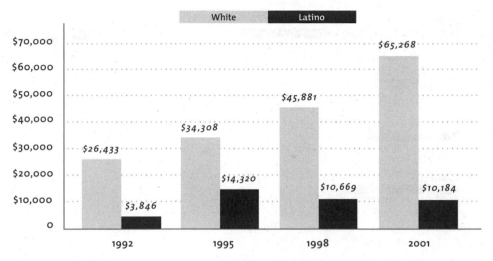

Source: Bárbara J. Robles's Calculations, Survey of Consumer Finances, Board of Governors, Federal Reserve Bank System, 1992–2001.

in more bricks and mortor investment activities. One example of immigrant asset accumulation is investment in tangible assets such as property, other homes for rental purposes, and business investments. Rental income often substitutes for pension and retirement income. Even as primary homes for Latinos display the segregated values of the homes, rental properties and rental income play a role in retirement strategies.

Retirement income is essential for the well-being of those past their prime working years. The gap in pensions between Latinos and other groups in inflation-adjusted dollars is grim. Recall that the Social Security Act exempted farm workers and domestics from coverage. Latinos and black Americans have the least participation in private pensions,

thrifts, and IRA accounts compared to white Americans, and to a comparable degree the category used by the Survey of Consumer Finances called "other." Presumably, other includes Asian and Native American communities as well as those who did not self-identify as white, black, or Hispanic. This lack of retirement pension income indicates that family and Social Security play substantial roles in determining the continued standard of living of the elderly in many communities of color.

Another very important aspect of wealth accumulation is the intergenerational bequests that occur from parents to children. The capacity to purchase a home, using inheritances as down payments, or begin a business, using start-up capital from a gift,

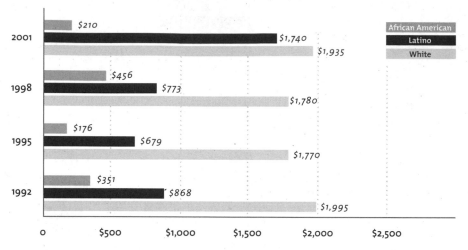

FIGURE 4-13
Mean value of rental income
(in 2001 dollars)

Source: Authors' Calculations, Survey of Consumer Finances,
Board of Governors, Federal Reserve Bank System, 1992–2001.

often becomes possible due to transfers of wealth in the form of income, homes, or portfolios received from parents. The Survey of Consumer Finances asks respondents if they have been recipients of gifts and/or inheritances. The data clearly map out who has benefited from such transfers. Additionally, these transfers buffer many families from serious economic instability brought about by unemployment, a divorce, or a serious health crisis in the family.

Government policies that aided many families during the late 1940s and 1950s, through the GI Bill and FHA/VA mortgages, helped increase the likelihood of inherited transfers from one generation to the next. That not all Americans were able to

benefit from these policies can be seen generations later in the low amount of wealth accumulated by many families of color. We saw that the loss of land for many Latinos during the late nineteenth and early twentieth centuries set them on a path of low wages and wealth reversals. As generations have accumulated small wealth portfolios, the continued family size becomes another obstacle in wealth transfers from parents to children. Moreover, current economic crises and educational expenditures create dilemmas about acquiring pensions and portfolios for retirement and future transfers to children. Current asset-building policies such as Individual Development Accounts (IDA) disqualify many working-poor and low-income families from these matching savings accounts by imposing net worth eligibility requirements. In *colonias*, for example, many families own their land and have some equity in their homes (home values in colonias range from $10,000 to $24,000) and earn $5,000 to $14,000 dollars a year. Yet, these same families that seek to provide opportunities for their children are disqualified from participating in IDAs because their assets are over the $10,000 threshold. Their homes cannot be leveraged for educational opportunities for their children. But an IDA could provide a pathway out of poverty for *colonia* families.

Policies that expand home ownership and education (like the GI Bill), specifically targeted to low-income families, would be instrumental in reversing the wealth gap between working-poor communities of color and their more affluent neighbors. Additionally, children's investment accounts (called "baby bonds" or "child trust funds") that are currently being implemented in Great Britain (and being discussed in Australia and New Zealand) may be a way to close the wealth inequality gap. Each child at birth receives an endowment of $400 to $1,000, and at subsequent birthdays receives additional funds. By the child's eighteenth birthday, the fund has accumulated a sufficient amount to pay for the first year of college or a down payment on a home. Of course, there are obvious built-in incentives for parents to also contribute to the account, as their contributions combined with governmental contributions are more likely to cover college costs. This

FIGURE 4-14

Mean gifts and inheritance (in 2001 dollars)

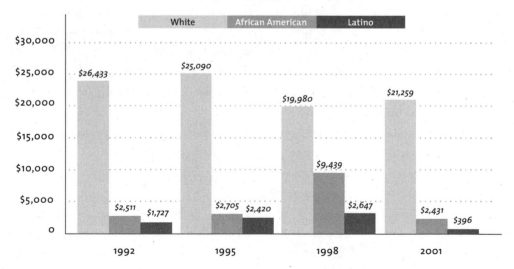

Source: Bárbara J. Robles's Calculations, Survey of Consumer Finances, Board of Governors, Federal Reserve Bank System, 1992, 1995, 1998, and 2001.

would have the added effect of releasing family funds to save for retirement and home ownership without trading off children's higher education.

We have not begun to tap into our innovative and imaginative collective talent on how best to reduce the wealth gap. One important way that we can begin to do so is by mapping out past policies that had a significant impact on increasing and stabilizing the upwardly mobile working class and the semistable middle class and crafting new policies that incorporate the best of what we know has already worked.

WHAT CAN WE DO WITH ALL THAT WE KNOW?

To combat the growing wealth inequality in the United States, we need to continue to push for fair political and media representation of communities of color. We need images of the positive aspects of communities of color engaging in social change at the micro level.

Our academic discourse has infected our policy debates and conversations with terms such as "at risk" and "permanent underclass" and "culture of poverty," indicating a defeated attitude toward proactive policy and program outcomes.

Policy makers are taking their cues from these academic experts, leading to a lack of imaginative and innovative programs to reduce wealth inequality. In essence, our researchers are telling us that as a country, we will continue to perceive our working poor and disenfranchised communities as deficits and a drain on public services. What this admits to is a failure of a research agenda that incorporates the voices of community members who are engaged in social change,

who are not waiting for government policies or academic models to create positive change in their communities. Community advocates and grassroots organizations are creating collaborative and innovative programs and alliances that exist below the research radar and are not included in policy-making dialogues. Our reliance on only empirical data has brought us a deficit mentality when crafting policies that are meant to address social and economic injustice. Dynamic community-based organizations in collaboration with community members dispel the culture of poverty assessment. There are many examples of communities organizing around issues they define as priorities, as opposed to "external needs assessment surveys" which do not employ many of the community's comparative advantages, nor do they account for community cultural factors. When communities engage in change, they set the parameters with new models and new ways of thinking about and dealing with old problems.

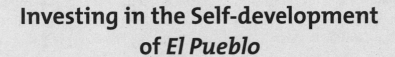

Investing in the Self-development of *El Pueblo*

La Union del Pueblo Entreo (LUPE),[101] located in San Juan, Texas (Hidalgo County), is an example of a community-based social and economic justice organization for change. Sustainability, respect for human dignity, and learning by doing are the prime pillars of the entire organizational philosophy of LUPE. Its three main programs which lay the foundation for permanent and sustainable change for community members, are:

Mano de Apoyo (Supporting Hands): responding to the immediate needs of people

Programa Escalera (Ladder of Opportunity Program): investing in the self-development of people

Juntos Adelante (Forward Together): transforming people and their communities through participation and advocacy

LUPE is the umbrella organization, but there are two affiliate or subsidiary organizations that provide additional resources that make Mano de Apoyo and Programa especially successful: Proyecto Azteca is a self-help affordable home ownership program where families build their own homes along the U.S.-Mexico border at a cost of between $13,500 and $24,500. Low-cost housing is possible when no builder, developer, or realtor are involved as middlemen. Also, Azteca Community Loan Fund offers emergency family loans, micro-enterprise loans, individual development accounts and other financial services so that predatory lenders and high-interest payday loans are less prevalent in the community.

Community members are also engaged in learning by doing through educational programs that are bundled along with the asset-building services. Community members can choose from literacy, English as a second language, GED,

(continued)

and citizenship classes; get financial and homeownership counseling; and receive information about the Earned Income Tax Credit (EITC). Finally, the leadership component is not part of the educational services provided by LUPE. Instead, wisely, LUPE defines leadership as qualities any community member can acquire or display through engaging in activities that add to community collaboration and community development. Every community has indigenous leaders who emerge as a community coalesces around its own internally defined needs and aspirations.

Too often, external advisers appear providing advice on the types of development projects that should be imported into the community, though despite good intentions they have little understanding of the aspirations or sustainability of community development programs and projects. Without community members engaged in their own self-defined and self-determined choices, sustainable community development has little chance of succeeding. The key to opening asset building opportunities for communities of color is to fully recognize that every community is unique. What works in an urban northeastern ethnic enclave or inner city will not necessarily work in a Southwestern semi-rural border region. Every successful community development program must contain flexibility and a capacity to modify elements of the program initiative in order to continually incorporate the changing dynamics of community members themselves. Word of mouth, community events, and community goals all play a crucial part in creating and promoting an evironment for change and proactive engagement. Here the key element of success is a community-created organization that becomes a resource for community members to take control of their own choices and become active members in their own organization, while engaging in community change. The improvement in economic security for families creates more resources for sustainable change in the community.

The Latino community in the United States today is diverse in two significant ways. First, Latino communities are not culturally monolithic. Spanish-speaking countries may have language in common, but institutions evolve differently, as do cultural traditions and behaviors. Although Mexican Americans are the largest Latino group (67 percent of total U.S. Latinos),[102] not all Latinos trace their roots to Mexico. Yet Latinos from the Caribbean, Central America, and South America often face the same experience in the United States: having to explain their cultural roots and attempt to educate their non-Latino U.S. friends, co-workers, and neighbors about the diversity of the Latino population in the United States.

Second, every Latino community has a range of generations with an immigrant experience and memories, either recent or in the past (some communities, such as those in Texas, New Mexico, Arizona, Colorado, Utah, California and Nevada, with roots that go back prior to the founding of the thirteen colonies). Most Latino communities are comprised of the foreign born, the native born with parents who were foreign born, and those with grandparents or ancestors who were foreign born.[103] This creates a very dynamic community, which is enriched by the diversity of the country of origin and the generational diversity that contributes to sustaining transnational ties, multilingual proficiency, and dynamic economic activity.

Latino communities have contributed to the economic growth of the United States through cultural exchange, participation in labor markets, the military, and civic life throughout the history of the nation. Latinos have also brought multilingual and cultural assets to U.S. business and diplomacy during a period of rapid globalization. These assets have yet to be fully employed and fully realized by many Latino families. The continual waves of immigration become a resource for Latino communities, and consequently, for the U.S. For example, many U.S. Latino families retain close ties with extended family in their home coun-

tries. This allows for a continual learning of cultural mannerisms and nuances by second- and third-generation U.S.-born Latinos, which are marketable assets that can then be translated into premium wages in a variety of U.S. occupations in the private and public sectors. This is a form of wealth and asset building in Latino communities that has not been identified as a benefit and resource for U.S. economic markets and institutions.

Aside from having bicultural and bilingual assets that can be leveraged to increase family and community wealth accumulation, U.S. Latinos also serve to export democratic and cooperative ideals to extended family members not residing in the U.S. This transnational exchange also serves as a form of patient capital, in the form of democratizing wealth and asset-building behaviors that ultimately benefit the United States in the long run, by creating strong allegiances and familiarity with U.S. customs and values.

Latino wealth inequality can easily be remedied through increased educational opportunities, financial market participation linked with financial literacy outreach, and access to home ownership counseling and mortgage markets. Government policy makers at local, state, and federal levels can contribute to wealth and asset building in communities of color by simply engaging in egalitarian actions that match stated policy and program goals. An important source of tax revenues can be had from incorporating Latino microbusiness activities and self-employment behaviors into mainstream markets and financial institutions. These activities are present in Latino communities but are not fully documented in local, state, or national databases. Families can benefit from establishing formal relationships with private and public sector institutions and markets. Community wealth and asset-building activities can continue to occur below the formal radar, or they can be brought into the mainstream via community-based organizations serving Latino low-income and working-poor communities, and partnering with government and financial institutions. We have the imagination, the innovative skills, and the capacity to democratize access to financial products and markets.

The real question is this: Will we continue to stipulate that there is only one middle-class model leading to the American Dream? Or are we willing to recognize that there are imaginative paths and egalitarian models that give rise to the American Dream in struggling communities of color?

Chapter 5

THE PERILS OF BEING YELLOW: ASIAN AMERICANS AS PERPETUAL FOREIGNERS

"Okage sama de."
"I am what I am because of you."
—Japanese saying

FROM ASIANS IN AMERICA TO ASIAN AMERICANS: OVERVIEW

Recently, a reporter went to China to track down information about General Tso, perhaps the Chinese name best known in the United States because General Tso's Chicken appears on almost every Chinese restaurant's menu. Most of his descendants still live in the valley where he was born in 1815, and they know all about his military service—but his chicken? How General Tso had a chicken dish named after him was a puzzle. They were flabbergasted when told that millions of Americans knew their ancestor's name in connection with a popular Chinese restaurant entrée.

Indeed, people in the United States know little about the Chinese, or about any Asians living either on the other side of the world, or living next door in these United States. The most well-known Asian American is probably Bruce Lee. Like General Tso, what is known about him is mostly a figment of U.S. imagination and marketing. In the United States, Asians—little distinction is made between the many nationalities—have always been shrouded in mystery, sometimes sinister, sometimes alluring—but always inscrutable, and always foreign.

People from countries in Asia know they "are who they are" because of the activities of their parents and grandparents, and family ties that go back generations. As with General Tso's relatives, ties to the land or region of one's birth, deep respect for ancestors, and extended families as the unit governing one's life form the basis of a person's identity. For Asian immigrants, those ties get loosened over time and distance, and older values and practices are challenged by the American way. Upon arrival, the process of trying to figure out who they are and how they fit into this very different society begins. Like other immigrants from all over the world, the Asians who come have often been among the sturdiest and most entrepreneurial, driven by the desire to better themselves, including the desire to create wealth for their families. While many did succeed along the way, and particularly today their success is much touted, their chances for success have continually been handicapped by something their ancestors would not have understood: the politics of race.

The story of race-based differences in the United States started well before the first Asian immigrants arrived from China. Asians too would get pulled into the whirlpool. Unlike Native Americans, Asians did not occupy this land before the Europeans came. Unlike Mexican Americans, Asians were not on land that was appropriated by the United States through conquest. And unlike African Americans, they were not brought here as property. They got here in the same way and for the same reasons that most Europeans did—crossing the ocean for economic or political reasons. In this land of immigrants, it would seem then that the Asian story should more closely follow that of people from European countries. People of Asian and European descent should both be insiders, in the mainstream.

Not so.

No matter how many generations an Asian family has been in the United States, no matter whether they are citizens or noncitizens, they are still considered perpetual foreigners, based on their physical appearances. Since first hitting these shores in the mid-1800s, Asians have been treated as "members of a racially subordinated group, not future citizens of America."[1] While currently they are seen as successful, they are still not considered to be "real" Americans. They are still identified by the nationality of their ancestors.

FIGURE 5-1
Home ownership rates, 2003

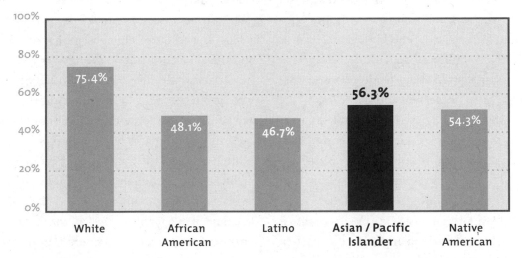

Source: U.S. Census Bureau, *Annual Statistics, 2003, Housing Vacancies and Homeownership*, Table 20.

If we were to imagine the racial economic structure as a solar system with whites in the center like the sun around which all other races revolve like planets, Asian Americans for the first one hundred years would have been in the outermost orbit; they were Pluto. All people of color were closer to each other in terms of economic status than any of them were to whites. But since 1965, Asians have moved closer to whites economically—they are now Mars—while other people of color are still far away in the outer orbits. But despite their proximate success, the social, political, and economic profile of Asians is quite different from that of whites. For example, even though the median incomes for whites and Asians are similar, Asians do not occupy the same range of professions as whites and are less likely to own homes. They are miss-

ing from the higher ranks of business and politics. Policies and practices from years past still affect their status, as does the turmoil of current world events and the shifting alliances in U.S. foreign policy.

Asians Need Not Apply

The most important exclusionary policy was already in place when the first Asians arrived in the 1840's. Only white people could become citizens. One of the first pieces of legislation passed by the newly founded United States of America, the 1790 Naturalization Law, stated that only "a free white person" could begin the naturalization process that would lead to citizenship. Over time, the 1790 law would be used to designate immigrants from one Asian country after another as nonwhite, which kept them from wealth-building opportunities offered to white immigrants only, the chosen future citizens of the United States.

Other policies specifically targeting Asians prevented them from sustained asset building in their new country. From the mid-1800s to the mid-1900s, many discriminatory state and local laws were passed; federal court decisions upheld those anti-Asian practices, such as Asian-only taxes, or laws restricting Asians from owning land.[2]

Finally, the classification of Asians as ineligible for citizenship played a part in the formulation of immigration laws that restricted the entry of Asians into the United States.[3] This stymied Asian population growth, as well as their political power and collective wealth-building potential. Asian men with families were prohibited from sending for their wives and children; other Asian men who were single were reluctant to go back to their homeland to find and return with a wife, because the law often did not allow re-entry. When families can't come in, then money flows out, sent home to support those left behind.

In spite of, or because of, the marginalization of Asians, within ethnic enclaves, there was a high degree of self-sufficiency and wealth creation, as business and service enterprises owned by Asians and serving Asian consumers sprang up. Asians were also able to carve out some niches for themselves that whites would not or could not fill, such

as Chinese laundries, or Japanese garden centers and nurseries.

It wasn't until the late 1940s and early 1950s, as a result of changed global politics and the alliances made in World War II, that most Asians who lived in the United States were given the right to become citizens, and as a result, to feel some measure of hope that they, too, could participate as equals in the United States. This transitional period also included one of the most shameful moments in U.S. history. During World War II, Japanese Americans, many of them U.S.-born citizens, were considered potential enemy agents and sent to relocation camps. Most lost their hard-won economic and social status. In spite of this setback, Asians overall were making economic and social progress. The first significant number of American-born and -educated Asians came of age in the 1960s, uniting for the first time as a conscious pan-Asian group, "Asian Americans," in time to join the Civil Rights and racial justice movements to push for full racial equality.

After 1965, with the passage of new immigration policies that finally opened the door for people from Asian countries, major demographic and economic changes occurred. Asians are a rapidly growing population today, and as an aggregated group, they have incomes and wealth that most closely approach the economic status of whites. But in spite of their successes, Asian Americans are still not equal. They still lack the social and economic security afforded whites. They do not hold economic or political power. And when past history and current attitudes and practices are examined, it remains doubtful that Asians will reach full equality with whites any time soon.

Even today, Asians are still seen as foreigners, even when they have been here for generations. As Angelo Ancheta argues in *Race, Rights, and the Asian American Experience,* "[A]nti-Asian subordination is qualitatively different from anti-black subordination. Rather than being centered on color, which divides racially between the superior and the inferior, anti-Asian subordination is centered on citizenship, which divides racially between American and the foreigner. Asian Americans are thus perceived racially as foreign outsiders who lack the rights of true 'Americans'." They remain vulnerable to sudden changes in attitudes and practices due to changing U.S. relations with the countries of their ancestors' origins. Look how easy it was in 1999 for the government to assume that Wen Ho Lee, the U.S. physicist working at Los Alamos Nuclear Laboratories, was a spy for China, and to subject him to months of solitary confinement; the suspicions turned out to be unjustified. After the September 11, 2001, attack on the World Trade Center, South Asians were beaten and murdered because they looked to some like Arabs (also stereotyped as inevitably foreign), and deportations have increased once again.

As Asian Americans have gained ground, new feelings of resentment have grown toward them from other peoples of color, who have been in the United States longer but who still lag behind. Caught in the middle, Asian Americans must be careful not to become pawns for those who favor continued white economic supremacy.

WHO ARE "ASIANS" ANYWAY?

Defining Asian America

In creating an Asian/yellow race out of people of many hues from various parts of the world, U.S. history has obscured the enormous differences among Asian nationalities. Each group has arrived at different times, with different cultures, different relationships between their home countries' governments and the U.S. government, and under different rules that determined what economic class of immigrants came from that country. Recent immigrants from Southeast Asia have come under refugee policies, and many are of peasant background, while South Asians have come as recruits for high-tech jobs and many are Western-educated professionals. In the 2000 census, "Asian" was defined as "people having origins in any of the original peoples of the Far East, Southeast Asia, or the Indian subcontinent. For example, Cambodia, China, India, Japan, Korea, Malaysia, Pakistan, the Philippine Islands, Thailand, and Vietnam."[4] The "for example" covers a lot of territory!

Reliable data on Asian Americans is impossible to come by, for a variety of reasons. First, many people who are here without documents do not want the government to know they exist, so people from some Asian countries are undercounted. Peter Kwong in his 1997 book, *Forbidden Workers: Illegal Chinese Workers and American Labor,* tells what happened after the *Golden Venture* ran aground in 1993 with 293 undocumented Chinese aboard. The subsequent uproar led to tougher immigration policies, including summary deportation of people arriving without papers.[5] These restrictive measures did little to stem the tide; it just forced many immigrants underground.

The census has always been a political tool, not simply an account of who's here. The first census of 1790 was instituted in order to determine each state's number of representatives in Congress, using a method that would maintain the balance of power between North and South. African slaves were counted as three-fifths of a person, not in order to give them three-fifths of the white man's rights, but to bolster the number of representatives that slave states could send to Congress. Chinese were first counted in 1860, and Japanese in 1870. In the early years, race was decided by the cen-

sus taker, eyeballing the person who answered the door; one's race was determined by the census taker's visual assumptions. It would be another one hundred years until other specific Asian nationalities were included: in 1970, the same year that "Hispanic origin" was added. In the years between, Asians were simply an "other." On the positive side, since the 1960s, census data have also been used to apportion federal funding to alleviate poverty. In 2000, many community activists encouraged Asians, whether documented or not, to fill out the census, in order to draw attention to needs that would otherwise remain hidden.

Second, as census information began to be filled out by household members themselves rather than census takers, people had to decide on their own identity, which is a very subjective matter. In one mixed race Asian/Anglo family for example, one sibling might say white, while another might check the Asian box. Many people of mixed race, particularly in the younger generation who have not experienced the worst aspects of segregation, want to acknowledge all their races and ethnicities, which has resulted in a system where people can select more than one racial category[6]—the Tiger Woods phenomenon. Today, many identify as mixed race.

Third, people themselves began to use the census as a political tool. In 1990 there was an "Asian or Pacific Islander" category added. Native Hawaiians and Pacific Islanders presented arguments that separate categories were needed to call attention to their particular economic conditions, so their specific issues would not get swamped by larger Asian groups.[7] They got a separate box in the 2000 census. While Native Hawaiians were only 3 percent of the larger category in 1990, they are 60 percent of the new category.

For this chapter, because of the changing racial and ethnic categories in the censuses taken over many decades, it is difficult to use data that is completely comparable. We will include Native Hawaiians and Pacific Islanders in some instances where more detailed data is not available; but in general, we will try to stick with Asian-only information, to honor the desire for separation. The story of Native Hawaiians, given that these are peoples indigenous to a country whose queen was illegally overthrown by U.S. businessmen and taken as a U.S. possession, is more similar to that of Native peoples than to Asians, who were immigrants coming to an already existing political entity, the United States.

Marking Posts in Asian American History

Asian American history has different key dates and historical milestones than other races. While each racial group's stories affected the others, they did not move in parallel. There are three major periods in the Asian wealth story.

The first period lasted nearly a century, from the California Gold Rush to the eve of World War II. People came in waves from different Asian countries based on the desire of U.S. agribusiness for Asian labor and on the economic and political conditions in their countries of origin. Each successive wave of immigrants worked hard to gain a toehold in the U.S. economy—only to lose it and slip backward, one after the other. This period was marked by exclusion from the American Dream, through denial of citizenship, discriminatory laws affecting income and wealth building, and through immigration policy.

World War II marked the threshold of a new era in Asian/white relations, when Asians became accepted as permanent members of the United States through federal policies. Between 1941 and 1965, substantial progress was made. While this was a time of considerable financial gain for many Asian Americans, it was also a period of considerable loss for others, notably Japanese Americans. Moreover, the number of Asians in the United States was still kept so small through immigration quotas that in many parts of the country, to see an Asian was like spotting a being from outer space.

The third period began in 1965, which continues to the present. Race-neutral immigration laws were enacted that opened the door to a new wave of migration from Asia. Increased Asian immigration was also due to more liberal refugee policies in combination with the large number of people coming into the United States as a result of the Vietnam War. More recently, well-educated Asians have been recruited by U.S. hospitals and businesses. The massive influx of Asians from diverse countries and the class nature of that migration brings us to the present day.

FIRST PERIOD, 1850–1941: A "CHINAMAN'S CHANCE"

The Creation of the Yellow "Race"

The most important federal policy that would exclude Asians from wealth-building opportunities was the 1790 Naturalization Law, which stated that only "a free white person" was eligible for citizenship. Every country determines who can be citizens, but the United States, a new country of immigrants from many places, invented "white" as a unique criterion. Over time, immigrants from many countries who might have considered themselves English, or Dutch, or Norwegian learned that they were none of the above. They were white, and whiteness brought legal and economic benefits.

The criteria for citizenship are set by choice. Contrast the 1790 law to that of Haiti, which gained independence in 1804. Both people of French and African ancestry lived in Haiti, since it was a French colony with an economy based on slavery; but in their constitution, it was declared that all citizens were legally black, thus extending equal rights to all who lived there, regardless of color.

Even without the Internet, word of the streets paved with gold in the United States spread around the world, catching the imagination of the adventuresome from every part of the globe. The Gold Rush brought both a massive wave of Irish immigrants and the first wave of immigrants from Asia: the Chinese. One could have said of the Irish the same thing that Ronald Takaki, in *Strangers from Another Shore: A History of Asian Americans,* said of the Chinese: "Though they were driven by 'necessity,' they were also stirred by 'extravagance.'"[8] While 325 arrived in 1849, by 1870, there were 63,000 Chinese in the U.S., and 77 percent were living in California.[9]

It was not a foregone conclusion that the Irish were white. Many of the whites who were of British origin weren't sure about the Irish; anti-Irish cartoons showed them as resembling orangutans, red-headed monkeys. Nor was it a foregone conclusion that Asians were *not* white. What exactly did it mean to be "white"? There were "scientific" racial categories, and most Asians were put in the Mongolian race box, not the Caucasian. But could Mongolians be white, since white is not a race? Wanting the benefits of the law and of citizenship, Asians used the courts to argue that they were worthy enough to qualify. Over time, every different nationality of Asian that came to the United States in this first century filed suits claiming that they had a *right* to be white. But over several decades and many lawsuits, the courts eventually decided that no Asian group would gain entry to the "whites only" club—a club providing material benefits for its members.

The Chinese were the first to fail the whiteness test. In 1853, George Hall was convicted of murdering Ling Sing, a Chinese man, on the strength of one Caucasian and three Chinese witnesses. In *People v. Hall,* the decision was overturned on appeal by the California Supreme Court in 1854, and Hall was released on the grounds that Chinese witnesses should not have been allowed to testify against a white man. California law stated that "no black or mulatto person, or Indian, shall be permitted to give evidence in favor of, or against, any white person." The chief justice ruled that the witnesses were "Indian" (Native American) since the hypothesis of the day was that Indians were descendants of Asiatic people who had migrated across the Bering Strait thousands of years earlier. The Chinese were, therefore, ineligible to testify against whites. [10]

Next, the Japanese tried their luck. In 1914, Takao Ozawa applied for and was denied the right to become a U.S. citizen because of his race. Ozawa had lived most his life in California, attended school at the University of California, and had moved to Hawaii. He was working for an American company, and he was raising a family. After his request was denied, he took his case to court. The court upheld the naturalization denial, ruling that he was ineligible because he was not white. He appealed the decision, and it eventually reached the U.S. Supreme Court in 1922. Ozawa told the court that he was honest, of good character, had no connection to Japan or Japanese organizations, and that he felt like a "true American." The High Court rejected his appeal because he was "not Caucasian." [11]

This argument was noted by Asians from India, who thought this decision gave them a good shot. Several lower federal courts in 1910 and 1913 held that Asian Indians were Caucasians and therefore eligible for citizenship; between 1907 and 1923, about seventy Asian Indians were granted citizenship. The 1922 Ozawa ruling that the Japanese were not Caucasians and therefore not white seemed to reinforce their argument, that since they were Caucasian they were also white and could, therefore, be naturalized.

When Bhaghat Singh Thind was denied naturalization, he took his case to the Supreme Court in 1923. This time, he lost. In a reversal, the Court ruled that Asian Indians were Caucasian—but not white! A "white person," they clarified, "was not to be defined simply on the basis of race [as the Ozawa case suggested], but rather in accord with popular definition." "You don't look white to me," in the eyes of someone already in the white club, became a legal standard! Whiteness became a social race, that could confer legal status, supplanting the old categories of Mongolian, Caucasian, and so on that had been used in earlier legal cases. Over the course of seventy-five years, Asians played a key role in defining race in the United States. With the Thind decision, they took their place in the U.S. racial hierarchy: like other peoples of color, at the ready for economic exploitation or exclusion, whichever suited the needs of U.S. capitalism at any particular moment of history.

Being protected by the rule of law is of enormous importance. After the decision that Chinese could not testify against whites in court, the consequences were chilling; Chinese could not protect themselves from theft, assault, or even murder—and the lesson was not lost on whites. In the late 1850s, for example, many Chinese miners were driven from the mines, beaten, robbed, and killed, and the perpetrators had virtual immunity. It is impossible to know how much wealth in the form of savings or mine holdings were lost.

Compare this with the Armenian experience. Due to genocide in their homelands in western Asia, fifty thousand Armenians came

to the United States. In 1909, they were declared "Asiatics," and were denied the right to become naturalized citizens. But the U.S. Circuit Court of Appeals reversed that ruling and declared that Armenians were Caucasians and white. Thus, when California prohibited noncitizens from owning land, Armenians were not restricted, and of eighteen thousand Armenians in California in 1930, some became wealthy farmers.[12]

The Civil War does not loom large in Asian American history. However, because race was so central to that conflict, it was bound to affect Asians as well. The first sentence of the Fourteenth Amendment, passed in 1868, explicitly grants citizenship to all persons born in the United States; this would benefit the children of Asian immigrants. It also granted legal due process and protections to all persons, not just to citizens or to whites, so that Asians could finally seek justice in the case of theft or murder.

On the other hand, in 1870, when citizenship rights were extended to include those of "African nativity and people of African decent," [13] Asian immigrants were still excluded under the 1790 Naturalization Acts. An amendment to the 1870 law to include Chinese was rejected.[14] Denial of naturalization rights remained in effect until World War II.

WHITES "SUPERSIZE" THEIR PROFITS

In 1865, the first Chinese were hired for the construction of the Central Pacific Railroad. By 1867, twelve thousand Chinese were employed by the railroad, representing 90 percent of the total workforce. The savings derived from the underpaid employment of Chinese were enormous. If the company had used white workers, it would have had to pay them for board and lodging. By using Chinese workers, railroad owners increased their profit by one-third. As Teresa Amott and Julie Matthaei point out in their book, *Race, Gender, and Work*, "White employers achieved higher profits by using Asians as low-wage replacements for white workers and as strikebreakers."[15] The Chinese workers were even forced to work in the winter of 1866, sometimes under snowdrifts "over sixty feet in height . . . with shafts to give them air and lanterns to light the way."[16]

In the 1870s, the Chinese supplied much of the cheap labor for California's agricultural industry, an industry that still relies today on the labor of noncitizens whose underpayment falls outside the concern of the mainstream. Chinese workers also represented 46 percent of the labor force in San Francisco's four key industries: boots and shoes, woolens, cigars and tobacco, and sewing, earning less than white workers doing the same jobs.[17] By 1870, San Francisco was the ninth leading industrial city in the United States, a leadership position based on squeezing profits out of underpaid Chinese labor.

The Chinese provided much of the labor for public works projects, beginning in California and then other parts of the West Coast. Thousands worked to reclaim much of the land that is now San Francisco, and the California delta of the Sacramento and San Joaquin rivers was made agriculturally productive by levees, drainage ditches, and irrigation systems that were built by underpaid Chinese labor.[18] But the Chinese were not allowed to purchase any of the land or to live outside of Chinatowns.

Taxation Without Representation

Tax policy has always been a tool for the distribution of resources. The Chinese were targeted for special taxes, fees, and regulations in the early 1850s, including a tax simply for working! Sometimes these laws didn't specifically state that only the Chinese would pay this tax or that fee: allegedly race-neutral or universal policies are nothing new, but have been used similarly throughout U.S. history to target a non-white group.

The first major tax aimed at the Chinese was California's Foreign Miner's Tax, which required a monthly payment of $3 by every foreign miner. Since most of the foreigners who were mining were Chinese, this was essentially a Chinese tax. Other states followed suit. While the original purpose was to drive the Chinese out of the mining industry, the Chinese miners who remained occupied a lower financial tier than white miners. The tax turned out to be a tremendous source of revenue for the state of California. The law remained in effect until it was voided by the Civil Rights Act of 1870. By the time of its repeal, California had collected $5 million from the Chinese, and the Foreign Miner's Tax accounted for over 25 percent of California's annual budget. Not only did the tax come out of Chinese pockets, but the government jobs and services that the revenue produced went almost entirely to whites. This was a direct transfer of resources from Chinese to the white community—taxation without representation or benefit.[19]

Love and Marriage Made Illegal for Chinese

A common pattern of immigration to the U.S. from anywhere in the world was for working-age men to emigrate first. If things went well, the men would plan to either go home with their earnings or, for those men with families, they would send for their families to join them in the United States.

But the Chinese were prohibited from following this custom. Unlike any other group, including other Asians, the Chinese were denied family life. The specific exclusion of Chinese women by law curtailed most of their dreams for asset building. In 1875, Congress passed the Page Law, supposedly to exclude prostitutes, but it was enforced so vigorously that it effectively stopped Chinese women from trying to enter.[20] In 1870, five years before the Page Law was enacted, the ratio of men to women was fourteen to one.[21] Fifteen years after the Page Law was passed, in 1890, the sex ratio stood at an appalling twenty-seven to one.[22]

But maybe a Chinese man would fall in love with a white woman? Not allowed! In 1880, California was the first state to pass an antimiscegenation law directed at the Chinese. The law prohibited marriages between whites and Negroes, mulattoes, or Mongolians.[23] Many antimiscegenation laws remained in effect until the Supreme Court struck them down in 1967.[24]

The attempts at discouraging Chinese family formation and thus driving the Chinese out were successful. Most Chinese men never had wives or children in the United States. Between 1850 and 1882, 330,000 Chinese entered the United States, but 150,000 (47 percent) eventually returned to China.[25] The exclusion of women came at a critical time for the Chinese, and it "truncated the natural development of the community." Instead of building assets in the United States like white immigrants, the men who did remain (including many who could not afford the passage home) would send money back to China for the support of their immediate or extended families there; most were never able to establish a financial or familial stake in the United States.[26] Without enough women and with continued economic exploitation, the Chinese community had been dealt a severe blow, but the final stroke was yet to come.

A Nation of Immigrants Rejects Asians

Immigrant bashing is often stirred up in times of economic downturns. In the late 1870s and early 1880s, white fears of an "industrial army of Asiatic laborers"[27] swept the country. Thirty years of economic oppression, physical brutality, and antimiscegenation laws aimed at the Chinese were, apparently, not enough to calm these fears. White people lynched and murdered Chinese people,[28] rioted and burned down Chinatowns, and the authorities looked the other way. In an economic crisis,[29] with high unemployment and rising prices, the Chinese made handy scapegoats—even though they comprised

Ad for washing machine, 1886, four years after Chinese Exclusion Act *(Library of Congress)*

only 0.002 percent of the population. This racist sentiment followed the Civil War: Union victory did not mean that whites were imbued with the spirit of antiracism. On the contrary, whites did not want another non-white race to become a problem; denying entry to Asians was a preventive measure.

Congress responded to the hysteria with

THE COLOR OF WEALTH

the first and only immigration act to specifically target one group for complete exclusion. The Chinese Exclusion Act of 1882 gave the Chinese the distinction of being the only nationality to be deemed unworthy of entry, prohibiting Chinese laborers from coming to the United States for ten years; these exclusionary policies were made permanent in 1902.[30] The Chinese were the first illegal aliens. Like undocumented immigrants in later years, the Chinese found ingenious ways to get in—such as crossing the southern border dressed as Mexicans![31] The exclusion policy stayed in place until 1943.

As with the decisions about whiteness, the exclusion of other Asian nationalities would follow. Chinese exclusion led capitalists in agriculture to look for another source of cheap Asian labor. Particularly in Hawaii, Japanese workers were recruited. When they began to move to California in large numbers, white disapproval rose. The Japanese became the next excluded group, under the Immigration Act of 1924.[32]

The 1924 legislation, as finally enacted in 1929, was also significant because it marked the beginning of a "national-origins-based quota system."[33] It provided numerical limits for the number of people who could enter each year from various countries. This new system lasted, for the most part, until 1965.[34]

Next, it became the turn of Asian Indians, who also were a source of agricultural labor. In 1917, Congress created an Asiatic "barred zone" for restricted immigration.[35] The zone included those areas where the people were generally of a darker complexion, and where there was very little Christian influence. Besides India, the barred zone included such present-day countries as Indonesia and New Guinea to the south, Vietnam to the east, Mongolia and Kazakhstan to the north, and Turkmenistan and Pakistan to the west.

Ironically, because there was a constant need for cheap labor, when one Asian group was excluded, another was recruited, creating a revolving Asian door in and out of the United States.

The Filipinos' experience added a twist. The Philippine Islands became a U.S. possession in 1898, when the United States defeated Spain in the Spanish-American War. The status of Filipinos, who started arriving after the turn of the century, was different from other Asians; they were "American nationals," not foreigners or aliens. They were free to enter, but they still could not become citizens. The Filipinos were exempt from restrictive immigration laws, so they filled the demand for farm labor created by excluding the Chinese, Japanese, Koreans, and Asian Indians.[36]

Filipinos soon found themselves facing similar kinds of discrimination to what other Asian groups had faced, in spite of their nonforeigner status, their strong Catholic traditions, and the fact that most could speak English, having been taught by American teachers in the Philippines.[37] Since Filipinos were neither white nor of African nativity or descent, they were also

Working Twice as Hard to Be Equal
by Meizhu Lui

"You have to work twice as hard to be equal," my parents would say to me, when I complained that my white friends didn't have to stay home and do homework for the long hours that I did.

My father arrived in the United States in 1920, when he was about twelve, traveling with his father, uncle, and male cousins. He settled into the bachelor society of Seattle that was typical of Chinatowns. His father and grandfather also had been "sojourners," men who lived most of their lives in the United States, returning home to China only for brief visits every seven years if they could afford it. Four generations of men in my family lived and worked in the United States before a woman entered the picture.

My father was put into a third-grade classroom, but, knowing no English, of course he had no clue what was going on. The Chinese were so marginalized that when he died at age 95, after nearly eight decades in the United States, he still spoke with a strong Toisanese accent.

But my father was one of the more fortunate Chinese. He studied English in a YMCA program and soon caught up in school. An uncle had been able to open a store catering to other Chinese, and my grandfather worked there, too. Public universities like the University of Washington and the University of Michigan were affordable, and tolerance increased in the thirties and forties. He majored in chemistry and worked twice as hard as others. His diligence caught the eye of his professors, and he was recruited to do research work on a government contract on the eve of World War II. He almost returned to China to help in the rebuilding of that country at the end of the war—but the head of the Biochemistry Department offered him a permanent job, and he stayed.

My mother came on a special student visa, which was very unusual for women in those days—but very lucky for my dad! The Exclusion Acts were ended, and in the mid-1940s, I became one of the first children to be born into a Chinese family in the United States. In 1952, my parents finally decided that they would make a commitment to this country, and became citizens. (continued)

The strategy of his generation was to work hard and to show whites that Chinese can make contributions as professionals. Working in the same department from 1942 to 1976, he was able to earn a decent salary, buy a house, and join a 401(k) that provided for a comfortable retirement. My father was a very mild-mannered and peaceful man; I rarely heard him even raise his voice. But I do remember that he felt hurt at seeing whites get promoted faster, and he felt that as the only person of color on the staff, he "could not raise his head." He credited the Civil Rights Movement for improving the status of Asians as well as African Americans. In the seventies, after twenty years of citizenship and fifty years of residency, he finally felt entitled to equal rights and equal treatment.

While his story is one of success, it is still true that he worked twice as hard as his white counterparts and still was not economically equal.

subject to the restrictive laws that were applied to those ineligible for citizenship. Many Filipinos, for example, were denied land-ownership opportunities because of the alien land laws, even though they were not aliens, but nationals from a U.S. colony.[38]

The 1930s Depression heightened racial animosity toward Filipino workers, helping to lead to the passage of the Tydings-McDuffie Act in 1934.[39] The Act promised the Philippines commonwealth status and independence in 1946. While that sounds magnanimous, the main purpose of the law was to immediately cut off Filipino immigration. The Tydings-McDuffie Act divested Filipinos of their status and privileges as foreign nationals; their legal status changed to alien. The Filipinos too got caught in that revolving door of Asians.

Thousands of hungry and poor Filipinos were cut off or denied New Deal relief benefits during the Great Depression.[40] White immigrants faced tough times during the Depression as well, but they were never denied relief benefits and job opportunities because of race.

This Land Is My Land; This Land Is Not Your Land

Landownership is one of the main bases for wealth accumulation. The first restrictions on landownership for Asians occurred as early as 1857, when the Chinese were barred by law from exercising mining claims, in several western states. All these laws culminated in the 1913 federal Alien Land Law.

The Chinese population had dwindled after 1882, but the Japanese population was rising. Unlike the Chinese, Japanese men were allowed wives and families, because the Japanese government was stronger and able to negotiate on behalf of its emigrants. As the Japanese began to think of the United States as their permanent home, they tried to accumulate enough wealth to buy land.[41] But in 1907, Californians began to agitate for a bill to deny landownership to those not eligible for citizenship. The 1913 Alien Land Law restricted noncitizens from owning land and from leasing land for more than three years at a time.[42] The overwhelming support it engendered led to similar laws in Washington, Arizona, Oregon, Idaho, Nebraska, Texas, Kansas, Louisiana, Montana, New Mexico, Minnesota, and Missouri.[43]

To get around the law, many Japanese bought land under a corporation name or under the names of their children, born in the United States after the Fourteenth Amendment, who were citizens by birth. As a result, between 1913 and 1920 Japanese landownership in California experienced strong growth, from 26,707 to 74,769 acres. In response, a law was passed in 1920 stating that aliens ineligible for citizenship could not lease or own land in the names of minors. Additionally, they could not own stock in any corporation owning real property. Three years later, this bill was amended to make it illegal to "acquire, possess, use, enjoy, cultivate, occupy, and transfer real property," which closed off all access to leasing land as well. This led to a drop in landownership by Japanese from 74,769 to 41,898 acres and leased acres from 192,150 to 76,397.[44] Every mountain the Japanese tried to descend, they were cut off at the pass.

A 1925 Kansas law prohibited Asian ownership of land, and it was amended in 1933 to prohibit Asian inheritance of land. Since inheritance is the major method of passing wealth on from generation to generation, Kansans covered all the bases to ensure property rights for whites only. Kansas finally repealed this law in 2002, but Florida and New Mexico still have state constitutions that ban Asians from owning or inheriting property.[45]

Making Lemonade from Lemons: Ethnic Economies

Due to the often violent antagonism of whites to Asian workers, and due to their forced segregation into ethnic enclaves, Asians had no choice but to resort to self-employment.[46] Laundry work was one of the few opportunities open to the Chinese. Unlike a retail or restaurant business, a laundry could be opened with a small capital outlay, and the Chinese laundryman did not have to speak much English to run his business. Besides, both cooking and washing were jobs that were considered "women's

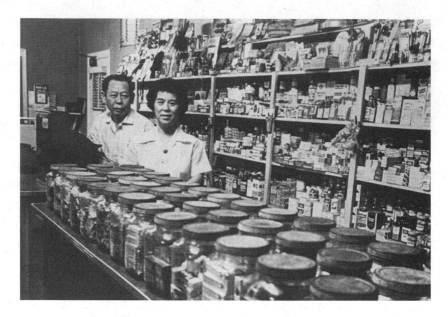

Store owned by Chinese American family, the Huie's, in Little Rock, Arkansas, in the 1930s
(Crystal K.D. Huie)

work." For white men to open such businesses themselves would be demeaning. (Even today, certain low-wage, low-status jobs are filled largely by men of color and women, such as food-service work in restaurants, cleaning offices, or nurse's aides. White men in such jobs are rare.)

But even for these businesses that no whites would want to have, special ordinances were passed to prevent Asians from accumulating wealth. The laundry ordinance passed in San Francisco in 1873 required each laundry employing one horse-drawn wagon to pay a $2 fee each quarter of the year; those with two wagons were required to pay a $4 per quarter fee; and those with no wagon had to pay a $15 per quarter fee. The ordinance was obviously aimed at the Chinese, as they were the only laundry washers to pick up and deliver by foot. San Francisco also banned the use of poles for

peddling vegetables, an ancient Chinese method. In 1880, San Francisco passed the Anti-Ironing Ordinance aimed at shutting down Chinese nighttime laundries.[47] In spite of all these barriers, by dint of hard work and long hours, the Chinese were still able to save and accumulate assets.

They started unique businesses within the community, such as helping their illiterate compatriots write and send letters home. While some businesses met legal needs, others helped those coming in illegally find a way to get in. In 1916, for example, Lee U Ong, a shopkeeper who could sell only Asian imports because the law prevented him from competing with white shopkeepers, made most of his money in buying, selling, and concocting false identities for illegal Chinese immigrants. (When birth records were destroyed in the 1906 San Francisco fire, Chinese could claim that they were born in the United States, the sons of those already here.) Whites were also involved in this "paper son" industry; Lee had people on the inside, at the Angell Island immigrant detention center in San Francisco, on his payroll.[48] Within the Chinese enclave, successful business people owned rooming houses, restaurants, and markets.

The Japanese were even more successful than the Chinese. The Japanese banded together and supported each other's small business and agricultural ventures, and created their own economic zones. As Ronald Takaki describes it, "The formation of the Japanese urban economy was sudden and extensive. Between 1900 and 1909 the number of Japanese businesses jumped from 90 to 545 in San Francisco and from 56 to 473 in Los Angeles. By 1910, a sizeable ethnic economy existed to serve the Japanese community. There were 3,000 establishments and 68,250 Japanese in the western states—a ratio of one business per twenty-two persons."[49]

Asian Exclusion and Asian Wealth

The 1880–1920 period is known as the "Great Migration," when about twenty-seven million arriving immigrants passed through Ellis Island, New York.[50] It was not only a great migration, but a great white migration. The number of Asian people in the continental United States only increased

from 105,000 in 1880 to 195,000 in 1920.[51] Had immigration laws allowed Asians to enter in numbers similar to whites, the demographics and economic data for Asians compared to whites would be far different today. As a group, they would have controlled much more aggregate wealth and very likely would have been better represented in Congress and state and local governments.

Not being seen as white and lacking a substantial population base, Asians could not gain the political power to change many of the unjust laws. Sucheng Chan, in *Asian Americans: An Interpretive History,* writes: "Unlike their European counterparts, who could participate in the electoral process after they acquired citizenship, Asian immigrants were unable to influence politicians to address their needs. Asians, who could not cast individual votes nor act as a voting bloc, had no political voice whatsoever."[52] It would take the much larger African American community to produce fundamental civil rights reforms decades later.

The impact of legal restrictions on Asian wealth creation on the U.S. mainland is particularly clear when you contrast the Chinese in California with those who were originally conscripted labor in Hawaii in the 1860s. Many of these Chinese laborers married Hawaiian women or left the plantations to start businesses. At the time, Hawaii was still ruled by a Hawaiian monarchy; it was not conquered and annexed to the United States until 1893, and there were no

Hawaiian laws restricting Chinese from owning land or businesses. They were so successful that today, while only 5 percent of Hawaii's population now identifies as Chinese, this is the most affluent racial group. Unfortunately, the Chinese have jumped ahead of the native population, thereby creating another kind of unfair wealth disparity.

Many Japanese in Hawaii also moved from plantation work to work in cities, and bought land. By 1930, 49 percent of retail stores in Hawaii were Japanese-owned. The Japanese owned temples, shrines, language schools, and banks. With the addition of a Japanese hospital, the number of doctors, dentists, and attorneys rose as well—the creation of a Japanese middle class was well on its way. Assets rose from $2,333,333 in 1910 to $28 million in 1930.[53] With whites in a minority, those assets were not lost during World War II as they were for Japanese on the mainland. Today, Asian Americans occupy most political offices in Hawaii, since economic and political power go hand in hand.

Lesson of Exclusion: Educate the Kids

The hope of the future for the waves of Asian immigrants who were excluded from citizenship was placed on their U.S. born children. For example, the passage of the 1924 Japanese exclusion law was a turning point in the lives of the Issei (immigrant, or first) generation: they no longer had a future in their adopted land except through their children. So the Issei were willing to sacrifice much, even necessities, to ensure that their children could go to college and get good jobs.[54] It helped that Asian cultures, under the influence of Confucius, gave the highest social standing to scholars, not to businessmen, as did those in the United States.

The Asian immigrants' response to oppression was usually to work hard, to strongly resist when they could, and to insist their children get good educations. By the 1930s, some Asians were able to attend public universities such as City College in New York, San Francisco State, or the University of California. But because of employment discrimination, they still ended up working in their parents' laundries or restaurants.[55] It would take a change in foreign policy toward Asia and the labor shortages of World War II for the education strategy to bear fruit.

But given the history of government policies regarding its Asian residents, it is no wonder that through the 1940s, the common phrase "a Chinaman's chance" meant that your odds for success were only slightly better than zero. During the course of the first period, Asians constantly fought for equality and greater opportunity. As early as 1876, the Chinese Six Companies wrote to President Grant, refuting charges made against the Chinese for being un-American.

The Chinese were accused of having no wives, and of not purchasing real estate—the very rights denied to them. The Six Companies's arguments could well be used today to advocate for wealth-building policies for those who are still left out:

> It is charged that the Chinese are no benefit to this country. Are the railroads built by Chinese labor no benefit to the country? Are the manufacturing establishments, largely worked by Chinese, no benefit to this country? Do not the results of the daily toil of a hundred thousand men increase the riches of this country? Is it no benefit to this country that the Chinese annually pay over $2,000,000 duties at the Custom House of San Francisco? Is not the $200,000 annual poll tax paid by the Chinese any benefit? And are not the hundreds of thousands of dollars of taxes on personal property, and the foreign miners tax, annually paid to the revenues of this country, any benefit?[56]

THE SECOND PERIOD, 1941–1965: DOING THE ONE-STEP TWO-STEP

Shifting Fortunes

World War II was a watershed event in terms of the status of Asians in the United States and their rights to build assets. In the previous hundred years, Asians had largely been denied citizenship, and for those who did not go home, their wealth-building opportunities were mostly in their own communities, out of the sight of whites, or in the loopholes of policies, such as putting property in the names of their citizen children. Wealth building was a scramble to find a new loophole whenever an old one was closed.

Throughout that first period, Asian countries were relatively weak and largely irrelevant in terms of U.S. foreign policy. World War II changed all that. Japan was a powerful enemy, as the bombing of Pearl Harbor, the event that brought the United States into the war, made clear. China was an important ally, since it was at war with Japan even before the outbreak of World War II. Korea, India, and the Philippines were also on the U.S. side. These new alliances and the need for a unified populace in time of war with both citizens and non-citizens needed to support the war effort, led to some internal policy changes.

At the war's end, the good news was that because many of those relationships with Asia were now positive ones, and because of the exemplary sacrifice and bravery of the all-Japanese Regimental Combat Team and the 100th Infantry Battalion, Asians gained greater acceptance and economic opportunity.

However, during this second period, both Japanese and Chinese Americans would find their wealth-building opportunities hampered by policies and practices arising from the U.S. government's foreign policies. Rather than being treated as American citizens, which many of them now became, they were treated as foreigners loyal to the countries of their ancestors. On the dance floor of race relations, Asians were doing the one-step two-step, stepping forward, stepping back.

World War II: U.S./Asian Alliances Abroad and Within

Because the United States and China, Korea, and the Philippines were on the same side, attitudes toward people of these nationalities changed. In 1943, the Magnuson Act repealed the Chinese Exclusion Act of 1882, making Chinese immigrants finally eligible for citizenship. This was followed by the passage of the War Brides Act in 1945, which allowed approximately six thousand Chinese women to enter the United States as brides of men in the armed forces; and then in 1946, an amendment to this act put Chinese wives and children of U.S. citizens on a non-quota basis.[57] After the 1940s, the percentages of men and women of Asian descent became more equalized, and family life—taken for granted by most everyone in the world—became normal for Asian Americans at long last.

When the Philippines gained independence in 1946, Filipinos in the United States were also allowed to become naturalized citizens. From 1946 to 1965, thirty-three thousand Filipino immigrants entered the United States and nearly half came as wives of American servicemen.[58] Asian Indians were also finally given naturalization rights in 1946.

The war brought the nation together, as people of all races were needed both in industry and the military. In 1941, President Franklin Roosevelt outlawed racial discrimination in the defense industry, and created the Fair Employment Practices Commission.[59] The Chinese suddenly found the doors for employment open to them, especially in the defense industries, where labor shortages were acute. Everyone in the Chinese community, including women and children, participated in the war effort. Young Chinese men were eager to go to war (citizens and noncitizens); 22 percent (13,499) of all Chinese adult males were drafted.[60] Koreans and Filipinos similarly found new opportunities, and also enthusiastically joined the war effort.

With greater acceptance, previously closed doors for wealth creation opened up. The Alien Land Laws were finally repealed by the Supreme Court in 1948. The law was "nothing more than outright racial discrimination," the Court declared. In spite of the changes in public sentiment and the law, many Asians would still find it difficult to buy homes outside of their segregated communities. The National Housing Act of 1934 laid the groundwork for continued segregation; the Federal Housing Authority's underwriting manual listed race as the most important criterion for granting housing loans: "If a neighborhood is to retain stability, it is necessary that properties shall be continued to be occupied by the same social and racial classes."[61]

As Asians started feeling more welcome, more decided to make the United States their permanent home. The repeal of all the exclusion acts culminated in the Immigration and Naturalization Act, or McCarran-Walter Act, of 1952. The passage of this act was a sign of the change in attitude toward Asians on the part of the government. It finally expanded the 1790 Naturalization Act rights to include Asians, and gave immigration preferences to family members of those already in the United States. While the quota system it put in place followed the national origins restrictions of the 1924 legislation with continued token quotas for Chinese (only 105 per year),[62] it did drastically increase the numbers of Asians who successfully filed for U.S. citizenship.

With greater acceptance, Asians pursued the American Dream with a vengeance. Many of those who had served in the military took advantage of the GI Bill. As jobs opened up, the traditional thriftiness of Asians led to savings for home ownership. The educational strategy for the second generation began to pay off, as professional jobs with good pay and good benefits opened up. For the first time, Asians joined the economic mainstream.

Japanese: The Enemy Within?

But there was a major setback during the war. In one of the ugliest and most racist government actions in U.S. history, Japanese Americans—even those who were U.S. born and citizens, even those who had never set foot in Japan—were incarcerated as suspected enemies of the United States.

On the eve of World War II, 63 percent of Japanese were Nisei (second-generation, American-born Japanese).[63] What was life like for these U.S. citizens before the war? While they attended public schools and had American names, they encountered housing discrimination. While they were above the national average in education, they were denied jobs. In 1940, Los Angeles, for example, had no Japanese firemen, policemen, mailmen, or public school teachers. While this was not the government's policy, exclusionary hiring practices were the unofficial norm.[64]

The Japanese attack on Pearl Harbor made those circumstances seem like a bed of roses. The United States immediately made policies that took away the jobs, the homes, the businesses, and the wealth of Japanese Americans. The years of hard work, the money saved, and the land assets acquired, through whatever legal loopholes there were in the maze of barriers put in front of them, were simply gone. In 1941, the assets of the Issei, first-generation Japanese, were frozen. In 1942, the U.S. Justice Department began mass investigations, and raids, and seized property. Throughout the 1940s, the California Justice Department actively enforced the Alien Land Law and confiscated lands declared illegally held by the Japanese. By the end of 1946, it had made claims against more than sixty Japanese landowners.[65]

After Pearl Harbor, hysteria began to build; the Japanese were considered by the public to be a threat to national security. The Japanese business sector at that time was worth approximately $140 million in California. Executive Order 9066 stated that the military could expel anyone from their home. Both home ownership and business ownership suffered dramatically as a result of these measures.

In an unprecedented denial of civil rights, it was decided that as a preemptive measure, all Japanese would be removed from California's coastal zone. In the most drastic measure ever enacted against potential enemy sympathizers, a War Relocation Authority was set up to do the job. The Census Bureau helped by releasing census lists. Why did Japanese fare worse than Germans or Italians? In 1940, Japanese was a *racial* category in the census. "German" and "Italian," on the other hand, were used solely to refer to countries of birth. When the census data was released, all Japanese, regardless of birthplace or citizenship, were "Japs" and potential enemies.[66]

The removal order set in motion a blatant transfer of assets mostly from Japanese to whites. The Japanese had just one week to dispose of their homes and businesses.[67] Many hastily sold their property. In California and Oregon, Japanese Americans were no longer allowed to own land.[68] White neighbors and speculators bought Japanese farms, houses, and businesses at a fraction of their worth, enriching themselves at their interned neighbors' expense.[69] Sometimes white men posed as FBI agents and visited Japanese homes to warn them that evacuation was imminent, and then their confederates in fraud would visit immediately afterwards to make an offer on their property at a very low price, such as $5 for a refrigerator[70] or a quarter for a washing machine.[71] One internee said, "It is difficult to describe the feeling of despair and humiliation experienced by all of us as we watched the Caucasians coming to look over our possessions and offering such nominal amounts, knowing we had no recourse but to accept whatever they were offering, because we did not know what the future held for us."[72] White people made oral agreements to care for or pay for the property of those removed, and when some later violated the agreements, there was no legal recourse.[73] Three-quarters of Japanese farmers were unable to return to their farms after the war;[74] many became tenant farmers on white-owned land.[75]

One Generation Loses, Another Generation Gains

In 1914, Tetsuo Takayanagi's father came to the United States because he had heard that if you could make it to the United States and stay six years, "you'd be all set"— you could become a "permanent resident." He started working as a cobbler, since it didn't take much capital to do this work. As he progressed, he sent away for a picture bride, and started a cut-flower business. Home ownership was forbidden to Japanese, and he couldn't become a citizen himself. So the way around the problem was to buy a house in his son's name, since Tak, as Tetsuo is still fondly called, was U.S. born and therefore a citizen.

The Japanese bombed Pearl Harbor when Tak (Tetsuo) was around twenty years old. The Japanese in Berkeley including his family were rounded up, and sent to camp Topaz in Utah. With only one week to prepare, they were fortunate enough to find a Mexican family to live in their house rent-free and to look after it while they were gone. For this reason, while some Japanese homes were ransacked or taken over, theirs was okay. If you had a job or a sponsor and promised not to return to California, you could leave the camp. Luckily, Tak's sister had not been living in California, and had moved to Washington, D.C. She was able to get American friends to sponsor Tak and their father to go to Virginia.

Like other Nisei (second-generation Japanese), Tak was drafted into the army. Nisei before World War II could be drafted, but had always been de-activated, that is, they were not allowed to carry guns. They were also not allowed to join any other branch of the military. But now there was a need for people who could speak Japanese. Tak was given two choices: he could go into the segregated Japanese 442nd or be tested for language school. If he failed the test, he would go into the 442nd. He passed the test. After basic training and language school, he was shipped to General MacArthur's headquarters in the Philippines. Three months later, Japan surrendered. The U.S. military then occupied Japan, and they needed Japanese speakers, so Tak spent the next 6 months in Japan with the counter intelligence corps. The native population appreciated the presence of the Japanese-

(continued)

speaking Nisei. He said, "It was depressing to see Japan completely leveled." He lived with other military officers, who had Japanese servants. "Those servants saw me not as Japanese but as American."

One day, he happened to get into a conversation with his company commander in a bookstore when they were both off duty, and he expressed his interest in architecture. By chance, the commander had gone to the Institute of Design in Chicago, and wrote Tak a letter of recommendation. He was able to use the GI Bill to enter the Institute. A professor from Harvard invited him and some fellow graduates to finish at Harvard, and he went on to become a successful architect. The GI Bill gave Tak an unprecedented opportunity.

Tak says that "World War II was a watershed for Japanese Americans. It dispersed us across the country, and we could see what the rest of the country was like." And the house in California? Tak's family sold it to a Mexican congregation as the site for a church.

The story is not without tragedy, of a truly unexpected sort. His father had traditional Japanese cultural values and was firmly the head of the household and the breadwinner before World War II. But after World War II, after all the changes he had suffered, he perceived himself to be a burden to his kids. He took a trip home to Japan. Instead of returning, he committed suicide.

The cost in personal sacrifice of the first generation, the Issei, was immeasurable.

By November 1942, 119,803 Japanese men, women, and children, both citizens and legal immigrants, had been forcibly removed from their homes and put into hastily constructed camps in the barren interior of Arizona, Utah, and other states. Housing for one hundred thousand was thrown up in twenty-eight days. They left nearly $200 million in property behind. Japanese losses were estimated at $67 million to $148 million in 1945 dollars.[76]

Japanese Americans were banned from serving in the Navy. Two special battalions of segregated Japanese American troops were formed, the 100th and the 442nd. Many Japanese were recruited and signed up right out of the camps. They felt that if they served well in the U.S. military, they would not only be making a sacrifice for their country, the United States, but also for their families and for all Japanese Americans. They hoped that exceptional service would gain the respect and trust of the American public. Because of their knowledge of the Japanese language, between two thousand and three thousand men were also used to gather military intelligence. Technology was primitive, and this type of work usually put them in close proximity with enemy forces, and, therefore, in great danger.

In the end, *not a single incident* of espionage or treason was found to have been committed by Japanese Americans throughout the course of World War II. The enormous losses and the heroism and unquestionable loyalty of the Japanese American battalions did indeed turn the attitude of the country around. The fact that the Japanese Americans from Hawaii and the mainland distinguished themselves in the U.S. military also destroyed the myth of their loyalty to Japan. In the postwar years, they were accepted into U.S. society more than before the war. This was an incredible moment: for the first time, by dint of their own colossal bravery and effort, an Asian group won public acceptance based on their own actions, and not on those of people in their home countries.

World War II brought out some of the worst and some of the best in American principles and values. At the war's end, Japanese Americans were allowed to return home and start over again. When they got home, many were not welcome, and their land and property was gone. There were no loans available for farmers to start over. Many small business owners went back to working as janitors. However, the Japanese once again exercised their resourceful spirit. They created new niches. Having lost their farms, they started the first greenhouse nurs-

eries, or worked as gardeners. Some soldiers got an education through the GI Bill. While they had been thrown several steps back, they put one foot in front of the other, and started again.

As a footnote to this story, the interrelationships of Asians in the United States can be complex. In 1943, the Filipinos benefited at Japanese expense: the California attorney general reinterpreted the land laws and decided that Filipinos would be allowed to lease lands, and encouraged them to do so, particularly land from which the Japanese Americans had been forced.[77]

Reparations—Forty Years Later

But what about all the wealth lost during the war years? In July 1948, President Truman signed the Evacuation Claims Act to help Japanese Americans regain some of their losses caused by their internment. This was a rather meager program. Under the act, twenty-three thousand claims were filed, asking for about $132 million; out of those claims, the government paid out $38 million dollars.[78] Meanwhile, $200 million was paid to white-owned companies that claimed the loss of foreign property.[79]

It wasn't until 1980 that public demands were made on the U.S. government to answer for its unjust treatment of its own citizens. The National Coalition for Redress and Reparations, an organization of Japanese

Americans, helped to promote the voices of those who had served time in the camps, who had lost so much of their property, money, and lives, and who had suffered silently for forty years. Congress created the Commission on Wartime Relocation and Internment of Civilians to investigate, and make recommendations. In 1983, the CWRIC found a "grave injustice" had been done to Japanese American people.[80] Congress finally passed the Civil Liberties Act of 1988, giving a formal apology and a payment of $20,000 to each of the survivors of the internment camps. President Ronald Reagan said it was time to end "a sad chapter in American history."[81]

The Enemy Within (Reprise)

The acceptance of Chinese during World War II was short-lived. In the late forties and early fifties, Americans became increasingly concerned about the growing communist threat. In 1949, the Soviet Union exploded its first atomic bomb and the Chinese Communist Party took control after winning the Chinese Civil War. In June 1950, communist North Korea invaded South Korea, the United States intervened to defend the South, and then China entered the war on the side of the North. The Korean War lasted from 1950 to 1953, and ended in a draw. However, it had repercussions at home.

Once again, the treatment of Chinese Americans as perpetual foreigners came into play. The FBI hunted down alleged communist sympathizers—any Chinese person who was not a supporter of Chiang Kai-Shek and his dictatorial government in Taiwan. Under the demagogic Senator Joseph McCarthy, the anticommunist hysteria ruined the lives of people of all races, but the Chinese were thought particularly suspect. Thousands of Chinese were investigated, and jailed, had their citizenships revoked, and were financially ruined. No Chinese person was ever found guilty of sharing any secrets with China or trying to instigate a communist takeover of the United States. But many lost jobs, income, assets, community respect, and even their lives. In 1951, in New York, under the 1917 "Trading with the Enemy Act," the U.S. government shut down the progressive *Chinese Daily News* and investigated all sixty-five hundred subscribers. Several Chinese subscribers were deported. Under the act, no banks could send money abroad for those suspected of ties with the enemy. Three laundry workers were jailed, accused of funding the communists. The truth was that they were, like so many immigrants, making remittances to their families back home. Two men committed suicide as a result of the harassment.

The chill of the cold war froze many Chinese out of asset-building activities. While whites and blacks also were wrongly accused of being communists and also lost assets during the McCarthy era, the Chinese were the only group targeted *as a nationality*, once again proving that at any moment, Asian Americans can suffer the consequences of being perpetual foreigners.[82]

The Second Generation

In spite of McCarthyism and the cold war, Asians began to prosper in the postwar years. Because of stereotypes that Asians "didn't speak good English," Asians were initially steered into engineering, science, and math, both consciously by teachers and unconsciously by word-of-mouth stories suggesting jobs that would likely be available to an Asian. Many found their way into jobs in industries like engineering at General Motors in Detroit, academia at universities, or scientific research in private industry and government. Many of these positions included health benefits and retirement plans, which provided a cushion for life's unexpected problems. While limiting occupational options is never great, these jobs were certainly better than those jobs offered to African Americans or Latinos, who were steered into manual labor jobs.

For the large numbers of Asians who fought in World War II, the GI Bill helped them get a leg up in asset building. While most colleges practiced discrimination in admitting blacks and Latinos, Asians did not

experience exclusion. It is interesting how racial stereotypes change: from the dirty and unscrupulous outcast, their new image was becoming that of a harmless brainy nerd with a propensity for hard work.

With their new jobs and acceptance, home ownership became an available option to many, and they began to leave Chinatown behind, and buy homes in white communities (they were allowed to because they didn't have the numbers to be threatening). While not among the richest Americans, they began to live comfortable, upper-middle-class professional lifestyles. For those who came of age during the war years, many remembered what it had been like to live in an anti-Asian climate, and they were grateful for the opportunity to finally get a foothold on Gold Mountain (the Chinese name for the destination of those early immigrants in the 1880s, filled with hope by the gold rush.) The journey was longer than expected, but late was better than never.

But for their children, those born in the forties and coming of age in the sixties, working twice as hard to be equal was not good enough. One button worn by radicals had a picture of a hand holding chopsticks, with the words "yellow power" underneath. They gained entry into all occupations, and demanded full equality—for themselves and their children, for their communities, and for all those formerly left out of the American dream.

THE THIRD PERIOD, 1965 TO 2000:
THE ASIAN LEAPFROG

The Asian Population Explosion

Changes in immigration policy caused an Asian population explosion.

While opportunities increased in the post–World War II era for Asians already in the United States, it took another twenty years for immigration policy to change significantly. As we have seen, the refusal to allow Asians to enter this nation of immigrants, and then to refuse those allowed to enter to become citizens, is a major reason for the marginal Asian presence in the United States economy.

Unlike the Civil War, which did not greatly affect Asians, the Civil Rights Movement was a pivotal moment not just for blacks, but for all people of color, and women as well. In fact, the numbers show that Asians benefited more than blacks in the post–Civil Rights Movement. One of the results of the Civil Rights Movement was to open the door to immigrants who were not from Europe.

The Immigration Act of 1965 (also known as the Hart-Celler Act) was signed by President Lyndon Johnson as a corrective measure to nearly a century of discrimination against immigrants on the basis of race, and Asians had borne the brunt of those exclusionary policies. The new law's significance was that it changed the basis for United States residency from national origin to having skills or professions needed in the United States. Family reunification was a second principle within this new immigration policy. Because the nation's reputation as a democratic country was at stake, as scenes of racial violence were projected around the world, the Kennedy and Johnson government acted to change that global perception.

Since 1965, the new wave of immigrants from Asia have had a different profile than previous waves: more people from middle-class and professional backgrounds (as opposed to farmers and rural folk), more people coming with the goal of settling permanently (as opposed to sojourners), and families (as opposed to single men).[83]

To fill labor shortages, there have also been a number of times when workers with specific skills have been recruited. For example, nurses from the Philippines were sought out and enticed to the United States in the 1980s with economic incentives and jobs waiting for them. More recently, professionals from India have been invited to join U.S. technology companies.

From Cambodian Refugee to American Worker

Vanny Taing, her husband and daughter, and a handful of other relatives escaped Cambodia in 1979 to a refugee camp on the Thai-Cambodian border, after four years under the genocidal Khmer Rouge regime. She was twenty-one years old. Vanny had another daughter upon arriving in the United States, and her husband took English classes and went to a vocational school to become an auto mechanic, benefits provided under the Refugee Act of 1980. The family lived in a public housing unit in greater Seattle.

In 1989, with the help of family members and a loan, they were able to purchase an affordable home in the same area. Being home owners immediately changed their status. But with the additional financial stress that came from owning a home, when her three children all enrolled in school, Vanny had to enter the workforce. The tech industry at this point had taken off, and had become a major source of employment for Southeast Asian immigrants in regions such as Seattle and Silicon Valley.

Vanny got her first job assembling circuit boards at $4.25 an hour. She stayed with the company for two years, and later applied to another company, where she received a higher starting wage of $7 an hour. She began gaining a sense of confidence, or what she considers "toughness," that she had only remembered having as a child. She began taking more English classes at a community college and joined the local gym.

Her husband, who was also dealing with the personal trauma he experienced in Cambodia, became threatened by her growing independent nature, and became increasingly abusive and controlling. After years of abuse, she decided to file for divorce. It was an incredibly difficult decision for her to make; "to be a Cambodian woman is to have a husband," she was told. As a result of the divorce, she and the children stopped interacting with the Cambodian community, because she did not want to risk being ostracized by people unsupportive of her in her painful situation.

Although she had the freedom to file for divorce, the expenses of the lawyer's fees, a single income to support three children, and paying a mortgage made

(continued)

Vanny rethink her decision. Vanny was under an incredible amount of stress, emotionally and economically. She looked into obtaining welfare assistance, but was told that in order to receive assistance she would need to give up her house to qualify. "No way" would she do that, she said. "I am already poor and they want me to be even more poor." She began to work as much overtime as she could.

Her workplace has been a site of both personal empowerment and exploitation. She is a circuit board inspector, which consists of inspecting and cleaning circuit boards, changing the chemicals used to clean the boards, touching them up, and filling out the paperwork for company work orders. There is a separation between the labor and corporate sectors of the company. Vanny, along with other people of color, work downstairs, where toxic fumes permeate the air and their actions are closely monitored. Workers are only allowed to speak English while working, and they are now only allowed to use the bathroom during breaks. This is in contrast to the staff upstairs, which is comprised mostly of white men who are in a chemical-free environment and who are not subject to the bathroom-break policies. Before Vanny's promotion to inspector, she replaced three white women at once, yet was paid the rate per hour of one worker. Despite the unequal treatment Vanny experiences, she contends that "I am pretty smart to have this job and do all that I do with no education." Vanny knows that she does not get close to the amount of money she deserves for her work, but she takes comfort in the fact that her struggles will be worth it once her children all graduate from college and benefit from the numerous sacrifices she has made throughout her life. Perhaps "pretty smart" is an understatement.

Since September 11, her job has become increasingly demanding and competitive. Her hours were cut from sixty hours to thirty-five. Vanny's job, like other positions held by women of color, is vulnerable to the economy's shortfalls. She doesn't know how secure her job will be in the future. She places her hopes in her children, trusting that if her job were to disappear, they would be financially secure enough to support her.

Other policies also changed Asian demographics. The disastrous Vietnam War led to programs that brought in two waves of Southeast Asians as refugees. The first wave in the 1970s was composed of Vietnamese military families; many had skills and education. Later, more working-class Vietnamese also came, and refugees from Vietnam,

FIGURE 5-2

Poverty rate of Asian nationalities in the United States

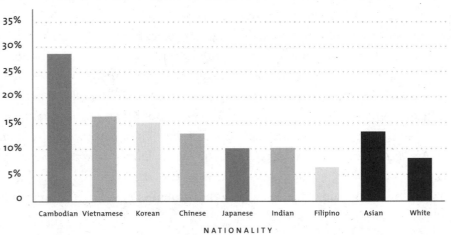

Source: U. S. Census Bureau 2000, Summary File 4.

Cambodia, and Laos, who often came from peasant backgrounds. These immigrants would fall to the bottom of the U.S. economy. And recently, trade rules that allow corporations the freedom to move overseas to find cheaper labor have created disruptions in Asian economies, forcing illegal economic emigration from Asia again. There have been news reports of horrible incidents, in which Chinese immigrants have suffocated to death as they tried to sneak across the border in poorly ventilated boxcars.

But the biggest news is growth: the population of Asians and Pacific Islanders in the United States (there was a single combined category on the census until 2000) more than doubled between 1970 (1.5 million) and 1980 (3.7 million), and then it doubled again between 1980 and 1990 (to 7.3 million). Between 1990 and 2000, the growth rate was 48 percent, compared to 13 percent for the total U.S. population.

Asian Wealth: Bipolar Disorder

While the mean and median assets of blacks, whites, and Latinos are available, there are no comparable figures for Asians. Even in the new data source book, *The New Face of Asian Pacific America: Numbers, Diversity and Change in the 21st Century*, wealth and asset data are missing.[84] However, we can draw some limited conclusions from the available information.

The Asian population has a unique economic profile. It is "bipolar" with people concentrated at both ends of the economic strata—like an hourglass. There is a greater percentage of people in the higher quintiles (fifths) and in the lower quintiles than other racial groups, and a smaller percentage in the middle income and wealth brackets. If we were to look at just income figures, it would seem that Asians are doing even better than whites. But if we were to look at just poverty rates, it would seem that Asians are doing *worse* than whites.

For Asians, statistical averages obscure the fact that the Asian demographic is top- and bottom-heavy. From looking at the aggregated numbers, some conclude that Asian Americans are "outwhiting whites." This is misleading, because it masks the differences in economic status among Asians—wealth gaps exists within the Asian category itself—and because it causes Asians who live in extreme poverty to be overlooked by the general public and by policy makers. Nearly 30 percent of Cambodians live in poverty, one of the highest poverty rates of all nationalities in the United States. However, it is still true that overall Asians have leapfrogged over other groups of color in economic status.

ASIAN AMERICANS IN THE ECONOMY: A DIFFERENT REALITY

How Data Obscures Asian Realities

From the numbers, it looks like Asian Americans are number one. In 1990, it was reported that Asians had a median income of $36,000, while whites had only $31,100. Why is that?

First, Asians do not live everywhere whites live. Over half of the Asian population lives in just three states: California (4.2 million), New York (1.2 million), and Hawaii (0.7 million). In those states, Asians are mostly concentrated in urban and suburban areas. If Asian income is higher than average, it's partly because very few Asians are working in states with low wages and low costs of living. If you compare whites and Asians in those cities with the highest Asian density, then the median income for Asians becomes $37,200, and for whites it is $40,000. Although lagging whites, Asians are indeed economically better off than African Americans or Latinos; in those same cities, the median income for blacks is $24,100, and for Latinos, $25,600.[85]

A second factor is the difference in family size between Asians and whites. Asian households are larger, so if you looked at income per person (per capita), Asian income would be less than that of whites. (See Figures 5-3 and 5-4.) For example, in Hawaii, the average white family size was 2.46 people, while that of Asians was 2.97, and that of Native Hawaiians was 3.75.

A third factor is that a few Asians have achieved enormous wealth. Charles Wang, the CEO of Computer Associates, took home $655 million in 1999. He was the only nonwhite among the 150 highest paid CEOs in 2005. Average that into all Asian salaries, and he pulls the average up.[86]

Finally, the distribution of income and wealth differs widely by nationality. Asian Indians are largely clustered at the higher end of the economic spectrum; Cambodians are at the bottom. (Sometimes the bipolarity exists *within* a population, such as the Chinese. There are many new arrivals living in extreme poverty, while many established Chinese professionals enjoy high standards of living.)

New Arrivals Skew the Picture

Since most wealth comes from inheritance, it is harder to talk about wealth accumulation in the United States when there are such a large number of immigrants in the Asian demographic. Some come with no money at all, others may bring wealth with them from home, so their wealth status cannot be credited or blamed on U.S. policies. The 2000 census recorded 11.9 million U.S. residents who identified themselves as Asian alone or in combination with one or more other races, making up just over 4 percent of the total population. In 1990, the population was 7.3 million. With such a rate of growth, obviously many are relatively recent arrivals. Two out of three Asians, or eight million, in

the United States have parents who were born abroad and were not U.S. citizens. Of those, only half are naturalized citizens. Since this book is concerned with the intergenerational accumulation and transfer of wealth that took place within the United States, the large numbers of immigrants makes the current Asian economic data comparable only to Latinos.

For example, recent Chinese immigrants represent the third largest group of immigrants to the United States, after Mexicans and Filipinos. Between 1965 and 1984, a total of 419,373 Chinese immigrants arrived, almost as many as the 426,000 Chinese who came between 1849 and 1930. The Chinese community went from being 61 percent American-born in1965 to 63 percent foreign-born in 1984, from citizen to immigrant once again.[87] Between 1984 and 1990, the Chinese population in the United States doubled again, to 1,645,000.[88] In 2000, the Chinese numbered 2,314,537; add in those who identified as a mixture of Chinese and another race, and the total was 2,734,841. When we look at the data for the Chinese, both recent immigrants and older residents are combined.

The only Asian group that is not a population of immigrants is Japanese Americans. Because of the Marshall Plan after World War II, in which the United States invested in rebuilding the Japanese economy, there has been no economic or political reason for the Japanese to leave their home country.

Income

If you took every Asian household in the United States and lined them up from the lowest to the highest income, the family in the middle has the median income. If you took all incomes, added them together, and then divided by the number of households, you would have the mean, or average, income. The "Asian" bar in the graph is the average of all Asian nationalities.

As mentioned, an Asian household is usually larger than a white household, since Asians bring their extended family structure with them when they arrive, and live in larger groups by choice. Because families often arrive with few resources, sometimes they do not have the choice of having adequate living space. When a landlord is busted for violating housing codes, sometimes there are three families living in a one-family apartment. The median household income chart (Figure 5-4) shows that only two Asian nationalities earn *less* than whites.

Per capita income data tell a more realistic story. Looking at the incomes of each working person, only two Asian nationalities earn *more* than whites.

At the top end of the Asian economic hourglass, second-and third-generation Asian Americans have unquestionably made economic leaps far beyond their immigrant parents' economic status.

Some immigrants who have come to work as professionals have arrived close to the top. South Asians (people from Bangladesh, Bhutan, India, the Maldives, Nepal, Pakistan, and Sri Lanka) are the best example of immigrants who have high

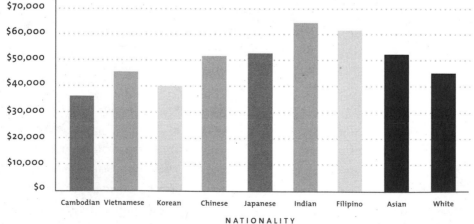

FIGURE 5-3
Median household income of various Asian nationalities in the United States

Source: U. S. Census Bureau 2000, Summary File 4.

FIGURE 5-4

Per capita income, 1999

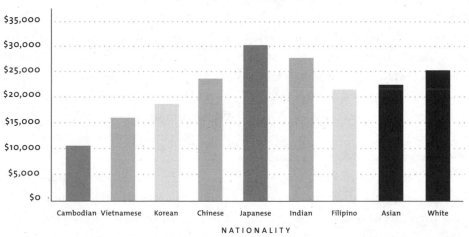

NATIONALITY

Source: U. S. Census Bureau 2000, Summary File 4.

incomes and wealth. Most have immigrated since the 1965 Immigration Act took effect. According to the 2000 Census, there are over two million South Asians in the United States today.

All subgroups of South Asians have very high levels of education compared to the general U.S. population. Many Indian physicians, pharmacists, nurses, and other medical professionals were allowed to immigrate during the 1970s. Also, many Indians came as foreign students, completed their master's or Ph.D. programs, and changed their status to permanent residents.[89] In 1990, 30 percent of Asian Indian workers were in professional occupations, compared to 14 percent of white workers. They are more highly represented in the professional category than any other immigrant/minority group, and medical professionals make up a large proportion of that category. Two factors other

than education have been important to Asian Indians' high-income occupational level. First, they are fluent in English (as a result of British colonization), and second is many of them have completed graduate programs in the United States.[90] Their skills are highly sought after. In 2001, Microsoft and other high-tech companies lobbied hard to get federal officials to double the number of foreign high-tech specialists allowed to come to the United States to work. Forty-four percent of those were from India.[91]

But once again, international factors have affected the South Asian community. Racist attacks against Asian Americans spiked significantly across the country after the World Trade Center was attacked on September 11; singled out as targets were Indian and Pakistani Americans, especially Sikh Americans, a religious group often mistakenly perceived to be Arab because many

Sikh men wear turbans and have long beards. In some places, South Asian businesses have been burned to the ground.[92] As with the Chinese during the McCarthy era, they have been investigated, harassed, arrested, and deported. It is the latest example of how being perceived as foreign can threaten the economic security of Asian groups.

While some Asian subgroups are in well-paid professional jobs, as a group they do not attain the income levels of whites. At both the top and the bottom of the employment ladder, it is still commonly assumed that Asians will work harder for less pay than whites, so they are still considered a good deal for white employers. Professionals bump up against a racial glass ceiling, so that they cannot reach the top of the management ladder—still a white male preserve. In 1991, Congress created a Federal Glass Ceiling Commission, and its 1995 study found, for example, that "Asian/Pacific Islanders held less than one one-hundredth of one percent of all corporate directorships."[93] Asians are also limited to fewer occupations and industries. They are three times more likely to be scientists and engineers than their numbers would predict; in those fields, they also hit a glass ceiling.[94]

Success as professionals has not come to all Asians. Compared to the Chinese, the recent Filipino immigration has been largely invisible, and yet it has been much larger. Over the last three decades, the Philippines sent more immigrants to the United States than any other Asian country and, until recently, was the second largest source of U.S. immigrants after Mexico. In 1990, Filipino Americans numbered over 1.4 million, up 90 percent from 770,000 in 1980.[95] In 2000, it was the second largest subgroup of Asians, with 2,364,815 people (including Filipinos of mixed race).[96] The recent wave is due to the economic crisis in the Philippines.

Many Filipino immigrants are well-educated professionals such as engineers, scientists, accountants, teachers, lawyers, nurses, and doctors.[97] But for those not recruited for a job, coming to America can result in downward mobility. According to Stephanie Yan, the daughter of Filipino immigrants, before emigrating many doctors in the Philippines study to be nurses, jobs they are more likely to find in the United States.

Filipinos from professional backgrounds are finding jobs in the lowest-paid sectors of the workforce—nannies, maids, home care workers, and food service workers. When looking at Filipinos as a whole, they remain in subordinate positions in relation to some other Asian groups and whites, whether educated or less educated, skilled or unskilled.[98]

Asians are the least likely to be unemployed. In 1990, 67 percent of all Asian Americans compared with 65 percent of all Americans were working. Again, these numbers mask differences in ethnicity; for example, the Hmong people from Laos had only a 29.3 percent labor participation rate, while Asian Indian men had an 84 percent rate.

At the bottom end of the scale, Asians also experience greater poverty rates than the general population. About 14 percent of all Asians lived in poverty in 1989; the rate for the nation was 10 percent. Again, there are enormous ethnic differences. The 1990 Census data revealed that 47 percent of Cambodians, 66 percent of Hmong, 67 percent of Laotians, and 34 percent of Vietnamese were impoverished. While at one end of the scale Asians do better than other minorities, at the low end, poverty rates among Southeast Asians are much higher than those of other minority groups such as African Americans (21 percent) and Latinos (23 percent).[99]

Education

Education continues to be an important part of the Asian strategy for social and economic advancement. Even low-wage parents doing manual labor place all their eggs in their children's educational baskets. Forty-four percent of Asians and Pacific Islanders (API) age twenty-five and over had a bachelor's degree or higher in 2000. The rate for all adults twenty-five and over was 26 percent. Eighty-six percent were high school graduates; the rate for all U.S. residents was 84 percent for all adults age twenty-five or higher. One in seven APIs over the age of twenty-five, or one million people, has an advanced degree.

However, the returns on their educational investments are not equal to whites. In 1988, the U.S. Commission on Civil Rights reported, according to Deborah Woo, that "after controlling for education, work experience, English ability, urban residence, and industry of employment . . . 'Asian descent' continued to have a negative effect on one's chances of moving into management."[100] Moreover, in a National Science Foundation survey of eighty-eight thousand scientists and engineers, they found that even when Asians did become managers, whites in similar positions earned *twice* as much.[101]

Looking at income data from California, where most Asians reside and work, one can see that if Asians are a model minority, as claimed by many, they are not getting the benefits that would be expected. Whites with no high school diploma, can expect to earn $26,115 a year; Asians, $18,517. Whites with a bachelor's degree can expect $44,426; Asians, $33,758. With a doctorate, whites earn $77,877; Asians, $59,603.[102] While this earnings gap is smaller than it is for black and Latino graduates, there's still a significant penalty for being Asian American.

WEALTH: ASIANS AND WHITES

Home Ownership

A home is usually the first important asset that a family acquires, so home ownership and home values are a way of estimating how Asian wealth compares to whites.

The Chinese have been particularly successful in increasing their home ownership assets. Since the 1960s, they have been able to buy homes in white suburbs without being driven out by the neighbors. In a few places, they have created Asian suburbs that equal those of whites in home values. In California, Monterey Park could be called a "Chinese Beverly Hills."[103]

But the advances still do not add up to equality for Asians overall. In 2003, the Department of Housing and Urban Development released an eleven-city study that focused exclusively on discrimination in the housing market against Asian Americans.[104] The eleven cities studied were Anaheim/Santa Ana, Chicago, Honolulu, Los Angeles, Minneapolis, New York, Oakland, San Diego, San Francisco, San Jose, and Washington D.C. These metropolitan areas account for 77 percent of all Asians and Pacific Islanders living in the United States. The study revealed that Asian and Pacific Islander seeking to buy homes experienced "consistent adverse treatment" relative to

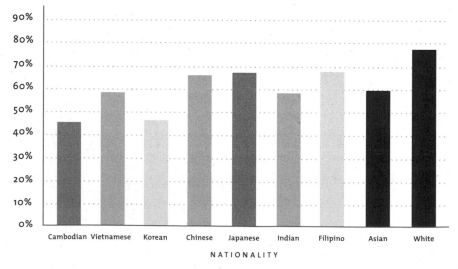

FIGURE 5-5
Percent of households in owner-occupied unit

Source: U. S. Census Bureau 2000, Summary File 4.

comparable whites 20 percent of the time, with "systematic discrimination"[105] occurring in housing availability, inspections, financing assistance, and agent encouragement.

According to the U.S. Census 2000, the average value of homes owned by Asian Americans was $199,300, compared to the white average of $123,4000. Once again, this reflects bipolar disorder: those who have money have quite a lot, but there are also a greater percentage of Asians living in overcrowded conditions than whites. Windy Sengsethuane, a young Laotian immigrant who came to the United States with her family in 1979, gives another reason for the Asian home ownership and home value figures. As a child, she worked with all her family members plucking chickens to make a little cash to supplement her mother's $30-a-day job cleaning the homes of white women. When they bought a house, it was using the combined resources of the parents and children; they all own it together, and numerous relatives chip in on the mortgage payments. They bought a house that was big enough to accommodate all the family members. While counted as an owner-occupied home of relatively high value, the owner is an extended family, Asian style.[106]

Business Ownership

In 1997, there were 913,000 Asian- and Pacific Islander–owned businesses in the United States. They employed more than 2.2 million people and generated more than $306.9 billion in revenues. Asians are 4.2 percent of the population, and own roughly 4 percent of the nonfarm businesses, an almost proportionate share. However, Asian- and Pacific Islander–owned firms generated 52 percent of all minority-owned business revenues. Between 1992 and 1997, the number of Asian-owned businesses increased about four times as fast as the total number of businesses (30 percent versus 7 percent). The average receipts for API owned businesses was $336,200 lower than the average for all firms ($410,600), but higher than that for all minority-owned firms ($196,600).[107]

Again, there are big differences among Asian groups in terms of ownership of different assets. The Chinese are entrepreneurial, and small business ownership has flourished. Whites and blacks alike eat Chinese food—such as that ubiquitous General Tso's chicken! What used to be viewed as strange cultural practices, such as acupuncture or kung fu, have become popular and lucrative businesses.

Koreans are particularly successful small businesspeople. The Korean population in the United States grew from 10,000 in 1960 to 69,130 in 1970 to close to 800,000 in 1990.[108] An overwhelming majority of post-1965 Korean immigrants were from the middle class and had held professional and white-collar jobs in Korea. However, due to limited English skills and the fact that many U.S. firms do not accept professional certificates acquired in Korea, they have faced dif-

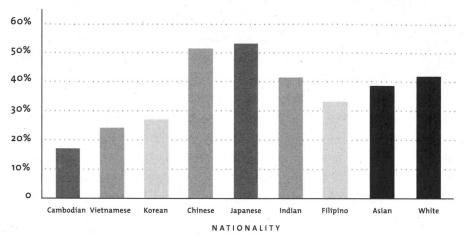

FIGURE 5-6

Percent with any interest, dividend, or rental income of various Asian nationalities in the United States

Source: U. S. Census Bureau 2000, Summary File 4.

ficulty in obtaining similar professional jobs in the U.S.[109]

Therefore, many in this wave of Korean immigrants have brought money with them to the United States to start their own businesses. The sizable number of business enterprises is one of the most distinguishing features of Korean immigrants. Another way they have accumulated start-up capital is through rotating savings accounts, where a group of people all put equal amounts of money into a fund, and then take turns drawing on the accumulated funds. The grocery and liquor store is one of the most common Korean small businesses. Unlike the Chinese and Japanese, who started businesses in their own communities serving their own nationalities, most Korean businesses are not located in areas that serve Koreans. They largely serve a clientele that

has been neglected or abandoned by U.S. businesspeople: blacks, Latinos, or Puerto Ricans.[110] This niche has helped build wealth for Koreans.

On the other hand, it has produced misunderstandings based on cultural differences, and interracial conflict that has also led to the loss of wealth. In Los Angeles in 1991, a Korean shopkeeper shot a young African American woman, who allegedly was shoplifting. This led to riots, and the trashing of many Korean-owned shops, resulting in the loss of millions of dollars worth of capital. In New York, Korean small grocery owners were employing Central American immigrants at very low wages. Boycotts against them also hurt their businesses. Immigrants who do not understand the dynamics of race when they come here, or who adopt racist attitudes toward other peoples of color once they get here, are at peril of being both instigators and victims of racial violence.

As people gain wealth, that wealth takes increasingly different forms. Length of time in the U.S., income levels, and jobs with benefits are all factors explaining why some Asian groups have higher interest, dividend, and rental income than other Asians, other people of color, and even whites.

Public Benefits

Southeast Asians (including Vietnamese, Laotians, Cambodians, Hmong, and the ethnic Chinese from those countries) were able to break new ground in terms of getting a helping hand from Uncle Sam as they tried to enter a new country. They came as part of the largest refugee exodus to the United States in our history. According to the 2000 Census, there are close to two million Southeast Asians in the United States today. Because of the obligation the United States government felt it had toward the people it had drawn into the Vietnam War, for the first time, the United States created an unambiguous refugee policy, which had previously been ad hoc. The Indochina Migration and Refugee Assistance Act of 1975 and the Refugee Act of 1980 defined "refugee" and created assistance programs.[111] They provided for expanded domestic refugee assistance programs, giving Southeast Asian refugees access to government-funded benefits. From

1975 to 1986, the United States spent approximately $5 billion in cash, medical assistance, and social services primarily for Southeast Asian refugees.[112]

While it may seem like refugee status would give this group a jump-start on wealth building, the circumstances of the war and the migration were so traumatic that the benefits afforded refugees hardly scratched the surface of what was necessary to enjoy basic aspects of life. The refugees left their countries in fear and crisis. Very few have the chance to even think about the long-term consequences of their migration prior to leaving, and most came with very few resources with which to start a new life. For example, 61 percent of the members of the first wave of Vietnamese refugees to arrive in the United States in 1975, had less than twenty-four hours to prepare to leave, and 83 percent had less than one week. Not only do refugees bring less capital with them than voluntary immigrants, refugees also have no access to their country of origin; voluntary immigrants, on the other hand, often retain advantageous trading relationships with their home countries and may return home to arrange deals, recruit workers, or borrow money.[113]

When an economic scapegoat is needed, Asians and other immigrants continue to be handy. Saying that poor people and immigrants consume too many of our tax dollars, the 1996 welfare reform bill cut off benefits to both legal and non-legal immigrants — not only cash benefits and food stamps, but also access to Medicaid. Before this change, nearly 30 percent of Southeast Asian Americans were on welfare, the highest participation rate of any ethnic group.[114] Immigrants continue to be subjected to taxation without the right to publicly funded benefits, much as for the Chinese 150 years ago. The Immigrant Reform and Immigrant Responsibility Act also passed in 1996, and it imposed sanctions against employers who hire people who are in the United States without papers. Before, even those here illegally had workplace protections.

ASIAN WEALTH – THE WAY FORWARD

Equal/Comparable Opportunity for Asians

When the first Asians began to arrive in any numbers, whites reacted in fear of "the yellow peril." As we have seen, the real story has been more about the perils of being yellow.

As we examine the Asian story of wealth building, we find a tapestry interwoven with many stories. Each nationality has lived a different history here. Asians of different nationalities living in the United States have been separated from each other by language, culture, how long they have been in the United States, and animosities between their home countries. Even today, recent immigrants live among people from their own countries, not with Asians as a whole; an Asian American community is not fully defined.

What needs to be done to ensure that the path for newer immigrants, who now need to take their first steps in asset building in this country, more resembles that of European immigrants than that of their Asian forebears? What government actions can eliminate the Asian color line?

First, foreign policy must be disengaged from the treatment of people of Asian origins within the United States. From Japanese internment to the Wen Ho Lee espionage case, Asian loyalty has been questioned, leading to discriminatory practices that limit Asian entry into the mainstream. Those types of policies, first practiced against Asians, are now being used against Arab Americans, and must be opposed by all those who are democratically minded.

Second, government programs investing in asset-building activities should be available to all residents. Asian immigrant high school students should not be barred from getting college scholarships or paying in-state tuition rates; it's cutting off our noses to spite our faces to deny opportunities to those with the talent and drive to get ahead.

Third, we need new asset-building programs on the scale of the old GI Bill, but the

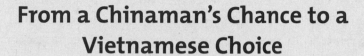

From a Chinaman's Chance to a Vietnamese Choice

Fields Corner in Dorchester, Massachusetts, was a depressed neighborhood in 1970, home to mostly working-class whites. White flight from the 1950s to the 1980s to the suburbs resulted in abandoned urban pockets that became resettlement locations for new immigrants, such as the Fields Corner neighborhood. It offered affordable housing and access to public transportation. The first wave of Vietnamese refugees in the area, even though they had no financial assets, were generally middle-class, and educated, and received some cash assistance and medical care under U.S. refugee policy. Their new neighbors in the 1970's were not welcoming, to put it mildly: one Vietnamese was murdered and others suffered attacks. But they had no place to go. They stayed, and used their small federal subsidies to help start their professional careers or small businesses.

The wealth-building strategies utilized were similar to those used by preceding immigrant groups. Mainstream loan assistance was not accessible due to language, cultural, and systemic barriers. For example, the Vietnamese were not familiar with the U.S. banking system, and did not deposit their money or use credit cards. Instead, collective efforts among family members and close friends gave the community its start. Small family-owned business ventures have been a major source of asset-building for the Vietnamese; they enable all members to contribute to the family income or "collective capital."

During the recession in the mid-1980s, real estate prices were low, and storefronts in the Fields Corner area were renting for between $600 and $700 a month. At the same time, blue-collar assembly line jobs which paid decently and didn't require specialized skills or mastery of the English language, were readily available. Businesses were relatively inexpensive to start. One native Vietnamese asset-building strategy is the formation of a group of mini-investors, a *hui*: a network of five or more people who pool their money together, with the understanding that whoever needs the money to start a business, or buy a house, or car will take the money as start-up capital and repay it with interest. The strategy relies on the

(continued)

trust of each participant to repay the money, or what might be called "community capital." If an individual does not repay the loan, their reputation in the community is tainted and they will no longer be able to share the pooled capital.

One type of facility that was popular in the 1990s during the economic boom was the work center. Work centers function as temp agencies; they contract with individuals to work at companies temporarily. The center receives a lump sum payment from a company, takes the taxes out of the payment, then pays the worker in cash. Many of these work centers are now Vietnamese-owned.

These collective wealth-building strategies have led to the proliferation of Vietnamese-owned businesses and services in the Fields Corner neighborhood and beyond. The community has found a niche for itself, in the hardwood floor industry (which is dominated by Vietnamese companies in the Boston metro area), nail salons, construction, real estate, restaurants, and, more recently, gift shops, legal services, translation, and remittance services. These businesses respond to the need for bilingual and bicultural services, creating and fulfilling their own supply and demand.

Along with the increase in Vietnamese-owned businesses and homes in Fields Corner came the desire to sustain its prosperity. Vietnamese economic activities had changed a depressed area into an economically vibrant one; now, they didn't want whites to gentrify what had become the economic heart of their community. In 1994, a group of young Vietnamese professionals decided to establish the Vietnamese American Initiative for Development (Viet-AID), a community development corporation that would examine and implement long-term strategies for community empowerment. The organization's success is illustrated in its campaign to create a community center in the neighborhood. Viet-AID began planning for this $5.1 million community center in 1996. The community center project became a way to organize the Vietnamese community. People in the neighborhood were first asked to define what they would want the community center to include, and were also approached for donations, which totaled $200,000. Private foundations and corporations were later approached with the understanding that the project was a community-driven effort. The community center opened in 2002. The center provides a senior drop-off location, an afterschool program, day care services, office space for other community-based organizations, a library, and a space for meetings and social events. Not only is it a space for the Vietnamese, but it has

(continued)

been offered as a resource for all groups in the neighborhood to use. The Vietnamese used their internal resources and their cultural values to develop the center. They pooled their individual and collective wealth and used it to leverage support from mainstream Boston financial institutions. They extended their idea of community beyond themselves and beyond Fields Corner.

The fact remains that 18 percent of individuals in the Fields Corner neighborhood still live below the poverty line;[116] 38 percent of those are Vietnamese families. However, it makes a big difference when people are not isolated, and can become part of a network that can provide the hand up that all of us need at various moments in our lives to make it in America. Their model resembles the best from Asian history: building local economies and creating both individual and community wealth. But they also incorporated mainstream methods: founding a nonprofit service organization; forming a community development corporation; and connecting the Vietnamese community to mainstream networks with access to capital.

next round needs to ensure that people of color get their full advantages.

Any new program to bring people into the middle class must be culturally appropriate. Factoring in the cultural beliefs and practices of Asians to ensure their inclusion in program implementation will be necessary to achieve this goal: definitions of family, credit worthiness, money handling, and community values are not the same for every nationality. For example, if an Asian family does not have a credit card because they only use cash for transactions, other means of judging their ability to pay a mortgage need to be allowed, and different mortgage products need to be designed.

Choosing Our Seat on the Bus

The status of Asian Americans in the United States is still uncertain. Asians have more access to wealth-building opportunities than they ever have had before, and the economic gap between Asians and whites is narrowing. But as the century progresses, Asians must define their own place in the racial hierarchy. In an interview with Bill Moyers, the Japanese American poet David Mura talked about the choice his father faced about where to sit on the bus. David's father was in a Japanese internment camp in Jerome, Arkansas, during World War II. Given a weekend pass, he caught a segregated bus.

Whites urged him to sit in the front, and blacks invited him to sit in the back. David used this incident to describe the Asian American dilemma: "America has offered Asian Americans honorary white status. But that status is predicated on a deal: you don't sit at the *very* front of the bus. . . . You don't *ever* drive the bus, and you must pay *no* attention to what's happening to people on the back of the bus."

The question remains, "Where will we sit?"[115]

Besides the adage that you don't have a "Chinaman's chance," there was a mocking children's rhyme in the 1950s that went: "Ching Chong Chinaman, sitting on a fence, trying to make a dollar out of 15¢." Today, many Asians have indeed made a dollar out of 15¢. Now they have a chance—and a choice. They can join the forces that want to close the door of opportunity once they themselves have gotten through. Or, as the Vietnamese did in Fields Corner, Asians can choose to share their newly acquired wealth with those who are still left sitting on the fence.

Chapter 6

CLIMBING THE UP ESCALATOR: WHITE ADVANTAGES IN WEALTH ACCUMULATION

"I don't think white people owe anything to black people. We didn't sell them into slavery; it was our ancestors. What they did was wrong, but we've done our best to make up for it."

—SIXTEEN-YEAR-OLD HIGH SCHOOL JUNIOR
INTERVIEWED BY THE *Los Angeles Times*[1]

White Americans typically have assets more than ten times greater than Americans of color. This difference was created not only by government policies that impeded wealth building for people of color, but also by policies that actually boosted white wealth—policies like land grant and homestead programs, low-cost mortgages, farm loans, and Social Security checks, all at times available only or mostly to white people.

It's hard for many white people to accept the reality that they profited from these government-promoted white advantages. In particular, white people who don't have anywhere near the median white assets, $120,000, find it hard to

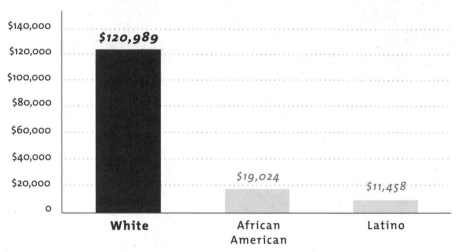

FIGURE 6-1
Median net worth, 2001 (in 2001 dollars)

Source: Bárbara J. Robles's analysis of Federal Reserve Bank Survey of Consumer Finances data.

believe. "My grandparents were dirt poor," some have said. "I'm in debt—I don't have any wealth." Responses like these reflect the understandable skepticism about how universal government help to white people has been.

To answer this skepticism, the white wealth numbers can be separated into two parts. White assets are high partly because the U.S. elite is and has always been composed overwhelmingly of white men. The biggest slaveholders, the most ruthless robber barons, and the present day CEOs all skew the white averages up.

But most white people are not wealthy elites. White people are almost three-quarters of the U.S. population (in the 2000 Census), and at times have been an even greater share of the population. The vast majority of them were not slave owners,

didn't own factories, and don't now have million-dollar stock portfolios. Most white people get their incomes from wages, and if they have any assets, they came from savings or from modest inheritances.

Yet even if we remove the wealthy elite from the picture, white working people still have, on average, more assets than people of color. One way to see the difference between the superrich and ordinary white people is to compare mean and median wealth. (If you lined up all the white families in the United States, the family in the middle of the line has the median amount of wealth. The mean is the average, the total wealth divided by the number of white families.) In 2001 the mean was $546,785, far greater than the median of $121,254. The vast majority of white families don't have anything close to the average amount of

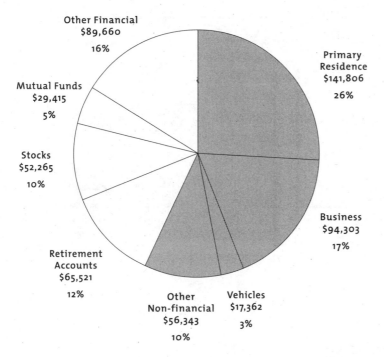

FIGURE 6-2
White mean family assets = $546,785

Other Financial
$89,660
16%

Mutual Funds
$29,415
5%

Stocks
$52,265
10%

Retirement
Accounts
$65,521
12%

Other
Non-financial
$56,343
10%

Vehicles $17,362
3%

Primary
Residence
$141,806
26%

Business
$94,303
17%

Source: Survey of Consumer Finances, Board of Governors,
Federal Reserve System, 1992–2001.

elderly former home owners, and some are students and other young people.

More than half of white families have retirement accounts; a majority owns some stock. Only 13 percent have zero or negative assets (compared with 31 percent of African Americans and 35 percent of Latinos), and some of those are young adults just starting out. Only a very small share of white adults have no assets at all throughout their middle years.

Of course, knowing that they don't have much company among other whites isn't much comfort for impoverished white people, who do number in the millions despite their relatively small share of the entire white population. And, of course, facing prolonged unemployment, health crises, or low wages can be terrifying even for a family with assets. Rural land ownership, in particular, sometimes does little or nothing to help pay mounting bills. Yet facing hard times without assets, as so many people of color do, is even scarier.

Many white people have heard stories of their great-grandparents or grandparents' poverty, whether after immigration or during the Great Depression or other economic

over half a million dollars; a small number of multimillionaires and billionaires are pulling the average up. The biggest socioeconomic group in the United States is white working-class home owners with a high school degree but no college degree, and their household incomes tend to be below $40,000 a year.

But even the modest assets of the typical white family are greater than those of most families of color. Asset ownership is very common among white working people. Three-quarters of white households are home owners; and of the renters, some are

FIGURE 6-3
Home ownership rates, 2003

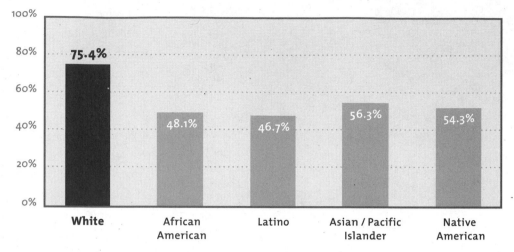

Source: U.S. Census Bureau, *Annual Statistics, 2003, Housing Vacancies and Homeownership*, Table 20

FIGURE 6-4
Mean asset ownership, 2001

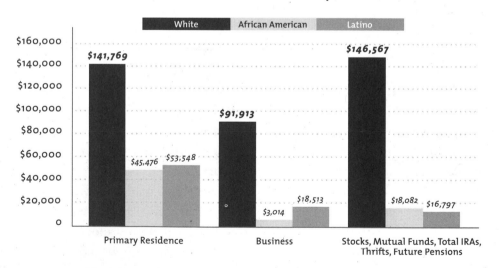

Source: Bárbara J. Robles's calculations of Federal Reserve Bank Survey of Consumer Finances data.

hardships. But at all times in U.S. history, poor white people were not as poor, on average, as poor people of color. It is true that wave after wave of European immigrants found only low-paying, dirty, dangerous jobs, along with prejudice from

FIGURE 6-5
Median family income, 1999

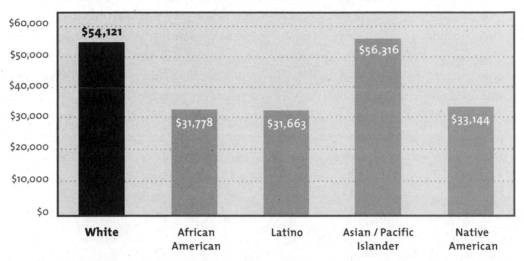

Source: U.S. Census Bureau, *Historical Income Tables*, Table F-5, *Characteristics of American Indians and Alaska Natives by Tribe and Language, Census 2000*, Table 10.

native-born Anglo Americans. But almost always, their jobs were not the worst jobs; they were a step above jobs held by workers of color. And almost always, the prejudice diminished enough by the second or third generation to allow some minimal accumulation of assets by some people in each white ethnic group.

This chapter tells both stories: the policies that supported the vast enrichment of elites *and* the comparatively smaller advantages given to white working people at the expense of their fellow workers of color. It retells many of the stories in the last four chapters, shining the spotlight this time on public sector boosts to white people's net worth.

White people can be proud of the hard work of their grandparents, their parents, and themselves and still recognize that hard

work is only one ingredient in acquiring assets. The right to own property and establish businesses, access to credit, access to education, jobs, and promotions, political representation, access to courts to settle disputes, a safety net for times of unemployment and disability, and government subsidies and contracts: all these also play roles in building assets. And all of these have been consistently available to white people, and frequently denied to people of color. Economic development requires government infrastructure, and this has been provided for the vast majority of the white population, in ways that often excluded or impoverished people of color.

White working people can also be proud of the labor struggles and sacrifices their ancestors made to win basic economic security and still recognize that time after time these struggles were won through a devil's bargain of accepting opportunities and benefits that excluded people of color. Sometimes employers' divide-and-conquer techniques lowered white wages as well, but too often white working people waged struggles explicitly to exclude people of color from the opportunities they enjoyed. Government policies were only one ingredient in causing the racial wealth gap; discrimination, violence, and political pressure by white individuals, unions, property owners, and employers were the other ingredients. And the governments, for the most part, were elected by white majorities.

As white author Paul Kivel writes in *Uprooting Racism,* "It is not that white Americans have not worked hard and built much. We have. But we did not start out from scratch. We went to segregated schools and universities built with public money. We received school loans, Veterans Administration (VA) loans, and housing and auto loans when people of color were excluded or heavily discriminated against. We received federal jobs, military jobs, and contracts when only whites were allowed. We were accepted into apprenticeships, training programs, and unions when access for people of color was restricted or nonexistent."[2]

LAND GRANTS OF INDIAN LAND FROM EUROPEAN MONARCHS

The first governments to give white people assets in North America were the monarchies of England, Spain, France, and Holland, which awarded millions of acres of Native Americans' land to their countrymen in the sixteenth and seventeenth centuries.

In the 1500s and early 1600s, shortages of land had grown to crisis proportions across Europe. Monarchs saw colonization as a way to export the increasing numbers of unemployed and disruptive landless men, among other goals.[3]

Spain's American colonies grew rapidly, gaining control of the greatest amount of land throughout the Southwest and Caribbean, because in the 1500s Spain conquered the vast Aztec empire with its twenty-five million people.[4] Spanish settlers in particular were notable for not doing any manual work themselves. Indigenous people of Puerto Rico and other Caribbean islands were forced, often at gunpoint, to work for particular Spanish landowners.[5]

Large numbers of former English serfs were sent to the English colonies as bondsmen, forced to work off their transportation costs for a number of years, usually seven.[6] It wasn't always easy for them to become landowners, even after their period of

Inherited Assets? Who, Me?
by Betsy Leondar-Wright

White people who inherit assets—that sounds like someone else, not me!

Here's how I've usually thought about it: My family's not especially rich. The assets my partner and I own—a condo and some retirement savings—were saved dollar by dollar from our earnings, not from any intergenerational transfer of wealth from our families. I didn't inherit anything when my grandparents died. My father accumulated half a million dollars during his working life, but then spent it all on a catastrophic illness, greatly reducing the odds that I would inherit much. Of course, I got intangible privileges from being white and middle class, like a college education and a way of talking that matches how employers talk, but I didn't directly get any cash from my family.

But as I researched this book, I remembered my great-uncle, Paul Rasmussen.

Uncle Paul's father was a third-generation shoemaker who owned his own shoe store in Denmark. Uncle Paul was born in the United States, and worked in a shoe factory in Quincy, Massachusetts. Eventually he started a shoe factory to produce his own shoe designs. The family story is that he invented the saddle shoe, which became a big hit after World War II. He sold the shop and retired in his forties—the only owning-class person in our family tree.

When he died over a decade ago, he left me $2,500 in his will. I gave $500 to an anti-sweatshop group as a gesture of payback to the shoe factory workers, and kept $2,000.

When my partner and I were trying to buy our condo five years ago, it was hard to come up with the down payment and all the fees. My $2,000 inheritance from Uncle Paul really did help us become home owners without being penniless afterward.

So I have more assets because my ancestors had assets. Uncle Paul no doubt got assistance (such as permits and bank loans) to start his shop that factory workers of color couldn't have gotten in the 1930s. And Uncle Paul presumably had a leg up on the other shoe factory workers who had ideas for new shoe designs because of his shoe store–owning father. My ancestors had assets in part because they were European American. (continued)

> *Here's another way Uncle Paul's assets will affect my net worth over my lifetime: He left my mom enough money to greatly lessen the chance that my sisters and I will have to support her in her old age. This is an advantage more common among white people, to be free from the necessity of caring for the older generation financially. I can save for my retirement because my mom not only has Social Security, but she also inherited money to support her retirement.*

indenture was over. The original settlers of New England towns made themselves shareholders of the town, and then in many cases distributed additional land only to themselves, even when most land within the town was unallocated.[7] The pressure to find more land for landless ex-bondsmen was relieved by confiscating more Indian land. The Massachusetts Bay charter explicitly allowed Indian lands to be taken without compensation. Roger Williams was expelled from the colony in part for objecting to this policy. Between 1660 and 1710, as the Eastern seaboard became more crowded,

209 new settlements were formed on the northern and western frontiers of New England, on land opened up by battles with Native Americans.[8]

In the Narragansett Swamp Fight of 1675, thousands of Wampanoag women, children and elders were massacred alongside the Narragansett warriors, who sought to defend them against the English. Fifty-five years later, in a cruel gesture, the colony of Rhode Island awarded Indian land to the families of colonial veterans of the massacre. The colony gave seven townships to 840 descendants of such veterans.

COLONIZING THE EAST WITH SERVANTS AND SLAVES

Land was abundant in the New World, but labor to work the land was scarce. Landowners all over the American colonies turned to coercing workers—and gradually a racial caste system was institutionalized with laws that defined whose labor was coerced and whose labor was paid.

At first, religion and landownership, not

race, were the bases for political rights. All New England colonies and states except Rhode Island had official state churches until the early 1800s. Citizen rights in most colonies were restricted to Protestants; Protestant Christians of African ancestry had no less formal status than white servants; and some Africans did own land, earn wages, and have white servants.[9] Jews, Catholics, and other religious minorities were prohibited from settling in the New England colonies.[10] Irish servants had a longer period of indenture than English servants under Virginia colonial law.[11]

But gradually, throughout the 1600s, racial distinctions were put into law. In 1640, three runaway Virginia servants were caught: the two white ones got a four-year extension of their contract, while the black one was sentenced to servitude for life.[12] In the 1640s, Virginia was the first colony to allow the sale of African slaves and to treat them and their descendants legally as property.[13] By the 1650s, there were about a thousand slaves in Virginia; free Africans had fallen to the bottom of the caste system; and there was a huge new group of white people now free after finishing their terms of service.[14] A 1663 Virginia law prohibited English female servants from doing fieldwork, but allowed African women to work outside.[15] In 1666, in Northampton County, Virginia, 32 percent of European bond laborers became landowners at the end of their terms, compared with 16 percent of African American bond laborers.[16] Eventually, all the southern states enacted slavery into law.

Native American slavery, though not as well known as African slavery, was also gradually coded into law. War captives were sold as slaves, for example by the Massachusetts Bay Colony after the Pequot War.[23] Usually they would be sold to the West Indies, as Indians enslaved in their homelands were

too difficult to control and often able to escape, and local slavery tended to sour relations with tribes that were the colonists' military allies and trading partners.[24] Nevertheless, there were thousands of Indian slaves by the end of the 1600s.[25]

"Divide and conquer" was one motivation for creating distinctions by race among servants and laborers. There were many rebellions in which white, black, and Native American servants were allies. Some were small groups running away together; others were large, organized, armed insurrections, such as Bacon's Rebellion in Virginia in 1676. In the process of suppressing such uprisings, landlords and colonial governments codified a racial caste system into law. Tenants and servants—now mostly white—began to get more rights and benefits.[26] At the same time, African slavery was institutionalized.

South Carolina was the first colony founded as a slave colony, in 1670.[27] The Carolina low country was suitable for huge plantations, and the planters there started buying African slaves from the West Indies to do their labor. Rice became a major cash crop in South Carolina in the late 1600s because some slaves brought rice-growing skills from West Africa.[28] Georgia started with a prohibition on slavery, but reversed it in 1751 when their lower-class English plantation workers proved too few and too inexperienced to clear the land and make tobacco farming profitable.[29] By 1776, Georgia's population was thirty-three thousand whites and fifteen thousand slaves.[30]

The Template for Work Without Rights

Even in periods when white economic status declines, the racial wealth gap grows, because people of color fall even further behind.

It's not only when white people are given boosts to their net worth that the racial wealth gap grows. At times when nonelite whites are losing out financially, people of color often lose even more, widening the gap. In *The Invention of the White Race*, Theodore Allen gives a great example of this from the 1600s.

Compared with labor law in England, the systems set up by the governors of the Eastern colonies rescinded labor rights for workers of all races. Even the lowliest serfs and vagrants in England had some right to compensation and some rights to refuse coerced labor. These rights were whittled away in the colonies, despite explicit terms in the Virginia Company charters of 1606 and 1609: The Royal intent, they said, was that all English colonists "shall have and enjoy all liberties, franchises and immunities of free denizens and natural subjects . . . to all intents and purposes as if they had been abiding and born within this our Realm of England." These constitutional principles were violated when wage laborers were reduced to the status of chattel servitude, unpaid and bound to a particular landowner.[17]

To induce poor Englishmen to move to the colonies, the Virginia Company initially offered them one hundred acres on a tenant-sharecropping basis, but after 1616 this land guarantee was no longer offered.[18] Landowners were, however, still given fifty more acres for every servant whose transportation from England they paid, which resulted in vast plantations owned by wealthy landlords.[19] Homeless children were rounded up in England and sent to Virginia, supposedly as apprentices who worked without wages for seven years, and women were forced onto ships for the colonies and sold to settlers as wives.[20] Suits were brought to the colonial courts objecting to these violations of English law.[21]

Theodore Allen claims that this degrading of English bondsmen and bondswomen from free-will wage workers to indentured servants was the template for African slavery.[22] Coerced labor without basic rights became the norm in the colonies, but was increasingly applied more severely to African and Indian laborers than to whites, and remained legal for people of color even after basic freedoms were legislated for white workers.

The luxurious lifestyle and rapid accumulation of wealth by the huge plantation owners was made possible by the work of slaves.

Theodore Allen believes that there could have been a different and more just history if Virginia planters had made the decision to pursue a slower-growing, diversified economy like New England's instead of a quick-buck tobacco economy, and if white, black, and Indian servants had continued their early solidarity, instead of whites succumbing to divide-and-conquer techniques.[31] This imaginary United States, without racial castes, would clearly have been better for white working people as well as for people of color.

WE THE WHITE PEOPLE OF THE UNITED STATES

At the time of the Revolutionary War, half of the wealth of the colonies was owned by 10 percent of the population—white men with over 2,000 pounds of property each, who collectively owned one-seventh of the population as slaves.[32] These wealthy white landowners dominated the Continental Congress and set up the laws of the new nation for their own benefit.[33]

The war was financed by the profits of slavery. Slave traders were among the wealthiest New England revolutionaries. France was paid in tobacco for its military assistance, and the tobacco plantations used slave labor.[34] Ironically, independence was won thanks to slavery. Without independence from Britain, emancipation would have come sooner, as England abolished the slave trade in 1791, and British slaves were freed in 1834.

One cause for which the war was fought was the right to steal Indian land. The British were limiting westward expansion, patrolling the western border to prevent squatting on their allied tribes' land. Tenant farmers and new immigrants were clamoring for land, sometimes organizing insurrections, and the revolutionary leaders focused attention on rebellion against these limits to westward expansion onto Indian land, diverting attention from the desire for land reform.[35] The most common payment for service in the Continental Army or state militias was western land, which made paying for the war possible without major tax increases on landowners.[36] In the South, some soldiers were also paid in slaves captured from loyalists' farms.[37] To reward Revolutionary War veterans, Congress passed the "extinction" of Indian claims to nine million, five hundred thousand acres of land.[38]

The Constitution gave nonelite white men more rights and took some from African Americans. It specified that white men "bound to service for a Term of Years" would count as full citizens for purposes of taxation, voting, and representation, but slave states would get extra representation in Congress based on three-fifths of the slave population, despite the lack of voting rights for slaves.[39] This gave Southern voters greater clout than Northern voters, so almost a century of congressional decisions favored the slave-owning South.

After the war, full citizenship for all European American men gradually became the reality, with a corresponding decrease in rights for people of color. In the early 1800s, in Connecticut, North Carolina, Tennessee, and New York, men without property were given the vote via legislation that also disenfranchised free black men.[40] At first many states restricted citizenship to Protestants;

Jews and Catholics could not be naturalized. But the first act of the U.S. Congress, the Naturalization Act of 1790, allowed only white male immigrants to become citizens, after two years of residency and proof of "good character" and loyalty to the Constitution.[41] [42] But these hurdles were minimal compared to the roadblocks set in the path of non-European immigrants, Indians, Mexicans, Asians, and Native Americans, the vast majority of whom were completely excluded from political participation in the new country. Since they were denied any role in making the laws of the land, only white interests would be represented in the political arena.

RICH OFF SLAVES' LABOR

For fifty of the first sixty-four years of U.S. history, the president was a slave owner.[43] George Washington owned five plantations totaling eight thousand acres. At his death he owned 123 slaves and his wife's estate had 153. If his wealth were adjusted for inflation, he would be the fifty-ninth richest American of all time, according to a 1996 survey that ranked Bill Gates thirty-first.[44] Thomas Jefferson owned ten thousand acres of land and 185 slaves.[45] James Madison estimated that he spent $12 to $13 on yearly upkeep per slave, and earned $257 per slave per year.[46]

The majority of slaves were owned by 4 percent of the southern white population;[47]

most whites were not slave owners. As of 1860, one-third of Southern white people had no assets of any kind, including slaves and land.[48] And most slave owners were not the big plantation owners, but owned five or fewer slaves, especially among the immigrant, urban, frontier, young, Indian, and black slave owners.[49]

But nonelite whites got economic opportunities based on slavery as well. Nonslave-owning employers could rent slaves as cheap labor.[50] Textiles were the first large American industry, employing people in trade and manufacturing all over the East, based entirely on cotton cultivated by slaves.[51] More land for cotton was the impetus for pushing Native Americans out of Tennessee, Alabama, Louisiana, Mississippi, and other areas where cotton was being cultivated by 1820. Many small farmers became large cotton farmers and slave owners by settling in these newly conquered areas.[52]

Joe Feagin writes in his book *Racist America*:

> *Without slave labor it seems likely that there would have been no successful textile industry, and without the cotton textile industry . . . it is unclear how or when the United States would have become a major industrial power. There was not a New England merchant of any prominence who was not then directly or indirectly involved in this trade. As the 19th century progressed, the sons and grandsons of the earlier traders in slaves and slave-related products often became the captains of the textile and other major industries in the North. The business profits made off enslavement were thereby transmitted across generations.*[53]

Thanks to the contemporary reparations debate, many scholars have attempted to estimate the total lost wages foregone by slaves, as well as the total wealth created for white America by their labor. Several of these attempts are collected in Richard F. America's book, *The Wealth of Races*. One article estimated that slaves accounted for about 15 percent of all privately owned assets in the United States before the Civil War, totaling over $3 billion in 1860.[54] Another calculated the value of slaves'

unpaid wages as $1.4 trillion, adjusted for inflation up to 1990, or $56,000 each if divided among twenty-five million African Americans.[55]

Wealth in the form of slaves amounted to just under $500 per white person in the South in 1860, according to a calculation in which the number of slaves is multiplied by the average price paid per slave. At a modest 6 percent return on these human assets, this implies a $30 average annual income for every white Southerner—a high amount given that the national per capita income in 1860 was $144.[56] In 1850 in South Carolina, the state with the highest earnings from slavery, the average slave owner earned $565 a year from slavery, and the average white resident earned $53.[57]

The wealth created from slavery in 1860 has been calculated as equal to about three or four times the total income of whites in the South. In the 1980s, American net worth was also calculated at between three and four times as high as total income; so the wealth from slavery was about as high in relation to income in the antebellum South as all forms of wealth—stocks, bonds, property, bank accounts, etc.—were in the 1980s.[58]

Theodore Allen documents land transfers over the centuries from 1666 to 1860 in Northampton County, Virginia. As wealth became more concentrated, European Americans had a 46 percent lower rate of land ownership in 1860 than in 1666. African Americans, by contrast, had a 98

Coming to Terms with Profiting from Slavery

Some white families can trace the origins of their assets to slave ownership or the slave trade. Katrina Browne discovered that she is the great-great-great-great-granddaughter of a major Rhode Island slave trader, Mark Anthony DeWolf. She organized family members to research their history.

Ten of them took a journey retracing their ancestors' route in the "triangle trade" between Ghana, Cuba, and Rhode Island. She has now turned this journey into a movie, *Traces of the Trade*, about how one family confronts and attempts to take responsibility for the privilege that grew from the crimes of their forebears.

The family discovered that three generations of DeWolfs made eighty-eight voyages to West Africa and the Caribbean, and grew wealthy off their human cargo. They eventually owned forty-seven ships, a slave auction house in Charleston, sugar and coffee plantations in Cuba, and a rum distillery and cotton mill in Rhode Island. Bristol, Rhode Island, grew into a prosperous seaport because of the DeWolfs' successful ventures.[61]

Katrina Browne and her family confronted grisly evidence of the suffering on which their ancestors' wealth was built: a whip and iron shackles in a cousin's basement, and a legend of a captain on a DeWolf ship who threw ill slaves overboard, and cut off their hands if they clung to the side.[62]

The DeWolf family fortunes dwindled after the slave trade was outlawed in 1808, but some Rhode Island businesses and institutions built on slave profits, such as Brown University, still exist today. Katrina Browne, with her dedication to exposing the New England slave trade and her ancestors' role in it, is a role model of a white person taking responsibility for the privilege passed down through generations and struggling to find a way to repair the damage done by it.

percent lower rate of land ownership.[59] "If the proportion of land ownership among African Americans had declined, but only as much as the ratio of land ownership among European-Americans, an estimated 30,000 landholdings would have been in the hands of the 53,000 free African Americans in rural Virginia in 1860."[60]

The Civil War grew out of a power struggle between slave owners who wanted more land for railroads and plantations, and immigrants and other would-be homesteaders who wanted western land kept available for small farm settlers.[63] Whether the new western states would be slave states or free states was the major political controversy of the day, pitting Southern slave owners against land-hungry Northern whites for access to western land. The Free Soil movement called for inexpensive western homesteads and a ban on slavery in western territories, as well as a ban on free black people there.[64]

After the Civil War, land originally promised or given to freed slaves was distributed to white veterans. After Lincoln was assassinated, President Johnson helped white plantation owners get back the land distributed by the Freedmen's Bureau,[65] evicting some black farmers by force.[66] Tax-delinquent land in the South was sold off, but far more went to white Northern speculators than to freed slaves.[67] The sacrifices of so many Union soldiers, both white and black, killed, wounded, and impoverished in the war, were traded for far too little improvement in African American life.

WESTWARD EXPANSION ONTO INDIAN LAND

"What good man would prefer a country covered with forests and ranged by a few thousand savages to our extensive Republic, studded with cities, towns, and prosperous farms, embellished with all the improvements which art can devise or industry execute, occupied by more than twelve million happy people, and filled with all the blessings of liberty, civilization and religion?"

—President Andrew Jackson,
Second Inaugural Address, 1833[68]

The British colonial administration forbade any settlement by English colonists west of the Appalachians, in order to keep control of trade and avoid conflicts with Indian tribes needed as allies against the French.[69] Squatting without the permission of English or Indian leaders was common, and was the cause of most Indian attacks on settlers.[70]

After independence, there were some limited efforts by the federal government to remove squatters from Indian land. In debates in Congress on Indian land policy, those who wanted to respect tribal land rights lost.[71] The federal government displaced the last Native Americans east of the Mississippi and supported the massive westward migrations of whites.

Many white settlers took their slaves with them, seventy-five thousand to Kentucky and Tennessee alone.[72] After the cotton gin was invented in 1791 and more cotton could be processed, the demand for land accelerated the migration to the Deep South and the Southwest.[73] Cherokee, Chickasaw, Choctaw, and Creek land was perfect for growing the most profitable kind of cotton, which increased white pressure on the federal government to displace these tribes.[74]

In Andrew Jackson, the land-hungry cotton planters found the leader of their dreams. A hero of the War of 1812, he then led a campaign against the Creeks of Mississippi, in which his troops and Cherokee warriors surrounded and massacred eight hundred Creek men, women, and children.[75] Then, from 1814 to 1824, by using threats, attacks, bribery, and deception, he negotiated nine treaties with the Cherokees, Chickasaws, Choctaws, Creeks, and Seminoles that gave massive amounts of land to the white government.[76] Jackson personally benefited from these treaties. A longtime speculator, he had bought a $100 share of five thousand acres of Chickasaw land in Mississippi twenty years earlier, in 1796, then sold a portion but kept the rest. After the treaty with the Chickasaws, he sold the remainder for $5,000.[77]

More than half a million white settlers moved to Kentucky, Tennessee, Alabama, Mississippi, and Louisiana from 1810 to 1821; almost a half million others moved into Ohio, Indiana, Illinois, and Missouri.[78] Jackson was elected president in 1828, after which there were few government impediments to wholesale takeovers of Indian land by whites.[79] He refused to enforce treaties, laws, and court rulings protecting native land rights.[80] In 1830, Jackson signed the Indian Removal Act, which forced seventy thousand Cherokees to walk the Trail of Tears to Oklahoma, with one-third dying on the way.[81]

Millions of acres were then transferred from public to private ownership—twenty million acres in 1836 alone.[82] Who would get the vacated Indian lands was the subject of political struggle. Railroad companies, banks, land companies, and wealthy individuals were given huge tracts or bought them at low prices. They would then divide the land into small plots and sell them to settlers at high prices. In 1860, speculators owned half the private land in Minnesota and one-quarter in Illinois and Iowa.[83]

Protests over land speculation led to reforms in the form of government homesteading programs. Squatters who settled on land with no official sanction were called "pre-emptors." The Pre-emption Act of

1841 legalized this widespread practice.[84] Over thirty-five million acres was transferred from public to private land ownership in 1855 and 1856.[85]

Then the Homestead Act of 1862 gave millions of acres to white settlers. Some of them were white women.[86] Women gained new rights to own property as the country grew, but almost always, only white women could benefit.[87] The last huge wave of federal land grants and sales was from 1883 to 1887, when sixteen million acres were distributed each year.[88] Overall, 1.5 million families got ownership of 246 million acres of land from the various homestead programs, nearly as much land as California and Texas combined.[89] One study estimates the number of Americans living today who are descendants of homestead recipients at forty-six million.[90]

Land grant and homestead policies varied, but most typically, a head of household would file a claim for 160 acres, paying a tiny amount per acre, and gaining title to the land after clearing, building a house, and living on it for a set number of years.[91] By the end of the century, three-quarters of white families owned their own farms, thanks to government assistance.[92]

Some immigrants, in particular Germans and Scandinavians, became homesteaders; as long as they had filed citizenship papers, they were covered by the homestead policies. But most homesteaders were not immigrants; they were second- or third-generation European Americans seeking better land.

In 1835, a Norwegian settler wrote home to say that in the U.S., "whether native born or foreign, a man is free to do with [land] what he pleases"; he had been successfully growing "Indian corn" in New York, but since he could buy public land in Illinois at $1.25 an acre, he planned to move there and farm more acres.[93]

In some cases, land distribution was explicitly limited to white settlers.[94] For example, an 1826 law barred African Americans from any pre-emption rights.[95] Then the U.S. Land Office in 1857 decided to deny public land grants to African Americans.[96] In other cases, there were not explicit racial restrictions, but in fact few people of color were able to benefit. The transportation and start-up costs were over $1,000, an amount impossible to save on black laborers' wages.[97] White hostility and sabotage also stopped would-be black homesteaders.[98] If a black family and a white family claimed the same land, the courts almost always honored the white claim.[99] The few African Americans who went to California with the promise of a land grant found that the state didn't regard their ownership as legal.[100]

As white people swarmed west, Native American tribes continued to defend their lands, especially the Cheyenne, Arapaho, Kiowa, and Comanche on the high plains.[101] In contrast to the myth of the rugged individualist pioneers celebrated in countless western, government assistance enabled and smoothed the western migration. Western pioneers followed trails that cut through Indian hunting grounds, with armed conflicts frequent. In the Treaty of Fort Laramie in 1851 and the Treaty of Fort Atkinson in 1853, the federal government paid an annuity for safe passage for wagons.[102] To open land for white settlers, the U.S. Army waged battles with the Sioux in Nebraska in 1845 and in Minnesota in 1862, and with the Navajo in New Mexico, all of which resulted in Indian loss of land.[103] White settlers often participated in attacks on Native Americans, especially after the U.S. Army went east for the Civil War.[104]

The western market economy was created and integrated into the national economy largely through federal interventions: Indian removal, land distribution, and railroad subsidies.[105] The railroad companies were given one hundred million acres of land at no charge, eventually owning over 10 percent of the land in the United States, and they became the nation's most powerful industry, winning more public subsidies through lobbying and bribery.[106] They created thirty thousand miles of track from 1865 to 1873, laid by underpaid and overworked workers, mostly Chinese and Irish.[107] The railroads had an interest in more farms along their routes so that they could get the business of hauling their crops, so they formed land companies to buy up land along their rights-of-way and to recruit settlers.[108] Similarly, they had an interest in the development of the coal, iron, lumber, mining, and machine industries, all of which

boomed once the transcontinental railroad was completed.[109]

Buffalo and bison were another asset transferred from people of color to white people. Plains tribes used them for food, clothing, and shelter. White settlers slaughtered them en masse, not only for sport or for profit, but also to starve the Indians off their land.[110] Once the railroads were complete, a profitable market in buffalo hides developed. The Santa Fe railroad shipped over one hundred thousand a year to the East.[111] A farmer or shopkeeper could kill fifty to sixty buffalo a day, while professionals killed over five thousand per season, selling them for $2.50 each.[112]

Tribes on reservations owned the land collectively, until the Dawes Act of 1887 broke them up into individual allotments. Land that was not allotted was given to white settlers.[113] Forty million acres were allotted to Indians and ninety million went to white people.[114] Tribes protested the land division, in particular the Chickasaw, Choctaw, Creek, Cherokee, and Seminole tribes, whose treaties explicitly forbid division.[115] Cattle-ranching nations such as the Cheyenne and Sioux found their land made useless by division, as it was unsuitable for farming, and cattle couldn't graze on tiny allotments. In theory, provisions of the act protected Indians from any white takeover of their allotments for twenty-five years, and also exempted them from taxation.[116] But in reality, they lost much of the land through fraud, illegal purchase, court cases, "incompetence" hearings, and murder.[117] Over generations the Indian lands were carved into smaller and smaller parcels, as they were divided among heirs, and unusable tiny plots were abandoned. The Bureau of Indian Affairs managed these unusable parcels and leased them for very low rents to white ranchers.[118]

CONQUERING MEXICO

Just as white people were handed Indian land in the Midwest and West, white people were handed Mexican land in the Southwest.

In the 1820s, just after Mexico won independence, Anglo (English-speaking white) settlers began moving to Texas, squatting on land "sold" by speculators who didn't own it for 1¢ to 10¢ an acre.[119] Anglos gradually became the majority of the Texas population under Mexican rule,[120] because the governments of Spain and then Mexico had encouraged new settlers to occupy sparsely inhabited northern Mexico. The desire for more land for Anglo settlers was the impetus behind both the fight for Texan independence and the Mexican-American War. Anglo Texans started a revolt in 1835, in part because of the prohibition on slavery passed by Mexico in 1830.[121] In 1837 they took Texas from Mexico and started the Lone Star Republic. Citizenship was granted to all white men, and only white men, living in Texas on the day of independence. The Republic gave public lands to landless white Texans. Steve Austin, for whom Austin, Texas, is named, gave one-quarter as much land to blacks as to whites who settled in his colonies.[122] Indians in Texas were rounded up during the Lone Star Republic period and moved to reservations in Oklahoma.[123] Even in the two Indian towns with federal recognition—where, officially, native people were allowed to remain—Anglos overran the town and claimed most of the land.[124]

The Treaty of Guadalupe Hidalgo ultimately resulted in a massive transfer of land from Latinos to white people throughout California, Arizona, New Mexico, Nevada, Utah, parts of Colorado, and small sections of what are now Oklahoma, Kansas, and Wyoming.[125] The treaty guaranteed that land titles previously awarded by the Spanish or Mexican governments would be respected. But the true goal of land for Anglo settlers was evident in the ways that the treaty was unenforced.[126] Racial categories unknown in Mexico were used to determine who got to keep their land. Political rights and land rights were given only to those categorized as white. *Mestizos*, Indians, and African Mexicans had fewer or no rights, depending on the state.[127]

By the 1850s, Congress was allowing each state and territory government to determine the citizen status of Mexicans in their area.[128] Anglos took over Mexican-owned land rapidly after this reversal.[129] By 1851, thirteen Anglos had bought 1.3 million acres from 358 Mexicans in sales of dubious legality.[130] Other Anglo men married wealthy Mexican women, which gave them ownership of their land.

Land ownership by Mexicans in the new states and territories fell from 60 percent in 1850 to 29 percent in 1860, with almost all the land going to Anglos. In Nueces County, Texas, in 1883, 100 percent of the land was owned by Anglos.[131]

The Homestead Act of 1862 let settlers claim 162 acres of public land and gain title to it by clearing and farming it.[132] While the act didn't mention race, its goal was to enable white people to become landowning farmers, according to a classic 1878 study by Seymour D. Thompson, *A Treatise on Homestead and Exemption Laws*.[133] The homesteading program was open to citizens of the United States and immigrants eligible for naturalization, which meant white immigrants.[134] (Mexican Americans gained citizenship in 1898, but the Homestead Act was only in effect until 1889.)[135] It's ironic that this race-biased program took off at the very period when the United States is often glorified for taking a stand against the racism of slavery in the Civil War.

In New Mexico, some major *criollo* (white Spanish) ranchers kept their land and stayed in political power by allying themselves with Anglo leaders.[136] But for people of color in New Mexico, the story was dif-ferent. Anglo real estate investors came to New Mexico and bought up land at low prices from people who didn't have the right documents to prove their title. The New Mexico surveyor general for the most part approved only the claims of Anglo investors.[137]

In Arizona, as in the other states, Anglos poured into the new state and settled on Mexican land. Copper and other mines employed landless *mestizos* from the territory and migrant Mexican workers, and brought large profits to their Anglo owners. Between 1838 and 1940, over $3 billion in metal was extracted from Arizona mines.[138]

White settlers got encouragement and assistance to move to California in the 1840s. President James K. Polk pronounced that California's harbors "would afford shelter for our navy, for our numerous whale ships, and other merchant vessels employed in the Pacific Ocean, and would in a short period become the marts of an extensive and profitable commerce with China, and other countries of the East."[139]

The gold rush began in 1849; almost one hundred thousand white people came to California, and suddenly there was new pressure to find land for all of them to live on.[140] The Free Soil provisions of the California state constitution passed in 1849 not only banned slaves from California, but banned free black people as well.[141] Indian villages were destroyed, by order of Congress, and Indians were killed or moved to reservations, reducing the native population of California from 310,000 in 1850 to 50,000 in 1855.[142] Once the railroad arrived in the 1870s, the pace of Anglo land takeover increased, as fortunes could be made shipping products from California mines and ranches back east.[143]

By the 1880s, there were hundreds of thousands of white people in California. They owned the best land and worked the best jobs, and Mexicans of color, including former landowners, fell into peonage, working for housing and food only, or into a lower tier of wage work alongside recent Chinese immigrants.[144] This two-tier economy, with Mexicans of color at the bottom, continued over the following century, and continues today.

For many decades there seemed to be enough western land for all the white people who wanted some. But after 1910, Indian and Mexican land was virtually all claimed, and the crowds of poor white immigrants in the cities had nowhere to go. Industrialists saw them as a source of cheap labor, and textile mills were built to take advantage of their desperation. [145]

WAVES OF WHITE IMMIGRANTS

Millions of white Americans today have parents, grandparents, or great-grandparents who emigrated from Europe during the huge wave of U.S. immigration from 1850 to 1920. Many have heard stories of the hardships and prejudice their relatives encountered in the New World, and these stories sometimes lead immigrants' descendants to deny that they have any privilege by virtue of being white.

This resistance is bolstered by conservative scholars who argue that white immigrants faced the same barriers of discrimination as African Americans but were able to overcome them through hard work and family values, a path they advocate for poor people of color.[146]

It is true that the United States was unwelcoming to many immigrants at the turn of the twentieth century. Ethnic and religious prejudice was often virulent, and government assistance was usually nonexistent. But it is also true that the poorest and most despised European immigrant had employment opportunities, including government jobs that African Americans never had—or in some cases had but promptly lost when this new source of cheap labor appeared. In general, the second or, at most, third generation escaped the most appalling tenement conditions.

Prejudice against poor immigrants was not encoded into law as obstacles for people of color were, although the government did little or nothing to protect immigrants against "No Irish need apply" rules, gentile-only workplaces, or the lynchings of Italians. New immigrants had difficult choices between keeping their native languages, names, and communities or pushing their children to become more "American" and assimilate—but, unlike people of color, most of them at least had this choice.

Immigration from northwestern Europe, which had predominated in the eighteenth and early nineteenth centuries, increased in the late 1800s. Scandinavian immigration doubled. These light-haired Protestant immigrants encountered little prejudice and no official opposition to assimilation or naturalization as they moved to rural areas in the Midwest where there was no overcrowding problem.[147] They were considered the same race as white Americans, while Jewish, Slavic, Irish, and southern Italian and other Catholic immigrants were commonly considered racially different.

The Nativist movement of the 1820s to 1850s aimed to exclude certain immigrants from American society, especially Catholics.[148] The American Party, popularly called the Know-Nothings because they swore to answer all inquiries about the party by saying "I know nothing," campaigned on an anti-immigrant and, in particular, anti-Catholic platform, and won many elections in the 1850s. There were Know-Nothing state legislators in Massachusetts, Delaware, and Pennsylvania, and a Massachusetts governor, and seventy-five members of Congress were elected in 1854.[149] Irish military companies were disbanded and Irish men banned from the police force and state agencies in Massachusetts (ironic, in light

of their predominance two generations later).[150]

The Jacksonian movement, the Nativists' political opponents, envisioned a racial caste system in which all men with only European ancestry were in the upper, white caste, and below them all Indians, Mexican *mestizos*, and black people.[151] The Jacksonian vision prevailed, for example, in the policies of President Theodore Roosevelt, and the Know-Nothing viewpoint shrank to a minority position never again achieving political power. In its glory days, however, it managed to impose hardships on many new immigrants by rallying prejudice against them.

Jewish Immigrants

The worst era of institutionalized American anti-Semitism was early in the Republic, especially in Massachusetts and other colonies in which citizenship was tied directly to Christianity. By 1800, however, Jews could vote and hold political office everywhere except in Maryland and New Hampshire.[152] Social and economic discrimination continued, but was rarely institutionalized by government policy. In the Immigration Act of 1907, the "head tax" paid by each new immigrant was increased from $2 to $5 with the goal of keeping out poor Russian Jews in particular,[153] but once in this country, Jewish immigrants were able to become citizens.

Jews in Europe had congregated in trades such as tailoring because they were barred from owning farmland and from many occupations. Similarly, Jews in the United States who weren't manual day laborers tended to be self-employed as pushcart peddlers, because major employers excluded them.[154] European Jews had sometimes been confined to ghettos; most Jewish immigrants to the United States were limited to overcrowded and squalid tenements in neighborhoods like New York's Lower East Side, in part by housing discrimination elsewhere.

The police not only looked the other way during mob violence against Jews, but sometimes the police joined the mob.[155] A wave of anti-Semitism in the 1920s resulted in a drastic cutback in Jewish immigrants from over 120,000 at the beginning of the decade to fewer than 7,000 at its end.[156] Discrimination by hotels, colleges, and employers worsened in the 1920s.[157]

But as the New York garment industry boomed after the 1880s, it was Jews and not African Americans who got the sweatshop jobs that gave them a toehold in the U.S. economy and the ethnic connections to start garment-related businesses of their own.[158] And Jewish arrivals, like other immigrant groups, founded and joined a network of ethnic charities and mutual-aid organizations to help orient them and keep them above the lowest poverty level. Anti-Semitic and Christian nation movements and hate groups have never been absent from the U.S.

landscape, but they have never won major political power either.[159]

Eastern European and Italian Immigrants

Eastern European and southern Italian immigrants were despised simply for their poverty and their cultural differences from northwestern Europeans. The provision of the 1891 Immigration Act barring people who might become public charges was arbitrarily enforced to keep out southern and eastern Europeans.[160] As their numbers swelled anyway, through what is now referred to as illegal immigration— 2,450,877 Italians and 1,597,306 Eastern Europeans arrived between 1901 and 1910[161]—a literacy requirement was imposed for entry to keep them out.[162] By contrast, there were fewer than one hundred Asian immigrants per year during this period.

In 1901, Woodrow Wilson contrasted "the sturdy stocks of the north of Europe" with the new "multitudes of men of the lowest class from the south of Italy and men of the meaner sort out of Hungary and Poland, who have neither skill nor energy nor an initiative of quick intelligence."[163] An 1893 *Los Angeles Times* editorial opined:

If we can keep out the Chinese, there is no reason why we cannot exclude the lower classes of Poles, Hungarians, Italians and some other European nations, which people possess most of

the vices of the Chinese and few of their good
qualities, besides having a leaning towards bloodshed and anarchy which is particularly their
own.[164]

But these widespread prejudices never translated into a prohibition of voting rights or naturalized citizenship. Italian immigrants, like the Irish, used municipal jobs to get ahead at a time when the private sector limited them to menial, low-paid jobs.[165] "For several decades southern and Eastern Europeans formed an ambiguous middle stratum of the racial order, between the native-born whites and old European immigrants above them, and the American Indians, blacks, Asians and Mexicans below," write Chip Berlet and Matthew Lyons in *Rightwing Populism in America.*[166]

Irish Immigrants

Because Irish people were considered an inferior race by their British colonizers, and this view spread to the English Americans across the Atlantic, and because potato famine refugees were some of the most desperately poor people to arrive on U.S. shores, Irish immigrants endured the worst treatment of any European nationality, and for the longest time.

The U.S. Census before the Civil War divided people into three categories, native born, foreign, and Irish.[167] Irish people were not only seen as a separate race,[168] but as a

virulently hated race. Irish people were referred to as "niggers turned inside out," and African Americans were called "smoked Irish"; both were meant to be insulted by comparison to each other.[169] The stereotypes of both were similar: drunken, lazy, animal-like, and stupid.[170]

Before the Irish potato famine of the 1840s, a sizable minority of Irish immigrants was able to become farm owners, although most began as laborers.[171] After the famine began and the numbers of Irish Catholic immigrants grew to two million by 1850,[172] landownership became a rarity.[173] The new wave of Irish immigrants was poorer than early Irish immigrants had been.[174] Virtually all Irish immigrants in large eastern cities worked as unskilled laborers—94 percent in Boston in 1850[175]—most as workers on canals, railroads, construction, or docks, jobs that had been previously done mostly by African Americans.[176] Most Irish women worked as domestic servants.[177] By 1870, 22 percent of Irish American households lived in desperate poverty.[178]

Some Irish Americans have argued that Irish immigrants were worse off economically than African slaves.[179] Frederick Law Olmsted repeated a statement made to him by an Alabama official of a stevedoring company, who said he hired Irish laborers because "niggers are worth too much to be risked here; if the Paddies are knocked overboard . . . nobody loses anything."[180] Death rates were extremely high among Irish and Chinese railroad workers. Yet Irish immi-

THE
NEW DECLARATION OF "INDEPENDENCE."

"..FOR TWENTY YEARS NO MORE
CHINESE LABORERS SHALL COME TO THE
UNITED STATES; ..AND NO COURT
SHALL ADMIT CHINESE TO
CITIZENSHIP.

WHICH COLOR IS TO BE TABOOED NEXT?

FRITZ (to Pat). "If the Yankee Congress can keep the *yellow* man out, what is to hinder
hem from calling us *green* and keeping us out too?"

Political cartoon in Harper's Weekly linking Irish immigration with Chinese, 1882.
(*Library of Congress*)

voters was an immigrant, but in 1854 the figure was one in seven, and a plurality of the increase was Irish Catholic. By 1850, 42 percent of the foreign-born people in the United States were Irish.[184] The party that welcomed them was the party that grew the fastest.[185] The Democratic Party was the proslavery party, and its platform hinged on the uniting all white voters as a superior racial caste.[186] It opposed homestead laws, but most Irish immigrants were not interested in leaving the cities for a rural farm.[187] The Federalist Party was alarmed by this influx of new voters into its opponents' party, and proposed restrictions on Irish voting rights, but they failed to get them enacted into law.[188]

Government provided stepping-stones to prosperity for Irish Americans in the form of municipal jobs, unavailable to people of color. Before the Civil War, only one Boston police officer was Irish, and by 1900 there were one hundred. The first Irish mayor of Boston was elected in 1884, and by 1906 virtually all Boston political figures were Irish.[189] In part, Irish Americans gained dominance of New York and Boston munic-

grants in fact had access to jobs that African Americans didn't.

The hardships of Irish laborers still left them more fortunate than unemployed Irish immigrants. In the 1840s and early 1850s in Boston, 97 percent of the residents of one almshous, 75 percent of all county jail prisoners (hence the term "paddy wagon"), 90 percent of all truants and vagabonds, and 58 percent of paupers were Irish.[181]

Yet despite this mistreatment, Irish Catholic men never lost rights essential to building wealth: the right to vote, the right to immigration, and the right to naturalization.[182]

The Democratic Party and Irish Americans were responsible for advancing each other.[183] In 1830, only one in thirty

ipal jobs and contracts by denying them to African American people.[190]

Who's White?

In 1909, Armenian immigrants were classified as "Asiatics" and thus denied naturalized citizenship.[191] Four Armenians sued the federal government for citizenship on the grounds that they were white. It is ironic that they had to sue to be considered Caucasian, given that Armenia is in the Caucasus Mountains.[192] Unlike Japanese, Chinese, Hawaiian, and Burmese people who had lost similar lawsuits, they won their case, on the grounds that the term "white" referred to

anyone not "Negro" or "Indian."[193] Citizenship brought the Armenians the right to own land in California after aliens were barred from owning property in 1913, and some of the state's eighteen thousand Armenian immigrants became major landowners and raisin producers.[194] They arrived at the same time as many Japanese immigrants did, speaking as little English, but zoomed ahead in wealth because of the valuable designation "white."

Court decisions on white status were based on a mix of supposedly scientific criteria and the common understandings of the day, leading to a mess of contradictions.[195] Syrians were deemed white in 1909, 1910, and 1915, but not in 1913 or 1914. Asian

1940 certificate of naturalization for Chinese American woman marks her race as "White."

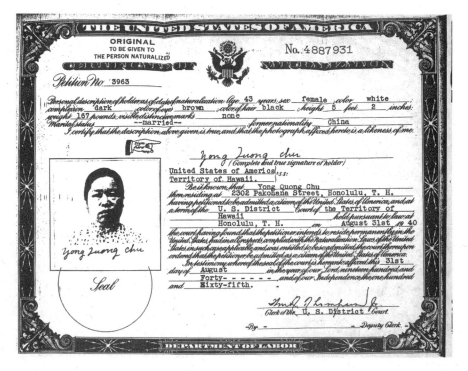

Indians won white status in 1910, 1913, 1919, and 1920, but not in 1909, 1917, or after 1923.[196] The persistence of immigrants in suing for whiteness is evidence of the financial and social benefits that came with white status. After all, no one sued to be considered Asian, much less black.

A new wave of nativism and anti-Semitism swept the United States in the 1920s. Vice President Calvin Coolidge wrote an article for *Good Housekeeping* called "Whose Country Is This?" saying, "[B]iological laws show us that Nordics deteriorate when mixed with other races."[197]

New laws stopped the flow of European immigrants. In 1921, Congress enacted a quota system for each European country of origin, limiting the number of new arrivals to 3 percent of the 1910 Census numbers of foreign-borns from each country. Then, in 1924, the quotas were lowered to 2 percent of each group's numbers in the whole population—not just the foreign-born population—of the 1890 Census, which raised the northwest European quotas while lowering all others.[198] The Italian quota, for example, fell from forty-two thousand to four thousand, and the Polish quota from thirty-one thousand to six thousand.[199] Jewish would-be immigrants, who were scattered among various Eastern European countries, were the most heavily affected; Jewish immigration slowed to a trickle.[200] One year after the 1924 legislation took effect, the commissioner of immigration said that virtually all immigrants now "looked exactly like Americans."[201]

Quotas posed impossible barriers for many, and those who did arrive from certain undesirable countries were met with discrimination. But despite these various levels of prejudice and barriers to immigration, people already in the United States faced two different degrees of opportunity encoded into law, one for all white people and one for all people of color. This is not to dismiss the struggles against hate and discrimination that white ethnic groups faced in the New World. But they had a degree of government representation and protection that made education, home ownership, livable wages, and savings achievable dreams by the second generation, at a time when these were impossible for almost all people of color. White immigrants and people of color lived under two different sets of economic rules, both harsh—but only one with an escape hatch.

There was a glimmer of hope for people of color in 1917 when the Supreme Court overturned municipal laws barring people of color from moving to majority-white neighborhoods.[202] But the real estate industry responded by creating a national code for realtors and bankers to enforce segregated housing and put restrictive covenants into deeds to prevent white home owners from selling to people of color.[203] The code said, "[A] realtor should never be instrumental in introducing into a neighborhood a character of property or occupancy, members of any race or nationality, or any individual whose presence will clearly be detrimental to property values in the neighborhood."[204] White people, even noncitizen immigrants of despised ethnic groups, could almost always live wherever they chose.

THE NEW DEAL: A BETTER DEAL
FOR WHITE PEOPLE

Like the colonial period, the Great Depression of the 1930s was an example of a time when the racial wealth gap widened even as white people lost economic ground. The Depression caused greater hardship for people of color than for white people, yet most of the government aid went to whites.

African Americans were laid off at a higher rate than white workers, and as desperate white unemployed people sought any available job, no longer were certain low-status occupations, such as hotel, garbage, and domestic work, reserved for black workers.[205] In southern cities, over half of African Americans were unemployed by 1932.[206] In New York, Philadelphia, Chicago, and Detroit, while the unemployment rate was 23 percent for white men and 14 percent for white women in 1932, for black men it was over 40 percent, and for black women 55 percent.[207] Industrial wages fell by 20 percent by 1930,[208] and black wages were already much lower than white wages.

The Depression did not automatically lead to federal aid to destitute Americans. President Herbert Hoover's administration actually cut government spending in response to falling tax revenues, giving little to unemployed workers besides "pick your-

self up by your bootstraps" advice.[209] Only when threatened with massive organized protest—labor strikes, veterans' marches on Washington, tenant groups blocking evictions—did President Franklin Roosevelt's administration begin to pass its historic proworker legislation.

Key congressional committees were controlled by southern members of Congress, who wanted their white constituents' sharecroppers and domestic and agricultural workers to be excluded from any federal aid. Thus, to get his New Deal policies through Congress, Roosevelt made compromises that in effect gave benefits and protections only to mostly white nonagricultural workers.[210]

Public works jobs were offered primarily to white unemployed men; those given to men of color were generally lower-wage, and less skilled jobs.[211] The rules of the Public Works Administration were intended to prevent such discrimination, requiring black men to be hired in proportion to the racial balance in each occupation in the 1930 Census, but these good intentions didn't become the reality.[212] Southern employers and officials openly defied the antidiscrimination clauses. A Georgia official said, "There will be no Negroes pushing wheelbarrows and boys driving trucks getting forty cents an hour when the good white men and white women, working on the fields alongside these roads, can hardly earn forty cents a day."[213]

Union members were sometimes given preference for public jobs, at a time when many unions restricted membership to whites.[214] Minimum wage rules were sometimes bent to allow employers to pay black workers less, and some employers fired blacks rather than pay them an equal wage.[215]

The Civilian Conservation Corps in 1933 was employing over two hundred thousand white young men and fewer than ten thousand young black men, and housing them in segregated camps in the South.[216] These numbers improved later in the decade; in 1935, 10 percent of CCC workers were black.[217] Despite the efforts of CCC administrators to use the program for black advancement, with implementation left in the hands of racist local officials, most job training and promotions went to white workers.[218]

Once the Works Progress Administration (later called the Works Projects Administration) was formed in 1935, two-thirds of the white relief recipients in New York got WPA jobs, while only one-third of black relief recipients were hired.[219] The WPA put over three million people on the federal payroll. Construction projects were chosen at the local level, and in the South tended to benefit white communities.[220]

Wages were set and staff hired at the local level, usually on terms favorable to white workers.[221] Of more than 10,000 WPA supervisors in the South, only eleven were black.[222]

Millions of white families survived the Depression with federal paychecks, while most unemployed and impoverished people of color were not hired for public works jobs.

The National Industrial Recovery Act of 1932 was designed to stop the Depression-era trend of lower wages and longer hours by setting federal standards. But minimum wage and maximum hours requirements mostly improved conditions for white workers. Wages in the New York garment industry, which was full of white immigrant workers, rose by 30 percent to 60 percent by 1934.[223] On the other hand, when the NIRA set a minimum wage of $12 a week for cotton workers, plantation owners fired black workers rather than give them such a raise.[224]

After a wave of militant strikes and union protests, the National Labor Relations Act of 1935 (the Wagner Act) was passed to protect industrial workers' rights to organize unions and bargain collectively with employers, the legal framework that has benefited union workers ever since.[225] But the bill was dubbed the "Negro Removal Act" by bitter African Americans, who saw it as legitimizing whites-only unions.[226] Both the labor rights in the Wagner Act[227] and the federal minimum wage established by the Fair

Labor Standards Act of 1938 didn't apply to domestic and agricultural workers, jobs held by most people of color.[228] Among women, 30 percent of white women benefited from the act, while only 10 percent of black women did.[229]

In the rural South a higher percentage of white than black families got relief from the Federal Emergency Relief Administration.[230] Benefits in some areas also were higher for whites than for blacks,[231] for example $32 versus $19 a month in Atlanta.[232] The work programs that white men were steered to continued longer than the relief programs. When federal relief was discontinued in 1935, it was mostly African Americans and white women who lost their source of income.[233]

Social security was the broadest and most enduring program created by the New Deal, yet because domestic and agricultural workers were not covered by old age assistance, only among white people were most seniors covered.[234] In 1939, Congress added survivor benefits to Social Security, thereby transferring the mostly white widows of employed men covered by Social Security away from Aid to Dependent Children, which thereafter became a disproportionately African American program—and, not coincidentally, a stigmatized program with benefits far below the poverty line.[235]

Foreclosures on homes and farms were part of the downward spiral of the Depression, as banks became cautious about lending. The Home Owners' Loan Corporation (HOLC), created to help home owners and stabilize banks, gave all of its loans to white home owners, and thus a greater proportion of white home owners avoided losing their homes during the remainder of the Depression.[236]

The Federal Housing Administration was not explicitly a white program, but realtors and hostile neighbors kept families of color out of white neighborhoods, so in practice it was almost impossible for a family of color to get an FHA loan anywhere.[237] The FHA also encouraged restrictive covenants in deeds to prohibit sales to people of color.[238] Its manuals for appraisers encouraged channeling loans toward white home buyers.[239] It institutionalized the practice of redlining, marking certain neighborhoods as off-limits for loans.

Not only was there discrimination in FHA mortgages, but almost all Veterans Administration mortgages went to white families.[240] Since banks faced less risk with federally insured mortgages, they stopped issuing home loans without such insurance; as a result, the New Deal housing programs actually made it even harder for a family of color to buy a home than during the upsurge of discrimination in the 1920s. This is one of many examples of supposedly race-neutral policies that in fact increased racial disparities in assets.

The Housing Act of 1937 authorized tax-free bonds for local governments to build public housing projects and provided federal subsidies for low-income tenants' rent.[241] Virtually everywhere, local public housing authorities built projects in segregated neighborhoods and selected tenants by race.[242] For example, a huge public housing development of eighty-two thousand apartments was built near Philadelphia with federal underwriting, and it was 100 percent white until the 1960s.[243] Overall, 282 of 400 public housing projects developed by the U.S. Housing Authority between 1937 and 1942 were for white families, and just forty were racially integrated.[244] White projects tended to be located in suburbs and black projects in inner-city neighborhoods.[245]

The Agricultural Adjustment Administration distributed its aid almost entirely to white farmers.[246] Even worse, some planters who were paid to keep their cotton farms idle in order to boost cotton prices evicted their black sharecroppers,[247] and the cash aid was used to mechanize farms and lay off black farm hands.[248] Because of these unintended effects, the law was amended in 1934 to give tenants half the agricultural assistance payments, but often planters took the checks to apply toward the tenant farmers' debts—and sometimes took them by force when the tenants were black.[249] Over 90 percent of the payments meant for tenants went to the landowners.[250]

Similarly, the Farmers Home Administration (FH) gave loans to help mostly white farmers keep their farms. Later, in the 1950s, FH loans were sometimes denied to black farmers in retaliation for joining the NAACP or registering to vote.[251]

During President Roosevelt's second term, the forces within the federal government opposed to racial discrimination gained strength, and the number of WPA jobs and the amount of relief going to African Americans increased.[252] But racist local governments continued to find ways not to cooperate with federal rules and to channel aid to white people.[253]

The New Deal is frequently held up today as a model for the positive effects of an activist government. And for white Americans, it is true that programs created in the 1930s wove an almost Europe-like safety net. But the overall effect of the New Deal on the racial wealth gap was to widen and institutionalize it. Millions more white families owned homes, belonged to unions, and counted on social security checks for retirement at the end of the 1930s than at the beginning. Americans of color, on the other hand, ended the decade shut out of home ownership and stuck in segregated neighborhoods, dislocated from rural southern communities, impoverished and with a chronically high unemployment rate.[254]

WORLD WAR II AS A BOOST TO WHITE PEOPLE

When the United States entered World War II, defense jobs opened up for people unemployed during the Depression, including people of color, but even more for whites. The defense industry openly discriminated against African Americans. For example, the North American Aviation company issued a statement in 1941 saying, "'While we are in complete sympathy with the Negro, it is against company policy to employ them as aircraft workers or mechanics . . . regardless of their training. . . . There will be some jobs as janitors for Negroes." [255]

Not only did the Roosevelt administration not object to this discrimination, it responded to the growth of the defense industry by terminating some New Deal programs, including the relief program that aided many still-unemployed people of color.[256] White median income in 1947 was double the black median income, according to the U.S. Census.[257]

The most blatant transfer of assets from people of color to white people during the war was the internment of 110,000 Japanese Americans, two-thirds of them U.S. citizens, from 1942 to 1945.[258] The rationale was that they might have loyalty to an enemy nation, but racism was clearly involved, as German and Italian Americans were not interned, and neither were

Japanese people in Hawaii, where racial attitudes were less biased.[259]

With Japanese people under deadline to dispose of their homes and businesses,[260] white neighbors and speculators bought Japanese farms, houses, and businesses at a fraction of their worth, enriching themselves at their interned neighbors expense.[261]

After the war, many New Deal programs, including the Fair Employment Practices Committee, were dismantled by a congressional coalition of southern Democrats and northern Republicans.[262] This meant that the massive discrimination faced by the returning GIs was not against federal law.

The Servicemen's Readjustment Act of 1944, better known as the GI Bill, provided a number of benefits to servicemen returning from World War II. Benefits included help in job placement, unemployment compensation for up to a year after returning, mortgage loans, and tuition for up to four years of education and training.[263]

Of sixteen million returning veterans, over two million went to college on the GI Bill, and over five million went to vocational school.[264] They were by far disproportionately white. Many went into well-paid professions: 450,000 became engineers; 240,000, accountants; 238,000, teachers;

91,000, scientists; 67,000, doctors; 22,000, dentists; 17,000, writers and editors.[265]

Job placement was run by the United States Employment Services (USES). Local USES centers had discretion over who got placements and unemployment benefits, and white staff funneled the good jobs and benefits to white veterans. White veterans in job-training programs learned radio repair, machine and electrical work, photography, carpentry, business, and diesel engineering; black veterans learned dry cleaning and tailoring.[266] While black veterans were being referred to menial jobs, 86 percent of the referrals to skilled jobs were to whites.[267]

Another major benefit under the GI Bill was low-interest, long-term mortgage loans for first-time homebuyers insured by the Federal Housing Authority (FHA) and the Veterans Administration.[268] Most of these loans went to white veterans buying homes in the suburbs; with these loans, suburban home ownership became cheaper than renting in the inner city.[269] In St. Louis County between 1943 and 1960, for example, five times as many FHA mortgages were issued to the mostly white area of the county as were given to those in the racially mixed city of St. Louis.[270] Of the 67,000 mortgages insured under the GI Bill in New York and the suburbs of northern New Jersey, over 66,900 went to white veterans.[271] The number of homes in the United States grew by 13 million from 1945 to 1954, and 40 percent of them were purchased with Veterans Administration mortgages.[272] A total of $120 billion in new housing was financed by the VA and FHA by 1962, 98 percent of it for white home owners.[273]

Many billions of dollars of equity were accumulated by white people thanks to government help not available to people of color. These FHA and VA recipients are the parents of the baby boomers, and their homes form a substantial part of the record-setting $10 trillion in inheritance now being passed down to the baby-boom generation.

SUBURBAN SPRAWL

Thanks to discriminatory postwar policies, as the 1950s progressed, more and more white people lived in new suburban homes, and more and more people of color lived in overcrowded and substandard inner-city apartments.

The flood of government money turning white families into suburban property owners included not just mortgage insurance, but also the construction of water and sewer systems for the new suburbs.[274] The suburbs also got a boost from the federal government through highway construction. The building of roads to connect suburban commuters with downtown workplaces—for example, in Los Angeles, Houston, and St.

Louis—destroyed already scarce housing in neighborhoods of color, while increasing options for white families.[275]

The population of white people in the suburbs increased by twenty-two million from 1960 to 1977, four million of them moving from central cities. Meanwhile, the inner-city black population rose by six million, and the number of African Americans in the suburbs grew by only half a million.[276] In the suburbs, ethnic differences among white people grew less important, and they began to define themselves simply as "white," in contrast to people of color.[277] Corporations began to close urban manufacturing plants and relocate them in the suburbs, convenient to white job seekers.[278]

A study of home ownership in greater Los Angeles found that white people were more likely to become home owners and tended to buy earlier in life than black people, and that that gap was wider in 1980 than in 1970.[279] White people paid 15 percent less than black people for similar housing in the same neighborhood, the study also found.[280]

Not only did white Americans need less money for real estate, but they also continued to have more income. The white unemployment rate was always much lower than that of other racial groups, and white wages were always higher. A study by the Office of Urban Programs at the University of California at Berkeley School of Business Administration analyzed how much white people would have lost if they had had the same unemployment rates and wage levels of African Americans from 1929 to 1984. They concluded that the difference would be $638 million in 1984 dollars.[281] Another group of economists concluded that employers gained $25 billion in 1980 by paying African American workers less than white workers.[282] As of 1984, white median income was $24,000 and black median income was $13,000.[283]

Nevertheless, white Americans perceived blacks' small gains after the Civil Rights Movement as much greater than they actually were. This misperception was one basis for the white backlash in the 1970s and 1980s. Author Martin Carnoy describes this trend in *Faded Dreams:*

In the 1970's, white working- and middle-class backlash against the black power movement and against black economic gains became a major political factor that shaped government action. Ronald Reagan's election would not have been possible without it—neither probably would have been the high-unemployment/low-wage economic strategy pursued by both Carter and Reagan. Most members of the white working class who voted for a conservative approach to economic growth—Reagan Democrats and blue-collar southern Republicans—did so because they blamed economic problems on government antipoverty and other social programs inextricably identified with inner-city blacks.[284]

Later, he reports a

[b]acklash against affirmative action . . . was a building block of the new politics. So were

antiunionism, low inflation, and, implicitly, slow or no growth in real wages and greater income inequality. The last two should have been very unpopular with the mass of American voters, but when presented as a precondition of economic competitiveness, economic growth, and lower tax rates, they lost their negative edge. Conservatives were also successful in making "welfare" spending a symbol of New Deal economic policy. They blended minorities of color and welfare into inseparable images and, to boot, expanded the minority identity to include crime and violence. As inflation rose and real wages fell, economic insecurity increased in the white working class. . . . Insecurity and fear fueled the success of conservative politics, which in turn played to rising popular feelings among whites against social spending, taxes, and affirmative action.[285]

HANGING ONTO JOBS DURING DEINDUSTRIALIZATION

Millions of industrial workers lost their jobs in the waves of plant closings in the1970s and 1980s, but white workers were less heavily affected by deindustrialization than workers of color, in part because of government policies. Just from 1966 to 1973, corporations moved over a million American jobs to other countries.[286] Even more jobs moved from the Northeast and Midwest regions to the South, where unions were scarce and wages were lower. New York City alone lost six hundred thousand manufacturing jobs in the 1960s.[287] This trend concentrated wealth in fewer hands. Working people overall had lost 4 percent of national income by 1975 due to foreign investment by U.S. corporations.[288]

Federal policy encouraged plant closings and did very little to mitigate their effects. Tax credits for foreign investment and foreign tax payments encouraged companies to move. While deindustrialization was happening in the 1970s, the federal government spent more in the southern states than in the affected areas: the Northeast and Midwest states averaged 81¢ in federal spending for each tax dollar they sent to Washington; southern states averaged $1.25.[289] As plants closed, laid-off workers suffered thirty times the suicide rate of Americans as a whole, as well as more alcoholism and physical and mental illness.[290] Meanwhile, companies passed the benefits from lower wages onto their mostly white shareholders.

Media images of these displaced workers usually showed young white men. But, in fact, they were disproportionately African American. The U.S. Commission on Civil Rights found that during the recession of 1973 to 1974, 60 percent to 70 percent of laid-off workers were African American in places where they were only 10 percent to 12 percent of the workforce.[291] In five cities in the Great Lakes region, the majority of black men employed in manufacturing lost their jobs between 1979 and 1984.[292] One reason was seniority: white workers had been in their jobs longer, and so had an advantage for keeping them during cutbacks.

Another reason was geography. Just a couple of generations after blacks and Puerto Ricans moved to northern industrial cities for the jobs, the jobs disappeared.[293] The northern cities that lost the most jobs were some of those with the largest populations of people of color,[294] and they sank into poverty and chronically high unemployment as few heavily white areas did.

White families also had more of a cushion to survive job losses than black families. In 1971, black median income was 60 percent of white median income; by 1980, the portion had fallen to 58 percent.[295]

As dramatic as the shift of jobs from the North to the South and overseas was, the shift of jobs from the city to the suburbs was equally drastic. In the 1950s and 1960s, white people moved to the suburbs and commuted to the city; in the 1970s and 1980s their jobs joined them in the suburbs.[296] The majority of new manufacturing jobs in the 1970s were located in the suburbs, while manufacturing employment fell almost 10 percent in center cities.[297] In the Los Angeles area, for example, plants were closing in the city while plants opened in

the San Fernando Valley and Orange County, then mostly white areas.[298] Suburban white people had a greater and greater geographic edge in job hunting.

But white working-class men did in fact have fewer well-paying unionized manufacturing jobs available to them by the 1980s than in the postwar industrial boom, and this setback fueled the politics of backlash.

As runaway inflation and plant closings made most Americans less economically secure in the late 1970s, right-wing think tanks and politicians pointed to the modest progress of African Americans as a cause for white working-class troubles. "Unqualified black people took your jobs" became a rallying cry. Of course, black progress did not cause stagflation or deindustrialization. In fact, any particular jobs or benefits forgone by white workers because black people now shared some access to government largesse were no doubt dwarfed by the many jobs and tax revenues created by the now higher earnings and spending of African Americans. But the progressive voices saying this commonsense view were often drowned out by right-wing voices. The New Deal coalition, with its vision of an activist government, began to unravel, as some white voters began to vote for more conservative politicians, putting their perceived racial interests ahead of the economic interests they shared with people of color.

AFFIRMATIVE ACTION FOR WHITE PEOPLE
BEGINS A COMEBACK IN THE 1980S

The Reagan administrations of the 1980s made dramatic policy shifts in favor of white people. In a few cases, such as affirmative action reversals, policy changes were explicitly based on racial categories. But more often, the racially disparate effects were de facto (in practice), not de jure (in law). Decisions about budget cuts, farm subsidies, and criminal justice were made without explicit reference to race but had the effect of advantaging white people, while harming people of color.

Sometimes the white backlash cut off its nose to spite its face, as budget reductions aimed at people of color in fact made white working-class people more economically insecure as well. Some economists have shown how white wages are kept lower because of the divide-and-conquer effects of racial discrimination. When the income gap between people of color and white people is wider, white average incomes are lower; when the gap is smaller, white average incomes are higher. [299] In 1985, black median income was only 58 percent of white median income, according to the U.S. Census Bureau. [300]

Republican Party rhetoric since the 1980s has implied that only people of color need government help, due to their own character flaws, while white people are home owners and overburdened taxpayers employed in the private sector. Of course, this is not true: poor people in the United States have always been mostly white, and millions of white renters and white unemployed and underemployed people have benefited from government antipoverty programs. White women were major beneficiaries of affirmative action. But the rhetoric was persuasive in convincing lower-income white people to vote in a block with white financial elites.

In his provocative book *The Possessive Investment in Whiteness: How White People Profit from Identity Politics*, George Lipsitz describes how conservative politicians have persuaded white voters to act against their own economic interests:

By generating an ever repeating cycle of "moral panics" about the family, crime, welfare, race, and terrorism, neoconservatives produce a perpetual state of anxiety that obscures the actual failures of conservatism as economic and social policy, while promoting demands for even more draconian measures of a similar nature for the future. The neoracism of contemporary conservatives plays a vital role in building a countersubversive consensus because it disguises the social disintegration brought about by neoconservativism itself as the fault of "inferior" social groups, and because it builds a sense of righteous indignation among its constituents that enables them to believe that the selfish and self-interested politics they pursue are actually part of a moral crusade.[301]

President Reagan cut the budgets of most domestic federal programs, most notably housing. Military spending was the only area that greatly increased during the Reagan administrations, and the military procurement industries disproportionately employed white men. In 1985, a group of economists projected the racial employment effects of a hypothetical shift of a million jobs to military supply industries like aerospace, communications, and electronics and away from health, education, and social services, based on 1980 gender and race employment data. They found that white men would gain 386,000 jobs from the shift, white women would lose 320,000, black men would break even, and black women would lose 66,000 jobs.[302]

Affirmative action programs, which had begun in the 1970s to put some small limits on historic white and male advantages, were first eroded by court challenges before President Reagan took office. The 1978 *Regents of the University of California v. Bakke* case sounded a warning bell of attacks to come.[303] Allan Bakke sued the University of California at Davis medical school for rejecting his application, claiming his grade

point average (GPA) was higher than sixteen students of color who had been admitted. But the facts don't bear out his claim that he was discriminated against because he was white: his GPA was also higher than thirty-six white students admitted, and lower than at least one student of color.[304] Bakke had also been turned down by several other medical schools with no affirmative action programs, probably in part because he was thirty-six years old.[305]

There were also five students admitted that year because their parents had attended or donated to the school, and his suit did not object to their admissions.[306] In fact, there have been no legal challenges to so-called legacy admissions to colleges anywhere in the United States. Since the 1950s, 20 percent of Harvard undergraduates have been admitted because their parents had gone to Harvard. In California and Virginia, out-of-state children of alumni of the state universities have been given the same preference as in-state applicants.[307]

Bakke, in short, was an opportunist with a racial ax to grind. However, the Supreme Court did order him admitted to the medical school and prohibited quotas for particular numbers of people of color, while upholding in vague language the validity of affirmative action efforts to create an overall diverse student body.[308] This decision opened the door to more white people to try to use the courts to get college admissions and jobs they otherwise wouldn't have gotten.

In 1986, the Supreme Court overturned a

collective bargaining agreement in Michigan that preserved diversity among teachers by allowing layoffs of senior white teachers instead of newer black teachers to remedy past discrimination. Justice Powell, writing for the majority, wrote "the rights and expectations surrounding seniority make up what is probably the most valuable capital asset that the worker 'owns,' worth even more than the current equity in his home."[309] While this was no doubt true of the experienced white teachers, the income security of teaching jobs was certainly an even greater share of the assets of the newer black teachers.

In Richmond, Virginia, white contractors had been given 99.33 percent of city construction business between 1973 and 1978, even though half the population was African American.[310] A City Council decision to set aside 30 percent of construction contracts for businesses owned by people of color was overturned by the Supreme Court, allowing the historic white advantage to continue. Justice O'Connor explained why the discrepancy in contracts was not necessarily due to discrimination by saying, "Blacks may be disproportionately attracted to industries other than construction."[311]

After these setbacks, colleges, government agencies, and employers had to circumscribe their affirmative action programs to very narrow goals and activities to avoid federal lawsuits.

Attacks on affirmative action grew more organized and bolder in the 1990s. Organizations such as the Center for Individual Rights (CIR) actively solicited white plaintiffs willing to sue to re-establish white advantages.[312] Their first cases were all against state universities with affirmative action programs, in Texas, Michigan, and Washington state, with mixed results.[313] In 2002 CIR's Michigan case was considered by the Supreme Court, which upheld the looser of the two contested programs and banned the more energetic and numerical one.

After California's Proposition 209 was approved by voters in 1996, black admissions to the University of California at Berkeley's Boalt Hall School of Law dropped 80 percent the next year.[314] The voters enabled many more white people to become lawyers than would have done so if the school had been free to set its own admissions policy.

The results of all these policies of the 1980s on the racial wealth gap were striking. White people gained assets during the decade, increasing their median net worth from $71,500 in 1983 to $84,900 in 1989. African American net worth, meanwhile, fell from $4,800 to $2,200 over the same period, and Latinos' fell from $2,800 to $1,800.

THE NINETIES BOOM WENT MOSTLY
TO WHITE ELITES

The economic boom of the 1990s was a bust for those without assets. Stock prices and home prices soared, while wages first stagnated, and then rose very slowly. Those who got rich were those who owned stock and real estate—mostly wealthy white people. Over 85 percent of stock market gains from 1989 to 1997 went to the wealthiest 10 percent of Americans.[315]

In 1998, the Federal Reserve's Survey of Consumer Finances found that just over half of white households owned stock; only 30 percent of African American households did.[316] And on average, white households with stock own five times as much as black stockowners; 23 percent of total white households' assets are invested in stock, compared with only 11 percent of total black households' assets.[317]

Similarly, home ownership was more common among white people in the 1990s. From 1992 to 1998, the white home ownership rate rose from 69 percent to 72 percent.[318] Meanwhile, black home ownership actually fell from 48 percent to 46 percent, and Latino home ownership rose just slightly, from 43 percent to 44 percent.[319] Most white families could take advantage of the real estate boom, and most families of color could not.

Largely as a result of the growing values of stock and real estate, white families' median net worth rose from $71,300 in 1992 to $120,989 in 2001, while the net worth of most families of color actually fell.

The growing sectors of the U.S. economy in the 1990s created jobs that required computer skills and other advanced education. And this education was easier for white people to get, in part because of government policies.

First, white students tend to go to better funded schools from kindergarten through twelfth grade. The non-profit Education Trust analyzed Census Bureau data to compare state and local funding based on the predominant race of the school district. They found that the quarter of districts with the highest white enrollment got $6,684 per student, $902 more than those with the lowest white enrollment.[320] In twenty-two states, the state sends substantially more money per student ($100 or more) to the whitest quarter of school districts. For example, New York sends $1,339 more.[321]

At the college level, the government assistance that students of color especially depend upon has been harder to get. During the 1980s, tuition rose 146 percent at private colleges, but Pell grants (the main federal scholarship program) only rose 47 percent. As a result, students turn to loans more than in the past. Nellie Mae, a national lender of student loans, found that the median student loan debt was $13,000 in 1997, and almost all students also had additional debt, such as credit card debt.[322] Nellie Mae surveyed students who dropped out and didn't finish their undergraduate degrees, and found that students of color were more likely to cite excessive debt as their reason for dropping out than white students were.[323] Thus, the higher education needed for the well-paying jobs in the new high-tech economy has been more targeted than in the past to students whose parents can afford the tuition—disproportionately white students.

In 2003, President Bush weighed in against "racial preferences" in the University of Michigan's admissions policy, then under consideration by the Supreme Court. As usual, the twenty-point advantage given to black, Latino, and Native American applicants was the only one under attack, not the ones that favored whites. Students from low-income backgrounds also got twenty points, but these points couldn't be combined with points for race, so in effect they boosted low-income white and Asian students.[324] Applicants from the Upper Peninsula, a rural white area, got sixteen extra points on the 150-point scale.[325] Graduates of the highest-quality high schools—mostly white—got another ten points, and those who took Advanced Placement and honors classes—not as available in schools with predominantly students of color—got another eight points. And then of course there is the kind of preference that the president himself benefited from, the legacy advantage given to children of alumni, which at Michigan earned four points.[326] Compared to just twenty points awarded by race, this added up to fifty-eight points available to an almost all-white pool of students and unavailable to almost all applicants of color. Antiracism activist Tim Wise comments, "But while the first of these are seen as examples of racial preferences, the second are not, hidden as they are behind the structure of social inequities that limit where people live, where they go to school, and the kinds of opportunities they have been afforded. White preferences, the result of the normal workings of a racist society, can remain out of sight and out of mind, while the power of the state is turned against the paltry preferences meant to offset them."[327]

CONCLUSION: WHITE RESPONSIBILITY TO INSIST ON ASSET-BUILDING ASSISTANCE FOR ALL

How much money did all these advantages in government policy bring to white people?

Melvin Oliver and Thomas Shapiro in their 1995 book *Black Wealth/White Wealth* found that differences in income, occupation, and education only accounted for about 29 percent of the difference between white and black families' assets in 1988; over 70 percent of the difference was related just to race.[328] They called this "the costs of being black," but it could also be called the benefit of being white. In 1983, David Swinton estimated that 40 percent to 60 percent of the difference in income between black and white Americans came from present and past discrimination, and he calculated a total $500 billion debt to African Americans.[329]

The debate over reparations for slavery has brought a flood of defensive reactions from white people, all claiming they aren't to blame and haven't benefited from racism. Are individual white people to blame for the legacy of discrimination in government assistance? In most cases, no. But as beneficiaries of white advantages in a democracy supposedly based on the principle that "all [humans] are created equal," white people have a responsibility to speak up for widening the circle of government support to include everyone.

Clearly, government assistance in asset development works: after centuries of preferential treatment in land policy, farm aid, housing subsidies, the safety net, education, etc., white people's net worth is much greater than people of color's net worth.

Clearly, the nation would benefit if people of color with no assets had the security of home ownership, good education, fair pay, savings, and retirement accounts.

Clearly, people of color alone, as 30 percent of the population, can't form a big enough voting block to successfully lobby for broad-based asset development programs that don't exclude them. White people need to step up to the plate as allies to organized efforts by people of color to win racial justice.

This is not only a moral imperative, but a pragmatic one as well. When the U.S. economy no longer systematically undervalues certain racial groups and nationalities, the floor will rise for all working people, including whites. As populist Jim Hightower says his daddy told him, "We all do better when we all do better."

Chapter 7

RAINBOW ECONOMICS: CLOSING THE RACIAL WEALTH DIVIDE

To be a poor man is hard. But to be a poor race in a land of dollars is the very bottom of hardship.

—W.E.B. DuBois[1]

THE COLOR LINE IN THE TWENTY-FIRST CENTURY

One hundred years ago, in 1903, W.E.B. DuBois prophetically wrote, " The problem of the twentieth century is the problem of the color line." Unfortunately, the problem of the twenty-first century is still the color line.

DuBois's quote about being a "poor race in a land of dollars" is also important to the economic unity of our nation. When everyone is in a roughly similar economic situation, people do not feel poor or resentful of others. There are still those among us who remember being children during the Depression of the 1930s. When it was the entire community that was down and out, and when people banded together to share what little they had, the sense that "we're in this together" helped people make it through the crisis. But if your little dinghy is stuck in the mud and the *Queen Elizabeth* comes sailing by and will not stop to give you a lift, then your situation becomes unbearable.

The economic and social problems in our society today are not caused by poverty per se. Rather, it is the growing inequality between the have-too-muches and the do-not-haves based on accidents of birth or luck which is tearing apart our body politic.

As we have seen in the previous chapters, while no one would contest that pulling hard on one's own oars is necessary to getting out of the shallows, it is usually not sufficient. Government tugboats pulled some dinghies ahead, and government freight weighed down others. The rules of the game have not been fairly written.

Mel King, an African American former Massachusetts state legislator and author of *Chain of Change*, talks about the history of race relations. He says, "This country was founded by white men of means. But sometimes my tongue slips and I say it was founded by 'mean white men!'" The ideological descendants of those original white men of means continue to set the economic structures and policies that determine how the nation's wealth is distributed. As a result, today the economic rift between the top 1 percent of the population and everyone else has grown to proportions comparable to the Gilded Age before the turn of the last cen-

tury. In 2004, the top 1 percent of the population owned one-third of the nation's total private wealth, while 18 percent of the people had no assets or lived in debt. We are experiencing a massive shifting of wealth from those with little to those with much. Fifty-one new billionaires were created in 2004, from 262 in 2003 to 313, middle-class and low-income people lost ground; and one million more fell below the poverty line.

Why isn't the American public up in arms?

As in the past, those who rule use the construction of race to produce a social hierarchy that legitimizes the transfer of wealth from people of color to whites, and that provides cover for the transfer of wealth from white working people to the corporate elite. In the years during and right after the Civil Rights Movement, most Americans agreed that no one should be judged by the color of his or her skin. But a conscious strategy to reverse that moral stand and to re-inflame racist attitudes was created by, among others, Republican presidential candidate George H.W. Bush in 1988. By invoking the image of a black murderer, Willie Horton, who committed a rape after being released on furlough during Michael Dukakis's governorship in Massachusetts, Bush was able to overcome Dukakis's seventeen point lead and keep the presidency. This use of racist stereotyping became part of a steady diet fed to the public for the twenty years, helping to put the brakes on the gains of the Civil Rights Movement, and to make judging people by their race seem more moral than to judge them by their character.

Racist myths provide easy explanations for the loss of economic status by white working people. It's easier to blame the family in the next neighborhood than to understand how corporate behavior or government policies are the problem. Current myth making includes repeating the falsehood that immigrants take jobs from whites and African Americans. In truth corporations take union jobs overseas to where wages are lower, allowing them to rake in higher profits that are distributed only to the top management and stockholders. Women of color on welfare are blamed for draining government coffers, while the true budget busters are tax givebacks to the already wealthy. Since September 11, it has been even easier to play on white fears of outsiders—including U.S.-born people of color—than to criticize U.S. policies in the Middle East.

There are positive American values that can be drawn upon as arguments for policies that bring all of us to the same economic starting line, and for closing the racial wealth divide. To the credit of those white men of means who founded the country, they did not advocate creating an aristocracy. It continues to be a basic U.S. value that all our children should be provided with the opportunity to succeed to the best of their ability. So many of the inventions that contributed to the growth of our economy came from individuals of limited means. We

love the rags-to-riches stories of people like Oprah Winfrey, who was born poor but became one of the richest people in the United States, with a net worth of $1 billion in 2004. If more people of color are able to contribute their talents, our society as a whole would be the richer for it.

Another shared American value is that a strong middle class makes economic sense. Henry Ford wanted to pay his workers enough so that they could afford to buy the cars they were making: "a car in every garage" became possible when workers made sufficient incomes. If only Henry Fords could afford cars, such a tiny market would have stopped the development of the massive auto industry that fueled economic growth and built the industrial capacity that was needed in World War II.

When groups of people are excluded from the economy, society loses productive possibilities. Millions of people, disproportionately people of color, are now incarcerated. If those dollars devoted to keeping people in jail were used for job and income creation, the money would circulate within our economy to the benefit of both workers and business leaders as well as all sectors of society.

While the task of reversing the tide toward inequality seems daunting, it can happen. At other times in U.S. history a winner-take-all system was in place. In the late nineteenth century, wealth accumulated in the hands of the new industrialist "robber barons," while laws gave more rights to corporations, which fed inequality. The Populist movement of rural farmers and urban workers built the People's Party in 1891, which pushed for ways to redistribute wealth through a progressive income tax.[2] However, the People's Party failed after only five years because of racism, when Southern farmers abandoned the party candidate and decided to vote Democratic and uphold white supremacy.

This time around, as we build a new movement for economic fairness, a commitment to solve the racial economic divide must be part and parcel of the agenda. Communities of color must be included not just as a tactical measure; racial equality must be a central governing principle. Gain for one sector of the population is not justice: no more wealth-building opportunities where "only whites need apply." To ensure inclusion, people of color must not only be followers, they must be leaders. Because people of color have been at the very bottom of the economy, raising the bottom lifts those *near* the bottom too; the Civil Rights Movement provided gains for women, gays, and people with disabilities. This time around, the goal of eliminating the color line can build a broader movement for economic justice in the twenty-first century.

FROM GROWING INEQUALITY TO SHARED PROSPERITY

In the introductory chapter, 1850 and 1950 were described as moments in the development of the racial wealth divide. We asked, "What can we envision for U.S. society in 2050—the period when the country's demographics shift so that the majority of people living here are of color? What if the color line were erased?" Imagine this:

➤ In 2050, the treaties between Native nations and the United States have been honored. Native peoples are no longer under the "guardianship" of the U.S. government. Land taken illegally has been returned in some cases. In others, tribes have bought back the white-owned areas between the checkerboard bits of land still owned by Native people after the division of tribal lands into individual plots under the Dawes Act back in 1887. The rights of others to use of Native land have been restricted (no, snowmobilers do not have the right to buzz around on sacred grounds).

➤ Native peoples have set up their own schools and universities, in which Native youth learn and thrive in a familiar cultural environment, in which interdependent learning, not individual competition, lays the basis for education.

➤ Dollars flow within reservations from new local businesses.

➤ Pollution from agribusiness, such as their massive pig and chicken farms, has sparked public outcry about the contamination of the waterways. Native Americans have led the way in teaching the rest of the country how to be stewards of the land and its resources; this knowledge brings them new wealth. All benefit from an improved ecology.

➤ By 2050, African Americans have used world courts to sue the U.S. government over the effects of slavery. The U.S. government agrees to set aside billions of dollars to bring African Americans to economic parity with whites. The money is raised through taxes on multimillionaires and on corporations. Companies and banks that illegally benefited from slave labor have also paid restitution to the families of their victims, thanks to the legal work that was begun earlier in the century. African Americans have chosen to use the dollars to take control of economic development agendas, to revitalize city neighborhoods, create affordable housing, and replace the Wal-Marts and the McDonald's that currently disfigure neighborhoods with local businesses. Vibrant, self-sustaining black communities with their own financial institutions which have existed briefly before, are flourishing again.

➤ Many African Americans choose to move back to the South. Majority African American cities and towns use their political muscle to win public offices and to experiment with economic methods that are designed to build the community as a whole, and not just enrich a few individuals.

➤ Through the use of participatory community-planning processes, the creation of land trusts, in which land is owned in perpetuity by the community so that individuals do not profit from a public good, and municipal investments in cooperative housing and businesses, individual profits are minimized and the sharing of public resources is maximized. The South is no longer the U.S. region of the greatest poverty and racial economic inequality.

➤ In 2050, the economy is transnational, but it no longer works only to the advantage of U.S. corporations. The strong workers' movements in South and Central America, in partnership with immigrant-led labor struggles within the United States, have overturned free-trade agreements, which gave free rein to private corporations and took away the right of governments to provide public services for its peoples. Venezuela, Brazil, and Uruguay started the trend toward progressive elected leaders who have concern for their working people, and who are willing to stand up to the United States; others follow suit.

➤ As the countries to the south refuse to accept structural adjustments to their economies, they reconstruct tax-funded social safety nets and place restrictions on transnational corporations, and their economies improve so that migration is no longer such a dire necessity. Mercosur, first negotiated in 1991 among 4 South American countries to create a common market, is a new economic powerhouse like the European Union, ensuring that South–Central America control its own natural resources and economic development.

➤ The Monroe Doctrine, in which the United States insisted on control over its backyard, is no longer operable. After the U.S.-Mexico border moved north in 1848, when half of Mexico was ceded to the United States, many Mexicans were cheated out of their land because of English-only transactions. They now have the last laugh. Because the Latino population has grown to 25 percent, southwestern states have two official languages. Proficiency in Spanish language and culture becomes a major advantage in finding jobs and doing business; the income and wealth of Latinos rise.

➤ In 2050, Asian immigration has increased the numbers and visibility of Asian Americans. They are no longer perceived as foreigners and viewed with suspicion. They are not only computer experts and doctors, but found in all occupations. With equal opportunity, Asians have not become white. On the contrary, they have rejected whiteness and have chosen instead a vision of a multicultural America, where no one has to give up their culture to be accepted.

➤ Interest in Asian theories and practices in health and well-being has continued to increase. Just as acupuncture was first considered a crazy idea and then was found to cure conditions from arthritis to drug addiction, other Asian therapies are now widely accepted and covered by national health insurance. Everyone benefits from a greater array of health care choices, with the monopoly of Western-style medicine broken.

➤ And the Chinese still make a good buck off of General Tso's famous chicken!

➤ And whites? One might think that with all the financial investment in communities of color, funded in part through a return to more progressive taxation, that the fortunes of whites would be declining in proportion to the rise in the fortunes of people of color. Not so. Poor and middle-class whites are also doing better than they were at the turn of the twenty-first century.

➤ In the early 2000s, the "war on terror," the attempt to privatize safety nets like social security, the monopoly power of companies like Wal-Mart, and tax cuts for the rich eroded their standard of living and their sense of security. The increasing strength of the economies of the European Union, Mercosur, and African and Asian economic blocs, as well as the failures of U.S. free-trade agreements to improve the economy, caused them to reject the notion that what's good for General Motors is good for the rest of us, or that giving more to the rich will cause wealth to "trickle down."

➤ In 2050, the majority of whites understand that they and their families benefited from years of affirmative action and have agreed that using public funds for new asset-building programs, particularly by investing in communities of color, is fair—and to their own benefit as well. The producing, spending, and investing power generated by redistributing wealth downward has expanded the economy as a whole. Whites see that their long-term interest lies not in the preservation of white advantage, but in the creation of a global economic system where wealth is broadly shared and relations of equality bring stability and peace.

Utopian dreams? These brief scenarios are not meant to be a blueprint. They are bits of a vision, offered to spark other people's imagination. As we trudge along trying to reach equality, beating back the obstacles thrown in our way, we all long to lift our heads from time to time to look far down the road at the shining world that is our hoped-for destination. A people without a vision will perish, and those with vision can accomplish the impossible.

Back in 1955, when repression was tightening in apartheid South Africa, it seemed crazy to dream of a country liberated from white rule. But that was the year that a multiracial assembly of South Africans gathered outside of Johannesburg for a Congress of the People, and proclaimed a Freedom Charter that inspired a sustained mass movement for a free South Africa.

All over the world, ordinary people are resisting exploitive structures and dreaming up new ones. What do the alternative economic visions of the future share? Success is measured by how well each and every family is doing, not by the number of dollars that change hands (which the Gross Domestic Producet measures); communities control their own land, labor, and economic development; and the different ways in which people of different races and cultures conduct their lives are respected.

POLICY STEPS TOWARD CLOSING THE GAP

Meanwhile, there are many small steps to be taken. The following section highlights some ideas old and new, and lifts up some examples of useful and innovative work being done to close the wealth gap. This list is by no means comprehensive, but perhaps it can spark more energy to tackle the issue of wealth building for communities of color, and for all those currently without economic security.

First Steps: Human Assets

Education has been an important tool in creating white advantage. It was a crime to teach African slaves to read and write; Latinos have been disadvantaged by English-only classrooms; Native Americans were forced into assimilationist school settings, and Asians had to sue to go to school with whites.

In today's economy, more than ever, you need an education to get ahead. Even for a menial job, a high school diploma is often required. Current mechanisms for public school funding—largely local property taxes—enable wealthier families in white suburbs who pay more property taxes to have more dollars invested in their public schools. Disparity in funding produces disparities in educational outcomes, and per-

petuates a class and race divide. The infusion of federal dollars to invest more in communities that are poor could help close the gap.

As unionized jobs in manufacturing have shrunk, higher education has become an even more important ticket to a job at a decent wage with benefits. Professor Hubie Jones, former dean of the Boston University School of Social Work and a longtime community activist, grew up with his single mom in Harlem, New York. Without the possibility and promise of free higher education at the City College, he says, he would not have had the motivation to work hard in school in order to get that ticket up and out. Gangs and drugs would have been the only option.

Free public universities came about in 1862, the same year as the Homestead Act, when the Morrill Act established land-grant colleges in every state. Their purpose was to provide knowledge and skills to the newly landed masses.[3] Public institutions of higher education were the ticket out of poverty for many people of color who could not afford tuition at private colleges. Today, affordable higher education is moving out of reach for many of our children.

The federal government spends $55 billion on student aid, but the mix has been changing. Seventy-seven percent of that aid is in loans, not grants, a reversal of past poli-

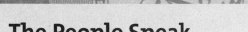

The People Speak

In the United for a Fair Economy racial wealth divide workshop, a middle-aged white man, Doug, is excited. "I was part of the Civil Rights Movement, and there's been so much progress. But when we stop paying attention, progress slows down. We need to keep on pushing for more laws and better enforcement."

An African American student raises his hand. "No one, especially the government, thought about protecting the people in my community from catastrophes that could wipe out their savings, like health crises. My folks didn't even have access to doctors. It was the Black Panthers who set up the first free health clinics for my people."

Later in the workshop, as the UFE workshop leader gives median family income data, a woman from Somalia is perplexed. "I don't understand. The measures don't fit us. In our culture, a nuclear 'family of four' isn't the unit we'd use to measure our wealth. Our family members—uncles, grandparents, sisters, brothers—even on the other side of the world put into and take out of the pot."

These comments point to pieces of strategies. Rule changes pushed by popular movements can change the rules of the game and help the disadvantaged gain ground. Community-based activities throughout the centuries have allowed peoples of color to protect their communities and to build wealth right under the noses of those who would exclude them; but like neighborhood health centers, these efforts can grow and become institutionalized when government funding is won. Finally, it must be remembered that even well-intentioned attempts to define and solve the problems of inequality often use a one-size-fits-all approach, and the size is usually the "white" size, not the right size. But even if the size fits African Americans, it may not fit Cambodians—indeed, even if the remedy fits Chinese, it may not fit Cambodians. In the twenty-first century, community involvement can promote culturally appropriate program designs.

cies. With tax cuts mostly for the wealthy, and the resulting budget shortfalls, states have been spending less on their public colleges, and tuitions have been growing at a faster rate than family income. The new welfare policies set in 1996 have led to a decline in enrollment of low-income women in college. Before the Temporary Assistance for Needy Families (TANF) program, forty-two states allowed women to count college attendance as employment in order to qualify for benefits: after TANF, only twenty-six states still allowed this option.[4] We can change the mix back again, and raise new taxes to invest in public colleges. A well-educated populace is the cornerstone of democracy, and the cornerstone is crumbling.

For those who don't speak English as their first language, English classes are the first stepping-stones to success. It is not possible to get a decent job without English skills. Some immigrants are not literate in their native language and need extended classes. Some come with degrees from other countries, and can learn English quickly. For all of them, long waiting lists for free or affordable classes prevent them from obtaining this skill so essential for entry of limited English speakers into the U.S. workforce. On the other hand, so that non–English speakers do not get cheated out of their assets, or miss out on the benefits of programs for which they qualify, English-only policies must be rejected.

One big health problem can wipe out a lifetime of savings. The cost of care for a premature baby in a neonatal intensive care unit can be $500,000. In 1999, one quarter of the families that filed for bankruptcy cited health problems and the related costs as the reason.[5]

A 2000 study found that people of color are more likely to be uninsured than non-Hispanic whites, and are less likely to have job-based health insurance.[6] Thirty percent of Latinos, 25 percent of African Americans, 20 percent of Asian Americans and Pacific Islanders, and 17 percent of Native Americans are uninsured.[7] (The relatively low percentage rate of uninsured Native Americans is mostly due to their access to Indian Health Services as opposed to private or Medicaid coverage.[8]) Medicaid, which cares for the poor in inner cities and rural areas, is increasingly underfunded, as states face budget crises.

Universal coverage is possible. In 1983, Hawaii received permission from the federal government to require all employers to provide insurance to employees. In 1993, they were able to pool all their public dollars to create one big statewide insurance system. Not only were they able to provide health, dental, and mental health coverage for all, but the system was also able to save public dollars through a competitive bidding system.[9]

Hitting a Stride: Income Assets

One of the main reasons that nonwhite people were shut out of asset building was because they were restricted to no wage or low-wage jobs. From African slaves in the South to Latino day laborers on the street corners of Los Angeles, people of color have been denied fair compensation for their labor power. They have been limited to jobs that whites did not and do not want, were excluded from unions, paid taxes to work, and have always been the last hired and the first fired.

Jobs are needed that provide the cash income to cover day-to-day needs, *with something left over to build savings,* the basis for financial wealth. Today, income disparity lays the groundwork for future wealth disparities. Thomas Shapiro, in *The Hidden Cost of Being African American: How Wealth Perpetuates Inequality*, analyzed the impact of income on wealth. Once basic living expenses are met, each additional dollar of annual income generates $3.26 in net worth over a person's lifetime. Wealth disparity grows because of differences in income. For example, the difference in net worth between someone making $30,000 a year and someone making $60,000 a year is nearly $100,000.[10] Income includes not just wages and salaries based on working, but cash supports for those who are unemployed, retired, or parents of small children.

In Bárbara Robles's class at the LBJ school at the University of Texas in Austin, students simply did not believe her when she told them that the minimum wage means a family must live on $10,000 a year. Over 27 million workers make less than $8 dollars an hour; of these workers, 16.8 million are adults twenty-five and over; more than 16 million are women; 22 million are white; 4.2 million are black; and more than 17.5 million

work full-time.[11] The present federal minimum wage of $5.15 an hour translates into an annual income of $10,712. The Economic Policy Institute has done several studies that reveal that an increase in the minimum wage would primarily benefit full-and part-time workers of low-income families,[12] which are disproportionately headed by single women of color. It would require raising the minimum wage to at least $8.10 an hour as of 2004 for a family of four to move above the official poverty line.[13] Around the country, people are organizing for more than the minimum wage: they are demanding a living wage. Since the cost of living varies across the country, communities are calculating costs particular to their cities. For example, in San Francisco voters approved a city living wage of $8.50 an hour in 2003; this will put over $100 million per year into the pockets of roughly fifty-four thousand workers.

And what about a maximum wage? In most countries, the ratio of CEO pay to worker pay has been around 40 to one. In the United States in 2004, the ratio of CEO pay to the average workers pay was 431 to 1.[14] Rep. Martin Sabo of Minnesota wants to curb that excess. His Proposed Income Equity Act would prevent corporations from claiming tax deductions on any executive pay that totals over 25 times what a company's lowest paid workers are earning.

The poorest group in the United States is women of color and their children. As Miami resident Thelma Brown puts it, "[C]ertified nursing assistants in Miami start at $5.75 an hour with no benefits. Day care costs ninety to one hundred dollars every two weeks per kid; then you have to pay rent, electricity, food, and everything else. A single mom can't live on one job at that rate."[15] They require government help to survive. For many years, it was mainly white women who received welfare payments. Attieno Davis, a longtime African American activist, remembers how empowering it was for black women in the 1960s to realize that they were *entitled* to these benefits, too. Latinos also were underenrolled, since no outreach was conducted in Spanish, nor were there Spanish-speaking workers in welfare offices. However, President Reagan's caricature of "welfare queens," stereotyped as a woman of color, created backlash. In 1996, the program changed to Temporary Assistance to Needy Families. To quality for the meager payments, women cannot have assets of more than $1,000 in some states.

One positive tax provision for the poor is the Earned Income Tax Credit (EITC). It was born out of the welfare debates in the late 1960s and early 1970s. At the time, President Nixon was proposing a guaranteed income to all families with children, regardless of whether the parent(s) worked. It is amazing today to remember that Nixon was proposing such a progressive policy. But Democratic senator Russell Long of Louisiana felt that the Nixon proposal would discourage people from working. His alternate proposal provided tax relief to low-income workers, rather than guaranteed income for all. The

EITC was passed in 1975. Its annual budget rose from $2 billion to $12 billion between 1980 and 1992.[16] According to the 2001 Census, forty-three million people were living in low-income working families with children, and two out of every three poor families with children had at least one parent working. The EITC has lifted more families with children out of poverty than any other government program.[17]

Low-wage workers use the money they receive from the EITC for investments in education and savings, as well as to help them pay daily living expenses.[18] In order to encourage savings, Ray Boshara from the New America Foundation suggests that a portion of EITC refunds could be channeled directly into a basic savings account.[19] The Center on Budget and Policy Priorities found that EITC funds are often spent locally, serving as an economic development tool for low-income neighborhoods.[20]

Decent pay and accumulation of assets is hard to come by if you are not allowed citizenship. As we have seen, immigrant status has been a major barrier to economic equality for people of color. Jeannette Huezo, a political refugee from El Salvador, has lived and worked in Boston for fifteen years. However, she had to leave four of her children behind when she fled, and they are not allowed to reunite; she has been sending money home to support them. Salvadorans in the United States send remittances back home that now amount to half of the Salvadoran economy. Being forced into low-paid jobs because of their tenuous legal status, coupled with the need to send money home, makes it difficult to build assets in either country. The National Coalition for Dignity and Amnesty developed a proposal for a federal Freedom Act. It would legalize undocumented immigrants currently living in the United States and create a status of "temporary residency" for future migrants, who would be eligible for permanent residency after three years.

People of color should be hired into jobs for which they are qualified and to rise to the level of their capabilities. Affirmative action, won through the Civil Rights Movement, did bring many more people of color into middle-income jobs where they could begin to save, buy homes, and build wealth. However, the gap is still not closed. Over their working lifetime, African Americans with a college degree can expect to earn $500,000 less than equally qualified white people.[21] Asians do fine getting in on the ground floor and moving up, but then encounter glass ceilings: an Asian with a college degree had median annual earnings in 1993 of $36,844; comparably qualified whites made $41,094.[22] The need for affirmative action and government enforcement of nondiscrimination laws is far from over.

Going the Distance: Financial Assets

Over the course of history, the federal government has used public resources to create wealth-building starter kits as well as continuing subsidies for whites, and has removed assets from people of color and denied them the benefits given to whites. In recent years, the white middle class has taken a hit: overall, it's shrinking, and general economic inequality has reached the levels of the Gilded Age at the turn of the last century. As a result, more and more academics, advocates, foundations, and public officials are recognizing that income alone is not enough to lift a family out of poverty. While this attention is not mainly because of wide recognition of the racial wealth gap, there is an opportunity to bring race into the conversation.

It's not that there aren't federal asset policies currently in place. The government spends approximately $355 billion a year in direct outlays and tax expenditures (allowing tax breaks for certain kinds of income). However, they are not named as asset policies, and they disproportionately benefit those who already have assets.[23] As we have seen, the net worth of people of color is far below that of whites.

While there are many ways to group asset-building opportunities, the Asset Policy Initiative of California has designed a framework that is simple and user-friendly. They see that strategies in four areas are needed. *Asset accumulation* is about policy strategies that encourage families to save; *asset leveraging* policies help low-wealth families use their limited savings to get loans for larger assets such as home and business ownership.

THE COLOR OF WEALTH

Unfortunately, if there are not *asset preserva-tion* assistance programs, often low-wealth people lose everything they have to predatory lenders. And finally, "*asset creation*" goes beyond individual strategies; communities can gain control over development in their own neighborhoods and rural communities.

ASSET ACCUMULATION

New thinking on how to help low-income people save money has been inspired by Michael Sherradan's groundbreaking book *Assets and the Poor: A New American Welfare Policy*. Sherradan and others recognize that income-support programs do not foster asset accumulation.[24]

Individual Development Accounts (IDAs) are nontaxable matching funds savings accounts that can be used—and used *only*—toward purchasing a home, retirement, education, starting a business, or other asset-accumulating endeavors. The outside matching source comes either from the public or private sector. Generally, the program has been targeted to the working poor, those who have a low but stable income in which some money can be set aside. Foundations and local banks have both provided funding to augment savings on the part of the poor. There are about 250 neighborhoods participating in IDA programs across the country, many in communities of color. The National Council of La Raza and the First Nations Development Institute have developed projects for Latinos and Native peoples.

Pilot IDA programs funded privately have encouraged policy change. According to the Corporation for Enterprise Development (CFED), since 1993, twenty-nine states and the District of Columbia have passed laws in support of IDAs. Thirty-two states have included IDA initiatives in their welfare reform programs and seven states have instituted state-funded IDA programs. In 1998, a federal pilot program of savings incentives for the poor was enacted, with $125 million over five years set aside for matching individual savings. While on the one hand this legislation helps to make the IDA idea more visible, it is not on a scale to be truly transformative.[25]

Another promising idea involves investing in our future: our nation's children. It is every parent's dream to leave their child a nest egg. And wouldn't it be great if everyone could be born with a trust fund! An impossible dream? Just such a program was instituted in England, sponsored by Prime Minister Tony Blair's Labor Party. In 2003, the British Parliament established what has become known as "baby bonds," a small child trust fund for each newborn in the country. Modest amounts of public funds will be deposited and invested for each newborn infant, and made available for withdrawal at the age of eighteen. If a child is given an initial deposit of $1,000, and then the parent makes a yearly contribution of $500, matched by another $500 from an outside source, this would translate into $40,000 available to eighteen-year-olds to use toward education, starting a business, or putting a down payment on a home.[26]

In 2005, a bill to create a similar program was introduced in Congress by an unusual alliance of conservative Republicans and progressive Democrats. The America Saving for Personal Investment, Retirement, and Education Act (the ASPIRE Act of 2005) proposed that a $500 KIDS Account be established for every newborn child. Children in households earning below the national median income would be eligible for a supplemental government contribution of up to $500. Additional benefits would include tax-free earnings, matched savings for lower income families, and financial education. Here is a program that provides a double incentive for lower income people to save: no taxes on the savings account, and matched government contributions for the poor.

Whether such new asset subsidiary programs should be universal or targeted to people of color is a strategic question. In any case, additional resources for outreach, translation, and other mechanisms to ensure inclusion must be part of the program.

Asset Leveraging

When you have some savings, you can either keep them, or use them to leverage more assets through making bigger investments.

Rotating savings and credit associations (ROSCA) have been an important strategy utilized by immigrant households in order to start a small business, purchase a home, or pay for a child's education. This strategy has origins in many different ethnic groups from East Asia, Latin America, the Caribbean, the Near East, and Africa. The Vietnamese ROSCA is called a *hui,* the Ethiopian is *ekub,* Jamaican is *partners,* Dominican, *san,* Korean, *keh,* and Cambodian *tong-tine.*[27]

A ROSCA is formed among family members, friends, and kin groups. They require participants (usually five or more people) to pay in a monthly sum agreed upon by the group. A participant can make a request to borrow the month's pool of money, or there may be an agreed-upon sequence for withdrawal—tax-and interest-free, since these transactions take place outside of the mainstream economic structure. This continues until all members have had access to the funds. The system is based on trust and social pressure. Thus, if members do not return the money at some point, their reputation in the community is tainted, something they are usually not willing to risk.

A *Philadelphia Inquirer* reporter sat in on a ROSCA meeting. "A Vietnamese *hui* group listened as one member asked to break the payout schedule and let her have that month's collection. . . . [T]he group sat in judgment on her needs, then let her take the tax-free, no-interest pot of $14,000." But because ROSCAs are part of an unregulated, unprotected financing system, they have no recourse in case of theft. While sometimes immigrants do not trust banks, banks also do not make it easy to deposit

ROSCA dollars. They treat deposits as belonging to an individual or household, and have no category to accommodate this unique form of savings. They report any deposit of more than $10,000 to the Internal Revenue Service. Without a financial institution to hold the money, one member has to keep the mounting dollars under his or her bed. A policy that recognized ROSCAs as a micro lending system, and allowed the money to be banked and borrowed tax-free, would build on existing community customs and help rather than hinder these activities.

Another way to use your small savings to leverage larger loans without worrying about a financial institution charging excessive fees and interest is to join a community credit union. The credit union movement was essentially a response to mainstream financial institution's neglect of marginalized groups. Community Development Credit Unions (CDCU) provide basic financial services such as check cashing and small loans at fair rates to their members within a restricted area or community.[28] They are member based and member governed; some are based in churches or community organizations. One of the problems plaguing poor communities is that the meager resources present in poor communities tend to flow out of them.[29] In response to this problem, CDCUs keep local money in the community, as well as draw in outside money.[30] The resources accrued from CDCUs are then channeled back into the community and are used to respond to its various needs.

Usually, the first asset leveraged from savings is a home to live in. Expanding opportunities for home ownership are critical in closing the racial wealth divide. Home equity is one of the first building blocks for wealth, and is the most significant source of assets for people of color. For blacks, 62 percent of their net worth is held in homes; for Latinos, 51 percent. For white families, housing accounts for only 32 percent of their net worth. Given the history of federal subsidies for home ownership for whites, targeted funding for people and communities of color is now needed.

The Community Reinvestment Act of 1977 (CRA) came out of community struggles demanding access to banks and mortgage companies. Evidence was compiled showing that financial institutions engaged in discriminatory lending practices based on race, age, and location, instead of on an applicant's creditworthiness. These discriminatory practices had contributed to the decline of low-income and minority neighborhoods. The CRA required banks to lend in low-income communities, and federal banking regulators were mandated to maintain a close watch on financial institutions to ensure that they were meeting the needs of local communities. Communities of color were successful in getting the federal government to use its powers to stop private industry from providing affirmative action in lending to whites.

Through the CRA, significant strides were made during the 1990s as major banking institutions, increase lending toward affordable housing and economic development to assist low-income people.[31] Over $20 billion has been invested in low-income neighborhoods and communities of color thanks to the CRA.[32]

ASSET PRESERVATION

Home ownership has been a double-edged sword for many home owners of color. It is a struggle first to gain access to fair loan terms, and another to try and keep the home. If we were to dig beneath the home ownership figures, which provide only a snapshot in time, we would find a lot more turnovers of home ownership among people of color than among whites. Lending predators target the weak—those unfamiliar with the rules of the game.

ACORN's Mary Gaspar described her ordeal: "Here's how my nightmare started: I got a check in the mail from Household Finance with an offer to refinance our home. . . . Household was misleading and dishonest. I received my first bill and it was $13,000 more than I thought it was going to be! I have seen how Household preys on people who are economically desperate as well as middle-class people like us." ACORN (Association of Community Organizations for Reform Now) responded by putting the public pressure on Household Finance by holding demonstrations at their annual shareholder meetings. They were joined in their efforts by members of United for a Fair Economy's

Responsible Wealth project. Proxy votes given to ACORN members by Responsible Wealth members who owned shares allowed Mary to tell her story—*inside* the halls of wealth, usually barred to the people of color whose hard-earned homes were being stolen from them. Having shareholders and ACORN members speaking with one voice brought Household to the table to discuss changing its behavior.[33]

Mortgage foreclosure has been another impediment to maintaining home ownership. A report done by the Family Housing Fund in Minneapolis found that the major reason home owners default on mortgage payments is job loss or a significant reduction in income; other causes include health emergencies and separation or divorce. While home ownership rates have increased, so have instances of foreclosure.

Foreclosure prevention is an important tool in stabilizing home owners at risk of losing their homes and neighborhoods by preventing houses from becoming vacant and boarded up. Between 1991 and 1997, the Mortgage Foreclosure Program (MFP) carried out by the Family Housing Fund assisted close to seventeen hundred home-owners and helped to reinstate the mortgages of over half of them within the St. Paul and Minneapolis area.[34] Foreclosure prevention counseling provides a more affordable way for home owners to stabilize their home ownership, compared to going through a mortgage insurer. It costs an average of $2,800 to help a home owner reinstate a mortgage, while with a mortgage insurer it could cost $10,000 to $28,000, depending on the insurer and the location of the home.[35] Ana Moreno, a housing consultant and who conducted the study, contends that "[p]rograms that promote home ownership for households with very low incomes need to be linked to the full continuum of homeownership support services—pre-purchase education and counseling, financial assistance, post-purchase support, and delinquency and foreclosure prevention."[36]

Even with a home, you can spend your final years in poverty, if you have no retirement account from which to draw. Social security was invented to protect U.S. workers from this risk: it is the country's most successful insurance program. While 10 percent of those over age sixty-five live in poverty today, without social security that rate would be almost 50 percent.[37] Occupations held mostly by African Americans and Latinos were excluded initially, but all employment sectors were included beginning in 1950. Social security was also expanded to include not only retirement benefits, but also benefits to disabled workers and the families of workers who have died.

Because people of color have less income from stock holdings or capital gains than whites, social security is especially important to them: it is the sole source of income for 40 percent of elderly African Americans. The shorter life span of African American men

means that both survivor and disability benefits go disproportionately to African Americans. While African Americans make up 12 percent of the U.S. population, 23 percent of children receiving social security survivor benefits are African American, as are about 17 percent of disability beneficiaries.[38]

Private pension plans are also an important asset. They provide retirement income, often as an employment benefit. The loss of unionized manufacturing jobs in the 1990s led to the loss of this asset for many. Laid off from auto and steel jobs which opened up to them during World War II, African Americans in particular have had to shift to jobs in the low-wage service sector, which do not provide employer-sponsored pension plans. In 2001, the mean value of the retirement account of a black family was $12,247, compared to $10,206 for a Latino family and $65,411 for a white family.[39]

For those who are fortunate to have jobs with pensions, there has been a change from defined benefit plans, in which workers receive a defined percentage of their wages, based on age and years of service, to defined contribution plans, in which employers and/or employees contribute a defined amount of money into a plan, but they do not guarantee that the money will still be there when you retire. The risk has been shifted to the worker. The AFL–CIO news related the story of Wanda Chalk, an African American employee at Enron. She had worked at Enron for fifteen years and had stock options worth $150,000, which was to generate income for her retirement. But due to Enron's fraudulent dealings, when Enron crashed, so did she. She lost her job, her stock value dropped to zero, and her retirement security went up in smoke.

Privatizing social security could produce the same effect. Preservation of assets, not risky schemes that could fail when you need the money most, needs to remain the cornerstone of retirement plans. As a society, we should not revert to a pre-Depression system, where our elders are at risk of dying in poverty.

ASSET CREATION

Even if a few individuals of color hold greater assets, that will not be enough to close the racial wealth divide. Just because in 2004 Bill Cosby was worth $540 million in assets, and just because the Unanues, owners of Goya Foods, were worth $700 million, it doesn't help those members of their racial groups who are stuck at the bottom. Assets need to be utilized to expand wealth for the community as a whole.

For example, Native land was given away to railroad owners and, in 1887, tribal land was broken into individual plots. Over the years, more and more Native owners lost their plots, resulting in a checkerboard pattern of landownership in what should have been tribally owned territory. In 2002, the Northwest Area Foundation, funded by heirs of James J. Hill, head of the Great Northern Railroad, who grew rich from the

displacement of Ojibwes in Minnesota, made voluntary reparations. They gave $20 million in seed money for a buyback. Now millions of acres are back under tribal control.

In the 1970s, the inner city of Battle Creek, Michigan, became an economically depressed area, due to the closing of a military base nearby; by 1990, there were fifty recognized crack houses within a mile of downtown. Battle Creek Neighborhoods Incorporated, a community development financial institution, stepped in. Their approach has been to focus on lending to people who are willing to buy particular community blocks rather than to buyers of housing units scattered throughout the city. Their loans come with a requirement to improve the property and to participate in improving the quality of life on the block. For example, they sponsor "best of neighborhood" contests—Best Front Porch, Best Back Yard, Best Group Effort—that encourage home maintenance and improvement. Brenda Sue Woods wasn't going to participate in the Porch contest at first, but then decided to try. When she took first place, "I was just screaming like I won something on The Price is Right." The emphasis on neighborhoods will enable housing values to rise in the area.

The Hawai'i Alliance for Community-Based Economic Development, a statewide nonprofit organization, provides loans not to individuals, but to groups. For example, a group of young people put in a proposal with the goal of "reconnection with their elders." One of the ways they used the loan was for a community van to transport those elders to needed services.

In a variety of locations, nonprofit organizations and government entities are experimenting with wealth-creation frameworks that are "inclusive, community-driven, and action oriented, protecting community, cultural, and environmental concerns while shielding individual private rights." [40] These efforts are road signs to the future.

PRINCIPLES FOR A FAIR ECONOMY

As we survey the wreckage from the swath of federal policies that have undercut the efforts of the nonwhite people of the United States to work hard, gain success, and contribute to their country, it is clear that a fair economy that closes the racial economic divide will need to be based on some new economic principles and some new policy-building processes.

First, we need an activist government that invests in people and communities from the bottom up. The current ruling axiom that a marketplace operating free from all government intervention will produce an economy good for everyone has been proven wrong more than once. The corollary—that giving more money to those who already have money will cause it to "trickle down" on the rest of us—has also been proven wrong: a "jobless recovery," as it was called in 2004, is not a recovery for those without jobs. Capitalism's invisible hand does not distribute resources or benefits equitably. On the contrary, it pours riches on some and knocks others off their feet.

In January 2003, United for a Fair Economy published a report called "State of the Dream: Enduring Disparities in Black and White," showing that the level of racial economic disparity was largely unchanged between 1968, the date of Martin Luther King's death, to 2001. For example, at the rate of improvement in black income compared to white income, it would take 581 years to reach income parity. [41] Thabo Mbeki, the South African president, while thinking about the problem of racial economic inequality in South Africa, looked at the report and compared the situation of African Americans in the United States to that of blacks in South Africa. He notes that in the United States, we have tried to use a free-market approach to solve the problem of inequality. From the data, he concludes that this approach has been a failure.

What's the alternative? Mbeki points to the European Union as an example of another method. Wealthier European countries are engaged in the redistribution of wealth across the Union, by investing in poorer countries. This allows the poorer countries to catch up and become producers and consumers. The assistance they receive is a temporary investment that produces rewards for both the rich and the poor countries.[42] For example, Europe invested heavily in the Irish Republic, whose economy had lagged behind due to years of political instability and friction with British-supported Northern Ireland. After just a few years, the Irish economy came roaring back. For the first time in centuries, people are immigrating *to* Ireland. Businesses flourished; jobs returned. Instead of the boom-boom trading of bullets, cross-border trading in commerce between Protestant Northern Ireland and the Catholic Irish Republic is booming. The so-called religious war has subsided, not just because of new political initiatives, but because economic interdependencies are replacing economic domination of one side by the other. Greater economic equality breeds greater social stability.

These methods could be applied to narrow the racial wealth gap in the United States. Investing public resources into people and communities of color, and allowing local control over the use of those resources, could reverse the effects of years of disinvestment.

Second, our economy must recognize and preserve assets that we hold in common. One of the greatest ways of creating wealth for whites was to take land held collectively by Native peoples and divide it into privately held pieces. Private landownership lies at the base of economic inequality.

One alternative was proposed by Henry George one hundred years ago. He proposed that property taxes be divided into a land tax and a tax on whatever is built on that land. His argument was that the land itself has no monetary value that any individual created; however, whatever is built upon the land is created by the owner. For example, a piece of land in the middle of New York is valuable because of all the infrastructure that surrounds it. If property taxes are divided into two rates, land being taxed at a high rate based on its social value, and the improvements taxed at another rate, then land in the middle of a city would not stand vacant or have run-down tenements on it. The high land tax would give the owners an incentive to use it rather than to hold it for speculation; the lower tax on the improvements would be offset by the revenue improvements the building would bring. In Pittsburgh, the two-rate property tax was in place for a number of decades. After a political struggle, it went to a one-rate tax in 2001, after which requests for building permits declined steadily. During its two-rate tax era, the annual value of Pittsburg's building permits greatly outpaced other Northeastern cities.[43] Philadelphia is now considering putting a two-rate property tax in place.

A third principle is that the nation needs new policies that support wealth building for the asset poor. For half a century, conservatives and liberals alike have focused only on income support for the poor. There is nothing wrong with constructing safety nets that enable people to survive for another day. But many of these programs remove incentives for savings, so that the poor cannot get ahead. In order to qualify for transitional assistance (welfare), a single mother cannot have more than $1,000 in assets in some states. She is forced to spend down her savings, ensuring that she and her children will stay in poverty. There are also asset limits to qualify for subsidized health insurance.

Those who already have assets get different policies. They are given incentives in the form of tax breaks to save and to invest even more. Over the last few years, the tax rate on dividend income was cut, which encourages the wealthy to buy even more stocks. But the rate on income from working hasn't been cut as much, and as the cost of living rises faster than incomes, those without investment assets can save even less. Reforms that allowed greater pretax deductions for retirement accounts favor those who can put aside thousands of dollars a year for their retirement but don't help those without money to put aside. The mortgage interest tax deduction gives home owners, but not renters, a tax break. All of these policies make the rich richer and the poor poorer.

In these chapters, we have seen instances of massive public investments to build a white middle and upper class. Millions of acres of land have been given away to white homesteaders; taxpayer-subsidized low-interest mortgage and business loans have been channeled to whites; and tax givebacks (another

form of government subsidy) have gone mainly to whites. After World War II, the GI Bill enabled the biggest class restructuring in U.S. history: anyone who served in the military was eligible for government-subsidized college tuition and a home mortgage.

These examples show that the poor can be brought into the middle class when they are given a boost by the government. Not everyone wanted to help low-income whites. When the GI Bill was first suggested, there were those who thought that allowing working-class white men to go to college would bring down the quality of higher education. A familiar argument for those who fought for affirmative action! But neither class or race origin predetermines success in education or occupation. Giving working-class whites and people of color an opportunity to move up and out of poverty demonstrates the success of investment in our people. Massive asset-building programs have been instituted in the past, and that can be done again.

Fourth, these new programs should be paid for through progressive taxation (taxing people with greater income and wealth at higher rates than those with less financial means), a principle agreed upon since the first income tax was enacted in 1915. Since most wealth has been created or aided by government action, taxes on wealth are fair.

Bill Gates, Sr., father of one of the richest men in the world, is a proponent of keeping the estate tax, which in 2006 is levied on estates starting at than $2 million (and that exemption rate is due to rise to $3.5 million in 2009). While some of the rich want to abolish the estate tax completely—not him. He notes that if it were not for tax-funded research that developed the Internet, or government-funded development of computer technology, or the education system that brought his son a highly skilled workforce, or the laws we have protecting corporations like Microsoft, his son would not have been able to achieve financial success. If Bill, Jr., had been born into a society without these prior social investments, he could have been just as smart, just as hardworking—and poor. Therefore, he concludes, the estate tax should be seen by those with wealth as their obligation to replenish the treasury which enabled them to make their fortunes. Revenues from concentrated wealth could reverse our society's drift toward aristocracy. Revenues from the estate tax alone, if it is preserved, will generate $662 billion over the next ten years.

A fifth principle is that policy proposals must be approached with a race lens, and that the involvement of people from different cultural traditions will be required. Any program will need community involvement, from the proposal-drafting stage to the implementation stage. Throughout these chapters we have seen that universal programs often have disparate effects, both intended and unintended. In earlier days, there were explicit exclusions, like the Alien Land Laws forbidding Asians to own land. Later, the exclusions became subtler. For example, Social Security didn't explicitly exclude blacks and Latinos, but by excluding agricultural and service work, the effect was the same. Federal housing policy didn't deny housing dollars to people of color, but drawing red lines around neighborhoods, on the basis of the seemingly neutral assessment that people in those neighborhoods were bad risks for loans, had the same effect.

Using a race lens would mean that "government and public bodies would attempt to weave policies of equality of opportunity and non-discrimination into the fabric of decision-making."[44] If such an approach were taken when the Social Security Act was enacted, farm and domestic workers, occupations held predominately by blacks and Latinos, would not have been excluded.

A roomful of white men will not be able to foresee the impact of policies they design on people of different races and cultures; this approach requires the active participation of the people for which the policies are intended. U.S.-style constitutions imposed on Indian tribes did not make tribal governments more democratic. Because the assets and barriers of each nationality will be different, policies will need to be crafted and adjusted to provide different paths to the same outcome. For example, the desired outcome might be adequate housing for all families. Voices of those like the woman from Somalia puzzled by the U.S. definition of a "family" need to be heard. Her family may include uncles and grandparents and clan members. In home buying, the ways to qualify as creditworthy cannot be one size

Closing the racial wealth divide

United for a Fair Economy's workshop ends on a note of hope. The trainer tells the group, "The racial wealth divide isn't natural or inevitable. Because it was widened by human beings who decided all these policies, it can be narrowed by democratically deciding on new policies. The United States can be held accountable for living up to its ideals of equal opportunity."

Then she positions five people across the floor of the room to represent the racial wealth divide: the person holding the sign "white" is standing far ahead of those holding the signs that say "African American," "Latino," and "Native American," and a little ahead of the person with the "Asian American" sign. As the group brainstorms policy changes that would narrow the racial divide, the trainer moves the people along the floor to represent whom that policy change would affect. For example, when someone says, "Tax the super-rich!," she asks the "white" person to take two steps backward, as most of the very wealthy are white. When someone suggests "universal health care," she asks those representing people of color to take one step forward, because people of color are more likely to be uninsured. Similarly, "more scholarships," "no more redlining," "rent control," and a "crackdown on employers who discriminate" all move the people of color forward.

The brainstorm goes on, and one step after another brings the people with the signs closer to each other. When at last a step is taken that brings them all onto the same line, a spontaneous cheer arises from the group. They've seen the possibility of equality.

fits all. The Vietnamese often do not use banking services. They tend to use cash for all transactions, but that doesn't mean they cannot meet their mortgages or pay off their loans. Latinos may qualify for a home-buying program, but unless there are Spanish-language materials and clarity about immigration status requirements, they may

never find out. Dollars for outreach and education need to be built into all programs.

The first step in building a movement for greater economic and racial equality is a change in consciousness. The myths of racial superiority and inferiority can be debunked, and the government's hand in creating racial categories and distributing economic resources by race exposed. We see that "the rich get richer and the poor poorer" is not a law of nature, but a man-made choice. We remember what brings us together as Americans: our shared value that work should be rewarded, and our belief that leaders are not born but rise from the ranks when given the opportunity.

Using these principles as guidelines, the specific policy agenda can be filled in. The various groups who are thinking and working on wealth building—grassroots activists, service providers, think tanks, academics, and government officials—need to be connected.

"I am concerned that African Americans not just demand a 'share' but to build a system that guarantees freedom and justice for everyone," stated Charles Hamilton Houston, architect of the *Brown v. Board of Education* lawsuit, in 1949.

Closing the racial economic gap is not just about dividing up the pie into fair shares. The economy is not a zero-sum game, in which some must lose in order for others to win. In employment, why narrow the pool of talent to only those with white skin? In business, why not tap the innovative spirit and cultural contributions of peoples of color? Why let some communities falter, when those community members might add their dollars into circulation, creating more demand and more jobs? Why waste public dollars incarcerating legions of young people of color, when with hope and opportunity they can build our future?

At the end of his life, Martin Luther King, Jr., made this prophetic statement: "There is nothing new about poverty. What is new is that now we have the techniques and the resources to get rid of poverty. The real question is whether we have the will."[45] As the twenty-first century ticks along, we can stiffen our will. We can end poverty, and we can close the racial economic divide.

NOTES

Chapter 1 OVERVIEW: THE
ROOTS OF THE RACIAL
WEALTH DIVIDE

1. Jones, Jeffrey, 2004.
2. Ibid.
3. Morin, 2001, A1.
4. Muhammed, et al., 2004, 7.
5. Ibid., 6.
6. PBS, "Interview with Melvin
Oliver," 2003.
7. Shapiro, 2004, 60–61, citing a
Kotlikoff-Summers study that estimates that as "much as 80 percent of
family wealth derives not from savings but from transfers of money
from generation to generation."
8. Ibid., 63.
9. Ibid., 64.
10. Ibid., 8.
11. Stanton, et al., 1889, 63–75.
12. Takaki, 1993, 154, 156.
13. Ibid., 195.
14. Wong, 1995, 65.
15. Reimers, 1989, 18.
16. Amott and Matthaei, 1991, 270;
Morales, 1986, 30.
17. US Census Bureau, Income,
Poverty, and Health Insurance
Coverage in the United States: 2004.

18. Capgemini, 2004, 6.
19. Computations from 1983 and
2001 Survey of Consumer Finances
in Wolff, "Recent Trends in Wealth
Ownership," 2004, pp. 30-31.
20. Ibid., 31.
21. Ibid., 12, 34.
22. Mishel et al., 2003, 413, Table
7.10.
23. Greenstein and Shapiro, 2003,
1–2.
24. Ibid., 2.
25. United for a Fair Economy,
Executive Excess 2005, August 2005.
26. U.S. Census Bureau, *Income,
Poverty, and Health Insurance Coverage
in the United States*: 2004.
27. U.S. Bureau of Labor Statistics,
Current Employment Statistics,
Table A-1.
28. ABC News, 1991.
29. Muwakkil, 2003.
30. Ibid.
31. Shapiro, 2004, 121.
32. Ibid., 53.
33. PBS, "Interview with Dalton
Conley," 2003.
34. Ibid.
35. Oliver and Shapiro, 1995, 169.
36. Glenn, 2002, 18–55.

37. Ibid., 68–69.
38. Reed, 2002.
39. Marable, 2000, 4.
40. Allen, 1997, passim.
41. Wilson, 1997, 39–46.
42. Carnoy, 1994, 53–55.
43. Feagin, 2000, Chapter 5.
44. Glenn, 2002, 238–239.
45. Ibid., 239.
46. Carnoy, 1994, 6–7.
47. Ibid., 10.
48. Ibid., 11.
49. Lipsitz, 1998, 27.
50. Gilbert and Eli, 2000, 164.
51. Marable, 2000, xxii–xxiii.
52. Applied Research Center, 2002,
19.
53. Feagin, 2000, 204.
54. U.S. Census Bureau, Population
Division, Gibson, Campbell and Kay
Jung, 2002, Table F-1. "Race and
Hispanic Origin, for the United
States and Historical Sections and
Subsections of the United States:
1790 to 1900."
55. Ibid.
56. Ibid.
57. U.S. Census Bureau, 2000
Decennial Census, Table PCH-1.
58. Ibid.

59. Marable, Manning, "Building Coalitions," in Jennings, *Blacks, Latinos, and Asians in Urban America,* 1994, 36–43.

Chapter 2
LAND RICH, DIRT POOR

1. U.S. Census Bureau, "The American Indian and Alaska Native Population: 2000," p. 11.
2. U.S. Census Bureau, 2000 Census Summary File 4, Table QT-P34 "Poverty Status in 1999 of Individuals: 2000."
3. Ibid., QT-P24 "Employment Status by Sex: 2000," QT-P20 "Educational Attainment by Sex 2000."
4. Taylor and Kalt, 2005, 28.
5. Ibid., 34.
6. Ibid., 36.
7. U.S. Census Bureau, 2000 Census Summary File 4, Table DP-4 "Profile of Selected Housing Characteristics."
8. Many Native people do receive some interest from federally controlled trust accounts such as the Individual Indian Monies accounts.
9. U.S. Census Bureau, 2000 Census Summary File 4, Matrix PCT92 "Interest Dividends, Net Rental Income for 1999 Households."
10. U.S. Census Bureau, "American Indian- and Alaskan Native-Owned Businesses 1997."
11. Pevar, 2002, 18–19.
12. Sutton, 1985, passim.
13. In the 1950s, the federal government "terminated" its relationship with several Indian tribes, thus effectively opening up their land for sale to non-Indians and ceasing all federal services to tribes.
14. Weatherford, 1991, 112.

15. Keoke and Porterfield, 2002, 6.
16. Axelrod, 1993, 23.
17. Ibid., 36.
18. Ibid., 1993, 59.
19. Ibid., 1993, 60–61.
20. Ibid., 1993, 61–62.
21. Ibid., 1993, 62.
22. Pevar, 2002, 46.
23. Chen, 2000, A1; Herbert, 2001, A17.
24. Woods, 1994, 1471, 1496–97; Pevar, 1992.
25. Pevar, 1992, xi.
26. American Indian Policy Review Commission, 1977, 99.
27. Pevar, 2002, 7; Deloria and Lytlen, 1984, 242.
28. Fixico, 1998, 88.
29. Axelrod, 1993, 141.
30. A region in the south-central United States, most of which comprises present-day Oklahoma, which in 1834 was set aside by the government specifically for the relocation of Indians from the southeast.
31. Axelrod, 1993, 142.
32. Abel, 1906, 412.
33. Matthiessen, 1984, 10.
34. Faimon-Silva, 1993, 215.
35. Shoshone-Bannock Tribal Enterprises. "Tribal History." http://www.sho-ban.com/history.asp, accessed August 2005.
36. U.S. National Archives and Records Administration. *Transcription of Homestead Act (1862).*
37. U.S. Library of Congress. "The Homestead Act Went Into Effect May 20, 1862."
38. U.S. National Archives and Records Administration. *Transcript of Pacific Railway Act (1862).*
39. Hartmann, 2002, 83–84, 90.
40. Baxter, 1995, 121, 136.
41. Hart, 1995, 92–97.
42. Ibid., 92–98.

43. Bartlett, 1974, p. 34
44. Ibid., 33; Amott and Matthaei, 1991, 106.
45. Menchaca, 2002, 257.
46. Project Underground, accessed August 2005.
47. Menchaca, 2002, 257.
48. Project Underground, accessed August 2005.
49. 24 Stat. 388, as amended, 25 U.S.C. Secs. 331-58.
50. Tyler, 1973, 95.
51. Iverson, 1994, 30.
52. Nabhan, 1989, 61.
53. Amott and Matthaei, 47.
54. McDonnell, 1991, 4.
55. Carlson, 1981, 149.
56. Amott and Matthaei, 1991, 47.
57. Iverson, 1994, 30.
58. Fixico, 1998, chapter 2, 27–53.
59. Ward and Aamodt, 2000.
60. Pevar, 2002, 299.
61. Lewis, accessed August 2005.
62. O'Brien, 1989, 78.
63. Ibid., 216.
64. General Accounting Office, 2003, 14.
65. Ibid., 14.
66. Native American Rights Fund, accessed August 2005.
67. Brinkley, 2003, A17.
68. Ibid., A17.
69. Ramah Navajo Class Action. "Affadavit of Charles A. Hobbs; U.S. Department of Justice.
70. *United States v. Navajo Nation* (01-1375), 263 F.3d 1325, reversed and remanded, as discussed in Lane, A19.
71. Lane, 2002, A19.
72. Cahn and Hearne, 1972, 5
73. Hurt, 1987, 174.
74. Ibid., 178–79.
75. Parker, 1989, 138.
76. O'Brien, 1989, 294.
77. Ibid., 83.
78. Pevar, 2002, 90.

79. Deloria and Lytle, 1984, 172.
80. Johnson, Troy R., 36.
81. Ibid., 35.
82. Pevar, 2002, 88.
83. Wilkins, 2002, 143.
84. Ibid., 288.
85. Ibid., 288.
86. Ibid., 143.
87. Ibid., 155.
88. Canby, 1998, 66.
89. Wilkinson, 1999, 280–283.
90. Ibid., 286.
91. Ibid., 283, 304–307.
92. Rosenthal, 1996, 253.
93. Canby, 1998, 354–357.
94. Gibbons, 2003.
95. Ibid.; Olson, M., 2003.
96. Pevar, 2002, 11.
97. Ibid., 11, 68.
98. Parker, 1989, 53.
99. Don Wharton, Native American Rights Fund, personal correspondence to author, January 2004.
100. Ibid.
101. Herzberg, 1977, 275.
102. Ibid., 275
103. Ibid., 285
104. Case study courtesy of the Native American Rights Fund.
105. *Worcester v. Georgia* 31 U.S. 515, 516 (1832); Pevar, 2002, 189–192.
106. *McClanahan v. Arizona Tax Commission* 411 U.S. 164 (1973).
107. *Oklahoma Tax Commission v. Citizen Band of Potawatomi* (1991) ruled that although states can tax sales of tobacco to non-Indians on tribal territory, they did not have the authority to enforce tax collection in Indian country. However, after years of harassment and political negotiations, many tribes in Oklahoma decided to enter into taxation compacts with the state. Bays, 2002, 198–192.
108. Bays, 2002, 192.
109. *Indian Country Today*, "Idaho coalition fights state tax bills aimed at reservation sales," Feb. 26, 2003.
110. Bays, 2002, 85.
111. USC, Title 25, Chapter 29, Section 2702; Mille Lacs Band of Ojibwe.
112. USC, Title 25, Chapter 29, Section 2710 ((b)(2)(b)(I v).
113. Forest County Potawatomi Foundation.
114. United Tribes of Wisconsin, Web site.
115. Minnesota Indian Gaming Association Web site.
116. Analysis Group/Economics Inc., http://www.cniga.com/facts/research_detail.php?id=8.

Chapter 3

FORGED IN BLOOD

1. Marx, 2002, 14, 40–42, 56–57.
2. Mills, C., 1997, 36–40.
3. Bureau of Labor Statistics, 2004.
4. Federal Reserve, *Survey of Consumer Finances, 2001*.
5. Ibid.
6. Ariel Mutual Funds/Charles Schwab, *2004 Black Investor Survey*.
7. Hine, Hine and Harrold, 2000, 27.
8. Ibid., 29–30.
9. Mills, C., 1997, passim.
10. Glenn, 2002, 18–26.
11. Okihiro, 2001, 28–54, 125–137.
12. Fuchs, 1990, 9–10.
13. Hine, Hine and Harrold, 2000, 53–54.
14. Ibid., 54
15. Marx, 2002, passim.
16. Jones, Jacqueline, 1998, 24.
17. Kranish, 2002, C1.
18. Fuchs, 1990, 88–89.
19. Marable, 2000, 4.
20. Fuchs, 1990, 90.
21. Ibid., 90.
22. Ibid., 90.
23. Ibid., 90.
24. Ibid., p. 91; Zinn, *A People's History of the United States,* 176.
25. Fuchs p. 91; Zinn, *A People's History of the United States*, 182.
26. Jones, Jacqueline, 1998, 259.
27. Fuchs, 1990, 93–94.
28. Marable, 1983, 140.
29. Fuchs, 1990, 91–94.
30. Ibid., 1990, 91–94.
31. Jones, Jacqueline, 1985, 33–35.
32. Davis, 1998, 113.
33. Westley, 1998, 458-459; Zinn, 1995, 187-194; Fuchs, 1990, 95.
34. Zinn, 1995, 196
35. Ibid., 200–202.
36. Ibid., 199.
37. Gilbert and Eli, 2000, 66–67.
38. Zinn, 1995, 203, 285.
39. Robinson, R., 2000, 211, citing John Hope Franklin, *From Slavery to Freedom.*
40. Marable, 2000, 142–143.
41. Carnoy, 1994, 162.
42. Westley, 1998, 464–465.
43. Gilbert and Eli, 2000, 13, 18–19.
44. See links to electronic copies of the text from University of Maryland (www.history.umd.edu/Freedmen/sfo15.htm).
45. Westley, 1998, 460.
46. Ibid., 460.
47. Zinn, 1995, 193.
48. Westley, 1998, 462.
49. Robinson, R., 2000, 205.
50. Gilbert and Eli, 2000, 65.
51. Robinson, 2000, 226, citing Yuval Taylor, *I Was Born a Slave.*
52. Zinn, 1995, 194.
53. Ibid., 196.
54. Jones, 1998, 243.
55. Westley, 1998, 461.
56. Amott and Matthaei, 1991, 154–55; Gilbert and Eli, 2000, 37.
57. Fuchs, 1990, 98; Zinn, 1995,

198–199.

58. Landrieu, 2005.
59. Fuchs, 1990, 98.
60. Gilbert and Eli, 2000, 28–29.
61. Fuchs, 1990, 109.
62. Ibid., 109.
63. Gilbert and Eli, 2000, 85.
64. Muwakkil, 2005.
65. Gilbert and Eli, 2000,32.
66. Ibid., 30.
67. Ibid., 30.
68. Ibid., 28–29.
69. Zinn, 1995, 204.
70. Fuchs, 1990, 97; Zinn, 1995, 278.
71. Gilbert and Eli, 2002, 32.
72. Fuchs, 1990, 102–10.
73. Gilbert and Eli, 2000, 84–85.
74. Jones, Jacqueline, 1985, 156–160.
75. Wilson, 1980, 66.
76. Ibid., 68.
77. Jones, 1985, 156–7.
78. Marable, 2005, 23 (in Conrad, Whitehead, Mason and Stewart)
79. Ibid.
80. White, 1919, 25.
81. Ibid., 25.
82. Newman, 1978.
83. Katznelson, 2005, 22.
84. Ibid., 32.
85. Conley, 1999, 36.
86. Katznelson, 2005, 32.
87. Ibid., 31.
88. Ibid., 42.
89. Ibid., 47.
90. Quadagno, 1994, 21; Abramovitz, 2000, 65.
91. Katznelson, 2005, 37.
92. Gilbert and Eli, 2000, 95.
93. Katznelson, 2005, 34.
94. Ibid., 38.
95. Ibid., 46.
96. Ibid., 46.
97. Abramovitz, 2000, 65.
98. Jones, 1998, 341.
99. Katznelson, 2005, 45.

100. Abramovitz, 2000, 66.
101. Gilbert and Eli, 2000,96.
102. Ibid.,102.
103. Jones, Jacqueline, 1998, 342; Gilbert and Eli, 2000, 96.
104. Gilbert and Eli, 2000, 99.
105. Ibid., 91, citing Robert Zabawa, "The Black Farmer and the Land in South Central Alabama, from 1818 to the New Deal."
106. Jones, Jacqueline, 1998, 343.
107. Gilbert and Eli, 2000,95.
108. Jones, Jacqueline, 1998, 343.
109. Ibid., 343.
110. Katznelson, 2005, 57.
111. Quadagno, 1994, 23.
112. Ibid., 23.
113. Jones, Jacqueline, 1998, 341.
114. Ibid., 341.
115. Ibid., 341.
116. Fuchs, 1990, 108.
117. Conley, *Being Black, Living in the Red*, 1999, 37.
118. Ibid., 37.
119. Quadagno, 1994, 23.
120. Ibid., 24.
121. Loewen, 2005, passim.
122. Gilbert and Eli, 2000,109.
123. Katznelson, 2005, 32.
124. Ibid., 33.
125. Fuchs, 1990, 155.
126. Ibid., 109.
127. Ibid., 155.
128. Gilbert and Eli, 2000, 111.
129. Fuchs, 1990, 157–158.
130. Katznelson, 2005, 113.
131. Ibid., 113.
132. Ibid., 100–101.
133. Ibid., 129.
134. Onkst, 1998, under "The Search for a Job and a Better Way of Life."
135. Kiester, 1994, 128(9); Katznelson, 2005, 116.
136. Onkst, 1998, under "The Education and Training Benefit, Part Two"; Katznelson, 2005, 135.

137. Katznelson, 2005, 120.
138. Ibid., 132.
139. Ibid., 130.
140. U.S. Department of Veterans Affairs, 3.
141. Onkst, 1998, under "The Search for a Job and a Better Way of Life."
142. Katznelson, 2005, 138.
143. Onkst, 1998, under "The Education and Training Benefit, Part One."
144. Katznelson, 2005, 137.
145. "GI Loans: Colored Vets Who Borrow Cash Prove Sound Business Investments," *Ebony* II. 10 (August 1947):23; *Los Angeles Tribune,* September 19, 1947; TINCF, R-101, F-454, cited in Onkst, under "The Search for a Job and a Better Way of Life"; Katznelson, 2005, 140.
146. Quadagno, 1994, 90.
147. Ibid.
148. Conley, *Being Black, Living in the Red*, 37.
149. Fuchs, 1990, 418.
150. Randall Robinson, 227.
151. Quadagno, 1994, 105-106.
152. Ibid., 105.
153. Ibid., 91.
154. Gilbert and Eli, 2000,107.
155. Westley, 1998, 441.
156. Fuchs, 1990, 416.
157. Lawson, 1976, 134.
158. Gilbert and Eli, 2000, 131.
159. Quadagno, 1994, 26.
160. Janofsky, 2005.
161. Quadagno, 1994, 27.
162. Fuchs, 1990, 165–166.
163. Ibid., 167.
164. Ibid., 168.
165. Ibid., 170–172.
166. Ibid., 173.
167. Zinn, 1980, 168.
168. Ibid., 166.
169. Bositis, 2001, 3.
170. Zinn, 1980, 166.

171. Lee, C., 1999, 147.
172. Ibid., 147.
173. Ibid., 148; Mills, K., 1993, 258.
174. Mills, K., 1993, 259.
175. Lee, C., 1999, 148; Mills, K., 1993, 259.
176. Lee, C., 1999, 150; Mills, K., 1993, 262.
177. Lee, C., 1999, 148.
178. Mills, K., 1993, 262.
179. Ibid., 271.
180. Quadagno, 1994, 97.
181. Ibid., 92.
182. Ibid., 92.
183. Fuchs, 1990, 417.
184. Ibid., 418.
185. Lipsitz, 1998, 8.
186. Ibid., 8.
187. Ibid., 27.
188. Ibid., 30.
189. Ibid., 6.
190. Quadagno, 1994, 111–112.
191. Ibid., 113.
192. Ibid., 109–111.
193. Ibid., 97.
194. Ibid., 98.
195. Fuchs, 1990, 419.
196. Quadagno, 1994, 91.
197. Katznelson, 164, citing Farley and Allen, 1987.
198. Oliver and Shapiro, 1995, 151.
199. Quadagno, 1994, 94.
200. Stone, 1993, 158.
201. Quadagno, 1994, 113.
202. Ibid., 113–114.
203. Mittal, 2000, under "The Perennial Crop of Bias."
204. Gilbert and Eli, 2000, 162.
205. Mittal, 2000, under "The Perennial Crop of Bias."
206. Gilbert and Eli, 2002, 163; Mittal, 2000, under "The Perennial Crop of Bias."
207. Gilbert and Eli, 2002, 161.
208. Mittal, 2000, under "The Perennial Crop of Bias."
209. Katznelson, 2005, 30.

210. Mittal, 2000, under "The Perennial Crop of Bias."
211. Gilbert and Eli, 2002, 162.
212. Ibid., 134.
213. Ibid., 134–135, citing Pet Daniel, *Breaking the Land*.
214. Ibid., 147.
215. Ibid., 149.
216. Ibid., 164.
217. Ibid., 164.
218. Mittal, 2000, under "The Perennial Crop of Bias."
219. Ibid.
220. Ibid.
221. Gilbert and Eli, 166–167.
222. Harris, 2000, 34.
223. Gilbert and Eli, 166–167.
224. Harris, 2000, 36.
225. Grant, 2001.
226. Mittal, 2000, under "The Perennial Crop of Bias."
227. Ibid.
228. Roediger, 1991, 12–13.
229. Carnoy, 1994, 162.
230. Fuchs, 1995, 442.
231. Johnson and Oliver, 1991, 544–545; Squire, 1982, 74.
232. Squire, 1982, 74–75.
233. Johnson and Oliver, 1991, 545–546.
234. Squire, 72.
235. Johnson and Oliver, 1991, 558.
236. Lipsitz, 1998, 15.
237. Quadagno, 1994, Chapter 2, 43.
238. Ibid., 67.
239. Ibid., Chapter 2.
240. Ibid., 73–75.
241. Fuchs, 1990, 389.
242. Ibid., 434.
243. Ibid., 2005, 443.
244. Katznelson, 148.
245. Fuchs, 1990, 388–389.
246. Albelda, et al., 1998, 33–34, citing John L. Palmer and Isabel V. Sawhill, eds, *The Reagan Record: An Assessment of America's Changing Domestic Priorities,* Urban Institute,

August 1984, based on data from the U.S. Office of Management and Budget.
247. Carnoy, 1994, 167.
248. Albelda, et al., 1988, 36–37.
249. Lipsitz, 1998, 15.
250. Quadagno, 1994, 113.
251. Stone, 1993, 159, 160; Carnoy, 1994, 167.
252. Quadagno, 1994, 113.
253. Ibid., 115.
254. Wolff, 2004, *Recent Trends in Wealth Ownership*, 1993–1998, Tables 7 and 8.
255. Lipsitz, 1998, 32.
256. Stone, 1993, 149.
257. Conley, 1999, 4; Conley, 2001, 2.
258. Hyman, 1996.
259. Simms, 1999.
260. Oliver and Shapiro, 1995, 8, 137, 182.
261. Bernstein, 2005.
262. Applied Research Center, 2002, 8.
263. Ibid., 19.
264. Ibid., 8.
265. Ibid., 19.
266. Ibid., 24.
267. Ibid., 12.
268. Ibid., 16.
269. Ibid., 16.
270. Lipsitz, 1998, 10.
271. Substance Abuse and Mental Health Services Administration, 1998, 13.
272. Chanse, 2002, 3.
273. Lipsitz, 1998, 11.
274. Robinson, Randall, 2000, 214.
275. Ibid., 214.
276. Levin, Langan, and Brown, 2000, 8.
277. Meierhoefer, 1992, 20.
278. Justice Policy Institute, http://www.justicepolicy.org/article.php?id=459.
279. US Department of Justice,

Bureau of Justice Statistics,
http://www.ojp.usdoj.gov/bjs/crim
off.htm#prevalence.

280. Uchitelle, 2003, A1.

281. Muhammad, et al., 2004, 1.

282. Uchitelle, 2003, A1.

283. Ibid.

284. Ibid.

285. Lee and Spriggs, 2004, 3, 27–28.

286. Uchitelle, 2003, A1.

287. Scott, 2004, B1.

288. Applied Research Center, 2002, 11.

289. Aratani, 2004.

290. Mishel, et al., 2003, 363–374.

291. From www.DiversityInc.com.

292. U.S. Census Bureau, *Income, Poverty and Health Insurance Coverage in the United States 2004*, September 2005, http://www.census.gov/hhes/www/income/income04.html.

293. Wilson, 1980, 1.

294. DiversityInc.com.

295. Michael Kinsley "Dead Wrong: The estate tax doesn't double-dip, and they know it," *Slate*, April 6, 2001. http://slate.msn.com/default.aspx?id=103874.

296. Forbes 400, 2004.

297. Throughout the 1980s and into the early 1990s, the number was zero.

298. Census Bureau, SIPP.

299. O'Reily and Lyons, 1993.

300. Center for Budget and Policy Priorities.

301. United for a Fair Economy, "Shifty Tax Cuts."

302. Center for Budget and Policy Priorities, April 26, 2004.

303. U.S. Census Bureau, August 2005, *Income, Poverty and Health Insurance Coverage*, 2004.

304. Little Gewirtz, 2002.

305. Ibid.

306. Ibid.

307. LeGates and Hartman, 1981.

308. Rose 1982, 148.

309. U.S. Small Business Association, 1999.

310. Ibid., 2.

311. Ibid., 3.

312. Ibid., 9.

313. *The Minority Business Challenge: Democratizing Capital for Emerging Domestic Markets*, The Milken Institute and Minority Business Development Agency, Sept. 2000.

314. Schomburg, center exhibit, 2004.

315. Speech by Ellison DuRant Smith, April 9, 1924, *Congressional Record*, 68th Congress, 1st Session (Washington DC: Government Printing Office, 1924), vol. 65, 5961–5962.

316. Schomburg, 2004.

317. Ibid.

318. Ibid.

319. Ibid.

320. Table B05006.

321. Ibid.

322. Schomburg, Center Exhibit 2004; Newland and Grieco, 2004.

323. Newland and Grieco, 2004.

324. Census Bureau, Table B05006.

325. Schomburg, Center Exhibit 2004.

326. Ibid.

327. U.S. Census Bureau, *Coming to America*, 4; Income, Poverty and Health Insurance Coverage in the United States: 2003, Table A-1.

328. Sowell, 1995, 41–49.

329. 319. *The Minority Business Challenge*.

330. Inman, 2000, 226.

331. Marable, 2005, 231–236.

332. Ogletree, 2002, 9.

333. Dudley Street Neighborhood Initiative, http://www.dsni.org.

334. Medoff and Sklar, 1995.

335. Ibid.

336. DSNI, http://www.dsni.org.

337. Ibid.

338. Ibid.

339. Medoff and Sklar, 1994, 287.

340. Ogletree, 2002, 9.

341. United for a Fair Economy, "Estate Tax Action Center."

342. Green, 2001, 17.

343. United for a Fair Economy, April 20, 2004.

Chapter 4
NEIGHBORS AND FENCES

1. *U.S. Census Bureau Current Population Survey*, 2003.

2. Huntington, 2004, passim.

3. Acuña, 2003 (5th edition); Velez-Ibañez, 1996.

4. Ybarra, 2004, Introduction.

5. Ramirez and de la Cruz, 2002, 1–2.

6. U.S. Census Bureau, *2000 Census Summary* File 3.

7. Amott and Matthaei, 1991, 68–69.

8. Ibid., 65–66.

9. Menchaca, 2002, 237,239.

10. Ibid., 242.

11. "Native Americans of North America," 2004.

12. Gonzalez, J., 2000, 44.

13. Amott and Matthaei, 1991, 71.

14. Menchaca, 2002, 216.

15. Amott and Matthaei, 1991, 71.

16. Acuña, 48–56.

17. This land loss had substantial effects on employment opportunities and options for Mexican-Americans. According to historian Ronald Takaki, the rural Mexican population was distributed in the following way: thirty-four percent were ranch farm owners, twenty-

nine percent skilled laborers, and thirty-four percent manual laborers. By 1900, these distributions changed to sixteen percent, twelve percent, and sixty-seven percent, respectively. These numbers show that institutions (such as courts, government) in this period not only caused substantial loss in land, but also put Mexican-Americans on an inevitable downward job spiral.

18. Menchaca, 2002, 215.
19. Ibid., 217.
20. Ibid., 234.
21. Amott and Matthaei, 1991, 73.
22. Gonzalez, J., 2000, 100-101.
23. Ibid., 100.
24. Ibid., 102.
25. Amott and Matthaei, 1991, 71.
26. Ibid., 72.
27. Menchaca, 2000, 246.
28. Ibid., 247.
29. Ibid., 250.
30. Ibid., 251.
31. Ibid., 252.
32. Ibid.
33. Ibid., 254.
34. Gonzalez, J., 2000, 46.
35. Menchaca, 256.
36. Crawford, 1989, Introduction.
37. Acuña, 2000, 282.
38. Rangel and Alcala, 1972, 307–391.
39. *Bracero* is a Spanish term meaning someone who works with their arms; an equivalent American folk saying would be someone who puts their shoulder to the wheel. This program continued until 1964.
40. The term "Wetback" refers to Mexican nationals swimming or wading across the Rio Bravo (Rio Grande) to get to the United States and in the process getting their backs wet.
41. U.S. Census Bureau, *The Hispanic Population in the US*.
42. Gonzalez, A., 2002, 66.
43. Amott and Matthaei, 1991, 262.
44. Morales, J., 29.
45. Ibid., 29.
46. Amott and Matthaei, 1991, 262.
47. Maldonaldo-Denis, 1971, 72–74.
48. Padilla, 1958, 1.
49. Amott and Matthaei, 1991, 263.
50. Morales, J., 30.
51. Padilla, 1958, 1.
52. Benson-Arias, 1997, 2.
53. Amott and Matthaei, 1991, 270; Morales, 30.
54. Ibid., 272.
55. Padilla, 1958, 3.
56. Rodriguez and Korrol, 1996, 14.
57. Maldonaldo-Denis, 1972, 154.
58. Ibid., 165.
59. Rodriquez and Korrol, 1996, 14.
60. Weisskopf, 1985, 119.
61. Morales, J., 37.
62. Steiner, 1974, 306.
63. Padilla, 1958, 2.
64. Morales, J., 39.
65. Rodriguez and Korrol, 1996, 12.
66. Morales, J., 37.
67. Steiner, 1974, 121.
68. Aquino, 2000, 10.
69. Ibid., 10.
70. Ibid., 11.
71. Rodriguez and Korrol, 1996, 16.
72. Camirillo and Bonilla, 113.
73. Chavez, 150.
74. U.S. Census Bureau, *The Hispanic Population in the US*, 15.
75. Ibid.
76. Ibid.
77. Ibid.
78. Paulin, 2003, 15–16.
79. U.S. Census Bureau, *The Hispanic Population in the US*.
80. U.S. Census Bureau, 2000 Census Summary File 1.
81. Randall, 2004.
82. Ibid.
83. U.S. Census Bureau, *The Hispanic Population in the US*.
84. U.S. Census Bureau, *Educational Attainment in the US*.
85. Darity et al., 2002, 847–853.
86. Gomez, 2000, 94–103.
87. U.S. Census Bureau, 2000 Census Summary File 1, Table PCT1 "Total Population."
88. Emergency Medical Treatment and Active Labor Act (1986) allows for the "emergency treatment" of undocumented workers. This is an unfunded mandate. Recent debates in Congress have indicated a reassessment of this legislation since overburden hospitals have been closing down emergency centers in urban areas with high concentration of immigrants (Senator McCain et al., Letter to the President, Jan. 9, 2003).
89. U.S. Census Bureau, *Current Population Survey 2003*.
90. Harkness and Newman, 2003, 97–98.
91. Glaser and DiPasquale, 1999, passim.
92. Boehm and Schlottman, 2001, passim.
93. Ross and Yinger, 2002, passim.
94. Center for Women's Business Research, 2001.
95. Robles, 2005, http://www.estey centre.com/journal/j_pdfs/robles3-2.pdf.
96. Ibid.
97. Edgcomb and Armington, 2003, http://fieldus.org/publications/IE_Latino.pdf.
98. U.S. Small Business Administration, 1999.
99. U.S. Census Bureau, *Educational Attainment in the US*.

100. Valenzuela, 1999, passim.

101. LUPE state director is Juanita Valdez-Cox and David Arizmendi is the director of Proyecto Azteca. They can be contacted at (956)782-6655 and jvaldez@lupemail.com for further information on LUPE and its programs.

102. Ramirez and de la Cruz, 2000, 1.

103. We wish to thank Dr. Lisa Peñaloza for reminding us of the need to emphasize Latino history in the United States and the importance of the Spanish exploration and colonial period.

Chapter 5
THE PERILS OF BEING YELLOW

1. Takaki, 1998, 31.
2. Gotanda, 1999, 138.
3. Hutchinson, 1981, 66.
4. Ibid.
5. Kwong, 1997, 4–5.
6. U.S. Office of Management and Budget 1997, under "Comments on Recommendations Concerning Reporting More Than One Race."
7. National Research Council, 2004, 311.
8. Takaki, 1998, 31.
9. Ibid., 31–33, 79.
10. Chan, 1991, 48; Takaki 1998, 102.
11. Takaki, 1998, 208.
12. Ibid., 15.
13. *Naturalization Act of July 14, 1870.*
14. Hutchinson, 1981, 57–58.
15. Amott and Matthaei; 1991, 194–195.
16. Takaki, 1998, 85.
17. Ibid., 87–89.
18. Wong, 1995, 75.

19. Takaki, 1998, 82.
20. *Act of March 3, 1875.*
21. Takaki, 1998, 40, 12.
22. Chan, 1991, 106.
23. Takaki and Mattaei, 1998, 330.
24. Amott, 1991, 204, 243.
25. Takaki, 1998, 116.
26. Chan, 1991, 104–105.
27. Takaki, 1998, 111.
28. Kitano, 1988, 12.
29. Wong, 1995, 62–63.
30. Takaki, 1998, 111–112.
31. PBS, 2002.
32. Takaki, 1988, 209; also see the U.S. Bureau of Citizenship and Immigration Service Web site that states that the law was "aimed primarily at the Japanese." www.immigration.gov/graphics/about/statistics/legishist/470.htm.
33. King, 2000, 212–213.
34. Gotanda, 1999, 137, 145, 147.
35. Chan, 1991, 55; *Immigration Act of February 5, 1917.*
36. Takaki, 1998, 316–320.
37. Ibid., 57.
38. Ibid., 328–331.
39. Kitano, 1988, 82.
40. Takaki, 1998, 332.
41. Ibid., 188.
42. Ibid., 203.
43. Ibid., 206–207.
44. Ibid., 205–206.
45. Akers, 2002.
46. Takaki, 1998, 92–93.
47. Wong, 1995, 76.
48. Parenti, 2003, 62.
49. Takaki, 1998, 186.
50. Reimers, 1989, 81.
51. Knoll, 1982, 310–311.
52. Chan, 1991, 47.
53. Hazama and Komeiji, 1986, 47.
54. Takaki and De Bary, 1998, 212–213.
55. Nee, 1974, 154.
56. Takaki, 1998, 113.
57. Wong, 1995, 65.

58. Liu, et al., 1998, 148.
59. Maharidge, 1996, 274.
60. Takaki, 1998, 373–374.
61. Woo, 2000, 101.
62. Wong, 1995, 65.
63. Takaki, 1998, 214.
64. Ibid., 218–219.
65. Ibid., 411–412.
66. Seltzer and Anderson, 2000.
67. Amott and Matthaei, 1991, 228.
68. Robinson, G., 2001, 231.
69. Berlet and Lyons 2000, 155; U.S. Congress Committee on Interior and Insular Affairs, 1992, 117.
70. U.S. Congress Committee on Interior and Insular Affairs, 1992, 131.
71. Robinson, G. 2001, 144.
72. U.S. Congress Committee on Interior and Insular Affairs, 1992, 132.
73. Ibid., 133.
74. Ibid., 241.
75. Robinson, G. 2001, 231.
76. Ibid., 144; U.S. Congress Committee on Interior and Insular Affairs, 1992, 118.
77. Agbayani-Siewert and Revilla, 1995, 140.
78. Knoll, 1982, 80.
79. Takaki, 1998, 138.
80. Kitano, 1988, 63.
81. Liebert, 8/5/88, A1; Liebert, 8/11/88, A1.
82. PBS, 2001.
83. Takaki, 1998, 420–421.
84. Lai and Arguelles, 2003, passim.
85. Woo, 2000, 34.
86. UFE and IPS 2005, 21.
87. Takaki, 1998, 421.
88. Wong, 1995, 67.
89. Sheth, 1995, 177.
90. Ibid., 178.
91. Zia, 2000, 210.
92. Marosi, 2002, A18.
93. Glass Ceiling Commission, 1995, 143.

94. Woo, 1995, 58.
95. Agbayani-Siewert and Revilla, 1995, 142, 134.
96. U.S. Census Bureau, 2000 Census Summary File 1.
97. Takaki, 1998, 431–433.
98. Kitano, 1988, 86.
99. U.S. Census Bureau, 1993, 9.
100. Woo, 2000, 54–55.
101. Ibid., 63.
102. O'Reily and Lyons, 1993.
103. Takaki, 1998, 425–426.
104. A summary of this study is found in the Department of Housing and Urban Development press release 03-060: "Metropolitan Housing Market Study Shows Asians and Pacific Islanders Face Housing Discrimination," July 1, 2003. http://www.hud.gov/news/release.cfm?content=pr03-060.cfm (accessed December 21, 2004).
105. Systematic discrimination is the difference between the percent of tests that a white is favored on a particular treatment indicator versus the percent of tests that a minority is favored.
106. Sengsethuane, 2005, 1.
107. U.S. Census Bureau, May 2001.
108. Min, 1995, 204.
109. Ibid., 208–209.
110. Mangiafico, 1988, 82.
111. Zia, 2000, 51.
112. Rumbaut and Kibria, 1995, 235.
113. Gold 1998, 72–73.
114. Thrupkaew, 2002.
115. Moyers, 1995, 304.
116. Viet-AID Web site.

Chapter 6
CLIMBING THE UP ESCALATOR

1. Schuyler, 1993, B4.
2. Kivel, 2002, 27.
3. Allen, Volume II, 14–26.
4. Amott and Matthaei, 68–69.
5. Allen, 1994, Volume II, 31–32.
6. Ibid., 14–26.
7. Martin, 1991, 149-161, 257–280.
8. Jones, Jacqueline, 1998, 114.
9. Allen, Volume II, 180–83, 186.
10. Fuchs, 1990, 9.
11. Higginbotham, 1998, 33.
12. Fuchs, 87.
13. Higginbotham, p. 26; Fuchs, 10.
14. Fuchs, 1990, 10; Higginbotham, 32–40.
15. Martinas, 5.
16. Allen, 1994, Volume II, 186.
17. Ibid., 51.
18. Ibid., 1990, 61.
19. Fuchs, 10.
20. Allen, 1994, Volume II, 68.
21. Ibid., 107–8.
22. Ibid., chapters 6 and 7.
23. Ibid., 37.
24. Wood, 1997, 75–76.
25. Allen, Volume II, 37.
26. Fuchs, 1990, 11.
27. Jones, Jacqueline, 1998, 24.
28. Wood, 1997, 64–65.
29. Jones, Jacqueline, 1998, 30.
30. Ibid., 32.
31. Allen, 1994, Volume II, 173.
32. Zinn, 1995, 79, quoting Jackson Main, *The Social Structure of Revolutionary America.*
33. Ibid., 74.
34. Feagin, 2000, 55.
35. Berlet and Lyons, 2000, 26.
36. Ibid.
37. Ibid.
38. Allen, 1994, Volume II, 205.
39. Roediger, 1991, 34.
40. Ibid., 57.
41. Fuchs, 1990, 16; Amott and Matthaei, 1991, 110.
42. Fuchs, 1990, 16.
43. Feagin, 2000, 6.
44. Kranish, 2002.
45. Feagin, 2000, 55.
46. Zinn, 1995, 33.
47. Oakes, 1982, 38.
48. Ibid.
49. Ibid., 39.
50. Ibid., 40.
51. Feagin, 2000, 52.
52. Fuchs, 1990, 90.
53. Feagin, 2000, 52.
54. America, 1990, 6.
55. Ibid., 9.
56. Vedder, 1990, et al., in America, 1990, 128.
57. Ibid., 129.
58. Ibid., 128.
59. Allen 1995, Volume II, 184–85.
60. Ibid., 184–85.
61. Robertson and Kerber, 2000, B1.
62. Ibid.
63. Feagin, 2000, 57.
64. Berlet and Lyons, 2000, 53.
65. Westley, 1998, 460.
66. Zinn, 1995, 193.
67. Ibid.
68. Fuchs, 1990, 82.
69. Bartlett, 1974, 8.
70. Ibid., 17.
71. Ibid., 26-28.
72. Jones, Jacqueline, 1998, 107.
73. Ibid.
74. Bartlett, 1974, 53–54.
75. Berlet and Lyons, 2000, 41.
76. Ibid.
77. Gonzalez, Juan, 2000, 36.
78. Fuchs, 1990, 92.
79. Bartlett, 1974, 30.
80. Berlet and Lyons, 2000, 41.
81. Ibid.; Amott and Matthaei, 1991, 53.
82. Bensel, 2000, 93.
83. Amott and Matthaei, 1991,

105–106.

84. Fuchs, 1990, 92.

85. Bensel, 2000, 293.

86. Fuchs, 1990, 83–84; Amott and Matthaei, 1991, 105–106.

87. Amott and Matthaei, 1991, 122.

88. Bensel, 2000, 293.

89. Shapiro, 2004, 190.

90. Williams, Trina, "The Homestead Act: A Major Asset-building Policy in American History," Center for Social Development, Washington University, 2000, cited in Shapiro, 190.

91. Amott and Matthaei, 1991, 105–106.

92. Conley, 1995, 35, quoting Oliver and Stone, *Black Wealth/White Wealth*.

93. Fuchs, 1990, 92.

94. Ibid.; Feagin, 2000, 61.

95. Fuchs, 1990, 92.

96. Gilbert and Eli, 2000, 13.

97. Ignatiev, 1995, 87.

98. Amott and Matthaei, 1991, 367.

99. Conley, 35, quoting Oliver and Stone, *Black Wealth/White Wealth*.

100. Ibid.

101. Bartlett, 1974, 33.

102. Ibid., 32.

103. Ibid., 33.

104. Ibid; Amott and Matthaei, 1991, 106–10.

105. Bensel, 2000, 294.

106. Berlet and Lyons, 2000, 58.

107. Ibid.

108. Bensel, 2000, 294–5.

109. Berlet and Lyons, 2000, 58.

110. Bartlett, 1974, 34.

111. Ibid.

112. Ibid.

113. Fuchs, 1990, 84.

114. Bartlett, 1974, 37.

115. Amott and Matthaei, 1991, 47.

116. Ibid.

117. Ibid.

118. Ibid.

119. Gonzalez, Juan, 2000, 41.

120. Ibid.

121. Amott and Matthaei, 1991, 71.

122. Menchaca, 2002, 238.

123. Ibid., 241.

124. Ibid.

125. Ibid., 216.

126. Amott and Matthaei, 1991, 71; Menchaca, 215.

127. Menchaca, 2002 215.

128. Ibid., 217.

129. Glenn, 2002, 148.

130. Gonzalez, Juan, 2000, 100.

131. Amott and Matthaei, 1991, 71.

132. Menchaca, 2002, 234.

133. Ibid., 235.

134. Ibid.

135. Ibid.

136. Amott and Matthaei, 1991, 72.

137. Menchaca, 2002, 250.

138. Gonzalez, Juan, 2000, 46.

139. Fraser, 2002, 45.

140. Menchaca, 2002, 261.

141. Berlet and Lyons, 2000, 65.

142. Menchaca, 2002, 257.

143. and Matthaei, 1991, 72.

144. Menchaca, 2002, 271; Berlet and Lyons, 2000, 65.

145. Amott and Matthaei, 1991, 108.

146. Feagin, 2000, 180.

147. Fuchs, 19990, 12 and 55.

148. Berlet and Lyons, 2000, 52.

149. Fuchs, 1990, 41.

150. Ibid.

151. Berlet and Lyons, 2000, 52.

152. Fuchs, 1990, 14.

153. Sachar, 1992, 286.

154. Ibid., 144.

155. Ibid., 274–275.

156. Ibid., 324.

157. Berlet and Lyons, 2000, 105.

158. Sachar, 1992, 145–146.

159. Ibid., 275–283; Berlet and Lyons, passim.

160. Sachar, 1992, 285.

161. Fuchs, 1990, 56.

162. Berlet and Lyons, 2000, 94.

163. Fuchs, 1990, 57.

164. Berlet and Lyons, 2000, 68.

165. Carnoy, 1994, 162.

166. Berlet and Lyons, 2000, 72.

167. Roediger, 1991, 133.

168. Jones, Jacqueline, 1998, 282.

169. Ignatiev, 1995, 41–42.

170. Roediger, 1991, 133.

171. Ibid., 139.

172. Fuchs 1990, 42.

173. Roediger, 1991, 145.

174. Ignatiev, 1995, 39.

175. Roediger, 1991, 145.

176. Ignatiev, 1995, 39.

177. Roediger, 1991, 145.

178. Fuchs, 1990, 46.

179. Roediger, 1991, 145.

180. Ibid., 1991, 146; Ignatiev, 1995, 109.

181. Fuchs, 1990, 45.

182. Berlet and Lyons, 2000, 47.

183. Ignatiev, 1995, 75.

184. Fuchs, 1990, 38.

185. Roediger, 1991, 141; Ignatiev, 1995, 69.

186. Roediger, 1991, 140.

187. Ibid., 141.

188. Ignatiev, 1995, 65-66.

189. Fuchs, 1990, 46–47.

190. Jones, Jacqueline, 1998, 283.

191. Lopez, 130; Takaki, 1993, 15.

192. Olzak and Shanahan, 1998.

193. Lopez, 1996, 61, 67.

194. Ibid., 130; Takaki, 1993, 15.

195. Lopez, 1996, 67–77.

196. Ibid., 67.

197. Sachar, 1992, 324.

198. Ibid.

199. Fuchs, 1990, 60.

200. Sachar, 1992, 324.

201. Fuchs, 1990, 60.

202. Lipsitz, 1998, 25.

203. Ibid., 26.

204. Ibid.
205. Goldfield, 1997, 202; Sitkoff, 35–36.
206. Sitkoff, 1978, 35–36.
207. Ibid., 37.
208. Levine, 1988, 1.
209. Ibid, 4.
210. Quadagno, 1994, 21.
211. Feagin, 2000, 64.
212. Sitkoff, 1978, 67.
213. Ibid., 49.
214. Brown, 1999, 110.
215. Sitkoff, 1978, 54.
216. Jones, Jacqueline, 1998, 341; Goldfield, 1997, 204; Sitkoff, 1978, 51.
217. King, 1999, 201.
218. Sitkoff, 1978, 74–75.
219. Brown, 1999, 110–111.
220. Goldfield, 1997, 205.
221. Ibid., 204–05; Brown, 1999, 110.
222. Sitkoff, 1978, 49.
223. Amott and Matthaei, 1991, 129.
224. Gilbert, 2000, 95.
225. Levine, 1988, 1–4.
226. Jones, Jacqueline, 1998, 343.
227. Lipsitz, 1998, 5.
228. Goldfield, 1997, 207.
229. Jones, Jacqueline, 1998, 342.
230. Brown, 1999, 105; Sitkoff, 1978, 36.
231. Sitkoff, 1978, 37.
232. Ibid., 49.
233. Brown, 1999, 111.
234. Sitkoff, 1978, 52.
235. Conley, 36.
236. Conley, 1999, 37; Jones, Jacqueline, 1998, 343.
237. Quadagno, 1994, 23.
238. Ibid., 24.
239. Lipsitz, 1998, 5.
240. Goldfield, 1997, 206.
241. Quadagno, 1994, 24.
242. Goldfield, 1994, 206.
243. Ibid.
244. Sitkoff, 1997, 67.
245. Goldfield, 1994, 206.
246. Gilbert, 2000, 96.
247. Ibid.; Jones, Jacqueline, 1998, 342.
248. Quadagno, 1994, 24.
249. Gilbert, 2000, 97.
250. Ibid.
251. Ibid., 134–135.
252. Sitkoff, 1978, 70; Brown, 1999, 105–106.
253. Ibid., 1978, 48.
254. Goldfield, 1994, 206.
255. Ibid.
256. Ibid.
257. America, 1990, 133.
258. Berlet and Lyons, 2000, 155.
259. Amott and Matthaei, 1991, 229.
260. Ibid., 228.
261. Berlet and Lyons, 2000, 155; U.S. Census Committee on Interior and Insular Affairs, 1992, 117.
262. Gilbert, 2000, 115.
263. Onkst, 2004, Introduction.
264. Kiester, 1994, 128; Katznelson, 2005, 116.
265. Kiester, 1994, 128.
266. Onkst, 2004, 528; Katznelson, 2005, 136–137.
267. Katznelson, 2005, 138; Onkst, 2004.
268. Quadagno, 1994 90.
269. Conley, 1999, 37.
270. Lipsitz, 1998, 6.
271. Katznelson, 2005, 140.
272. Ibid., 116.
273. Lipsitz, 1998, 6; Quadagno, 1994, 91, quoting from National Archives Record Group 207, National Committee Against Discrimination in Housing.
274. Lipsitz, 1998, 6.
275. Ibid., 8.
276. Ibid., 7.
277. Ibid., 7.
278. Goldfield, 1994, 331.
279. Ong and Grigsby, 1988, 602–03.
280. Ibid., 605.
281. America, 1990, 165–68.
282. Albelda, et al. 1988, 39.
283. America, 1990, 165–68.
284. Carnoy, 1994, 45.
285. Ibid., 210–11.
286. Squire, 65.
287. Fuchs, 1990, 418.
288. Squire, 65, citing Senate subcommittee report.
289. Ibid., 70.
290. Ibid., 66–67.
291. Lipsitz, 1998, 43.
292. Ibid.
293. Wilson, 1987, passim, 1997, Chapter 2.
294. Massey and Denton, 1993, 147.
295. Lipsitz, 1998, 18.
296. Johnson and Oliver, 1991, 544.
297. Ibid., 549.
298. Ibid., 544-545.
299. Albelda, et al., 1988, 39.
300. America, 1990, 133.
301. Lipsitz, 1998, 16.
302. Albelda, et al., 1988, 36.
303. Conley, 1999, 136.
304. Lipsitz, 1998, 36.
305. Ibid.
306. Ibid.
307. Ibid., 37.
308. Aziz, 2002, 8.
309. Lipsitz, 43.
310. Ibid., 44.
311. Ibid.
312. Aziz, 2002, 1; Biskupic, 2000.
313. Ibid., 8–9.
314. Conley, 1999, 137.
315. Collins, Leondar-Wright, and Sklar, 1999, 13.
316. Wolff, Table 9.

317. Ibid.

318. Ibid., Tables 7 and 8.

319. Ibid.

320. Education Trust, 5.

321. Ibid, 7.

322. Collins, Leonder-Wright, and Skylar, 1999, 46.

323. Ibid., 48.

324. Wise, 2003.

325. Ibid.

326. Ibid.

327. Ibid.

328. Oliver and Shapiro, 1995, 169.

329. America, 1990, 9.

Chapter 7

RAINBOW ECONOMICS

1. DuBois, 1903.

2. Collins and Yeskel, 2000, 129.

3. Brown, et al., 9.

4. Price, 2003.

5. Sklar, et al., 122.

6. Henry J. Kaiser Family Foundation, 2004, 1.

7. Ibid., 2.

8. Ibid., 4.

9. Department of Health and Human Services, 1993.

10. Shapiro, *Hidden Costs*, 2004, 52.

11. Sklar, et al., 2001, 90.

12. Collins and Yeskel, 2000, 182.

13. Ibid.

14. Anderson et al., 2005, 1.

15. Root Cause, 2003.

16. Christopher, introduction and under "Humble Origins."

17. Sklar, et al., 2001, 118.

18. Phillips, 2001.

19. Boshara, et al., 2004, 1.

20. Sklar, et al., 2001, 118.

21. Muhammad, et al., 2004, 7.

22. Woo, 1997, 104.

23. Shapiro, Thomas, power point presentation , 2004.

24. Sherradan, 1991, 3–7.

25. Brown et al., 17.

26. Shapiro, *Hidden Costs*, 2004, 185.

27. Ginsberg and Ochoa, 2003, B1.

28. Isbister, 1994, 2.

29. Ibid., 5.

30. Ibid.

31. Policy Link, 2003.

32. Ibid.

33. United for a Fair Economy, 2002.

34. Moreno, 1998, 6–7.

35. Ibid., 1.

36. Ibid., 17.

37. Orr, 2004, 14.

38. Spriggs, 2004, 18.

39. Muhammad, et al., 17.

40. Agres, 2005, 37.

41. Muhammad et al., 2004, 25.

42. Mbeki, 2004.

43. www.progress.org/cg/feet3.htm.

44. Ryan, 1999, 6.

45. King, Martin Luther, 1968.

SOURCES

ABC News, *Primetime Live*, September 26, 1991.

Abel, Annie Heloise. "The History of Events Resulting in the Indian Consolidation West of the Mississippi." *Annual Report of the American Historical Association*, Vol 1. (1906):235–450.

Abramovitz, Mimi. *Under Attack, Fighting Back: Women and Welfare in the United States*. New York: Monthly Review Press, 2000.

Act of March 3, 1875. 18 Stats at Large of USA 477.

Acuña, Rodolfo. *Occupied America: A History of Chicanos*. 4th ed. Menlo Park, CA: Addison Wesley Longman, Inc., 2000.

Agbayani-Siewert, P., and Revilla, L. "Filipino Americans." In *Asian Americans: Contemporary Trends and Issues*, edited by P.G. Min. Thousand Oaks, CA: SAGE Publications, 1995.

Akers, Joshua. "Kansas Repeals Anti-Asian Property Law." *Asian Week* (June 21, 2002). http://www. asianweek.com/2002_06_21/news_upfront.html (accessed December 15, 2004).

Agres, Bob. "Community Building in Hawai'I," in The Nonprofit Quarterly, Summer 2005.

Albelda, Randy, Elaine McCrate, Edwin Melendez, June Lapidus, and the Center for Popular Economics. *Mink Coats Don't Trickle Down: The Economic Attack on Women & People of Color*. Boston, MA: South End Press, 1988.

Allen, Robert. *Black Awakening in Capitalist America: An Analytic History*. New York: Doubleday, 1969.

Allen, Theodore W. *The Invention of the White Race: Racial Oppression and Social Control*. Verso Books, New York, 1994.

America, Richard F., editor. *The Wealth of Races: The Present Value of Benefits from Past Injustices*. Westport, CT: Greenwood Press, 1990.

American Indian Policy Review Commission. *Final Report Submitted to Congress, May 17, 1977*. Washington: GPO, 1977.

Amott, Teresa, and Julie Matthaei. *Race, Gender and Work: A Multicultural Economic History of the Women in the United States*. Boston, MA: South End Press, 1991.

Analysis Group/Economics Inc. "Economic and Fiscal Benefits of Tribal Government Gaming." Sacramento, CA: July 1, 1998. http://www.cniga. com/facts/ research_detail.php?id=8 (accessed 03/09/03).

Anderson, Sarah, John Cavanagh, Scott Klinger, and Liz Stanton. *Executive Excess 2005*. Boston and Washington, D.C.: Institute for Policy Studies and United for a Fair Economy, 2005. http://www.fair economy.org/press/2005/EE2005.pdf (accessed September 8, 2005).

Applied Research Center (ARC). "Race and Recession: A Special Report Examining How Changes in the Economy Affect People of Color." Oakland, CA, Summer 2002.

Aquino, Gabriel. "Distinctions in the Economic Integration of Puerto Rican Women in New York's Metropolitan Statistical Area." *Phoebe: A Journal of Feminist Scholarship, Theory, and Aesthetics* 13 (2000): 2. http://www.skidmore.edu/%7Egaquino/PR%20Fema1.pdf.

Aratani, Lori. "With jobs heading overseas, trade issues resonating with many." Knight Ridder News Service (January 25, 2004).

Axelrod, Alan. *Chronicle of the Indian Wars: From Colonial Times to Wounded Knee.* New York: Prentice Hall, 1993.

Aziz, Nikhil. "Colorblind: White-washing America." *The Public Eye* XVI.2 (Summer 2002).

Bartlett, Richard A. *The New Country: A Social History of the American Frontier 1776–1890.* New York: Oxford University Press,1974.

Baxter, John O. "Problems of Land Use Within a Portion of the Zuni Land Claim Area." In *Zuni and the Courts,* edited by E. Richard Hart. Lawrence, KS: University Press of Kansas, 1995:ch. 14.

Bays, Brad A. "Tribal-State Tobacco Compacts and Motor Fuel Contracts in Oklahoma." In *The Tribes and the States: Geographies of Intergovernmental Interaction,* edited by Brad A. Bays and Erin Hogan Fouberg. New York: Rowman & Littlefield, 2002: ch. 9.

Bensel, Richard Franklin. *The Political Economy of American Industrialization, 1877–1900.* New York: Cambridge University Press, 2000.

Benson-Arias, Jaime E. "Puerto Rico: The Myth of the National Economy." *Puerto Rican Jam: Essays on Culture and Politics,* edited by Negrón-Muntaner and Grosfoguel. University of Minnesota Press. (1997): 77–92.

Berlet, Chip, and Matthew N. Lyons. *Right-Wing Populism in America: Too Close for Comfort.* Guilford Press, 2000.

Bernstein, Nell. *All Alone in the World: Children of the Incarcerated.* The New Press, 2005.

Biskupic, Joan. "Case Could Reshape College Admissions." *USA Today.* Dec. 2, 2002:4A.

Boehm, T., and A. Schlottman. "Housing and Wealth Accumulation: Intergenerational Impacts." *Low-Income Homeownership Working Paper Series.* Boston: Joint Center for Housing, Harvard University (Oct. 2001).

Boshara, Ray, Reid Cramer, and Leslie Parrish. *Policy Options to Encourage Savings and Asset Building by Low-Income Americans,* New America Foundation, Discussion Draft. January 28, 2004. (from www.newamericafoundation.org).

Bositis, David. *Black Elected Officials: A Statistical Summary, 2001.* Washington, D.C.: Joint Center for Political and Economic Studies, 2001. http://www.jointcenter.org/ publications1/publication-PDFs/BEO-pdfs/2001-BEO.pdf (accessed September 5, 2005).

Brinkley, Joe. "American Indians Say Government Has Cheated Them Out of Billions." *New York Times,* Jan. 7, 2003:A17.

Brodkin, Karen. *How Jews Became White Folks and What That Says About Race in America.* Rutgers University Press, 2000.

Brown, Michael K. "Race in the American Welfare State: The Ambiguities of 'Universalistic' Social Policy Since the New Deal." *Without Justice for All: The New Liberalism and Our Retreat from Racial Equality.* Adolph L. Reed, editor. Boulder, CO.: Westview Press, 1999.

Cahn, E.S. and D.W. Hearne. *Our Brother's Keeper: The Indian in White America.* Washington, D.C.: New Community Press, 1970.

Canby, Jr., William C. *American Indian Law.* St. Paul, MN: West Group,1998.

Capgemini Group, *World Wealth Report 2004.* http://www.apc.capgemini.com/industry/finance/attachments/World%2520Wealth%2520Report%25202004.pdf&e=7507 (accessed December 11, 2004).

Carlson, L. E. *Indians, Bureaucrats, and Land: The Dawes Act and the Decline of Indian Farming.* Westport, CT: The Greenwood Press, 1981.

Carnoy, Martin. *Faded Dreams: The Politics and Economics of Race in America.* New York: Cambridge University Press, 1994.

Center for Budget and Policy Priorities. "Many States Cut Budgets as Fiscal Squeeze Continues." April 26, 2004.

Center for Women's Business Research. "Hispanic Owned Businesses in the US, 2002: A Fact Sheet." Washington, D.C.: 2003. http://womensbusinessreseach.org/minority/hispanic.pdf.

Chan, Sucheng. *Asian Americans: An Interpretive History*. Boston: Twayne Publishers, 1991.

Chanse, Samantha. "Whites Overcounted in Prison." *Color Lines* 5.1 (Spring 2002).

Chen, David. "Battle Over Iroquois Land Claims Escalates." *New York Times*, May 16, 2000: A1. Available on line at Indian Law Resource Center: http://www.indian law.org/SixN_NYT_2000-05-16.pdf.

Collins, Chuck, Chris Hartman, Karen Kraut, and Gloribell Mota. *Shifty Tax Cuts: How They Move the Tax Burden off the Rich and onto Everyone Else*. Boston: United for a Fair Economy, 2004.

———. Betsy Leondar-Wright, and Holly Sklar. *Shifting Fortunes: The Perils of the Growing American Wealth Gap*. Boston: United for a Fair Economy, 1999.

———. and Felice Yeskel. *Economic Apartheid in America: An Economic Primer on Economic Inequality and Insecurity*. New York: The New Press, 2000.

Conley, Dalton. *Being Black, Living in the Red: Race, Wealth, and Social Policy in America*. Berkeley and Los Angeles, CA: University of California Press, 1999.

Crawford, J. *Bilingual Education: History, Politics, Theory and Practice*. Trenton, NJ: Crane Publishers, 1989.

Darity, William, Jr., Darrick Hamilton, and Jason Dietrich. "Passing on Blackness: Latinos, Race and Earnings in the U.S." *Applied Economics Letters*, 9.13 (2002):847–853.

Deloria, Vine, and Clifford M. Lytle. *The Nations Within: Past and Future of American Sovereignty*. Austin: University of Texas Press, 1984.

DiversityInc website, www.DiversityInc.com (accessed August 2005).

DuBois, W.E.B. *The Souls of Black Folk*. Chicago: A.C. McClurg & Co., 1903.

Edgcomb Elaine L., and Maria Medrano Armington. *The Informal Economy: Latino Enterprises at the Margin*. Washington, DC: FIELD, Aspen Institute, 2003. http://fieldus.org/publications/IE_Latino.pdf (accessed 1/8/05).

Education Trust, "The Funding Gap: Low-Income and Minority Students Receive Fewer Dollars." Aug. 8, 2002. http://www.edtrust.org/main/documents/investment.pdf.

Faiman-Silva, S. "Multinational Corporate Development in the American Hinterland: The Case of Oklahoma Choctaws." In *The Political Economy of North American Indians,* edited by John H. Moore. Norman, OK: University of Oklahoma Press, 1993. 185–215.

Farley, Reynolds, and Walter R. Allen. *The Color Line and the Quality of Life in America*. New York: Russell Sage Foundation, 1987.

Feagin, Joe R. *Racist America: Roots, Current Realities, and Future Reparations*. New York: Routledge, 2000.

Fixico, D.L. *The Invasion of Indian Country in the Twentieth Century: American Capitalism and Tribal Natural Resources*. Niwot, CO: University Press of Colorado, 1998.

Foner, Eric, and John A. Garraty. *The Reader's Companion to American History*, sponsored by the Society of American Historians. Boston: Houghton-Mifflin, 1991.

Forest County Potawatomi Foundation. *Generations, Forest County Potawatomi Community 2001 Community Investment Report*. Milwaukee, WI: 2001.

Fraser, James W. *A History of Hope: When Americans Have Dared to Dream of a Better Future*. New York: Palgrave MacMillan, 2002.

Fuchs, Lawrence H. *The American Kaleidoscope: Race, Ethnicity, and the Civic Culture*. Hanover, NH: Wesleyan University Press, 1990.

Gibbons, Jim. See U.S. House of Representatives.

Gilbert, Charlene, and Quinn Eli. *Homecoming: The Story of African-American Farmers*. Boston: Beacon Press, 2000.

Ginsberg, Thomas, and Paola Ochoa (contributor). "Immigrants pool money, find success." *Philadelphia Inquirer*, Nov. 17, 2003.

Glaser, E., and D. DiPasquale. "Incentives and Social Capital: Are Homeowners Better Citizens?" *Journal of Urban Economics* 45 (1999): 354–384.

Glass Ceiling Commission. *Good For Business: Making Full Use of the Nation's Human Capital*. A Fact-Finding Report of the Federal Glass Ceiling Commission, Washington, D.C., March 1995. http://www.ilr.cornell.edu/library/downloads/key WorkplaceDocuments/GlassCeilingFactFindingEn vironmentalScan.pdf (accessed December 10, 2004).

Glenn, Evelyn Nakano. *Unequal Freedom: How Race*

and Gender Shaped American Citizenship and Labor. Cambridge, MA: Harvard University Press, 2002.

Gold, Steve, and Nazli Kibria. *Asian Americans Issues Relating to Labor, Economics, and Socioeconomic Status,* edited by Franklin Ng. New York: Garland Publishing, 1998.

Goldfield, Michael. *The Color of Politics: Race and the Mainsprings of American Politics.* New York: The New Press, 1997.

Gomez, C. "The Continual Significance of Skin Color: An Exploratory Study of Latinos in the Northeast." *Hispanic Journal of Behavioral Sciences* 22.1 (Feb. 2000):94–103.

Gonzalez, Arturo. *Mexican Americans and the U.S. Economy: Quest for Buenos Días.* Tucson, AZ: University of Arizona Press, 2002.

Gonzalez, Juan. *Harvest of Empire: A History of Latinos in America.* New York: Viking Press, 2000.

Gotanda, Neil. "Exclusion and Inclusion: Immigration and American Orientalism." In *Across the Pacific: Asian Americans and Globalization,* edited by Evelyn Hu-DeHart. Philadelphia: Temple University Press, 1999.

Grant, Gary R. Quoted in *Charlotte News and Observer,* July 25, 2001. http://www.newsobserver.com/ Sunday/ news/nc/story5101789p-506787c.html.

Green, Joshua. "Black Death," *The American Prospect,* 12.10 (June 4, 2001):16–17.

Greenstein, Robert, and Isaac Shapiro, *The New, Definitive CBO Data on Income and Tax Trends.* Washington, D.C.: Center on Budget and Policy Priorities, November, 2003.

Harkness, J., and S. Newman. "Effects of Homeowner-ship on Children: The Role of Neighborhood Characteristics and Family Income." *Federal Reserve Bank of New York: Economic Policy Review* (June 2003):87–107.

Harris, Hamil B. "Can't save the farm," *Black Enterprise,* 31.5 (December 2000):34–36.

Hart, E. Richard. "The Zuni Land Conservation Act of 1990." In *Zuni and the Courts,* edited by E. Richard Hart. Lawrence, KS: University Press of Kansas, 1995:ch. 12.

Hartmann, Thom. *Unequal Protection: The Rise of Corporate Dominance and the Theft of Human Rights.* Emmaus, PA: Rodale Books, 2002.

Hazama, Dorothy Ochiai, and Jane Okamoto Komeiji. *The Japanese in Hawaii. 1885–1985.* Honolulu: Bess Press, 1986.

Henry J. Kaiser Family Foundation. "New Report Provides Critical Information About Health Insurance Coverage and Access for Racial and Ethnic Minority Groups." Washington, D.C. Aug. 1, 2000. http://www.kff.org/ uninsured/upload/ 13342_1.pdf (accessed December 16, 2004).

Herbert, Bob. "Justice, 200 Years Later," *New York Times,* Nov. 26, 2001:A17. Also available online at http://www.hvk.org/articles/1101/252.html.

Herzberg, S.J. "The Menominee Indians: From Treaty to Termination," *Wisconsin Magazine of History* 60.4 (1977):267–329.

Higginbotham, A. Leon, Jr. *In the Matter of Color: Race and the American Legal Process: The Colonial Period.* Oxford: Oxford University Press, 1978.

Hine, Darlene Clark, William C. Hine, and Stanley Harrold. *The African-American Odyssey.* Upper Saddle River, NJ: Prentice Hall, 2000.

Huntington, Samuel P. *Who Are We? The Challenges to America's Identity.* New York: Simon & Schuster, 2004.

Hurt, R.D. *Indian Agriculture in America: Prehistory to the Present.* Lawrence, KS: University Press of Kansas, 1987.

Hutchinson, Edward Prince. *Legislative History of American Immigration Policy: 1798–1965.* Philadelphia: University of Pennsylvania Press, 1981.

Hyman, Wilton. "Empowerment Zones, Enterprise Communities, Black Businesses, and Unemployment." *Journal of Urban and Contemporary Law* 53:143. http://law.wustl.edu/journal/53/169 _.pdf (accessed September 8, 2005).

Ignatiev, Noel. *How the Irish Became White.* New York: Routledge, 1995.

Indian Country Today, "Idaho coalition fights state tax bills aimed at reservation sales," February 26, 2003.

Inman, Katherine. *Women's Resources in Business Start-Up: A Study of Black and White Women Entrepreneurs.* New York: Garland, 2000.

Isbister, John. *Thin Cats: The Community Development Credit Union Movement in the United States.* Davis,

CA : Center for Cooperatives, University of California, 1994.

Iverson, P. *When Indians Became Cowboys*. Norman, OK: University of Oklahoma Press, 1994.

Janofsky, Michael. "A New Hope for Dreams Suspended by Segregation," *New York Times*, July 31, 2005.

Johnson, James H., Jr., and Melvin L. Oliver. "Economic Restructuring and Black Male Joblessness in U.S. Metropolitan Areas." *Urban Geography* 12 (1991).

Johnson, Troy R., ed. *Contemporary Native American Political Issues*. Walnut Creek, CA: AltaMira Press, 1999. 17–71.

Jones, Jacqueline. *American Work: Four Centuries of Black and White Labor*. New York: W.W. Norton, 1998.

——— *Labor of Love, Labor of Sorrow: Black Women, Work and the Family, From Slavery to the Present*. New York: Vintage Books, 1985.

Jones, Jeffrey. *Blacks More Pessimistic Than Whites About Economic Opportunities*. Princeton, NJ: The Gallup Organization, July 9, 2004. http://www.gallup.com/content/?ci=12307.

Justice Policy Institute website, http://www.justice pol-icy.org/article.php?id=459 (accessed August 2005).

Katznelson, Ira, *When Affirmative Action Was White: An Untold History of Racial Inequality in Twentieth-Century America*, New York: W.W. Norton and Company, 2005.

Keoke, E.D., and K.M. Porterfield, *Encyclopedia of American Indian Contributions to the World: 15,000 Years of Inventions and Innovations*. New York: Facts-on-File, 2002.

Kiester, Edward, Jr. "The G.I. Bill may be the best deal ever made by Uncle Sam." *Smithsonian* 25.8 (Nov. 1994):128.

King, Desmond. *Making Americans: Immigration, Race, and the Origins of the Diverse Democracy*. Cambridge, MA: Harvard University Press, 2000.

King, Martin Luther, Sermon at the National Cathedral, Washington, D.C., March 31, 1968.

Kitano, Harry H.L., and Roger Daniels. *Asian Americans: Emerging Minorities*. Englewood Cliffs, NJ: Prentice-Hall, 1988.

Kivel, Paul. *Uprooting Racism: How White People Can Work for Racial Justice*. Gabriola, British Columbia: New Society Publishers, 2002.

Knoll, Tricia. *Becoming Americans: Asian Sojourners, Immigrants, and Refugees in the Western United States*. Portland, OR: Coast To Coast Books, 1982.

Kranish, Michael. "Washington Reconstructed." *Boston Sunday Globe*, Feb. 17, 2002:C1.

Kwong, Peter. *Forbidden Workers: Illegal Chinese Immigrants and American Labor*. New York: W. Norton and Co., 1997.

Lai, Eric, and Dennis Arguelles. *The New Face of Asian Pacific America: Numbers, Diversity and Change in the 21st Century*. San Francisco: AsianWeek, 2003.

Landrieu, U.S. Senator Mary L. "Senate Apologizes to Lynching Victims, Families for Failure to Act." News release from the Office of U.S. Senator Mary L. Landrieu, June 13, 2005.

Lane, Charles. "A Tale of Two Reservations," *Washington Post*, Dec. 2, 2002:A19.

Lawson, Steven F. *Black Ballots: Voting Rights in the South, 1944–1969*. New York: Columbia University Press, 1976.

Lee, Chana Kai. *For Freedom's Sake: The Life of Fannie Lou Hamer*. Champaign-Urbana, IL.: University of Illinois Press, 1999.

Lee, Cheryl Hill, and William E. Spriggs. *NUL Quarterly Jobs Report: New Findings on Recessions and their Impact on African-American Unemployment and Jobs*. Washington, D.C.: National Urban League Institute for Opportunity and Equality, January 2004.

Levin, David J. et al. *See* U.S. Department of Justice.

Lewis, David Rich. "Native Americans in Utah" on state of Utah Web site. http://historytogo.utah.gov/natives.html (accessed August 2005).

Liebert, Larry. "Congress Votes $1.25 Billion for War Internees." *San Francisco Chronicle*, Aug. 5, 1988.

Lipsitz, George. *The Possessive Investment in Whiteness: How White People Profit from Identity Politics*. Philadelphia: Temple University Press, 1998.

Little Gewirtz, Rivka. "The New Harlem: Who's behind the real estate gold rush and who's fighting it?" *Village Voice*. Sept. 18–24, 2002.

Liu, John M., Paul M. Ong, and Carolyn Rosenstein. "Dual Chain Migration: Post-1965 Filipino Immigration to the United States." In *The History and Immigration of Asian Americans*, edited by Franklin Ng. Fresno: California State University, 1998.

Loewen, James W. *Sundown Towns: A Hidden Dimension of American Racism*. New York: The New Press, 2005.

Lopez, Ian F. Hanley. *White by Law: The Legal Construction of Race*. New York: New York University Press, 1996.

McDonnell, Janet A. *The Dispossession of the American Indian: 1887–1934*. Bloomington, IN: Indiana University Press, 1991.

Maharidge, Dale. *The Coming White Minority: California's Eruptions and America's Future*. New York: Random House, 1996.

Maldonado-Denis, M. *Puerto Rico: A Socio-Historic Interpretation*. Translated by Elena Vialo. New York: Random House, 1972.

Mangiafico, Luciano. *Contemporary American Immigrants: Patterns of Filipino, Korean, and Chinese Settlement in the United States*. New York: Praeger, 1988.

Marable, Manning. *How Capitalism Underdeveloped Black America*. 2nd ed. Cambridge, MA: South End Press, 2000.

Marosi, Richard. "Study Finds Deadly Spike in Racial Violence Against Asian Americans," *Los Angeles Times*, March 11, 2002.

Martin, John Frederick. *Profits in the Wilderness: Entrepreneurship and the Founding of New England Towns in the Seventeenth Century*. Williamsburg, VA: Institute of Early American History and Culture, 1991.

Martinas, Sharon. *Shinin' the Lite on White: A Historical Overview of White Privilege*. San Francisco: Challenging White Supremacy, 2000. http://www.cwsworkshop.org/pdfs/WIWP2/5Shin_Light_White.PDF.

Marx, Anthony. *Making Race and Nation: A Comparison of South Africa, the United States and Brazil*. Cambridge: Cambridge University Press, 2002.

Massey, Douglas S., and Nancy A. Denton. *American Apartheid: Segregation and the Making of the Underclass*. Cambridge, MA: Harvard University Press, 1993.

Matthiessen, Peter. *Indian Country*. New York: Viking Press, 1984.

Mbeki, Thabo. "The Poor of the World Rich in Faith." *ANC Today, Online Voice of the African National Congress*. 4, 28 (July 2004). http://www.anc.org.za/ancdocs/anctoday/2004/at28.htm.

Medoff, Peter, and Holly, Sklar. *Streets of Hope: The Fall and Rise of an Urban Neighborhood*. Boston: South End Press, 1994.

Meierhoefer, B.S. "The General Effect of Mandatory Minimum Prison Terms: A Longitudinal Study of Federal Sentences Imposed." Washington, D.C.: Federal Judicial Center, 1992.

Menchaca, Martha. *Recovering History, Constructing Race: The Indian, Black, and White Roots of Mexican Americans*. Austin, TX: University of Texas Press, 2002.

Mills, Charles. *The Racial Contract*. Ithaca, NY: Cornell University Press, 1997.

Mills, Kay. *This Little Light of Mine: The Life of Fannie Lou Hamer*. New York: Penguin Books, 1993.

Min, Pyong Gap. "Korean Americans." In *Asian Americans: Contemporary Trends and Issues*, edited by Pyong Gap Min. Thousand Oaks, CA: SAGE Publications, 1995.

Minnesota Indian Gaming Association. Web site, http://www.mnindiangaming.com (accessed 02/27/03)

Mishel, Lawrence, Jared Bernstein, Heather Boushey. *The State of Working America, 2002–03*. Washington, D.C.: Economic Policy Institute, 2003.

Mittal, Anaradha, and Joan Powell. "The Last Plantation." *Earth Island Journal* 15.3 (Fall 2000). http://www.earthisland.org/eijournal/fall2000/wr_fall2000lastplant.html (accessed December 10, 2004).

Morales, J. *Puerto Rican Poverty and Migration: We Just Had to Try Elsewhere*. New York: Praeger, 1986.

Moreno, Ana. *Mortgage Foreclosure Prevention: Program and Trends*. Minneapolis: Family Housing Fund, December 1998.

Morin, Richard. "Misperceptions Cloud Whites' View of Blacks," *Washington Post*, July 11, 2001: A01.

Moyers, Bill. *The Language of Life: A Festival of Poets*. New York: Public Affairs Television, and A. David Grubin Productions, 1995.

Muhammad, Dedrick, Attieno Davis, Meizhu Lui, and Betsy Leondar-Wright. *The State of the Dream 2004: Enduring Disparities in Black and White*. Boston: United for a Fair Economy, 2004.

Muwakkil, Salim. "Racial Bias Persists," Knight Ridder op-ed, Sept. 27, 2003.

———. "So Very Sorry," *In These Times*, July 21, 2005. http://www.inthesetimes.com/site/main/article/2242/ (accessed September 8. 2005).

Nabhan, G. *Enduring Seeds: Native American Agricultural and Wild Plant Conservation.* Tuscon: University of Arizona Press, 1989.

Native American Rights Fund. http://www.narf.org (accessed August 2005).

"Native Americans of North America." *Encarta*, 2004. http://encarta.msn.com/encyclopedia_76157 0777_30/Native_Americans_of_North_America.html#p639 (accessed December 22, 2004)

Naturalization Act of July 14, 1870. 16 Stats at Large of USA 254.

Nee, Victor G. and Brett De Bary, *Longtime Californ'.* Boston: Houghton Mifflin, 1974.

Newland, Kathleen, and Elizabeth Grieco, "Spotlight on Haitians in the United States," Migration Information Center, April 1, 2004.

Newman, Dorothy. *Protest, Politics, and Prosperity: Black Americans and White Institutions 1940–75.* New York: Pantheon Books, 1978.

Nuñez-Portuondo, Ricardo, "Cuban Refugee Program," www.amigospaisguaracabuya.org/oagrn 014.html.

Oakes, James. *The Ruling Race: A History of American Slaveholders.* New York: Vintage, 1982.

O'Brien, Sharon. *American Indian Tribal Governments.* Norman, OK: University of Oklahoma Press, 1989.

Ogletree, Charles J. "Litigating the Legacy of Slavery," *New York Times*, March 31, 2002. Week In Review, 9.

Okihiro, Gary. *Common Ground: Reimagining American History.* Princeton, NJ: Princeton University Press, 2001.

Oliver, Melvin L., and Thomas M. Shapiro. *Black Wealth/White Wealth: A New Perspective on Racial Inequality.* New York: Routledge, 1995.

Olson, Michael D. U.S. House Resources Committee. 884. June 18, 2003.

Olzak, Susan, and Suzanne Shanahan. "Racial Policy and Racial Conflict in the Urban United States, 1869–1924," presented at the 1998 Annual Meetings of the American Sociological Association.

Ong, Paul M., and J. Eugene Grigsby III. "Race and Life-Cycle Effects on Home Ownership in Los Angeles 1970 to 1980." *Urban Affairs Quarterly* 23.4 (June 1988).

Onkst, David H. "First a Negro . . . Incidentally a Veteran: Black World War Two Veterans and the G.I. Bill of Rights in the Deep South, 1944–1948." *Journal of Social History* 31 (Spring 1998):517–43.

O'Reily, Richard, and Maureen Lyons. *Analysis of U.S. Census Data, 1993.* Cited on http://www.bol.ucla.edu/~tiffloui/glassceil.htm (accessed December 21, 2004).

Orr, Doug. "Social Security Isn't Broken." *Dollars & Sense*, 256 (2004).

Padilla, E. *Up From Puerto Rico.* New York: Columbia University Press, 1958.

Parenti, Christian. *The Soft Cage.* New York: Basic Books, 2003.

Parker, L.S. *Native American Estate: The Struggle Over Indian and Hawaiian Lands.* Honolulu, HI: University of Hawaii Press, 1989.

Paulin, G. "A Changing Market: Expenditures by Hispanic Consumers, Revisited." *Monthly Labor Review* 126.8: 12–35, Bureau of Labor Statistics, August 2003.

Pevar, S. *The Rights of Indians and Tribes.* 2nd ed. Carbondale, IL: Southern Illinois University Press, 1992.

Pevar, S. *The Rights of Indians and Tribes.* 3rd ed. Carbondale, IL: Southern Illinois University Press, 2002.

Phillips, Katherin Ross. *Who Knows About the Earned Income Tax Credit?* Washington, D.C.: Urban Institute, Jan. 1, 2001. http://www.urban.org/UploadedPDF/anf_b27. pdf, p.1.

Policy Link. "Community Reinvestment Act: Why use the tool?" http://www.policylink.org/Equitable Develop-ment/content/tools/56/20-all? (Accessed December 4, 2003).

Price, Derek, Lumina Foundation for Education, *Inequality in Higher Education: The Historic and Continuing Significance of Race,* panel on Colorlines Conference, Harvard Law School Civil Rights Project, Aug. 30, 2003.

Public Broadcasting Service. "Interview with Melvin Oliver," on Web site for *Race: The Power of an Illusion.* 2003. http://www.pbs.org/ race/000_ About/002_04-background-03-05.htm.

————. *Becoming American: The Chinese Experience*, a Bill Moyers special. 2002.

————. *The Chinatown Files*. Amy Chen, 2001.

————. "Interview with Dalton Conley," on Web site for *Race: The Power of an Illusion*. 2003. http://www.pbs.org/race/ 000_About/002_04-background-03-03.htm.

Project Underground. "Gold, Greed, and Genocide." Berkeley, CA: Project Underground. http://www.1849.org.

Quadagno, Jill. *The Color of Welfare: How Racism Undermined the War on Poverty*. New York: Oxford University Press, 1994.

Quigg, H.D., *South Dade News Leader*, April 14, 1966. www.cuban-exile.com/doc_176-200/doc0181.htm.

Ramah Navajo Class Action. *Affadavit of Charles A. Hobbs*. http://www.rncclassaction.santa-fe.net/fees 3e.htm.

Randall, Vernellia R. "Hispanic/Latino Americans: Laws and Policies—Selected Laws and Governmental Policies Affecting Hispanic / Latino(a) Americans," Feb. 24, 2004 http://academic.udayton.edu/ race/03justice/hispaw01.htm (accessed December 22, 2004).

Rangel, Jorge, and Carlos Alcala. "De Jure Segregation of Chicanos in Texas Schools." *Harvard Civil Rights–Civil Liberties Law Review* 7 (March 1972):307–391.

Reed, Jr., Adolph. Speech at *How Class Works* conference at State University of New York at Stony Brook, June 2002.

Reimers, David M. *The Immigrant Experience*. New York: Chelsea House Publishers, 1989.

Robertson, Tatsha, and Ross Kerber. "History Unchained: Delving Beyond Celebrated Abolitionists, New Englanders are Unearthing Painful Family Roots in the African Slave Trade." *The Boston Globe* Aug. 6, 2000: B1.

Robinson, Greg. *By Order of the President: FDR and the Internment of Japanese Americans*. Cambridge, MA: Harvard University Press, 2001.

Robinson, Randall. *The Debt: What America Owes to Blacks*. New York: Dutton, 2000.

Robles, Bárbara. "Latina Microenterprise and the U.S.-Mexico Border Economy." *Estey Centre Journal of International Law and Trade Policy* 3.2 (2002): 307–327.

Rodríguez, Carla E., and Virginia Sánchez Korrol, eds. *Historical Perspectives on Puerto Rican Survival in the U.S.* Princeton, NJ: Markus Wiener Publications, 1996.

Roediger, David. *The Wages of Whiteness: Race and the Making of the American Working Class*. London: Verso, 1991.

Root Cause. *Community Impact Report*. Miami, FL: November 11, 2003. http://users.resist.ca/~mangus/ CIR_eng.pdf (accessed 1/8/05).

Rose, Harold, "The Future of Black Ghettos," in *Cities in the 21st Century*. Gary Gappert & Richard Knight, editors, 1982.

Rosenthal, Harvey D. "Indian Claims Commission." *Native America In the Twentieth Century: An Encyclopedia*. Mary B. Davis, editor. New York: Garland Publishing, 1996.

Ross, Stephen L., and John Yinger. *The Color of Credit: Mortgage Discrimination, Research Methodology, and Fair-Lending Enforcement*. Cambridge, MA: MIT Press, 2002.

Rumbaut, R. "Vietnamese, Laotians, and Cambodian Americans." *In Asian Americans: Contemporary Trends and Issues*, edited by P.G. Min. Thousand Oaks, CA: SAGE Publications, 1995.

Ryan, Lorna. "Mainstreaming Equality—Weaving a Constant Thread. *Poverty Today* (April/May 1999): 6. http://www.cpa.ie/downloads/publications/PovertyToday/1999_PT_43.PDF.

Sachar, Howard M. *A History of the Jews in America*. New York: Vintage 1992.

Schomberg Center for Research in Black Culture, Exhibit. *In Motion: The African American Experience* 2004.

Schuyler, Rogena. "Youth: We Didn't Sell Them Into Slavery," *Los Angeles Times*, June 21, 1993.

Scott, Janny. "Nearly Half of Black Men Found Jobless." *New York Times*, Feb. 28, 2004: B1.

Seltzer, William, and Margo Anderson. "After Pearl Harbor: The Proper Role of Population Data Systems in Times of War." Presentation in March 2000 at the conference of the Population Association of America's annual meeting.

Sengsatheuane, Windy. "Ninjas, Dragons, & Other

Asian Myths." Boston: United for a Fair Economy, http://www.racialwealthdivide.org/resources/asian myths.html (accessed September 8, 2005).

Shapiro, Thomas. *The Hidden Cost of Being African American: How Wealth Perpetuates Inequality.* New York: Oxford University Press, 2004.

Shapiro, Thomas, power point presentation at Center for American Progress panel on wealth inequality, September 23, 2004.

Sherradan, Michael. *Assets and the Poor: A New American Welfare Policy.* Armonk, NY: M.E. Sharpe, 1991.

Sheth, Manju. "Asian Indian Americans." In *Asian Americans: Contemporary Trends and Issues*, edited by P. G. Min. Thousand Oaks, CA: SAGE Publications, 1995.

Shoshone-Bannock Tribal Enterprises. Tribal History. http://www.sho-ban.com/history.asp (accessed August 2005).

Simms, Margaret. "Job Creation prospects and strategies." *Focus: The monthly magazine of the Joint Center for Political and Economic Studies.* 27,4 (1999).

Sitkoff, Harvard. *A New Deal for Blacks: The Emergence of Civil Rights as a National Issue. Volume I: The Depression Decade.* New York: Oxford University Press, 1978.

Sklar, Holly, Laryssa Mykyta, and Susan Wefald. *Raise the Floor Wages: Wages and Policies That Work for All of Us.* New York: Ms. Foundation for Women, 2001.

Sowell, Thomas. *Race and Culture: A World View.* New York: HarperCollins, 1995.

Spriggs, William E. "Afircan Americans and Social Security: Why the Privatization Advocates are Wrong," *Dollars & Sense,* 256, (2004): 18.

Squire, Gregory D. "Runaway Plants," Capital Mobility, and Black Economic Rights." *Community and Capital in Conflict: Plant Closings and Job Loss*, John Raines, L. Berson and D. Grace, editors Philadelphia: Temple University Press, 1982.

Stanton, Elizabeth Cady, Susan B. Anthony, and Matilda Joslyn Gage. *History of Woman Suffrage: Vol. I 1848–1861.* Rochester, NY: Charles Mann, 1889.

Steiner, S. *The Islands: The Worlds of the Puerto Ricans.* New York: Harper and Row, 1974.

Stone, Michael E. *Shelter Poverty: New Ideas on Housing Affordability.* Philadelphia: Temple University Press, 1993.

Sutton, Imre, ed. *Irredeemable America: The Indians' Estate and Land Claims.* Tuscon: University of New Mexico Press, 1985.

Takaki, R. *Strangers from a Different Shore.* Boston: Little, Brown, and Co., 1998.

———. *A Different Mirror: A History of Multicultural America.* Boston: Little, Brown, and Co., 1993.

Taylor, Jonathan B., and Joseph P. Kalt. *American Indians on Reservations: A Databook of Socioeconomic Change Between the 1990 and 2000 Censuses.* Cambridge, MA: Harvard Project on American Indian Economic Development, 2005. http://www.ksg.harvard.edu/ hpaied/pubs/documents/AmericanIndiansonReservationsADatabook ofSocioeconomicChange.pdf (accessed 1/8/05).

Thrupkaew, Noy. "The Myth of the Model Minority," *The American Prospect*, April 8, 2002. http://www.prospect.org/web/printfriendly-view.ww?id=6231 (accessed December 16, 2004).

Uchitelle, Louis. "Blacks Lose Better Jobs Faster As Middle-Class Work Drops," *New York Times* July 12, 2003: A1.

United for a Fair Economy, "Estate Tax Action Center," http://www.faireconomy.org/estatetax/ (accessed December 19, 2004).

———. *Annual Report.* 2002.

U.S. Bureau of Labor Statistics, *A Profile of the Working Poor, 2001.* Washington: U.S. Department of Labor. http://www.bls.gov/cps/cpswp2001.pdf.

———. Current Employment Statistics, Table A-1. Employment Status of the Civilian Population by Sex and Age, http://www.bls.gov/ news.release/empsit.t01.htm (accessed September 2005).

———. *Usual Weekly Earnings of Wage and Salary Workers.* Washington, D.C.: October 20, 2004, p. 3. http://www.bls.gov/news.release/pdf/ wkyeng.pdf. (accessed December 19, 2004).

U.S. Census Bureau. 2000 Decennial Census, Summary File 1. Accessed through American Factfinder utility: http://factfinder.census.gov/ servlet/BasicFactsServlet.

———. *Income, Poverty, and Health Insurance Coverage in the United States: 2004.*

———. 2000 Decennial Census, Table PHC-1.

———. *2000 Decennial Census*, Summary File 3. Accessed through American Factfinder utility:

http://factfinder.census.gov/servlet/BasicFactsServlet.

———. *2000 Decennial Census*, Summary File 4. Accessed through American Factfinder utility: http://factfinder.census.gov/servlet/BasicFactsServlet.

———. *American Indian- and Alaskan Native-Owned Businesses 1997*, http://www.census.gov/prod/2001pubs/cenbr01-8.pdf.

———. *The American Indian and Alaska Native Population: 2000*, Washington, D.C. Feburary 2002. http://www.census.gov/prod/2002pubs/c2kbr01-15.pdf.

———. "Census 2000 PHC-T-1, Population by Race and Hispanic and Latino Origin for the United States, 1990 and 2000, " Washington, DC, April 2001.

———. *Coming to America: A Profile of the Nation's Foreign Born*. Washington, D.C., 2000, http://www.census.gov/prod/2000pubs/cenbr002.pdf.

———. *Current Population Survey (CPS)*, 2002 Annual Social and Economic Supplement. Washington, D.C., 2002.

———. *Current Population Survey*, 2003 Annual Social and Economic Supplement. Washington, D.C., 2003.

———. *Educational Attainment in the United States: March 2002 Detailed Tables*, Washington, D.C.: June 18, 2003. http://www.census.gov/population www/socdemo/education/ppl-169.html (accessed January 4, 2005).

———. *The Hispanic Population in the United States: March 2002 Detailed Tables*, Washington, D.C.: June 18, 2003. http://www.census.gov/population/www/ socdemo/hispanic/ppl-165.html (accessed January 4, 2005).

———. Population Division. *Historical Census Statistics on Population Totals by Race, 1790 to 1990, and by Hispanic Origins, 1970 to 1990, for the United States, Regions, Divisions and States* by Campbell, Gibson, and Kay Jung, Washington, D.C., September 2002.

U.S. Department of Health and Human Services, Substance Abuse and Mental Health Services Administration, *National Household Survey on Drug Abuse*. Rockville, MD: 1998.

http://oas.samhsa.gov/ nhsda/NHSDAsumrpt.pdf (accessed December 19, 2004).

U.S. Department of the Interior Bureau of Indian Affairs Tyler, S.L. *See* A *History of Indian Policy*, Washington, D.C.: Government Printing Office, 1973.

U.S. Department of Justice. Briefs submitted in *U.S. v. Helen Mitchell, et al.*, 1982. http://www.usdoj.gov:80/osg/briefs/1982/sg820135.txt; http://www.usdoj.gov:80/osg/briefs/1982/sg820220.txt.

———. Bureau of Justice Statistics, http://www.ojp.usdoj.gov/bjs/crimoff/htm#prevalence (accessed August 2005).

U.S. Department of Veterans Affairs. *World War II Veterans by the Numbers: VA Fact Sheet*. Washington, DC: undated. http://www1.va.gov/pspao/docs/WWII vetsfactsheet.doc (accessed September 4, 2005).

U.S. House of Representatives. Western Shoshone Claims Distribution Act, H.R. 884, by Jim Gibbons. Washington, D.C.: GPO, 2003.

U.S. National Archives and Records Administration. *Transcript of Homestead Act (1862)*. http://www.our-documents.gov/doc.php?doc=31&page=transcript.

———. *Transcript of Pacific Railway Act (1862)*. http://www. ourdocuments.gov/doc.php?doc=32&page=transcript.

U.S. National Research Council. Panel to Review the 2000 Census. *The 2000 Census, Counting Under Adversity*, edited by Constance F. Citro, Daniel L. Cork, and Janet L. Norwood. Washington, D.C.: National Academies Press, 2004.

U.S. Office of Management and Budget. *Revisions to the Standards for the Classification of Federal Data on Race and Ethnicity*. Washington, D.C.: Oct. 31, 1997. http://www.whitehouse.gov/omb/fedreg/1997standards.html (accessed December 21, 2004).

U.S. Small Business Administration, Office of Advocacy. *Minorities in Business*. Washington, D.C.: 1999. http://www.sba.gov/advo/stats/min.pdf (accessed 1/8/05).

United Tribes of Wisconsin Web site. http://www.unitedtribesofwisconsin.com (accessed 02/27/03).

Valenzuela, Angela. *Subtractive Schooling: U.S.-Mexican*

Youth and the Politics of Caring. Albany, NY: State University of New York Press, 1999.

Vedder, Richard, Lowell Gallaway, and David C. Klingaman. "Black Exploitation and White Benefits: The Civil War Income Revolution." In *The Wealth of Races*. Richard America, editor, Westport, CT: Greenwood, 1990.

Velez-Inaña, C. *Border Visions: Mexican Cultures of the Southwest United States*. Tuscon, AZ: University of Arizona Press, 1996.

Vietnamese American Initiative for Development website, www.vietaid.org (accessed September 2005).

Ward, Stephen R., and Jason B. Aamodt. "An Essay: Thoughts About Tar Creek, Tribal Environmental Jurisdiction, and Natural Resource Restoration of Tribal Lands." *Sovereignty Symposium 2000*. http://www.gardere.com/newsimages/TarCreek.pdf 4.29.03.

Weatherford, J. *Native Roots: How the Indians Enriched America*. New York: Fawcett Columbine, 1991.

Weisskoff, R. *Factories and Food Stamps: The Puerto Rico Model of Development*. Baltimore, MD: Johns Hopkins University Press, 1985.

Westley, Robert. "Many Billions Gone: Is It Time to Reconsider the Case for Black Reparations?" *Boston College Law Review* 40 (December 1998).

White, Walter. "The Causes of the Chicago Race Riot," *The Crisis* XVIII (October 1919): 25. Electronic reprint appears online at http://www.yale.edu/glc/archive/1126.htm (accessed September 4, 2005).

Wilkins, David E. *American Indian Politics and the American Political System*. Lanhan, MD: Rowman & Littlefield Publishers, 2002.

Wilkinson, C.F. *Fire on the Plateau*. Washington D.C.: Island Press, 1999.

Wilson, William Julius. *When Work Disappears: The World of the New Urban Poor*. New York: Knopf, 1997.

———. *The Truly Disadvantaged: The Inner City, the Underclass, and Public Policy*. Chicago: University of Chicago Press, 1987.

———. *The Declining Significance of Race: Blacks and Changing American Institutions*. Chicago: University of Chicago Press, 1980.

Wise, Tim. "Whites Swim in Racial Preference." AlterNet Feb. 30, 2003. http://www.altnernet.org /story/15223 (accessed December 21, 2004).

W.K. Kellog Foundation website, www.wkkf.org (accessed September 2005).

Wolff, Edward. *Recent Trends in Wealth Ownership, 1983–1998*. Annandale-on-Hudson, NY: The Levy Economics Institute (April 2000). http://econ-wpa.wustl.edu:80/eps/mac/papers/0004/0004047.pdf (accessed December, 15, 2004).

———. "How the Pie is Sliced: America's Growing Concentration of Wealth." *The American Prospect* 6 (1995). http://www.prospect.org/web/page.ww?section=root&name=ViewPrint&articleId=5015.

Wong, Morrison G. "Chinese Americans." In *Asian Americans: Contemporary Trends and Issues*, edited by P. G. Min. Thousand Oaks, CA: SAGE Publications, 1995.

Woo, Deborah. *Glass Ceilings and Asian Americans: The New Face of Workplace Barriers*, Walnut Creek, CA: AltaMira Press, 2000.

Wood, Betty. *The Origins of American Slavery: Freedom and Bondage in the English Colonies*. New York: Hill and Wang, 1997.

Woods, Mary Christina. "Indian Land and the Promise of Native Sovereignty: The Trust Doctrine Revisited." *Utah Law Review* 4 (Fall 1994):1471, 1496–97.

Ybarra, L. *Vietnam Veteranos: Chicanos Recall the War*. Austin, TX: University of Texas Press, 2004.

Zinn, Howard. *A People's History of the United States, 1492–Present*. Revised and updated version. New York: Harper Collins, 1995.

Zia, Helen. *Asian American Dreams: The Emergence of an American People*. New York: Farrar, Straus, and Giroux, 2000.

SUGGESTIONS FOR FURTHER READING

Acuña, Rodolfo. *Occupied America: A History of Chicanos*, 4th edition. New York: Longman Publishing, 1999.

Amott, Teresa and Julie Matthaei. *Race, Gender and Work: A Multicultural Economic History of the Women in the United States.* Boston: South End Press, 1991.

Barjas, Louis. *The Latino Journey to Financial Greatness.* New York: Rayo Press, A Division of HarperCollins, 2003.

Carnoy, Martin. *Faded Dreams: The Politics and Economics of Race in America.* New York: Cambridge University Press, 1994.

Conley, Dalton. *Being Black, Living in the Red: Race, Wealth, and Social Policy in America.* Berkeley and Los Angeles: University of California Press, 1999.

Glenn, Evelyn Nakano. *Unequal Freedom: How Race and Gender Shaped American Citizenship and Labor.* Cambridge: Harvard University Press, 2002.

Gonzalez, Juan. *Harvest of Empire: A History of Latinos in America.* New York: Viking Press, 2000.

Hare, Bruce. *2001 Race Odyssey.* Syracuse, NY: Syracuse University Press, 2003.

Jaimes, M. A., ed. *The State of Native America.* Boston: South End Press, 1992.

Johnson, Troy R., ed. *Contemporary Native American Political Issues.* Walnut Creek, CA: AltaMira Press, 1999. 17-71.

Kivel, Paul. *Uprooting Racism: How White People Can Work for Racial Justice.* Gabriola, British Columbia: New Society Publishers, 2002.

McDonnell, Janet A. *The Dispossession of the American Indian: 1887–1934.* Bloomington: Indiana University Press, 1991.

Menchaca, Martha. *Recovering History, Constructing Race: The Indian, Black, and White Roots of Mexican Americans.* Austin: University of Texas Press, 2002.

Pevar, S. *The Rights of Indians and Tribes.* 3rd ed. Carbondale: Southern Illinois University Press, 2002.

Robinson, Randall. *The Debt: What America Owes to Blacks.* New York: Dutton, 2000.

Roediger, David. *The Wages of Whiteness: Race and the Making of the American Working Class.* London: Verso, 1991.

Shapiro, Thomas. *The Hidden Cost of Being African American: How Wealth Perpetuates Inequality.* Oxford: Oxford University Press, 2004.

Takaki, Ronald. *Strangers from a Different Shore: A History of Asian Americans.* Boston: Little, Brown, 1989.

Zia, Helen. *Asian American Dreams.* New York: Farrar, Straus, and Giroux, 2000.

INDEX

affirmative action: and Blacks, 107, 108, 109-10, 111, 118, 128; and closing the racial wealth divide, 273, 279, 288; and education, 157, 167; and fighting poverty, 14-15; and Latinos, 156, 157, 158; in 1980s, 261-63; and perception and reality of economic inequality, 4, 5; and racial categories, 26; repeal of, 167; and role of government in wealth creation, 20, 22; and White advantages, 258-59, 261-63

Africa: and closing the racial wealth divide, 273; immigrants from, 124-25, 281

African Americans. *See* Blacks; *specific topic*

agriculture: and closing the racial wealth divide, 271, 289; and social security, 169; and White advantages, 252, 254. *See also* farming

Aid to Dependent Children (ADC) (1936), 93, 254

Alabama, 86, 99, 100, 237, 240, 248

Alaska, 31

Alien Land Law (1913), 192, 193, 198-99, 200, 289

Allen, Richard, 82

Allen, Theodore, 20, 234, 235, 237

American Dream, 133, 134, 176, 183, 199, 205

American Indian Movement (AIM), 66

American Revolution, 140, 235-36

American Saving for Personal Investment, Retirement, and Education Act (ASPIRE), 281

anti-Semitism, 246, 247, 251

antimiscegenation laws, 188, 189

Apache Indians, 144

Arapaho Indians, 241

Arizona: and Asian Americans, 202; land ownership in, 193; Latinos in, 140, 142, 143, 144, 145, 155, 160, 175, 243, 244; Native Americans in, 57, 71, 142

Arkansas, 48, 86, 140

Armenians, 186, 250

Asian Americans: and Blacks, 181, 218; categorization/ definition of, 24-27, 146, 181-84; and closing the racial wealth divide, 272, 274, 276, 279, 281, 289; and creation of the yellow "race", 184-86; and data uses/reliability, 182-83; diversity among, 220; first period (1850-1941) for, 10, 183, 184-86; in future, 220-24; history of, 10, 12, 183-84; image of, 177-224, 272; invisibility of, 25-26; lack of information about, 209; and Native Americans, 185; need not apply, 179-81; overview of, 177-79; population of, 158, 184, 195, 206, 208-9, 211, 214, 217, 219; and role of government in wealth creation, 19, 21; second generation of, 12, 205; in Second Period (1941-65), 183, 197-205; in Third Period (1965-2000), 183-84, 206-24; wealth gap among, 210-11; and Whites, 187-97, 209, 210, 212, 213, 214, 215, 216-20, 245, 247, 248, 250; women as, 188-89, 198, 207-8. *See also specific topic*

assets: accumulation of, 279, 280-81; of Asian Americans, 3, 196, 199-200;

and asset building assistance for all, 266; basic principles for management of, 30; of Blacks, 3, 75-77; Blacks as, 73-74, 78, 266; and closing the racial wealth divide, 24, 279-86; community, 176; creation of, 280, 285-86; and definition of wealth, 2; and fighting poverty, 16, 17; and income versus wealth, 8; of Latinos, 3, 76, 122, 132-36, 151, 159, 175; leveraging of, 279, 281-83; of Native Americans, 29-72; and perception and reality of economic inequality, 5, 6; preservation of, 280, 283-85;transformative, 8, 24; of Whites, 3. *See also* income; ownership; wealth; *type of asset*

"baby bonds", 280-81

Battle Creek Neighborhoods Incorporated, 285

Black Hills (South Dakota), 43-44

black power movement, 100, 107, 258

Blackfeet Indians, 51

Blacks: and Asian Americans, 181, 218; categorization of, 24-27, 144, 146; and closing the racial wealth divide, 269, 271, 274, 276, 278, 279, 284-85, 286, 289; diversity among, 122-25; freed, 82-83, 86, 236, 239, 244; Great Migration of, 88, 89-90; as immigrants, 122-25; Irish compared with, 248; and Latinos, 26, 74, 75, 76, 77, 112, 114, 115, 117, 127, 142, 144, 148, 158; overview about, 10, 11, 73-78; population of, 258, 284; as property, 73-74, 78, 80, 233; reproductive labor of, 83; and

ABOUT THE AUTHORS

Meizhu Lui is the executive director of United for a Fair Economy. She is a co-author of UFE's report, "The State of the Dream 2005: Disowned in the Ownership Society," and co-editor of *The Wealth Inequality Reader* (Dollars and Sense, 2004). She was a rank and file union activist for fifteen years in a workplace that was 40 percent African American, 20 percent Latino and 40 percent white. She organized in Boston's communities of color to build a coalition that challenged wealthy hospitals to provide more benefits to low-income residents.

Bárbara Robles, PhD, taught Latino public policy at the LBJ School of Public Affairs at the University of Texas at Austin from 1998 to 2005. She has a PhD in economics from the University of Maryland at College Park. Her next book will be *Rich Latino/Poor Latino: Wealth Inequality, Cultural Capital and Social Policy* (University of Arizona Press). She has presented at numerous academic conferences on Latino/a entrepreneurship, educational attainment, and consumer patterns. Her many publications include "Latino Family and Community Asset Building: The Southwest Border" (for the Annie E. Casey Foundation) and "Wealth Creation in Latino Communities," in *Wealth Accumulation in Communities of Color* (University of Michigan Press). She is a board member of United for a Fair Economy.

Betsy Leondar-Wright is UFE's communications director. A long-time economic justice organizer and researcher, she is the author of *Class Matters: Cross-Class Alliance Building for Middle-Class Activists* (New Society Publishers, 2005.) She is a co-author of UFE's report, "The State of the Dream 2005: Disowned in the Ownership Society," and co-editor of *The Wealth Inequality Reader* (Dollars and Sense, 2004).

Rose M. Brewer, PhD, is associate professor and Morse Alumni Distinguished Teaching Professor of African American & African Studies at the University of Minnesota and a contributing editor to *Souls*, an interdisciplinary journal of the Institute for Contemporary Black History at Columbia. She is the author of "Gender, Race and Social Policy: African Americans and the U.S. Social Welfare State," in *Women's International Policy Forum* (1998). She co-edited *Bridges of Power: Women's Multicultural Alliances* (New Society Publishers, 1990) and *Is Academic Feminism Dead?* (New York University Press). She is on the editorial board of the *National Journal of Sociology*. She was a long-time board member of United for a Fair Economy and of Project South: Institute for the Elimination of Poverty and Genocide. She co-founded and continues to be an active member of the Black Radical Congress.

Rebecca Adamson, a Cherokee, is founder and president of First Nations Development Institute (1980) and founder of First Peoples Worldwide (1997). She has worked directly with grassroots tribal communities and nationally as an advocate of local tribal issues since 1970. She has received several awards for her work. In 2003 she was one of ten honorees of the National Women's History Project. In 1996 she was awarded the Council on Foundations Robert W. Scrivner Award for creative and innovative grant making, and she was awarded the National Center for American Indian Enterprise Development's 1996 Jay Silverheels Award.

United for A Fair Economy, a national non-partisan organization based in Boston, Massachusetts, campaigns against growing income and wealth inequality and inspires action to reduce economic inequality.